Up the Capitol Steps

WOMEN AND POLITICS IN THE PACIFIC NORTHWEST
Series editor: Dr. Melody Rose, Portland State University

This series explores the many roles women have played in
Northwest politics, both historically and in modern times. Taking
a broad definition of political activity, the series examines the role
of women in elected office and the barriers to their role in the
electoral arena, as well as the examples of women as advocates and
agitators outside the halls of power. Illuminating the various roles
played by diverse and under-represented groups of women and
considering the differences among and between groups of women,
acknowledging that women of the Northwest do not experience
politics in a single, uniform way, are particular goals of this series.

PREVIOUSLY PUBLISHED:
Remembering the Power of Words:
The Life of an Oregon Activist, Legislator, and Community Leader
Avel Louise Gordly with Patricia A. Schechter

With Grit and By Grace:
Breaking Trails in Politics and Law, A Memoir
Betty Roberts with Gail Wells

Learn more about Barbara Roberts
— additional photographs, the text of her speeches, and much more — at
http://osupress.oregonstate.edu/book/up-capitol-steps

The photograph on the preceding page is courtesy of
Timothy Bullard Photography.

Up the Capitol Steps

A WOMAN'S MARCH TO THE GOVERNORSHIP

Barbara Roberts

Oregon State University Press • Corvallis

The paper in this book meets the guidelines for permanence and durability of the Committee on Production Guidelines for Book Longevity of the Council on Library Resources and the minimum requirements of the American National Standard for Permanence of Paper for Printed Library Materials Z39.48-1984.

Library of Congress Cataloging-in-Publication Data
Roberts, Barbara, 1936-
 Up the Capitol steps : a woman's march to the governorship / Barbara Roberts.
      p. cm. -- (Women and politics in the Pacific Northwest)
 Includes bibliographical references and index.
 ISBN 978-0-87071-610-2 (alk. paper) -- ISBN 978-0-87071-649-2 (ebook)
 1. Roberts, Barbara, 1936- 2. Governors--Oregon--Biography. 3. Oregon--Politics and government--1951- I. Title.
 F881.35.R63A3 2011
 979.5'043092--dc23
 [B]
                              2011020331

First published in 2011 by Oregon State University Press.
Second printing 2013.
Printed in the United States of America

Oregon State University Press
121 The Valley Library
Corvallis OR 97331-4501
541-737-3166 • fax 541-737-3170
www.osupress.oregonstate.edu

Contents

Dedication

To my two sons, Mike Sanders and Mark Sanders

For coping with a working mother during your youth
when I worked of necessity.
For later tolerating a political mother during your adult years
when I ran for office by choice.
Your patience, good humor, and pride in my accomplishments
meant more to me than you will ever know. I love you.

Acknowledgments

After more than five years of writing, research, editing, and rewriting to finish this book, the list of those who supported and assisted me has grown long—and longer.

Early on, when the book was still a dream, two women were there to dream with me: Maureen Michelson, the publisher of my book on death and grieving, and Dr. Melody Rose from Portland State University.

Some authors have readers. I had "listeners." My friends Rod Patterson and Terry Bean and my older son Mike sat for hours while I read new chapters to them for their reaction and input. Their patience, advice, and enthusiasm kept me moving, kept me writing.

High on the list of people who helped bring the manuscript to completion is the amazing and talented intern that Melody Rose and OSU Press sent to assist in the work of the final year's wrap-up of the book. Jessica Tollestrup typed, researched, formatted, read, and edited, plus cheered me on as deadlines loomed. I couldn't have done it without her.

Former staff members from my years as Governor and from the 1990 race for that office stepped up every time I requested their help on research *and* recall. Special thanks go to Marilynn Keyser, Anne Squier, Danny Santos, Kerry Barnett, Donnella Slayton, Rick Geistwhite, Kevin Smith, Sarah Johnson, and Carole Morse. Also, from my Secretary of State years: Felicia Trader and Craig Turley. And, from Frank's staff: Rick Hanson. Thank you all.

Several organizations and agencies were incredibly helpful when I needed material and background. At the top of the list are the Oregon Archives staff in Salem and Portland State University's Millar Library special collections staff. Also my thanks to the staff from the House and Senate at the Legislature, the Multnomah County Records and Archives Department, the president's staff at Mt. Hood Community College, Parkrose School District, the Center for American Women and Politics at Rutgers University, the Kennedy School of Government at Harvard University, and the Farmworker Housing and PCUN staff from Woodburn.

A special thanks to Drew Vattiat from *The Oregonian*, who helped me locate photographs from my political past, and Gerry Lewin, photographer, who generously shared his photo collection with me on an afternoon visit to his home. And I love Gerry's photo on this book cover. Photographs with no credit are from my personal collection.

My thanks to Chuck Johnson, who read the complete edited manuscript before it went back to OSU Press to put one more set of eyes on every page. He was there to cheer with me when the edits were done.

My gratitude to Tom Booth of OSU Press for helping me when the going got tough and I got frustrated. A special thanks for *hand-carrying* my two notebooks containing the final manuscript when I panicked at putting them into the U.S. Mail between Portland and Corvallis.

To Jo Alexander, a professional editor of extreme skill. She "felt" the story and also felt my pain at giving up some of my "pearls of wisdom" as we downsized the manuscript in the final edit process. Jo, you have a great eye for detail and could always see the "end product." Thank you, too, to Micki Reaman and Nancy Barbour for their help in promoting the book, and to David Drummond for the cover design.

Like a political career, a book does not become either a reality or a success without the support, assistance, and encouragement of others. Someone else must believe it is possible and that it matters.

To all those who helped and so many who encouraged me to complete the book … thank you, thank you, thank you.

B.R.

Introduction

I was the first woman governor in my native state of Oregon and among the first ten women elected governor in the United States of America. I hold a place in history, yet even now, after twenty years, there is a sense of nonreality about my life adventure.

More than fifteen years have passed since I left office as Governor of Oregon. I now feel ready to share that unique experience. The difficulty, for me, lies in knowing what to tell. Is my story simply a tale of political success as one of the first woman governors? Is my childhood an important element of my story? Does anyone care about the accomplishments of my gubernatorial term? Can I stomach a rerun of my most prominent political failure? Can I honestly define the line between the woman I am and the governor I became? Within my story are there elements that may inspire others? Where do I begin? Where do I stop?

Of the first ten women elected governor "in their own right" in America, elected between 1974 and 1997, four are already deceased. Governor Ella Grasso of Connecticut, the first, died of cancer in 1981. Governor Dixie Lee Ray of Washington, the second on the list, died of cancer in 1984. Governor Joan Finney of Kansas died of cancer in 2002. Governor Ann Richards of Texas died of cancer in 2006.

It is not always understood that being a governor is unlike being in Congress or the U.S. Senate or even serving as State Treasurer or State Attorney General. Governors are not merely one of a body or simply an elected executive leader in state government. Governors head state government with responsibility for billions of dollars and thousands of employees. They govern. They lead. In America, only the President has more single responsibility than the governors of our fifty states.

That may explain why I feel strongly that the earliest of our women governors have a fascinating tale to tell. And like Governor Madeleine Kunin of Vermont, author of *Living a Political Life*, I feel it is time for me to explore *my* piece of the puzzle, to help clarify what it was like to be one of our nation's female political trailblazers.

It is with that perspective that I set out to tell you my story.

B.R.

CHAPTER ONE

The Bombshell

I tentatively picked up the seven sheets of yellow legal paper and re-read the memo—the memo to myself. Not really a memo, I guess, but mental wanderings in an as-yet-secret world of my own political fantasy. These were the pages of both personal and political thoughts I had written in February of 1990 after Oregon's Democratic Governor, Neil Goldschmidt, called me at home to inform me he was likely to drop out of his reelection race in the next few days.

For two days I had been talking to myself on paper, reacting to his telephone call. Never again would I use the word "bombshell" loosely now that I knew what it was like to be the recipient of an honest-to-goodness verbal bombshell!

I was mid-way through my second term as Secretary of State and I was accustomed to campaigning statewide. Neil wasn't expected to have any Primary Election opposition but his fall race would be a competitive one. He was such a well-known, active governor, full of visionary ideas, that most political folks expected him to win. However, Republican Dave Frohnmayer, Oregon's Attorney General, would be a strong, experienced opponent.

Today, twenty years later, I find myself re-reading that long-ago memo and once again feeling the excitement, the anticipation, the near-confusion, and even an ounce or two of fear. I look at the date on the first page … Sunday, February 4, 1990.

The Governor called at about 8 p.m. (He said it was half-time of the Trail Blazers' game.) He called to say he would make his decision in the next forty-eight hours but he wanted me to know there was a strong possibility he was not going to run for reelection. He asked me to keep the call confidential. He said it was a "heads-up" call in case he decided to drop out of the 1990 governor's race. A forty-eight-hour "heads-up" ! He thought I might want to have "the next forty-eight hours for planning."

Forty-eight hours! I had planned on almost forty-eight months after the 1990 election to make my decision about running for governor in 1994 and to then to get my campaign organized for the race. I guess this is not a total surprise. With mounting rumors that Neil's marriage is in serious trouble and with Frohnmayer nipping at the Governor's heels poll-wise, a

1

tough race may not seem very appealing to Neil. It sounded, on the phone, as if he had some kind of a meeting with his close supporters today. In any case, I have a heads-up! The office of governor has shifted from day-dreaming status to something much closer to reality. Reality!!!! My God, how can Barbara Roberts running for Governor of Oregon be a reality?

The next few paragraphs in this short journal reflect feelings and emotions, even doubts that most political leaders keep to themselves. We always want to breed confidence for our voters and not tell them how frightening political leadership can seem, particularly when it hits you out of the blue.

I can't quite grasp the reality of it. My head is full of a hundred thoughts. My emotions are confusing. I feel close to tears but I'm not sure what these feelings mean: Happiness? Dreams coming true? Loneliness?

Loneliness is as close as I can come to explaining what I feel. How could I describe to anyone what I am experiencing, the emotional roller-coaster? ...

I'm too tired to be writing this but somehow even a few sketchy words seem in order on this unusual night in my life. I'll look back on this time later with a smile, I think. But also with the first reality of the loneliness.

My life is a movie script. Strangely I'm playing myself. I hope I am up to the role!!!!

On Monday I shared Neil's telephone call with my personal staff. Donnella Slayton, my executive assistant, went right to work helping me clean up every piece of paper on my desk and return every telephone call. We also did a complete in-depth review of my calendar. It was clear calendar priorities might change at any moment.

Patricia McCaig, who had managed my successful campaigns for Secretary of State, was out of the office on a week's vacation and in the middle of a move. When I called her at home there was a very long silence on her end of the line. I thought perhaps she had fainted ... or hung up. But within seconds she was ready to roll again. She was ready to put her considerable political skills to work again on the governor's race if and when the governor dropped out. She called an "emergency meeting" of our closest political insiders for Tuesday. We gave my supporters no hint of the agenda, but they came without hesitation.

The most significant message we received on that long-ago Monday was a call from the Governor's office requesting my full week's calendar! (The Governor wouldn't care about my schedule unless he planned to make an announcement.)

My notes from Tuesday, February 6, feel as real to me today as they were in 1990.

Funny things in my head today. I'm walking down the hall in the capitol; I put my shoulders back and find myself thinking about how I'd feel walking down these halls as Oregon's Governor. It was fun but I began to think people could actually see my thoughts.

Back in the office I signed a large stack of governor's appointment certificates. I've done this for over five years for two governors. But today each time I looked at Neil's signature on the Governor's line, I felt sad. I sensed he looked at that word as he signed each certificate. I remembered back to the day almost four years ago when he and I dreamed together about the Oregon we wanted to make happen. His vision was already clear … and exciting. Now, perhaps, that dream would be fading. The prospect made me sad.

Yet, in spite of the sadness of dreams unfulfilled, I began to sense the lineage as one leader follows another. Some dreams may die but new ones may emerge and blossom. I have my own dreams for Oregon, my own vision.

But there are questions, too. Can I be seen as strong enough? Will I be recognized as a leader? Will being female be a small or large factor in today's Oregon? Will the hundreds of speeches I delivered in every part of the state over the past six years count for something? I think so. I hope so!

Wednesday, February 7, 1990:
Today could be thought of as a one-sentence day: Today, Governor Neil Goldschmidt made the announcement that he would not seek reelection in 1990. (It is worth a comment here that there was never a second follow-up call from Neil.) The Governor also shared with the press and the state that he and his wife Margie were separating after twenty-five years of marriage.

Obviously for me, there is, on this dramatic day, a second sentence. Tomorrow I will announce my candidacy for Governor of Oregon.

Thursday, February 8, 1990:

Today, surrounded by family and close friends, in the Oregon Secretary of State's office, I held the press conference that made me an official candidate for governor. Press and media filled the office. My remarks went well. I handled the question period confidently. I felt strong and think that I looked professional. With only two days preparation it went incredibly smoothly. Every time I looked at Frank, he was beaming at me. How I love that man! And each time I looked at Dad he was teary-eyed! Two men who believe, above all others, that I can and will win. Tomorrow I will begin the journey to see if their belief in my abilities and in me is valid and realistic.

In many ways those memo pages represent a defining border in my life. On one side of the line, I am child, student, wife, mother, divorcée, single mother, new wife, and budding politician. Crossing the line to the other side, I am leader, governor, widow, academic, grandmother, author, and senior statesperson. I believe a single telephone call altered the remainder of my life. At age seventy-four, I look back and I feel a sense of disbelief about how so many different pieces fit together to produce who I became, even who I am now.

CHAPTER TWO

Small-town Girl

Few acts of chance have more influence on our lives than the family we are born into. I was one lucky little girl!

I was born in Corvallis, Oregon, on the first day of winter, December 21, 1936. I was born into a household filled with love and kindness and respect.

My mother was a farmer's daughter from Montana. My father was a preacher's son from Oregon. They met in an Oregon logging camp where my dad, Bob Hughey, worked in the mill and my mother, Carmen Murray, cooked for the work crew. They married in 1935, and were married for fifty-five years until my father's death.

As I think of the adult I became, I am aware there is a large amount of research about the outcome of birth order on a child's future success. As the firstborn child in my family, I am inclined to agree with the science that says that this particular birth position gives you some extra assets, a leg up. I am also swayed by more recent research that has asserted that most successful women in my age category had a very positive relationship with their fathers. Suzanne Braun Levine, a founder of *Ms.* magazine said it most interestingly, "A mother who praises her daughter is seen as cheerleading. When a father does that, he's bestowing." Terri Apter, a psychologist who did a four-year study on the subject, said, "Daughters often see their fathers as more objective than their mothers. Some women feel their mother thinks too highly of them, but they identify specific traits that their father appreciates, which boosts their confidence." Related research and articles indicate this impact is particularly strong with *elder* daughters.

My dad had two brothers but the greater influence on him was six sisters and a determined mother who raised most of her large family without a father in the household. My dad thought girls were real people and always declared he was thrilled to have two daughters and didn't feel shortchanged to have no sons. I believe, looking back, his declaration was factual but more important to me was the fact that I *believed* it and proudly shared my special status with friends all my life.

I am a descendant of Oregon Trail pioneers, the fourth generation of my family to be born in the state. My sister, Pat, was born two years later on December 20, 1938. We celebrated our December birthdays together for over sixty years until her untimely death in February 2001.

As far back as I can remember, our home was always filled with laughter and hugs, good food, and no bickering. My mother was a wonderful cook and a great pie maker. She had a cheerful disposition and, for all the early years of my life, sewed frilly dresses, little pinafores, and crocheted outfits for my sister and me. Because Pat and I usually had matching dresses, we were often mistaken for twins. Years of photos still exist of us; round cheeked, with blonde curls, standing or seated in our matching dresses and matched shoes and socks.

My father had a good singing voice, and every car trip, no matter how short, turned into a sing-along. As a kid I knew all the words to almost every song recorded by Bing Crosby and by the Mills Brothers. Dad's favorites were "Paper Doll" and "Red Sails in the Sunset," and no drive was complete without them. And additionally, at least once a week, Pat and I were serenaded to "Daddy's Little Girl."

How could I feel anything but loved? How could a little girl growing up in that household not gain the confidence that comes from feeling special?

My parents had a wonderful marriage, which only added to my sense of security and comfort. They kissed good-bye when they parted and kissed hello when they came back together, even on trips as short as a quick run to the grocery store. They made big decisions together and trusted each other's judgment on the small stuff.

Valentine's Day and my parents' August 13th wedding anniversary were considered real holidays in our home. My dad bought fancy lace-trimmed valentine cards and chocolates for his "three girls" every February 14th. Mother

Barbara Kay Hughey, age two

Family photo: Mother, Pat (age two), me (age four), and Dad.

and Dad exchanged sentimental cards, gifts, and love notes each wedding anniversary. Mother had over fifty years of these cards and notes saved away in her things when she died in 1998. Whatever there is about me that is *solid* came from that home and that upbringing.

My father gave up lumber mill work at the end of the 1930s and became a skilled machinist. In 1940 our family of four moved to Los Angeles, California. My mother's three brothers, her sister, their families, and mother's parents had all moved to the Los Angeles area. That clearly had an influence on the family decision to leave Oregon. Additionally, good jobs seemed plentiful in Southern California as the 1940s began. My dad was quickly employed and soon life seemed all about playing in the sunshine, roller skating and skinned knees, weekend baseball games and Sunday picnics, and lots of cousins, aunts, and uncles.

Just before my fifth birthday our world changed dramatically with the bombing of America's naval fleet at Pearl Harbor and the entry of the U.S. into World War II. Uncles and cousins went to war. My dad's plant was converted to war-time production. Dad, night foreman in a vital war industry, was exempt from foreign battlefields but quickly took responsibility as an air raid warden in our neighborhood. If the warning siren went off, and as searchlights scanned the skies for enemy planes, Dad would slip on his warden armband and his official helmet and make certain every light in our home was turned off. While he patrolled the neighborhood streets, we huddled close to Mother in our darkened house and waited for the all-clear siren and for Daddy's footsteps at the front door. Only then were we safe again.

Mother and Dad were also active with the Red Cross blood bank. They were volunteers and blood donors throughout the war years and for the next forty years. Years later, one New Year's Eve afternoon, my dad came by, unannounced, and informed me that at age thirty it was time I became a blood donor. Off we drove to the local Red Cross and a new generation of blood donors was launched in my family. Dad and I were type O negative, the universal blood type, and we felt an extra obligation to donate regularly.

Looking back at World War II, I believe my sense of duty, my commitment to public service, was born in those war years. The patriotism of the period was strongly felt. We learned to ration meat and other foods and gasoline. We planted "victory gardens." We did without chocolate. We donated our beloved rubber dolls to the rubber drive for the war effort. We felt weepy but it was for "our boys in uniform." We understood that it mattered.

I started school during that period—kindergarten. Even in school, the war was part of everyday life in our art projects, our music programs, and "show-and-tell" time. And school brought another change for me. For reasons still unclear to me, children in the Los Angeles school system were required to be called by their first name. My given name was Barbara Kay but I had always gone by my middle name. I was "Kay." Kay was me! Now at school, I became Barbara. This dual identity was confusing for a five-year-old. That name change labeled me for the rest of my life. As school records followed me through three states from kindergarten through high school, it was just easier to let people call me the name that matched those school records. And for over sixty years I've remained "Barbara," but almost all my cousins still address me as "Kay." And it still feels natural and right. When I married twice and changed my *last* name twice it was not the new experience for me that it was for most women in America. I'd been there.

When World War II ended in 1945, my parents decided that Los Angeles might not be the best location to raise two little girls. They thought we'd be safer and more sheltered in some small Oregon town. They wanted my sister and me to experience the sense of community that comes from small-town living. So from the city of Los Angeles, burgeoning in postwar growth, we were suddenly living next to a small country highway with the Yamhill River bordering our back yard, four miles from the closest small town, and attending a one-room school without indoor plumbing!

Gold Creek School was one half mile from our house and on school days we walked along the road single file, beside the highway, taking extra care when the big noisy logging trucks thundered by. The one-room school had only a big closet for coats and boots and lunch pails, and then the classroom with various-sized desks to fit the wide range of ages being taught in that single room. Our teacher, Mrs. Petite, was a tall Native American woman with big, rough hands and gentle eyes and voice. I had come from a huge Los Angeles school and almost literally stepped back into another century. Yet I've always been grateful for that experience. I learned to read and to study while other activities were happening all around me. I learned how long I could hold my breath in an outhouse! I found that when my assigned school work was complete, there were still many learning opportunities available to me.

After two and a half years at Gold Creek, my family moved the nine miles to Sheridan, the town where my dad worked at the Sheridan Machine Shop (later to be impressively named Sheridan Gear and Manufacturing). I still consider Sheridan, Oregon, my home town. Sheridan had a population of two thousand when we moved there in 1949. It had the same population when I moved away after high school graduation in 1955. Most people in the area worked in farming, logging, or timber mill jobs. We had one movie theater, one bakery, one doctor, one dentist, one lawyer, and one CPA. We also had two drugstores, two clothing stores, two gas stations, two taverns, two appliance stores, two grocery stores, two cemeteries, and a single funeral parlor. And lest you think my small town was devoid of sophistication ... Sheridan had a jewelry store, a beauty parlor, a bank, a weekly newspaper, a Masonic Lodge, a small city library, and several churches. And in times of emergency, we had *a* police officer and a volunteer fire department.

In those years, most moms didn't work. Most town kids walked to school, rain or shine. Most dads stayed married to the moms. You knew everyone's parents and *never* called them by their first names. You knew who were cousins to whom and to which church families belonged. You recognized most folks' cars so you could usually tell who was visiting whom.

I remember when I was in high school, eating my lunch at home, I saw two cars enter the roadway up on cemetery hill. As I watched from the kitchen window for the next few days, those same cars appeared every lunch hour. My young mind finally put two and two together. I knew the cars. I knew the two parents from two separate families. I was shocked when I figured it out. When I brought the incriminating facts to my parents, Dad said, "Yes, we've seen the cars. It may not be right but it is not our business. You are not to repeat what you've seen." Finally, the cars stopped meeting and the female parent moved away with her two daughters. I never told the story to anyone.

Small towns had disadvantages as well as advantages.

When my sister, Pat, and I first started elementary school in Sheridan, we were almost an oddity. We had once lived in California, our father didn't work in agriculture or the timber industry, and we hadn't started first grade with all the other kids in our class. A new child in town was pretty rare.

In the summer of 2004, four of the women I went to school with in Sheridan came to spend three days with me in my Portland townhouse. Amazingly, they could *all* remember my first day in school in Sheridan. They remembered the teacher bringing me to the front of the classroom and introducing me to all the students. They remembered it clearly. I had no memory of that day. And, even more strange, they remembered their young female reaction: "Why couldn't it be a good-looking new boy? Why did it have be a cute little blond girl?" We've all been friends for over fifty years and I had never heard that story before.

My sister and I loved school in Sheridan. We fit in very quickly and made lots of new friends. Less than a year later, as fourth and sixth graders, both Pat and I were selected by our classmates to be junior pioneer court members for Sheridan's annual celebration and rodeo. One mother complained openly and bitterly that our selection was inappropriate since we were "outsiders" and didn't come from local pioneer family stock. Many years later, when my parents were doing our family genealogies, they discovered Dad's Oregon Trail ancestors had actually homesteaded in the Sheridan area, before relocating to Southern Oregon. My mother, still irritated at that long-ago slight, immediately popped up with: "So who's a pioneer now?!" My mother was not only competitive, but was truly protective of her two daughters.

That minor slight aside, Sheridan was a fun, secure, safe, happy place to grow up. Pat and I belonged to Girl Scouts and then Rainbow Girls. We were active in a wide range of school activities. Mother was our Girl Scout leader. Dad coached our girls' summer softball league team. I was the team's catcher. Soon Pat was on the tumbling team and a strong member of the high school volleyball team. I was editor of the high school newspaper, a student body officer, president of the Service Club, did speech competition and school plays. And Pat and I were both high school cheerleaders.

By the time I was a freshman in high school, Mother was working at the weekly newspaper office, the *Sheridan Sun*, as a linotype operator. Dad was now foreman at the only machine shop in town. He belonged to the Masonic Lodge, eventually becoming Worthy Master of his lodge. Both Mother and Dad, and later Pat, were members of the Order of Eastern Star, the women's arm of the Masonic Lodge. Our family was clearly a member of the community. My parents had been right about leaving Los Angeles and starting again in a small Oregon community.

My parents attended every event Pat and I were involved with— school plays, volleyball games, Rainbow Girls ceremonies, high school band and chorus concerts. Pat played the clarinet. I sang alto. Mother and Dad were cheering Sheridan fans at every high school football and basketball game, even those in neighboring towns. All the kids in town knew our parents. When Pat and I weren't teaching some boy to dance in our living room on Saturday afternoon, we were playing cards with friends at the kitchen table and sharing one of Mother's delicious pies.

In the summer I picked strawberries and green beans to earn extra money for my school clothes. I would put the next fall's school wardrobe (wool sweaters and pleated plaid skirts) on lay-away at the local mercantile and then work like the dickens to pay off the items before the summer crop harvest season ended. I was a *driven* crop picker. I reasoned that if I were going to get up that early and get that dirty, I was going to make some money at it! I was usually in the top three pickers among all the local kids who rode the old school buses out to harvest berries and beans. I admit it might also be accurate to say that I was just a *tad* competitive! The money was an incentive. My place as a top picker was a status symbol!

Yet summer wasn't all work. My girlfriends and I owned bicycles and several of us often packed a lunch, tied a towel to the handle bars, and rode out to a swimming place in a wonderful, sparkling, little country creek. On a hot day that cooling stream was totally inviting. The added attractions were the local farm boys who showed up after their chores were done to cool off in that same swimming spot. We went to school with these boys from September to June but during the summer months we didn't often see them in town. These bike rides were always presented as biking and swimming excursions and an opportunity to earn points toward our Girls Athletic Association letters. We would never have confessed that these bike rides also turned into a great opportunity to practice our flirting skills. The truth be known, I never learned to swim. However, one summer I did learn to kiss underwater.

There was a great deal of freedom growing up in a small Oregon town in the 1950s. We walked or rode our bikes to visit our friends at home or to meet them for a Coke. We walked to the movie house and met our classmates. We dated young and held hands with our boyfriends during the movies. Later we rode to school events with sixteen- and seventeen-year-old dates. Sometimes we were even permitted to ride to or from school in a boy's car. But we were kept in line by the fact that every adult in town was keeping a watchful eye on us. If someone saw you in a boy's car headed to "park" at the old cemetery, they were not hesitant to mention it to your father the next day at the barber shop or the volunteer fire department. Talk about it taking a "village to raise a child."

I believe it is accurate to say I was popular in high school. I was an A student. I was involved in all kinds of school activities. I had boyfriends *and* girlfriends. I found it easy to be a big frog in a small pond. I don't know if I would have had such broad opportunities to try my wings in a big school.

I learned some life skills growing up in a small town. First, in order to make things happen, almost everyone needed to pitch in and help. If you wanted to have a parade, first you worked together to build a float, and then you also rode on the float. I thought the whole world operated that way. By the time I was a teenager I had little concept of the role of *spectator*. I was never good on the sidelines. I always loved being part of the parade.

Small-town experience also taught me the danger of gossip. When you are new in a small town you haven't yet learned about the interrelationships that exist in a somewhat closed community. Whispering about a classmate might be aimed directly at the ear of her first cousin! It was simply easier and safer not to gossip at all. It was a lesson that stayed with me. Many years later, it was a lesson that served me well in the political domain.

It all sounds idyllic and in many ways it was. However, there was little encouragement for girls to step forward, to lead, to question in the 1950s. High school girls did not become student body presidents. We were the secretaries of student bodies all over America. And just try and imagine this today: I was student body officer, class salutatorian, speech competition winner, cheerleader, editor of the school newspaper, all this and much more ... and no one *ever* suggested I think about college. It was the 1950s and in small-town, blue-collar U.S.A., girls married, had children, and disappeared into the kitchens of America. And nobody blinked. Nobody questioned. Not even those bright, motivated, energetic young women. Not even them.

I still have close friends from my high school years. We still spend time together. They knew my late parents and my late sister. I knew their parents and siblings. And they know me: small town girl, strawberry picker, cheerleader, student leader, governor.

We grew up together. As kids from the 1950s, the chance that any one of us could grow up to be a governor would have been laughable, silly to think about. We grew up together but *now* they tell me they aren't surprised I became governor. Well, they may not be surprised, but I'm shocked!

CHAPTER THREE

Growing Up Fast

I loved high school! It was a wonderful period of my life. I frequently hear adults lament the misery of their high school experience, and they say they never intend to be part of a class reunion or relive their teen years. That's not me. Those were wonderful years for me.

Although my small high school had limited academic options (no foreign languages, no journalism or drama classes, no tennis teams or advanced science classes), I worked hard at the classes that were available. I was a fast reader with good retention. I loved drawing colored maps in geography class and sewing garments in home economics. My favorite classes were bookkeeping and speech, two classes where I acquired skills that would become highly valuable later in my life. I made good grades and found the academic part of high school satisfying and rewarding.

However, I was definitely not a nose-to-the-grindstone type of girl. I found non-class activities around every corner that were fun and gave me new skills and experiences. For instance, for two years I was a student helper in the principal's office. I filed, delivered phone messages, posted tardy excuses on attendance records, and collected money for the athletic game buses. This experience allowed me to spend time with faculty members during their class breaks and lunch hours. It was eye-opening when I learned teachers had spouses, siblings, and even health issues. Some smoked. Some were divorced. Teachers were real people! What a revelation.

I was editor of the school paper my junior and senior years. Somewhat unusually, my high school paper was published weekly in the local community newspaper. So I was actually writing and editing for the entire community. Additionally, my columns had to meet the standards for newspaper submission. On top of that, my mother worked for the *Sheridan Sun* and was manually typesetting and checking my work. There was no such thing as "spell-check" way back then but, believe me, I made frequent trips to the dictionary to prevent my faculty advisor, the community newspaper editor, *or* my mother from discovering errors.

Some folks might say, "Of course, you loved high school. You were part of the popular clique." Funny, but I never saw myself that way. I was on the cheerleading team for all four years of high school. I dated basketball and football players. Most of my close friends and my sister, Pat, were in the same group. But I worked on the yearbook with a whole different set of students. I belonged to Rainbow Girls with girls who never considered cheerleading squad or football players. I picked summer crops with yet another bunch of teenagers. I often helped struggling students during study hall and sometimes went to dances with boys who never played sports.

Today, more than fifty years after graduating from high school, I can still pick up the phone and call almost all of my classmates. It is not about cheerleading or being governor, it's about our shared experience as small-town kids in the 1950s. We still dance the same way. We remember the lyrics to the same songs, songs that accompanied our growing-up years. We learned to dance and kiss and drive in the same town, in the same years. We shared secrets and we shared our lives. Who the hell cares about being a cheerleader fifty years ago? Not me! I care about still knowing friends who knew me way back when. I care about our shared history.

My high school years were also about dating. Dating in a small town has at least one notable liability—where do you go on a date? No bowling alley. No skating rink. No nice restaurants. There was one movie theatre where a new feature came only every three or four weeks. A date might mean a basketball game, an occasional sock-hop, or, on big nights, a drive to McMinnville (fourteen miles away) to a drive-in movie or to a local hamburger hang-out. Yet, for small town kids who knew nothing different, it all seemed just fine.

I dated a number of boys in high school, sometimes from Sheridan, sometimes from our rival town of Willamina, five miles away. I dated boys from my own class but more often guys a year or two older than me. My father's rule of thumb was I could sit in a boy's car in front of our house and talk for a while after a date. But when my dad decided the "talking" might be getting a little too serious, he would switch the front porch light off and on a couple of times. That signal meant: "Time to come in." If Dad thought my exit from the car didn't occur fast enough, the porch light flashed again. There was never a *third* signal. Most boys in town knew and liked my father and they didn't intend to get on his bad side.

After Christmas vacation in my sophomore year, I started dating a boy named Neal Sanders. Neal was a varsity basketball player who had moved from Durango, Colorado, to Sheridan. He was a senior and worked part-time at one of the local lumber mills. He boarded with the high school English teacher. It was very unusual to have a high school boy whose parents didn't live in town. My parents liked Neal and my mother looked for excuses to fix him a home-cooked meal or serve him fresh pie and coffee. He was a tall, lanky kid, six foot two inches tall, and my mother thought he looked underfed. Neal spent so much time in our home that he soon felt like a member of our family.

By the time Neal graduated in June of 1953, we were a steady item. After graduation he took a full-time job at the local plywood mill, bought a better car, and added some new clothes to his wardrobe. He felt pretty good about his life at that time, but by the spring of 1954 he was getting restless. He began thinking about the possibility of attending college but, for him, that seemed financially impossible. The only route to college he saw was through the military. So on April 1, 1954, he and his buddy, Bob Blair, left to begin a four-year enlistment in the U.S. Air Force. Four years! I was a junior in high school and the boy I loved was leaving for four years. This relationship no longer felt as if he was simply a steady boyfriend. I was seventeen and in love. It sounds so very young now. A popular song on the Hit Parade at the time was Nat King Cole's "Too Young." The song ended with the lyrics, "And then one day they may recall, we were not too young at all." At the time, those were my feelings, my sentiments about our relationship.

After Neal left, I continued to work hard on my high school classes. I stayed busy with my many school and community activities. I spent a lot of time with my friends. Yet Neal and I also kept up a romantic correspondence. Every day we wrote letters to each other. He wrote from basic training in San Antonio for three months and then from Biloxi, Mississippi. The letters grew more romantic and more serious with each passing month. Then in the late summer of 1954 he wrote the letter that changed my life: the proposal of marriage letter. At the same time he sent a letter to my parents asking for my hand in marriage. I was thrilled. I was filled with excitement and love and plans for the future. I said, "Yes." Yes, yes, yes. Two weeks later my parents announced our engagement in the Sheridan newspaper. I was about to enter my senior year in high school and my parents made only one stipulation about this engagement. I had to agree to graduate. That seemed an easy commitment to make at the time.

I entered my senior year of high school in September of 1954 engaged and happy. Several girls from my class had already dropped out of high school to marry. Some were already mothers. But I had promised my parents I would graduate.

In early October I received a letter from Neal, who was then in Air Force Electronics School in Mississippi. He told me he would have two weeks leave coming at Christmas time, followed by three more months of electronic schooling before he would be relocated to a new assignment. Most of the men with electronics skills were being shipped to European bases. Neal was clear that if he went to Europe, he wanted me to come with him. That could only happen if we were married.

Here was Neal's plan: he would come home on leave in December and we would marry. Then he would return to Mississippi and I would stay in school in Sheridan. In April he would be sent to Europe. In June, after my graduation, I would be flown to Europe as a military dependant, a wife, at Air Force expense. It was a grand plan. We imagined we would spend free weekends and his leave time touring Europe. It was all a pretty exciting dream for two small-town kids.

My parents finally agreed to Neal's plan. It seemed reasonable, considering our wonderful opportunity for European travel. We began making wedding plans. Our letters turned even more romantic, even more personal; I saved them, tied up in pretty blue ribbons. We counted the days until Neal's return to Oregon. On December 19, 1954, Neal arrived by military plane at the old Portland Air Base. As we embraced on the tarmac, him in uniform, it felt like a scene from an old movie. We had exactly one week to handle every detail before our wedding but that night, after nine months apart, the calendar seemed unimportant.

The next day we celebrated Pat's sixteenth birthday and had our required blood tests done. The following day I turned eighteen and we celebrated and still had time to meet with the minister who would be performing our wedding ceremony. In the next four days we picked up our marriage license, had our wedding rehearsal, and celebrated Christmas Eve and Christmas. On the afternoon of December 26, 1954, we were married at the local Methodist Church. After a short four-day honeymoon trip to Seattle, we arrived back home in time for the community New Year's Eve dance at the Willamina VFW hall. We entered the dance as husband and wife.

Friends and family were there to celebrate the New Year and our happiness.

Three days later Neal returned to Mississippi and I went back to high school. Not exactly a romantic first six months of marriage. We continued to write every day and awaited news of Neal's next assignment. Where would he be stationed? Where would I be flying off to after graduation? It was an exciting mystery.

Finally, in early April, the news of Neal's relocation came. It was not at all what either of us had expected. He was being sent to Harlingen Air Force Base in Texas, two hundred fifty miles south of San Antonio. The only place in the United States further south than this tip of Texas is the Florida Keys. Our dream of Europe was crushed, and yet we would be three thousand miles from Oregon. There wasn't a base in the continental United States that could have been a greater distance from home. We were both very disappointed.

I had two more months until graduation. I couldn't wait to be with Neal again. Our dream had certainly not been to reunite in Texas but you can't argue with the military. Texas it would be for three long years.

As graduation grew closer I began to feel sad about leaving my parents and my sister. A part of me felt very married. Yet another part of me knew how much I would miss my wonderful family.

My mother's parents came from California for my graduation. They had proposed that, after graduation, I would travel by car with them back to their home in Los Angeles, visit all my aunts and uncles and cousins there, and then go by train from Los Angeles to San Antonio, Texas. It sounded like a great adventure. I had traveled only once by train, as a child, during World War II, and I loved the idea of making the last leg of my trip by train. Well actually, not the *last* leg since San Antonio was two hundred fifty miles from Harlingen. That leg of the trip I would make with my husband!

I spoke on graduation night as salutatorian of my class. I felt very emotional as I delivered my remarks. The next morning I cried as I said good-bye. Pat was a weepy mess and I wasn't much better. My Grandpa Murray pulled slowly out of the driveway, giving everyone time for more waves and more tears. Grandma handed me a tissue as my Sheridan home went out of view. We rode silently for a number of miles as we headed south toward California and my new life.

The train trip from Los Angeles to San Antonio was indeed an adventure. I had never seen so many miles of nothing! For my very first meal on the train, the conductor seated me with an older man who spoke no English. My next dining car table mate was an older woman who talked incessantly about her stomach disorder and her bad feet—definitely not conducive to an appetizing meal. But I loved the movement of the train and slept easily to the sway. I found interesting people to visit with and soon even the bland scenery was a treat as each mile brought me closer to my new husband. The trip was only thirty-six hours but it felt like days.

As the train finally pulled into the San Antonio station, I already had my suitcases next to me, prepared to step onto the platform at the first possible second. I searched out the window for a glimpse of Neal. I didn't see him anywhere. I began to feel very anxious. What if he wasn't there to meet me? I stepped off the train, carrying my two inexpensive suitcases. Looking back, I must have been the picture of a scared, unsophisticated, small-town girl. Suddenly he was there. I was in his arms. The fear went away and I felt only love—and relief. He took my suitcases. We chattered madly at each other. He pointed toward the car without skipping a beat in our conversation. Neither of us could quit smiling!

We were in the car. We were in each other's arms. Months of loneliness melted away. God, how I had missed him. He started telling me about the duplex he had rented. I didn't care if it was a tent! It was going to be our very first home together. We were going home.

We had two hundred fifty miles we wanted to cover that afternoon and, believe me, that was going to happen. We decided to pull in to a drive-in restaurant for a quick meal before we headed to Harlingen. It was there I got my first taste of the South. In the drive-in parking area there were two outdoor drinking fountains, one labeled "colored only," the other marked "white only." For a girl from Oregon, this was a new and shocking experience. Growing up in an almost-all-white state, I had never seen such visible discrimination. To this day, I can still remember my sick feeling when I read those two signs. This would indeed be a new and different life.

We arrived in Harlingen just at dusk. There were lots of palm trees and citrus trees. It was tropical and quite muggy and warm. Neal pulled up in front of our furnished duplex. I had shipped most of our wedding gifts to him earlier and he had tried to make the place look like home. New sheets, new towels, even fresh flowers. He turned on the overhead fans, switched the radio to low volume, and welcomed me home.

One month later, the cockroaches drove us out of the duplex! We moved into a cute little cottage of a house … with exterminator services. We had no phone. I didn't drive. I knew no one and we had little money. When Neal left early each morning for the base, I was alone for the rest of the day. I walked a lot and kept our little house spotless. I wrote letters every day to my family and friends in Oregon. I found the heat stifling and tried to do laundry and housework early in the day. A few months later, wanting to add to his meager military salary, Neal decided to take a part-time job at the local television station. His electronics training helped him get the position. He now came home from the base every afternoon, changed out of his uniform, put on his civvies, ate, and left for his television job for the next five hours. Now I was really alone.

Well, not actually *alone.* I soon realized I was pregnant. I had morning sickness, afternoon sickness, and evening sickness! The only things that tasted good were banana popsicles and tomato juice. I couldn't face a glass of tomato juice for the next twenty years.

Our baby was due on the 20th of March. I was hoping for the 21st, my Grandpa Murray's birthday. In early March my parents came for their first Texas visit. I was so excited to see them. They, in turn, were *amazed* when they saw me … eight and a half months pregnant. We gave them a tour of our community, drove down to Padre Island on the Gulf of Mexico, and then took them back to our little house. We planned a nice visit the next day to Reynosa, Mexico, only thirty-five miles away and a still charming, unspoiled Mexican community. That visit was exciting for my parents who had never been out of the country. But it almost became more exciting than expected when I started having serious labor pains. My parents didn't feel dual citizenship and limited medical services were good ideas for their first grandchild so we headed back to the U.S. side of the border.

My parents were there for the birth of their first grandson early the next morning. I had missed my grandfather's birthday but Michael Scott Sanders' early arrival meant he was born on his father's twenty-second birthday, a totally unexpected gift. I always loved their shared birthday and found the numerical listing of their birth dates interesting. Neal was 3-4-34 and Mike was 3-4-56. No one, including me, had expected I would deliver a son. We hadn't even chosen a boy's name.

Speaking of names, by the time our son Mike was born, Neal Sanders had become Frank Sanders. His military records and then his temporary employment all used his first name and middle initial. I was Barbara to my friends, Kay to most of my family. He was Frank and also Neal depending on where he was. That name confusion continued throughout our lives.

However, now that we were Mama and Dada, that simplified the identity issue!

During the next two and a half years my parents made another visit to Texas, we made a month-long trip back to Oregon, and my sister, Pat, spent two weeks staying with us in the summer of 1957. She had just been a finalist in the Miss Oregon competition and she looked and felt like a million bucks.

Toward the end of 1957, we began to plan for Neal's Air Force discharge on April 1, 1958. But we had a complicated new issue to face. I was pregnant again and our second child was due at the exact time of Neal's military discharge date. We had little money saved and began to worry that if we waited until the new baby was born, we might get stranded in Texas. We *definitely* had no desire to stay in Texas and the timing of this pregnancy was really complicating our departure plans for Oregon.

We finally realized I needed to travel home to Oregon while my pregnancy would still safely permit that. Once again my maternal grandparents stepped up and announced plans to leave Los Angeles and drive all the way to southern Texas to transport Mike and me to California, where my parents would meet us. We would spend the December holidays in Los Angeles and then my parents and sister would take us home to Oregon to await the new baby and Neal's discharge. I was six months pregnant and I knew it would be a tiring trip. I hated to leave my husband for three months but I needed to go home to Oregon. It was the right decision.

I turned twenty-one on that endless drive from Texas to California. Pregnant, the mother of an almost-two-year-old, traveling with my grandparents, and in the middle of nowhere … I turned twenty-one. Hardly champagne and party hat time!

Me and Mike

After the Christmas and the New Year holidays, we left my mother's big happy extended family and headed back to Sheridan. The trip was wearing, but I reveled in the glorious vistas of trees and mountains and green valleys. I had really missed the green. Finally, we crossed the California/Oregon border. Now I truly felt I was going home. Six hours later I was back in the bedroom of my youth. As I crawled into bed it was almost as if I had never left ... except for Mike, already asleep in his corner crib, and the large mound under the sheets that clearly signaled my six-months pregnancy.

For the next three months I was pampered and spoiled. My mother's cooking and baking made it difficult for me to watch my weight. I was not allowed to lift Mike nor do any laundry, dishes, or housework. This was luxury I had never known, even as a child. Every afternoon, while Mike napped, I was instructed to put my feet up while Mother and I played our daily game of Scrabble. At this point the spoiling ended since my very competitive mother was not about to let me have an easy win at Scrabble. From Mother's high school basketball days, to growing up in rugged rural Montana, to having three athletic brothers, she played to win. Old friends visited. Mother and I grocery shopped together. Mother drove me to my doctor's appointments. And every night we talked and talked together — Mother, Dad, and me — making up for three years of missed visits. I loved every minute of it.

In February my sister, Pat, was married to Dwayne Turley, whom she had been dating for a few months. The wedding was held at the Sheridan Methodist Church, the same church where Neal and I were married. I was so far along in my pregnancy that I did not feel comfortable serving as my sister's matron of honor. Weddings always make me weepy but seeing my only sister married brought my hankie out from almost the beginning of the ceremony.

By March, the doctor began to wonder if this baby might arrive earlier than my April 1 due date. I had mixed emotions about this matter. If the baby came before April 1, the Air Force would pay my medical bills for the delivery but I would have to go through the birth without my husband. If the baby arrived later, I would have Neal there to hold my hand and soothe me but we would have a big medical bill and Neal would not yet be employed. But the baby would make the decision about when he or she was ready to arrive. And that is exactly what happened.

On the morning of March 26th I went into labor. We drove to the McMinnville Hospital (fourteen miles away), and I began a long, difficult labor. I silently wished for Neal's presence and support but was grateful as my parents took turns being with me. The delivery was complicated by the umbilical cord being wrapped around the baby's neck and my new baby arrived looking a not-so-healthy shade of blue. Even though he weighed 8 pounds, 4 ounces, my new son was immediately placed into an incubator. I was very frightened. Was he going to be all right? Had he been deprived of oxygen long enough to do any damage? The doctor said this was just a precaution but I wasn't fully convinced. Mark Jay Sanders had been born at 7 p.m. but I was not allowed to hold him until the next day. I was scared and emotional. I needed my husband's support but he was three thousand miles away.

When they finally took baby Mark out of the incubator and brought him to my bed, I was so relieved that I cried for several minutes. Thank goodness he was going to be all right. I checked every toe, every finger, every inch of his body. He squeezed my finger and opened his eyes. He was perfect.

A week after I came home from the hospital, Neal arrived back in Sheridan. I was overjoyed to see him. Neal marveled at his two sons and told me I was brave and extremely lovable. That's all I needed to hear! I felt as if we were finally a family again, all in one place, together. Yes, here we were, a married couple with two children, living and sleeping in a single bedroom. We had a small amount of savings and no job. Thank goodness for my parents. Those first weeks and months of starting over would have been almost impossible without them.

As the spring of 1958 turned into summer, Neal and I left my parents' home and moved the fifty miles from Sheridan to Portland and started a new life with our little boys. Mark was now three months old. Mike would soon be two and a half years old.

Neal had luckily found a position as a television cameraman at the studios of KOIN-TV, the CBS affiliate in Portland, as a result of his experience in electronics in the Air Force and his part-time job at the Texas television station. His pay was pretty good, and we had full family medical benefits. It was a great beginning for our little family.

We rented a brand-new two-bedroom duplex on the outskirts of Portland. I continued to be a full-time stay-at-home mother and housewife. It was such a wonderful period for me. We drove the fifty miles to Sheridan to visit with my parents at least twice a month. I loved my husband and children and I was happy to be back home in Oregon. These were good times. My sister moved to Portland and her first son, Craig, was born in August of 1958—another happy family change.

In 1959 we left our little duplex and moved a few miles away into the first home we owned—and it would turn out to be the only home the two of us would ever buy together. It was a brand-new three-bedroom ranch-style home with a fireplace, double garage, and a neighborhood of other young couples with small children. We were both so excited. We planted our front and back lawns, put in new shrubbery, and Neal built a beautiful retaining wall of red lava rock in our front yard. We fenced in the back yard area, bought a swing set, and planted a shade tree. We were living the American dream— or so it seemed.

The next year we enrolled Mike in a pre-school for four-year-olds. By then it was becoming clear that he had some problems. His speech was slow in developing. His communication habits were a little odd. Yet, at four, he was already reading. In the late 1950s and early 1960s if a child was neither blind, physically crippled, nor "retarded," there were few other diagnoses that defined a child with special problems. We felt that pre-school might stimulate Mike's communication abilities and give him better play skills with other children. After all, he was only four years old. His teachers said his ability to read and his demonstrated sense of humor were both signs of high intelligence. Our family doctor had no answers and no suggestions. Maybe I worried too much.

I learned to drive in 1960, got my driver's license at age twenty-four, and Neal bought a second family car. This was new freedom for me. I could do the grocery shopping, take Mike to pre-school, give the boys an outing in the local park, or just take them for a ride on a nice day. It was an independence I had not known before.

I was concerned about Mike but no one else seemed very worried about him. He avoided any eye contact, made odd gestures with his hands in front of his eyes, and seemed to live more and more in his own world. Neal wasn't willing to discuss this unusual behavior at any great length. It clearly made him uncomfortable. I would later learn that his reaction was quite typical for a male parent of a son experiencing any signs of disability. Oddly enough, for many men a less-than-perfect son is seen as a masculine shortcoming. Neal clearly loved Mike, but, for him, Mike's challenges were easier to ignore than face.

Mike began kindergarten in the fall of 1961, but he wasn't the only new student in our household. Three years after being discharged from the Air Force, Neal decided to take advantage of his G.I. Bill benefits. He registered as a freshman at Portland State College. He would be attending college full time during the day and working a full-time 3:30 p.m. to 11:30 p.m. shift at Channel 6. He would have only weekends to see his family and to keep up with his college studies and homework. It was a grueling schedule for him. As the months went by it became an increasingly lonely existence for me. I longed for the end of spring term and the start of summer vacation so I could once again have a husband with a more normal schedule.

I knew I needed something else besides the house and our boys to fill my time. I joined a local Toastmistress Club that met one evening a month to help its members become better public speakers. I had loved my speech classes in high school and thought this might be fun and useful. And it was. I met an interesting group of women, all older than me but full of fun and vitality. I looked forward to the monthly meetings, wrote diligently on any speaking assignments I was given, and faithfully practiced my presentations in front of my bedroom mirror, as instructed. Soon we were visiting other Toastmistress groups in our metropolitan area and I often represented our club in speech competitions. It was fun and stimulating. But I was ready for more.

I was soon reading Neal's textbooks, even helping him with his papers. I now understood how much I had missed by not furthering my own education. But he was the one with the G. I. Bill, the funding, the opportunity. Plus, his education was not just for him, it was for our whole family. I needed to be fully supportive. Already he had received a promotion at Channel 6. His bachelor's degree would open doors for him. The boys and I would also be beneficiaries. It all made perfect sense. Yet, it didn't keep me from wishing for my turn. Maybe someday my chance would come. Maybe.

CHAPTER FOUR

The Tough Years Begin

1962 is one of the years in my life that carries so many sad memories that I want to turn away from recording it on paper. This was the year that began a sea change in my life that was not to be reversed for many years, and in some cases the hurt would never be completely repaired.

The year started out pretty much in a pattern that our family had accepted as normal. Neal began his sophomore year at Portland State and was still employed at Channel 6. Mike began his first grade year in the Portland School District. Mark was in pre-school. I held down the home front and played chauffeur a great deal of the time.

In 1961 my parents had left Oregon to join another couple in the purchase of an old hotel and a separate restaurant in Tonopah, Nevada. It was a real adventure for them, but I missed having them in close visiting distance. My sister, Pat, had also moved away from the Portland area and lived over an hour's drive away, so we didn't get to see each other as often as we had before. I missed her. I missed having family close by.

Mike was still having problems, especially during school hours. At six years old he was still not completely toilet trained. At least a couple of times a week I had to drive to his school to clean him up and deliver a change of clothing. He had trouble concentrating on his school work. His lack of focus frustrated the teacher, and, in turn, her reaction upset Mike.

Finally, in the early spring, the teacher informed me that she was sending Mike home from school, not just for the day, but forever. Mike could no longer attend school. In 1962, children with disabilities had no legal rights to a public education. Even Portland, Oregon's largest school district, offered no special education classes of any kind. My son was sent home from school, kicked out of the first grade, and I had no recourse. I could not appeal to the school board, the courthouse, or the statehouse. It was 1962 and no state government in America, nor the federal government, gave these children with special needs any educational rights. What was I supposed to do? What would happen to Mike? Now his disability would be exacerbated by his also being uneducated. I went back to the school seeking some kind of help. They told me they would check around and get back to me in a few weeks.

About a month later the school called to give me a name and number at the Crippled Children's Division at the University of Oregon Medical School in Portland. The Center would be willing to see Mike and do some testing. I called immediately and made an appointment. Finally someone who could help. Finally someone who would have answers. I breathed just a little easier feeling there were now experts to help my son.

In late May Neal and I took Mike to his first appointment. They observed him at play, interacting with us, coloring, and just sitting (absorbed in his own world). They asked us dozens of questions. They set up more appointments for June and July. There would be many more tests.

In between Mike's medical appointments that summer, I drove to Stayton to see Pat at least once a week. She had had a baby girl in mid-June, the first granddaughter for my parents. It was such a joy buying cute little pink outfits for Kimberly after dressing four boys — Pat already had two boys — over the past six years. Pat couldn't wait until our parents came for a visit in September.

In mid-July, I went to California to be with Mother's family as we celebrated my Murray grandparents' fiftieth wedding anniversary. I took the boys with me, but Neal couldn't get the time off from work to join us. Our California trip was so much fun. I saw aunts, uncles, and cousins I seldom had the opportunity to visit. It was also wonderful to have time with Mother and Dad again. Pat decided she wasn't up to handling her three children in the car alone since summer was her husband's busiest work season and he was unable to make the trip with her. Her decision was one our whole family would always regret.

On August 22 I went back to the medical school to finally receive the report on Mike we had been nervously awaiting. The diagnosis was a devastating one. The doctor's label: "extremely emotionally disturbed." They recommended Mike be permanently institutionalized! These "experts" predicted Mike would never be able to go to school, never work, never be able to live independently. They had no hope for Mike's future. I was stunned. I thought I was going to vomit.

When I finally got control of myself, I asked where programs were located for children with Mike's problems. They indicated that Oregon really had no such public institutional services. There was, however, a special program for children in the State of Washington's mental hospital. I took the card they offered with the name and number and stumbled to my car. I had to maintain some emotional control to drive, especially since both of my boys were with me in the car. Once we arrived home I fixed lunch for the boys, found some cartoons on TV, and retreated to my bedroom. Behind my closed door I wept and wept. How could this be true? How would I be able to tell Neal? Mike was only six years old. How could I send him away?

Mike, Craig, and Mark, April 1961.

When Neal arrived home from the television station around midnight I gave him the terrible news. He wouldn't believe it. They were wrong, he said. They could name no cause. They could offer no cure. What kind of experts were these?

I slept fitfully that night. The next day I took Mike and Mark to Stayton to celebrate my nephew, Craig's, fourth birthday. I so needed to talk with my sister about this terrible news. Pat held me, sympathized, and told me she would be there for me during this ordeal—every step of the way.

The following day, another tragedy struck! My brother-in-law called. Pat had been in a terrible car accident. Her car had driven off the edge of a rural road and rolled down the embankment. Kimberly was dead. Craig and Pat, both injured, were in the hospital. Thank goodness, Scott, her other son, was not hurt. "Could you come to the hospital?" Dwayne asked. "Could you come right away?"

I hung up the phone and called my reliable teenage baby-sitter to stay with the boys for the night. I drove south on the I-5 freeway toward Salem and Stayton. I had to keep telling myself to concentrate on my driving. We didn't need another accident.

My God, only the day before Pat had been holding me, sympathizing about my pain over Mike's diagnosis. What would I be able to say, to do, to begin to ease this terrible loss for her? I was shaking as I stepped out of the car into the hospital parking lot. I was freezing cold in late August. As I stepped into my sister's hospital room, I saw not Pat, but my mother! My twenty-four-year-old sister had aged twenty years since I had seen her the previous day. We held each other and wept for a very long time. Then she wanted me to go and see Craig and find out exactly how he was. The hospital staff wouldn't take her to see him and she wanted the "straight scoop."

I stopped by the nurses' station and got the report on Craig. Four broken ribs, and one rib had punctured his lung. His face was badly scraped and cut on one side. He was hurting and very frightened. I walked quietly into Craig's hospital room in case he was sleeping. I immediately saw his injured face. It looked like raw hamburger. Only the day before he had been the happy birthday boy. Craig suddenly realized I was in the room and screamed out, "Auntie Barb, take me home."

I explained to Craig that he could not go home until the doctors and nurses fixed all his "owies." I told him I had just seen his mother and she had "owies," too. She sent him a kiss, I said. Did he want to send her a kiss? I would take it to her. He said, "Take it to her right now so she can get well." I waved good-bye and stepped into the hall. I couldn't seem to stop crying. My poor sister. My poor nephew. My poor little niece.

Pat asked me if I would be what we would call today Craig's medical advocate. Of course I would. Plus she asked if I would help Dwayne with the baby's memorial service. "I would be honored," I answered. Then Pat paused for a long time before asking when our parents would arrive from Nevada. "Tomorrow," I answered.

"They will never see my beautiful baby girl. They will never hold our Kimberly, Barb. Never. I should have gone to the wedding anniversary so they could hold her," Pat wailed. "I should have gone."

The next two days were like a nightmare. I visited the funeral home with my brother-in-law to make arrangements for Kimberly's little white casket, her services, the music, and her burial. I arrived back in the hospital just in time to hear Craig screaming, "Help me Auntie Barb. Help me. They are hurting me too much." I ran to his room to find the nurses moving him down the hall for new X-rays. I calmed

Craig and walked beside him to X-ray. Once Craig was done and asleep, I hurried to Pat's room. In this small community hospital she had been able to hear Craig screaming. I explained and told her that his X-rays showed improvement. Then, two hours later, Mother and Dad arrived at the hospital. It was a painful reunion. So many tears. So much regret. I had never witnessed such sorrow. Pat and Craig remained in the hospital for several more days. The doctors would not release Pat to attend Kimberly's memorial service. Dwayne promised Pat she would be there in McMinnville when their baby was placed in her final resting spot. That seemed to give Pat ease.

As we left the funeral home, the director took me aside and handed me a white envelope. Inside were two small locks of dark hair, each tied in a tiny pink ribbon. He said, "I know it is too soon to give these to Pat, but someday she will want these special mementos. You decide when you think the time is right for Pat. You'll know." Many years later, at a time I could never have predicted, I brought the white envelope with the little locks of hair back to my sister. I knew it was the right time.

The services were done. Pat and Craig came home from the hospital. Mother and Dad went back to Nevada and began plans to move home to Oregon. I went home to Portland and faced the decisions about Mike's future. The deadly tragedy our family had faced gave me new perspective about Mike. He wasn't *dead* and I couldn't permanently put him away as if he were. He deserved better. He deserved a chance. I didn't know how or when, but I would give my son a better future than the experts were recommending. Mike would not become another family tragedy.

CHAPTER FIVE

The Tough Years Continue

After searching out every option for Mike in both Oregon and Washington, there seemed to be only two choices available in 1962, one in each state, but the State of Washington's residential mental health program for children had no vacancies. The Parry Center for Children in Oregon, a private facility which then housed and treated "emotionally disturbed children," had only two vacancies that fall. Mike was offered one of those treatment slots. The Portland School District also taught a small number of classes in that center to the children being treated there.

The professional staff at Parry Center assured us they could really help Mike if they had him full time for a year of residential treatment. An entire year without my six-year-old son would be painful, but at least we were no longer talking about permanent institutionalization. After long, emotional discussions, Neal and I agreed to the year-long placement.

Mike was to arrive at Parry Center on the Friday following Thanksgiving. Neal and I and the boys drove to Parry Center and presented ourselves at the Administration Building. Two staff members met us in the lobby and took Mike's suitcase; we did hugs and kisses all around, and then they took Mike away to the so-called three-story "cabin" where he would be living. They took my six-year-old son for a year! Had we made a terrible mistake? Should I have kept Mike at home and tried to educate him there? What would this "treatment" do to my little boy? Who would protect him, who would soothe him? My heart ached as we slowly exited the agency's long driveway.

After a few months the financial pressure caused by paying for Mike's residential care required us to sell our home. The three of us temporarily moved into a nearby duplex. Yet it soon became clear that this would not be enough. We solved some of the money pressure when I became the residential manager of a three-building apartment complex just blocks from Portland State College and Channel 6. The arrangement meant we would have no housing or utility costs and almost no transportation expenses for Neal. It was a perfect location. Plus I could make extra money by cleaning vacant apartments for re-rental. Mark's new kindergarten class was only blocks away. We were also living closer to Parry Center.

Neal was in his second year of college. He bought a cute little red sports car, changed his college major to art, and he was seldom home. Between his job, his classes, and his new friends, his schedule seemed to leave little time for Mark and me. I began to worry that his only real commitment to family was our weekly visits to see Mike for an hour every Saturday morning. We all looked forward to visiting Mike and I usually brought treats and books for him on these visits. Mike and Mark were always so happy to be together again. They remained bonded. I was relieved and highly grateful for that.

A few months later, we started twice-a-week visits with Mike, and the staff discussed the possibility of his coming home one weekend a month. However, there was a catch. They wanted Mike to stay at Parry Center for a second year. They believed he was showing improvement plus there was nothing available for him on the "outside." If he was receiving no treatment and couldn't go to school, the staff felt he would slide backwards in his development.

We ended up with a negotiated arrangement. Mike would stay for another year at Parry. We would see him every Wednesday and Saturday evening. He would come home *two* weekends a month. On the Saturdays we visited Mike at the Parry Center, we would be allowed to take him out to dinner with us rather than staying in the Administration Building for our visits. It was an oh-so-much-happier arrangement for all of our family, including Mike.

I cannot share this story of my son's institutionalization and the constant hurt I felt without giving some historical context to what professional "experts" were saying and writing about children like Mike in the 1960s. The professional mental health treatment community generally accepted the then-current belief that these children—whom we would now term autistic—were the product of an unfeeling "refrigerator"mother who withheld real love and affection, severely damaging them emotionally. One of the most recognized experts, Bruno Bettelheim, author of the book *The Empty Fortress: Infantile Autism and the Birth of the Self*, was often quoted as the authority on these "damaged children." He went so far as to compare them to prisoners in a concentration camp, placing the parents in the role of the Nazi SS guards.

My son's counselor at Parry Center, who also acted as my liaison to Mike's treatment and progress, reminded me often that Mike's problem was not like heart disease or diabetes. He was not born with this emotional flaw, he reminded me; it was a result of my actions and behavior as a parent.

Can you imagine a young mother, still in her twenties, hearing an "expert" remind her of the blame she must accept for her child's condition if that child was ever to improve? Can you imagine the pain, the guilt, the confusion a young, loving mother would feel at those words? Sometimes I fought back, insisting that I had not created Mike's disability, but I often tired, as so much of the treatment world believed otherwise. Many years later mental health professionals would totally reject Bruno Bettelheim and his scientifically erroneous book. Mike's counselor from Parry Center would one day apologize to me for the extra misery his words had added to my already difficult situation. It was perhaps too little too late but I appreciated his brave apology and carried with more determination and comfort my belief that I was my son's advocate and never his source of damage.

During this period of time I began my first college classes … one three-credit class each term through the Extension Center at Portland State. While Neal finished his last two years at PSC, I could earn over twenty college credits. After he graduated, perhaps I could actually attend Portland State part time or transfer my credits to a community college program.

Part of me began to feel life was getting better. Mike would be home more. I was taking a college class every term. Mark was happy and doing well. My apartment-management job had diminished a lot of our financial pressure. Yet I knew that I faced a larger problem. My marriage felt less and less secure. Neal was seldom home and when he was there he seemed to have little interest in me or in doing anything with the family. He was distant and his mind seemed to be on other things.

One night Neal came home from work and announced he had found a little apartment close to the campus and was moving out on his own. I knew things weren't going well, but I was not prepared for this. He wasn't asking for a divorce, he just "wanted to have some space for a while." I was devastated and didn't know what to expect next. Would another shoe drop soon? Would I find he had someone else? Would he ask for a divorce later? Yet only a few months later Neal was back home with me. I felt we needed to make some changes if we were going to hold this marriage together. I gave up the apartment-managing position and took a full-time job as a bookkeeper in a construction firm, Cooper Construction. Maybe this would help us take the first steps toward a fresh beginning. We moved just east of Portland into the Parkrose area. It was a wonderful school district for Mark, and we found a nice rental house that we both liked and that gave us more space, much more elbow room than in the cramped apartment.

Neal, now a senior, continued at Portland State and was still working full time at the television station. He had moved from cameraman to floor director, to the control room. He was doing his first work at producing television specials and documentaries, and he loved his new position. I was still taking a single college class each term, in addition to my full-time job. Mike was home two weekends a month. Mark was a happy student in the first grade.

For a while everything seemed to have settled down. I started to relax. Maybe we had finally weathered the storm. With a good baby-sitter right next door I sometimes joined Neal after his television shift and we went out with his work colleagues. Neal and I even met some people involved in Democratic politics in our area and we started helping on some local political campaigns. It was nothing major, but we both seemed to enjoy it. It gave us something new and interesting in common. It seemed as if our relationship was repairing the scars created over the past few years. I was very encouraged. I loved him and wanted to make our marriage last. We would make this work, especially for our two boys.

Then suddenly everything fell apart! Neal dropped out of college only months before his graduation. I couldn't understand why he had quit. He had no explanation. He had worked so hard for so long to finish this degree. It made no sense. What was he thinking? His next decision was even more devastating. Neal announced he was leaving me again, this time to move in with a young woman and her little daughter.

I suddenly felt as if I was a character in a daytime television "soap," where the heroine moves from crisis to crisis, with a new challenge in every episode. I felt crushed. I had worked so hard to keep this family intact. After almost three years at Parry Center, Mike was coming home in a few months. Now his father was leaving.

I went into survival mode. I took my life a day at a time now: Getting Mark off to school. Doing my eight-hour shift at Lay's Construction, my new employer. Attending class one night a week. Visiting Mike. Volunteering to support our school budget election. And crying myself to sleep at night. A day at a time. A night at a time.

And then, after three months, Neal wanted to come home ... again. It was becoming a pattern—a very painful pattern. This time I was extremely doubtful. Once before such a marital reunion had failed. Why would this time be different? How many times could I face being rejected by the man I loved? We talked for several weeks and finally agreed that we would reunite and both of us would put real energy and commitment into making a solid marriage this time ... for us and for our two sons.

We began planning for Mike's coming home. We worked at reorganizing the boys' bedroom space and getting Mike ready for school. Mike had been so lucky to have been recently accepted into a new program funded by the National Institute of Mental Health. It would be one of ten experimental programs across the nation to try and determine if "emotionally handicapped children could be integrated into schools for normal children." The Parkrose School District had been chosen to house one of the programs for the next three years. Mike now had a label—a diagnosis—"autistic." Many of the children selected for the program were also autistic. It was almost a brand-new word in the American culture. When I used it to describe my son's disability, I usually had to spell it. Maybe a label would help our children get recognition and support. The timing for Mike's acceptance into the Parkrose Project could not have been better. He was ready to leave Parry Center, and we desperately needed a next-step program for him. And, as if by magic, there was the absolutely appropriate program right in our own community. In the fall Mike would enter school again after four years out of the classroom. It was so exciting. A new beginning for Mike plus our whole family would be together again.

The years that followed were good ones, especially where my sons were concerned. Mark was a bright, enthusiastic young student. His teacher reports were highly positive. Our refrigerator was covered with his 100 percent perfect papers and his school artwork. He was a very attractive boy, active and full of energy. His pre-school experience and basic intelligence had given him a strong foundation for school. I reveled in his early success.

Mike and Mark were, of course, now in the same school district, but they were in different buildings. Mike rode on a transportation van to the school where his special education program took place. Mark walked to his school, which was close to home. Attending different schools seemed a good situation during this time of Mike's readjustment to the public school setting.

Every day I remained thankful for Mike's new educational opportunity. He spent part of each class day in the special education classroom and part in his regular fourth and then fifth grade classrooms. Time on the playground and the cafeteria were integrated. Mike was learning to be part of the school setting and the children in his building were learning about our special-needs children. That was part of the intention of the federal education experiment. How fortunate we were to have this new program for our son. I tried very hard not to let myself think about the end of the three-year federal grant program. All of our parents hoped for a renewal of the program when the time came. With no state or federal laws in place to serve our children, this program was our only hope. We even did community fundraisers to keep the program operating during June and July, knowing our kids would regress if they had the normal three-month school vacation.

I was feeling so good about how Mike and Mark were doing, but I still worried about our marriage. Although Neal was outwardly working on his role as husband and father, there were other troubling signs. The big issue was his increased drinking. He drank every day, every night after work. When I gently raised my concerns about his drinking, he tried to reassure me that people could not be alcoholics when they drank only beer. Alcoholics, he mistakenly informed me, drank hard liquor or even wine. His drinking became an issue of ongoing disagreement between us. I tried not to nag, but my worry increased as months passed without improvement.

As the 1970s began, I had a strong sense that Neal was again having an affair. I recognized the signs. I so wanted it not to be true. But this time I sensed the liaison was not just another passing fancy but perhaps a serious relationship. I finally confronted Neal and got *total* denial. Still, I was not reassured.

Somehow challenges seem to come in bunches, and I now had another major worry. As the last months of 1970 approached, our

Parkrose Project parents learned that the federal government was not going to renew the grant for our children's education program. We all felt we couldn't simply take our children home with no hope of continuing their schooling. We needed help. We needed a champion to save our children's educational future.

Our parents' group reached out to State Representative Frank Roberts, who lived in the Parkrose School District. We told him about our children's crisis. We informed him of what we wanted. We were begging to change Oregon's education laws to give our special-needs children the educational rights every other child in Oregon enjoyed. Frank agreed to help us. He would have a legislative bill drafted and introduced and then assist us in getting the bill considered by the 1971 legislative session. We were all thrilled. Yet Frank was also clear we would need someone from our parents' group to present our story to legislators throughout the next months. None of us had the slightest idea how to be a lobbyist in the state Legislature. Frank offered to mentor whoever decided to take on the challenging new experience. Neal and I knew Frank slightly from our recent political activities, and I began to think that Frank's recommendation of one day a week in Salem was within the realm of possibility for *me*. I believed my boss at the construction company might consider giving me a day a week off work to lobby this important bill for my son. I felt Neal and I could afford the temporary loss of income.

I spoke to several members of our parents' group, and they all thought I was a terrific choice to lobby for our kids. My boss thought we could work around my new schedule for five or six months. I began to be excited about the prospect of doing this job. It was all but decided by Thanksgiving. I was now passionate about becoming my son's legislative advocate. Mike's future was in my hands. I felt a new sense of hope for all of our special children.

Hope. Hope can lift our spirits, give us strength, even build our courage. Yet hope can also vanish in a flash. In early December, Neal destroyed any hope of our marriage surviving. He announced he was in love with one of my best friends. He wanted a divorce. He explained that once we had celebrated the Christmas holiday, he would move into his own place. My suspicions had, unfortunately, been right. Not only had he been having an affair but an affair with my good friend Karen and it had been going on for quite some time. They had both lied to me over and over and over. I felt hurt and angry and cheated. He was ready to leave, not only me, but his two sons. Karen was prepared to walk away from her marriage and her three children. This time it was really done. I was devastated.

Two days after Christmas and one day after our sixteenth wedding anniversary, Neal left our home, moved out, this time for the *final* time. Our sons were twelve and fourteen. I had just turned thirty-four a week earlier. My future seemed like one big painful question mark.

What would happen to me? How could I adequately support my two sons? What would I tell my parents? My sister? My friends? More importantly, how could I tell my boys their father had left us and wouldn't be moving home again? And how would I be able to go to Salem and lobby for our new legislative proposal? The Legislature would go into session in less than three weeks. What could I do at this late date? All questions. No answers.

A year later I wrote a private poem about the pain and confusion I felt as my marriage ended in divorce. Somehow I never destroyed that revealing piece of paper. Looking at it now, I feel it may better describe how that loss felt at the time than anything I could write today to explain that emotionally damaging experience in my life.

I share, now, that long-ago expression of my pain and loneliness:

She reached.
Reaching out, responding to an offered love.
Reaching out to caress, and later to comfort.
Reaching out to bridge the crevasse of misunderstanding
And discovering nothing to grasp on the other side.
Reaching, nearly stretching, even as in darkness,
For some familiar object, some familiar warmth.
Then finding nothing as a guide, no longer reaching.
Finally returning outstretched arms to encircle only her.
And she reached no more.

CHAPTER SIX

Staying Afloat

As 1971 began, I had big choices on my platter: to lobby or not to lobby; to cut my income from five days to four days per week; to go with my head or my heart? Senate Bill 699 was ready. The question was: was I? My job was to stay emotionally and financially afloat. My boys needed my full-time attention. I didn't have the experience to be a lobbyist, and I certainly didn't have the money to buy as much as a cup of coffee for a state legislator.

Frank Roberts said I didn't need to spend money to lobby the Legislature. I just needed to tell them my compelling story about our children. I just needed to talk with all ninety members of the Oregon Legislature in the next six months, working only one day per week in the state Capitol! I just needed to meet with 3.75 legislators every Friday for six months! That—*and* convince those 3.75 lawmakers that my son had the same right to a public education that every other child in Oregon enjoyed. What should I do?

And then … Frank showed me the legislative draft for our bill proposal. There it was, in black and white. There, in print, was the future for our kids. Right at the top of the first page were the words, "Introduced at the request of the Portland Chapter of the National Society for Autistic Children." I could feel the tears coming. Our parent group had formed our own local chapter of the National Society for Autistic Children to advocate for all of our children. We had believed we could make a difference by organizing, stepping forward, and speaking out. Our children needed a voice. Now I asked myself how one collapsed marriage could be an excuse for giving up on our kids' educational future. I remembered the words from "The Impossible Dream": "Be willing to march into Hell for a Heavenly cause." I was hooked. I couldn't say no. I would wear my new label—lobbyist—with determination and pride.

Two weeks later I marched up the long flight of steps in front of the Oregon Capitol Building, prepared to change the world for the disabled children in my state. I was scared to death, almost flat broke, and didn't even know where to find the women's restroom. But before I was finished, I would find *that* room and much more.

Four days a week I worked my job as bookkeeper and office manager at Lay's Construction. One day a week I lobbied in Salem under the tutelage of Representative Frank Roberts. Seven days a week I worked to stretch every household dollar as far and as thin as it would stretch. The boys and I ate hundreds of tuna and noodle casseroles during those years and, believe it or not, my adult sons still love that dish. I tried to keep Mike and Mark feeling stable and supported with their father out of our home. Neal visited the boys once or twice a week and continued to reassure them that he would always be around even though they now lived in different homes. He sometimes took them over to his new apartment to show how easily their lives and relationship could work under this new arrangement. Sometimes Neal would call the boys after school to reinforce his presence in their lives. It helped the boys … and it helped me.

I continued my lobbying efforts in the state Capitol every Friday. I slowly began to feel more comfortable with the legislative setting as I gained knowledge about the committee process, the way legislative bills were amended, and Oregon's Ways & Means procedures, and met both Democrats and Republicans willing to give me their time and, eventually, their vote on Senate Bill 699. The work was demanding, but the more time I spent in the Capitol building, the more I learned and the more interesting people I met. In addition to the support and help Frank continued to give me, some of the professional working lobbyists offered their knowledge and experience in my challenging quest. I believe they were somewhat fascinated with the rumored early success I was gaining as a complete amateur. Plus in 1971 there were almost no women in the lobby except for the nurses' organization, the PTA, and one or two others. I believe those male lobbyists were partially enjoying the chance to show off their vast legislative knowledge to the new kid on the block. I listened and learned at every opportunity … and they usually bought the coffee.

In early April, Frank Roberts and I convinced the Senate Education Committee to hold a rare evening hearing. Parents, our special education teachers, grandparents, and my son Mike testified before the committee. Mike dramatically explained to the Senate committee members that for him special education wasn't special at all. For him, it was all there was.

That evening I also testified, as did my mentor and state representative, Frank Roberts. Joanne Hummel, the president of our sponsoring parent organization, and Sarah Brown, teacher of emotionally handicapped children in the Parkrose School District, both delivered strong testimony. Joanne ended her testimony saying, "Thousands of Oregon children are now barred from entering public school. ... This is a shameful, irresponsible thing to let happen." Sarah Brown pleaded, "Over one hundred years ago Oregon provided for the education of our blind and deaf children. Now we must take another step in providing an education for all of Oregon's children." I finished my prepared statement with these words, "As parents most of us know how rapidly a child grows to maturity. So, can you imagine the fears and despair of a parent of an emotionally handicapped child, watching his child grow too quickly to adulthood, while more studies are conducted without follow-up programs? I ask your support of SB 699 in the name of thousands of children waiting for help." Finally, Dr. Dale Parnell and Dr. Howard Smith from the Department of Education spoke in favor of SB 699.

The committee, at Frank Roberts' request, added their sponsorship to the bill and passed it out of committee unanimously that evening, sending it first to the Ways & Means Committee and then to the full Senate with a "Do Pass" recommendation. Two months later, on June 7, SB 699, now carrying $50,000 of state funding, passed the Oregon Senate without a single dissenting vote. I was thrilled. We were one step closer for our children. Yet I still had to gain at least thirty-one votes from the sixty-member House, and I also needed the signature of Governor Tom McCall. It was clearly premature for any kind of a celebration.

I had relentlessly pounded the marble halls of the Capitol. My feet became swollen and sore. I tired of hearing myself make the same presentation, the same case, to legislator after legislator. I explained to them that the lifetime potential of children like my son would be lost forever. As parents, we all paid property and income taxes like other Oregon citizens. Our children, I insisted, deserved at least a chance for an education.

Then, rather than assign our bill to the House Education Committee as expected, the Speaker sent it to the House State and Federal Affairs Committee. This was not a committee that usually handled education issues. I hoped that wouldn't turn out to be a problem. Well, it was anything but! For reasons I did not comprehend, SB 699 was put on a fast track. It came out of committee the very next day and, with unanimous consent, it went directly to the full House for a vote on that very same day! After six months of very hard and dedicated work, on June 8, SB 699 recorded fifty-seven votes out of sixty in the Oregon House of Representatives; two House members were excused and one was absent. Governor McCall signed the bill on June 29. Oregon now had the first law in the nation requiring special education for "emotionally handicapped" children. Imagine—I had actually made history! It would be a full four years before the federal law, PL94-142, would pass and give these educational rights to disabled children in all fifty states of our nation.

How does an amateur lobbyist shepherd a piece of legislation through the process, not only successfully, but without one dissenting vote? Looking back today, with all my years of political experience, it amazes me that I could have ever accomplished such a feat. Yet I had done it. I had moved the mountain of government. I had changed history for our special children. My mother sat with me in the Oregon House Visitors' Gallery and watched that amazing vote. Mother understood how much this meant to me and to her oldest grandson. She also knew what a lift this victory was for me in a life that felt so sad right then with my marriage ending and so many challenges.

My lobby assignment had been one of the most stimulating and productive experiences of my life. I discovered I loved the political arena, and I could actually change people's lives positively in that setting. I wanted to continue to find a way to make that kind of a difference. Looking back, even now, I feel real pride in setting that leadership standard for kids with disabilities. I had changed their lives and, in the process, had changed my own. However, it would be quite some time before I would fathom the *depth* of that life change.

Once our divorce became final in 1972, Neal and Karen made plans to marry. Neal came to the house the day of their wedding ceremony to pick up the boys. I had Mark and Mike all cleaned up in their best outfits, and I sent them off with their father for the festivities. Then I went to bed and cried for the next two hours. That day, his wedding day, the lesson was pounded home. He did not love me anymore. He loved someone else. He had another wife. He had another life. We had only two connections now—our sons and a monthly child-support check.

A few months after Neal remarried, he came to my house to inform me that he and Karen were moving to Southern California. I was shocked! He had promised the boys he would be there for them, seeing them every week, calling them on the phone, doing things together. The divorce wouldn't change that, he had told them. His remarriage wouldn't change that, he had said. He had promised my sons. He had said they could depend on him. Now, he was going away … more than one thousand miles away.

Neal left. Following close behind was my small but desperately needed $250-a-month child-support check. It had not occurred to me that he would stop helping support our two sons. He had never complained about his child support nor skipped a single payment. I called and pleaded for his financial help for the boys. Only a very rare support check appeared in my mailbox after that … and then nothing. In the 1970s there was little help with child-support collection and enforcement, especially across state lines. Another link was severed.

The boys and I moved to another part of the Parkrose School District and a smaller, less-expensive house. I quit going to lunch most days, saving the money for the boys' lunches at school. I watched every penny of my small paycheck.

Two interesting things occurred when I moved to the smaller house. When I tried to move my renter's insurance to the new location, the company refused to insure me again after they learned I was divorced. This made no sense to me. I pointed out that my husband had been a smoker, but I did not smoke, and that should be important with a fire insurance policy. The company representative informed me that the risk was not *my* smoking but rather that of visiting gentlemen who would share my household *and my bed* for the night. *They* were the risk factor. I was appalled. I hung up. I found another insurance agent and, even on my very tight budget, I paid my renters'/fire coverage premium gladly.

The second shocker came when I called to transfer my telephone number to my new address. Unfortunately, the telephone was still listed in my ex-husband's name. When I asked the phone company to list the telephone in my name, they suddenly required a rather large deposit. I informed the man on the other end of the line that I had been paying that phone bill for well over a year and I had the cancelled checks with my signature to prove it. He insisted he must have the deposit before the company could connect my telephone. I had no money for the deposit and asked if there might be an alternative. He informed me that if I had a male relative who could cosign for me, the deposit could be waived. I was furious but answered quietly that my father would be willing to sign for me. The telephone representative said, "I will mail the form to you immediately for your father's signature."

I calmly fibbed, "When the form arrives I will take it to my father at the nursing home since I need to deliver his welfare check anyway. He will be happy to sign the form." There was a rather long pause and then I added, "You asked me absolutely no questions about my ability to pay. I am thirty-six years old. I have been on my job for years. I pay all my bills on time, and yet you were unwilling to trust me to pay the bill I have already been paying for nearly eighteen months. However, you were willing to accept my father's signature without knowing a single thing about him except that he was a male. He could be a drunk or a drug addict or in a mental hospital or an old folks home. I want this phone in my name and I want it today. If it doesn't happen, I am going to repeat this entire conversation to every newspaper and radio and television station in the entire Portland area."

Two things happened on that long-ago 1972 day: I got a telephone in my own name and I became a feminist. Never again would I remain silent while I was treated like a second-class citizen. I didn't want special treatment. I wanted only to be recognized as the adult, responsible citizen that I was. Later I would sometimes wear a silver medallion necklace bearing the words of suffragist Susan B. Anthony: "Never another season of silence." It felt like my new life motto.

As Senate Bill 699 went into effect legally, the Parkrose School District applied for early funding from the new law's budget allotment. I was appointed to the state advisory committee created by the new legislation and then to the local committee for my own school district. Yet I wanted to keep an even closer eye on what was happening in my son's program. I believed being a member of the school board would guarantee me both access and the decision-making role to keep the local program intact. So in 1972, I ran for the school board. I lost. I lost my very first public election.

Perhaps I wasn't so politically adept as my legislative success had made me believe! I didn't like losing, and I determined I would not do so again. There would be another school board election in one year. Next time I would be prepared, informed, and involved in the local district. I volunteered for a vacancy on the school budget committee and was appointed. I began attending PTA meetings and rarely missed a school board meeting. Next time I would be ready.

With my limited finances I was no longer able to take classes at Portland State but I was definitely in a learning mode. I had become a Democratic precinct committeeperson two years earlier and was growing more active in my political party. I was serving on a Democratic committee studying issues for the upcoming county platform convention.

I joined the League of Women Voters and the Oregon Women's Political Caucus, both nonpartisan women's groups. I loved the experience of working with other women on political and policy issues. The LWV was focused on local, state, and national policy matters. The OWPC was *definitely* politically focused. The other active women's rights organization in Oregon at that time was NOW — the National Organization for Women. NOW may actually have preceded OWPC in Oregon, but the two organizations' agendas were somewhat different. NOW was centered around personal empowerment for women and introspective understanding of women in our culture. They offered support to women, especially those in personal transition. They were raising the consciousness of women in Oregon.

The Oregon Women's Political Caucus was an arm of the National Women's Political Caucus, and similar state groups were emerging across America. OWPC had local caucuses in Portland, Salem, Eugene, at the Oregon coast, and in the southern part of our state, which held monthly meetings and planned future activities, designed candidate-endorsement processes, and shared national updates. The state OWPC held an annual meeting where members from across the state came together to hear panels, listen to speakers, socialize, and "plot." It was at one of these state conventions that I was exposed for the first time to an upsetting and vivid program on domestic violence and the lack of legal protections for women victims. This would soon be added to the legislative agenda for OWPC. Our number one priority was keeping abortion legal and safe for Oregon women. We were also working on protecting reproductive rights in general, securing credit rights for women, putting gender equity into Oregon's insurance laws, and demanding equal pay for equal work. Ratification of the new federal Equal Rights Amendment that had come out of Congress in 1972 was now under consideration in all fifty states, attracting lots of attention and no small amount of controversy. Women activists were working diligently toward ratification by the Oregon Legislature in the 1973 session. There was, however, one other important part of the agenda for the Oregon Women's Political Caucus: electing women to public office. There had been only six women out of ninety legislators in Salem in the 1971 legislative session: Senators Betty Browne and Betty Roberts and Representatives Norma Paulus, Grace Peck, Nancie Fadley, and Fritzy Chuinard. We could do better. We must do better. There was usually a token woman on the Portland City Council and the Multnomah County Commission in those days, but across Oregon many city councils, county commissions, and school boards were all male. This situation was repeated across the nation. As women in Oregon and throughout the United States became more aware of and vocal concerning the inequities American women were experiencing, the modern women's rights movement blossomed. Helen Reddy then gave us a theme song when she belted out "I am woman hear me roar, in numbers too big to ignore ..."

As the legislative agenda for women's issues continued to expand, one of Oregon's noted women activists, Eleanor Davis of Portland, founded a new group: the Women's Rights Coalition, an umbrella group to be the legislative lobby arm for the progressive women's agenda. Membership included OWPC, NOW, the LWV, American Association of University Women, Soroptimists International, and other groups committed to the ratification of the federal Equal Rights Amendment and the broader agenda of the coalition. Eleanor Davis hired Gretchen Kafoury in 1973 as the first lobbyist in Salem for the coalition. By mid-February the Oregon Legislature had already ratified the federal ERA and the agenda expanded to other equity issues for women. In 1975 the coalition helped pass Oregon's highly controversial marital rape law. In 1977 the coalition's lobbyist moved legislation including the state's new domestic violence law, and in 1979, won the first major funding to support these new domestic-violence programs. Three of the coalition's first four lobbyists would later become successful elected officials. Gretchen would later serve as a state representative, a Multnomah County commissioner, and a Portland City Council member. Anne Kelly Feeney would be elected Multnomah County Auditor. Merri Souther Wyatt would become a long-term member of the Multnomah County Circuit Court bench. Pretty impressive results coming out of that women's coalition activity!

As the OWPC became more active and more politically committed, a second annual gathering emerged. Camp Tamarack in the pine forests of Central Oregon, a summer-camp location for girls, became the fall retreat for women activists from across Oregon. We came to camp and we bonded. In the safety of that forest we expressed our feelings, our frustrations, our hopes, and our dreams. We worked on issues, planned political strategies, debated politics, and relaxed. Without responsibilities for husbands, children, households, and jobs, we spoke openly, played poker, sang together, drank wine, and sunbathed on the old dock by the lake. The plans and memories we built at Camp Tamarack transformed a generation of Oregon feminists. Many of the women who participated at Camp Tamarack during those years would become not only recognized political activists but elected officials at every level of government for the next two decades. I don't think I ever missed a Tamarack gathering during these years. I have great memories of those times and the experience of sharing that setting with such wonderful, strong, dedicated women.

Meanwhile at home I was struggling with the new lessons of loneliness, carrying the load of both mother and father, trying to figure out how to distribute my limited money, my time resources, and my somewhat diminished energy. I tried to fill the weekends with inexpensive or free things the boys and I could do together. We would spend Saturday morning getting the house in shape so we could take a drive down the scenic Columbia River Gorge in the afternoon. We would rush through the laundry and vacuuming so we could visit my parents or my sister and her sons in Salem. Those visits always meant a big dinner with home-baked pie. More important, however, it was time with family that we all three needed. My family's support and love always lifted my spirits and made Mike and Mark feel more secure. My boys were especially happy to have time with my dad. Dad knew and understood the importance of the attention he gave my sons. His own father had left home when Dad was only ten. I felt such gratitude for his obvious affection for Mike and Mark. A step at a time, the three of us tried to work through our painful life changes.

I felt I was personally strong enough to stay afloat, but I needed to feel that my sons would also survive their father's absence. I particularly worried about Mark's growing anger toward his father.

His father was gone, the child support had stopped, and Mark grew more upset each year as birthdays and holidays were ignored by his father. His greatest anger was reserved for times when his brother's birthday went unacknowledged. Since Mike and his father shared their March 4 birth date, Mark knew that it was not simply a matter of forgetfulness. Mark was furious at his dad. It made me not angry but sad. What happens that permits a parent to ignore the special dates in their children's life? These times made me understand that survival included making certain my sons also reached adulthood with their self-confidence intact, feeling balanced, and maintaining the ability to love fully. There seemed likely to be some hard work ahead for me as a single parent. However, as time passed I began to recognize that I was not actually going to sink.

CHAPTER SEVEN

Climbing the Ladder

In the spring of 1973, I was elected to the Parkrose School Board. I had challenged a longtime male member of the board, and it was an unusually active campaign for an unpaid position in a small suburban school district. A number of parents who were long established in the area were willing to lend their support to my election efforts. They helped me do neighborhood coffees and even some door-to-door campaigning. I answered questions about our school budget, teachers' tenure, school lunches, and state graduation requirements. At one coffee I finally received a comment for which I had no response: "You seem smart and well-informed but I don't believe I can vote for a person who is divorced. That's a bad message for our community's children." I was truly speechless. Thank goodness, as it turned out, that particular citizen didn't represent the majority of Parkrose voters.

At the first school board meeting in July, I was seated at the board table with my shiny new nameplate clearly displayed on the table. I was greeted by the other four members of the board, the superintendent and assistant superintendent, and a number of school principals—all men. Tonight I would move to the other side of the board table, in many ways, never to return. I would no longer be an observer but would become one of the decision makers. I was excited and a little nervous. After all, the four other members of the board had been colleagues of the man I defeated. I didn't yet know if I would be fully accepted. I would test the waters before I jumped in. I had four years to prove myself. I didn't need to try and be a star on my very first night on the board. That turned out to be a good decision. Before the meeting was finished, I was being encouraged to comment and submit my opinions and ideas. Both board members and administrators alike seemed to welcome, my input. I felt included and accepted ... and relieved. This elected-official stuff looked pretty promising.

Looking back now, I remember feeling I had reached my political pinnacle. I was now an elected officeholder in my community. I was making policy decisions, discussing program changes in the high school, the two junior highs, and six elementary buildings. There would be teacher tenure votes, the hiring of principals, and way-too-many votes about repairing leaky school roofs. I found the whole process interesting, educational, and satisfying in terms of my need for intellectual growth. I couldn't afford my college classes any longer, but I had found a way to expand my knowledge base.

My parents were very proud that I was now an elected official. However, my mother found the fact that I had made friends with a handsome, single state representative, Frank Roberts, equally exciting. She reported my friendly status to relatives and friends. It would have been embarrassing if I hadn't been aware of the great pleasure she found in telling this story. I decided to just relax and let her enjoy it.

Even though my school board position was a nonpartisan office, my status as an elected official was now noted in most Democratic meetings I attended. The monthly Democratic Central Committee meetings gave me the chance to listen to speeches and debates on state, national, and international issues. I soaked up this new information and found myself hungry for more. Whenever my party held fundraising events, I was quick to volunteer to collect or sell tickets at the door. It was the only way I could afford to attend these paid gatherings. I was learning to recognize party regulars and elected officials by sight and by name. In turn, I was now becoming a more familiar face to active Democrats in my county. The volunteer party work I did in the first couple of years after my marriage ended was a life saver. This was one setting where single women could participate and not be expected to have a husband or boyfriend accompanying them. Events like picnics were fun and cheap and my boys could attend with me.

Still struggling financially, I finally found the courage to ask my boss at the construction company for a raise. Since the company was a union shop, all the painters and carpenters who worked for the company had very recently received a raise. When I pointed this out to my boss, he shook his head slightly and said, "Barbara, those men are all family breadwinners." I was startled, really shocked. Frank Lay was a very kind man. How could he not understand? I responded, "Frank, what do you think *I* am? I live on my wages and support my two sons. I'm a breadwinner, too." He replied, "But you have a second income: your child support." I had been so embarrassed about my former husband not paying his child support, only a few people were aware of the situation. I guess that had been a mistake.

"Frank, I haven't had a child support check in over a year and don't expect to see one again." My children had to come before my dignity.

I had set up the accounting books for Frank Lay's company and had been his very first employee. I was a one-person office: answering the phones, calculating and typing all the bids, handling the mail, the filing, the payroll, the banking, and the quarterly tax reports. His union employees had money going into their union retirement accounts, someone negotiating for their wages and health care benefits. I had no one to speak for me. The difference was clear. I received a small raise that day but I also became a lifelong supporter of labor unions.

I was facing some ongoing challenges with Mike and Mark at this time. For most of the past two years the boys had been in the same school building for the first time. Even though Mark was the younger brother, he was used to being protective of Mike. He felt he must be Mike's defender against the tormentors that disabled children frequently encounter; a fight would ensue, and I would get a call from school. It was a little awkward for the school principal to call a school board member when her son was in trouble.

One day yet another call came, but the tone of the principal was noticeably different. He said, "Barbara, Mark got into another fight today and got sent to my office. When I told Mark he could not fight his brother's battles, he responded, 'If I am not my brother's keeper, who is?'" The principal took a deep breath and said, "Barbara, I didn't have any answer to that question."

In spite of my pride in Mark's willingness to defend his brother, I knew he was paying a huge price. My bright, capable son was doing less well academically and showing more signs of teenage rejection of authority. Mark was growing increasingly angry with his father, and I couldn't seem to make him feel better. It broke my heart. I remembered the happy, quick, energetic boy he had once been. Sometimes we could talk and feel close. Other times Mark just seemed to slip away, leaving me without answers or a way to help him. I worried I was failing him.

I finally accepted letting Mark grow his hair long. A little harmless rebellion, I reasoned. I just needed to try and be sure the rebellion stayed harmless. I had a sense it was going to get more difficult and much more challenging.

CHAPTER EIGHT

Frank Roberts, a New Love

Frank and I had become friends — mostly *political* friends, I guess. The tremendous help he had given to me as he mentored me through the successful legislative passage of Senate Bill 699 in 1971 had given us a bond of mutual accomplishment. We saw each other at Democratic Party events and lived in the same neighborhood. Our paths crossed frequently. I thought he was wonderful and very attractive. Yet after my painful divorce I did not feel motivated to start encouraging a dating relationship *nor* did I feel desirable enough to start dating a man as distinctive and successful as Frank Roberts. I had heavy responsibility in raising my two sons alone. Plus, I carried another private burden, the parting message Neal delivered to me as he exited our home and our marriage; "No man is ever going to want you. Get used to that." I had been married since high school. Somehow I simply accepted his words and assumed that my shortcomings as a wife and woman had been the reasons our marriage had ended. At this point I had totally lost my self-confidence in that department and wasn't willing to risk being rejected again.

A year after the 1971 separation that led to the divorce, my son Mark, then fourteen, asked me bluntly why I had not started dating. I gave him some rather feeble excuse, not being able to tell my teenage son the more painful personal reason. Mark looked at me and responded, "Mom, you're a good-looking, smart woman. It's time you started dating again. You need some fun in your life." Mark was right but knowing it and doing something about it were two very different things.

A few months after that conversation with Mark, I rode with friends to a Democratic Party monthly meeting. Frank Roberts came and sat in the seat next to mine. I must admit, I felt pleased to have him there though somewhat self-conscious. After all, Frank was a divorced man and considered quite a catch, although he had a reputation as a little bit of a ladies' man. I had actually been warned by a couple of legislators' wives, during my lobbying effort, to avoid getting personally involved with Frank. "He'll just hurt you," one wife warned me. I responded, smiling, "Maybe I am the one who will hurt him!" But the truth was, I didn't feel nearly as confident as I sounded. Yet here I was getting *way* ahead of myself. Frank's seating choice may have been nothing more than a friendly gesture.

When the meeting was winding down, Frank asked if I would like to join a group going out for drinks. When I explained I had come with friends, he quickly added he would be happy to drop me at home later. A couple of hours later, Frank drove toward my home. My instincts told me that our relationship was in transition. We had crossed some kind of a line during the evening in our conversation, our warmth, and our "just friendly" status. Frank came in for coffee, but somehow the coffee was never brewed. Something more romantic and warm was brewing! Something more intimate.

When Frank left, we kissed goodnight. I had liked and admired Frank for so long, but this clearly personal evening was more than I had expected or dared to hope for. I had no idea what might come next but I felt happy and excited. The next morning I got Mike and Mark off to school and headed for work. I hoped for a call from Frank that day, but, in fact, he might not even know where I worked. The day went by. The evening passed without a call. The next day, the week, three weeks painfully slipped by without any contact from Frank. No call. No flowers. No note. My ex-husband had been right. No man would want me. I was devastated. I had made a fool of myself and likely ruined a growing professional friendship.

I skipped the next monthly Democratic meeting for fear of encountering Frank. I just couldn't face him.

After a full two months—two months!—Frank called. He asked if he could meet me after work. He needed to talk with me. I felt confused and had no idea what to expect. Our two cars met between my office and home, we parked, and Frank got into my passenger-side front seat. He smiled a little and began with, "I am so sorry. I don't know what I was thinking." I am sure I looked puzzled. He went on, "Barbara, I know your divorce was very painful and you are still at some stage of personal healing. That makes you vulnerable. I should never have taken advantage of that vulnerability. I have been so ashamed of myself I couldn't even call to apologize."

I protested, "Frank, I'm an adult. You don't have to protect me. There is no need to apologize."

"Barbara, we are friends, and I should have protected that friendship. The attraction I was feeling should have waited until you were less sad about your divorce."

Suddenly I was crying. The two-month wait was about concern for me, not rejection of me. I felt a tremendous personal relief. "Frank, could we go back to the part about the attraction you were feeling?" I asked through my tears. We both laughed. That moment became a new beginning for us. We were no longer just about a friendship but also about a warm, mature romance.

There was so much to know about Frank. In addition to being a state representative, he was also a longtime professor of speech communication at Portland State University. He was also a serious sailor with a twenty-two-foot Santana sailboat. The more time I spent with Frank, the more my world expanded. I started learning to sail. We attended speech department parties with his university colleagues. Frank's political friends and associates were frequently part of our social life. My son had been correct. There was, again, some fun in my life.

For most of the next two years, between 1972 and 1974, Frank and I were a "steady item." I became acquainted with his two adult daughters, Mary Wendy Roberts (a social worker) and Leslie Roberts (an attorney). Since both of my sons were teenagers, Frank spent time with them during his frequent visits to my home. He was very patient with Mike's sometimes unusual behavior and usually kept still when he felt confused about Mark pushing the boundaries of parental control. There were some bumps in the road as we both experienced each other's children but never any real roadblocks.

Frank and I had such special times together. He had a beautiful A-frame houseboat moored on the Columbia River. When we were alone, Frank sometimes read poetry to me in front of the fireplace, a thrilling, romantic new experience in my life. We took Mike and Mark out to dinner once or twice a week. Sometimes just the two of us spent a Sunday sailing on the Columbia. We laughed together often and, in spite of our age difference (twenty-one years), we shared very similar social and political views. I was happy and clearly falling in love. At the point our relationship began to feel more serious, Frank and I had an important and open conversation. Both of us had suffered failed marriages and now believed that without marrying again we could still have a special long-term relationship. It wasn't exactly a pledge, but it was a mutual understanding about our future. At the time it seemed a mature arrangement, honest and clear.

In 1972 Frank was running for reelection to the Oregon House of Representatives. Following the 1970 federal census and Oregon's 1971 re-districting, the entire Legislature was running in newly created single-member districts where *district* residency rather than *county* residency was now required. Frank was running in an area of the county where he had lived, but had not previously sought election. His primary election opponent was well known in the eastern part of the district but most political insiders assumed Frank would win handily. I, on the other hand, was worried about the race. Early in the campaign Frank's challenger sent out a political mailer showing a picture of Frank's houseboat and implying that Frank could simply pull up anchor after the election and float to another district if he wished. A houseboat was rather exotic to most voters and the mailer may have raised questions about Frank's residential stability.

Meanwhile, Frank was active recruiting, supporting, and fundraising for new Democratic candidates to the House. The Democrats had been in the minority for five legislative sessions, a decade, and were making a major push to retake the majority role. During the 1971 legislative session the sixty members of the House had been divided — thirty-four Republicans, twenty-six Democrats — so the Democrats would have to "swing" five seats to gain control, a tall order. Frank was considered the leading candidate for Speaker of the House if the Democrats gained control.

When the May primary date arrived and the votes were tallied in our county, Frank had lost to Troutdale Mayor Glenn Otto. It was a devastating political blow for Frank. He had been so focused on helping his Democratic colleagues statewide, he had not given enough attention to his own redrawn district, which had definitely not been designed to Frank's political advantage. He had been so accustomed to comfortable wins in the City of Portland part of the county that he had underestimated the impact of these new boundaries and new voters. Frank was crushed.

Suddenly the political experience that had brought me such fun and energized my political education now introduced me to the personal trauma a candidate can suffer in losing a political race. It is such a public loss. Your family knows. Your friends know. Your political adversaries know. It is in the newspapers, on television. Few losses in one's life are quite so visible, quite so public.

As summer began, Frank practically went into hiding. He stopped attending Democratic events. We ate *in* rather than *out*. It was summer and he wasn't teaching. He stayed home, depressed and embarrassed over his election loss. I gave him six weeks or so to grieve his political loss, and then I carefully confronted him about what he was doing. "Was winning the House back for the Democrats only important if you were a member?" I asked quietly. I informed Frank he could stay home and brood, but I intended to put my frustrations to work on the fall campaigns. I hated that he had lost his race, but I told him I would hate it worse if that loss had been in vain. The energy and time he had spent to recruit and help new candidates could result in a strong Democratic win in November, but not if we sat around licking our wounds. *I* was going back to work for our candidates.

Two days later Frank called: he wouldn't quite be ready for a party, but he was prepared to work on the late summer and fall campaign efforts. The other factor that helped draw Frank back was the fact that his older daughter, Mary Wendy, was running for the House for the first time and he could help on her campaign. I knew, however, that some days he felt sad not to be running himself, and I tried to encourage him to take breaks away from all the political activity.

When the November 1972 election finally arrived, a huge political shift had occurred in the Oregon House of Representatives. Although ten new Republican House members were elected, eighteen new Democrats had joined the sixty-member House; there were now thirty-three Democrats and twenty-seven Republicans. Among the new Democrats were Frank's daughter Mary Wendy, a future State Labor Commissioner; Earl Blumenauer, who would one day serve as a long-term member of Congress; Vera Katz, who would later become not only the first woman Speaker of the House but eventually a three-term mayor of Portland; and Frank's primary opponent, Glenn Otto. The other positive change in the upcoming 1973 session was a gain of four women House members—from five women in the 1971 session to nine. The state Senate would still have just two women members.

When the legislative session began, Frank took a leave of absence from the university and went on staff for the new Speaker of the House, Representative Richard Eymann. I missed seeing Frank on a daily basis while he was in Salem, but we had our weekends plus we were planning for a sailing trip to Mexico in the summer. Mike and Mark kept me busy being a mother. I had my full-time job at the construction company. My Parkrose School Board position was taking even more time than I had expected as I became chair and a senior board member. I was also busy doing volunteer activities for the Democratic Party.

At this point in time, Frank and I began another quiet discussion. No, not a conversation about marriage—Frank was considering running for the state Senate seat in our district in 1974. It was a brand-new Senate seat without an incumbent. It was a perfect political opportunity for Frank. But he had to decide if he felt too injured from his 1972 loss to come back into the political fray. He was simply considering the possibility.

Our August sailing trip to the Sea of Cortez in the Mexican Baja would mean trailering Frank's sailboat all the way south through California to the Mexican border, crossing into Mexico, and eventually launching the boat on the eastern shore of the Sea of Cortez. We would be accompanied by two close friends, Chuck Mendenhall, Frank's friend and longtime sailing partner, and Ann Mitchell, a houseboat neighbor of Frank's and a school counselor in the Parkrose School District. At that time, the waters of the Sea of Cortez were not charted or marked by safety equipment such as buoys. We finally located a couple of publications with hand sketches of the little bays and larger harbors. The books also contained descriptions of the Baja areas and comments on some of the tiny villages near the western shores of the Sea of Cortez. The area was quite isolated in 1973 with the Baja Highway not yet built. The four of us were enthused about this adventure.

My parents agreed to take my boys for ten days so I could participate in this sailing vacation. Ann and I would ride with the guys south, sail the length of the Baja, and then fly home to Oregon. Frank and Chuck would sail the boat both directions, up and down the Baja, and trailer the boat back to Portland.

The ship's log from that trip reads like one of today's reality television adventures. The Baja in August is hot, very hot, every day. Our boat motor went out; the winds were poor to nonexistent; we had no refrigeration. Some days we never saw another person or boat or even an airplane flying overhead. We sometimes commented that maybe we were the last four people left on earth!! The landscape was usually dry and barren, and there were sharks in some of the waters where we sailed. It was too hot to sleep in the cabin and we were forced to sleep outside on the decks. We lived on potatoes, fish, canned goods, and good rum with no ice. And I loved every minute of it! I returned from that trip nut-brown, very sun-bleached blonde, and madly in love with my captain. Frank returned from the trip just over a week later, also dark brown, with a bad cut on his leg from the boat motor propeller, and ready to run for the state Senate. I volunteered to manage his campaign as a part-time organizer.

I wanted to ask Frank if I made him a senator would he make me a senator's wife. However, long ago we had made a bargain. We had promised each other that we would be happy with a committed relationship that did not include marriage. I began to feel frustrated and angry about that long-ago bargain. I loved Frank and he often expressed his love for me. We were so compatible. Why couldn't he just propose to me? By now, he must understand that our relationship was something wonderful and special. Frank had been married twice before. Did he love me less now than he had loved those two women when he proposed to them? I was feeling upset and irritable.

After several months of brooding I decided I had to take some action. Before I headed over to see Frank that night I talked to my son Mark, now sixteen, about what I planned to do. "I am going over to break up with Frank tonight."

Mark looked at me, shocked. "Mom, you love him. Why in the world would you do that?"

I explained to Mark my dilemma. "I don't want to be mad at him anymore. It isn't fair. He has kept his part of the bargain. I'm the one with the problem and it is up to me to solve it."

Mark shook his head at me. "I think you're making a mistake, Mom, but you have to do what you have to do."

I arrived at Frank's place. He poured us a glass of wine and we sat down on the floor in front of the fireplace. My stomach was churning and I felt close to tears. I needed to do this and go home! Suddenly Frank turned to face me, looked me square in the eye and said, "I love you so much. I've worried for a long time that I am too old for you but I can't let that stand in the way of what I feel any longer. Will you marry me?"

I was stunned!

I was staring at Frank and had not responded to his words. He was waiting for a response. "Frank Roberts, I love you totally. My answer is almost sure to be yes but I need until tomorrow to give you my decision. Can you wait until tomorrow for my answer?" Frank laughed. "Babe, I'll wait as long as you want. I've had months to think about this. This probably comes as a surprise to you." I remember thinking, "Oh Frank, I may have considered this for much longer than you know!" Yet, before I could answer Frank, I had another chore I needed to take care of. We finished our wine, kissed good night, and I drove home.

I turned the key in my door and went straight to Mark's room, shook him awake, and said firmly, "Mark, you called Frank, didn't you? You told him I was coming over to break up with him. How could you?"

Mark was still shaking himself awake. "Mom, I never called Frank tonight. I wouldn't do that. What's all this about?"

I explained to my younger son that Frank had just proposed to me. "So what did you tell him?" Mark asked.

"I told him I would give him my answer tomorrow," I said. "I needed to be sure that this proposal hadn't been the result of you calling him. I wanted it to be what he wanted and not some kind of reaction to my being upset. The chance of this proposal happening tonight just seemed too much of a coincidence to be believable."

"Well, you better believe it," Mark laughed. "I had no hand in this at all."

I hugged my younger son and headed for bed. Tomorrow I would say yes to Frank's proposal.

On our wedding day.

On June 29, 1974, we were married on the large deck at the home of our friends Bob and Barbara Blakeley on a beautiful summer afternoon. Our families and a few special friends attended our brief wedding ceremony. Judge Berkley "Bud" Lent, a former state legislator, performed the wedding ritual. There are only a few snapshots from that day, no formal photography. I have never needed photographs to remind me of the day. The memories have remained clear and lasting. As lasting as the memories, so was the marriage. I guess one could say that this was a marriage built on a broken promise! Thank goodness both Frank and I were willing to set aside our pledge and let our strong love make the decision about our relationship and our future.

In May 1974 Frank won his primary election race for the state Senate seat by a solid margin, and the general election in November was a slam dunk. I was a senator's wife.

CHAPTER NINE

A New Political Partnership

When I arrived for our July 1974 school board meeting, there was a fun, sweet surprise for me. The school superintendent opened the meeting by removing my "Barbara Sanders" name plate from the board table and ceremoniously replacing it with a brand-new "Barbara Roberts" plate. He then solemnly announced, "If you change your name again you will have to personally pay for your next name plate." The whole room applauded and laughed. I felt such an integral part of my community, something I hadn't felt so clearly since leaving Sheridan at age eighteen.

In the next six months Frank would sell his beautiful A-frame houseboat (a sure sign of his love for me). We would now buy our first home together. Frank's new state Senate district covered parts of three school districts but we could purchase a home only in the Parkrose School District if I was to remain on the school board. This was not the usual consideration of a newly married couple as they begin house hunting. Such is the life of a political pair.

When Frank and I put our households together it was quite comical. He had sold all his major appliances with his houseboat. I had been renting for a number of years and most unfurnished rental houses and apartments at least included those appliances. So Frank and I, together, had four sofas, two dining-room sets, eight living-room end tables, three coffee tables, but no stove, refrigerator, washer, or dryer. Both our families suggested that perhaps this marriage might be a mismatch. However, we slowly succeeded in mixing and matching our furnishings and by Thanksgiving we were able to host our two families at our new home for the holiday. It was a perfect day for us ... or would have been ... if our water heater had not gone out leaving us with a kitchen full of dirty dishes, pots and pans, and no hot water.

As the 1975 legislative session approached, Frank and I began making plans to rent an apartment in Salem, so I could work as Frank's legislative assistant for the next six months. We made arrangements for Frank's nephew Brian Routh and his wife, Donna, to stay in our Portland home Monday through Friday and prepare meals and supervise my two sons. Mike was a senior in high school now. Mark was a junior. We would return home every Friday afternoon and spend the weekend at home. Brian and Donna were a younger married couple without children at this point and my sons seemed to feel quite comfortable with the arrangement. It was a big step for me to be away from my teenagers all week but we would talk on the phone most days and have weekends to catch up.

Frank and I found a very satisfactory apartment in Salem and in early January while Frank spent four days in the Capitol participating in legislative orientation workshops, I decorated our furnished apartment. We brought our wedding gifts, Christmas presents, so many special things to create a sense of home for us. I headed for the Capitol to get Frank and drive the hour back to Portland. We planned to return to Salem on Saturday afternoon with Mike and Mark so Frank and I could attend a big Democratic gala that evening. The boys could have an evening of television and food with us out of the way. The four of us would have Sunday free and then we would all attend the opening of the Legislature on Monday morning and watch Frank take the oath of office as a new state senator.

However, on Saturday we awakened to an ice storm that had hit the entire valley during the night. The roads were a mess and we decided it wasn't safe to drive to Salem for the Democratic event. We would drive down on Sunday after the weather had cleared and the road conditions improved. Just after sunset on Sunday we arrived in Salem and drove into the apartment area. Then we noticed the yellow police tape around a large portion of the parking lot and across the stairway area of one of the apartment buildings — our building. In the dark we began to see that our building was a charred, burned-out skeleton of its former structure. It was unbelievable. Two days before this was our perfect temporary home. Tonight all three floors of the building were black and smoldering. I started to cry. All of our things were destroyed — clothing, books, paintings, wedding gifts, jewelry, shoes, dishes, and photographs — everything gone. I calmed down, and we headed for the apartment manager's office. We found there was a spare apartment set aside for us. We had only our two suitcases in the car, a few hanging clothes, and two bags of groceries. Nothing else. I felt so sad — until the apartment manager told us that the young couple on the ground floor, directly below our apartment, had both died in the fire on Saturday evening. If the weather hadn't kept us in Portland, my two sons would likely have been trapped on the second floor of the apartment building the previous night while Frank and I attended the Democratic event. They could both be dead today. It was a very strange and sobering way to begin the legislative session.

On Monday, January 13, 1975, the Capitol ceremonies were both joyful and serious. I stood beside Frank at his desk as he was sworn in. Across the Senate chambers, Frank's older daughter, Mary Wendy, was also being sworn in as a new state senator. Frank's former wife, Betty Roberts, was already a seated member of the Senate. I looked at my sons in the Visitors' Gallery and they both smiled in acknowledgment of this special day.

On that day an Oregon legend finished eight years as Oregon's Governor. Tom McCall was both physically and politically a larger-than-life leader. In 1971 he had signed Senate Bill 699, my special education bill. In my mind, he would always be somewhat more famous because of that fact. I watched him deliver his final speech as Governor and accept his final standing ovation. I wondered how a political leader handles the transition to simply being a regular citizen again. Was it a tremendous relief or was there a sense of loss that came with this life change? Perhaps some of both.

Governor Bob Straub, a Democrat, was inaugurated that morning. He had won a very competitive primary election in May, defeating State Treasurer Jim Redden and state Senator Betty Roberts, and had defeated Republican Vic Atiyeh in the general election by a solid margin. The Democrats and the Republicans each held three of the six statewide offices, but the House was split thirty-eight Democrats, twenty-two Republicans and Frank was serving in a Senate chamber with twenty-two Democrats, seven Republicans, and one Independent. I knew how much Frank was looking forward to serving in the majority party after so many House sessions as a minority-party member. In fact, being in the majority gave Frank a chairmanship in his very first Senate session. He would be chairing the Local Government and Elections Committee and also serving as a member of two important and desirable committees: the Revenue Committee and the Transportation Committee.

During the 1975 session, state senators were still housed in the older parts of the Capitol building awaiting the construction of the new House and Senate office wings. Frank's office was located at the far end of the third-floor hall, through and *behind* a committee hearing room—not exactly prime real estate! Frank may have been a member of the majority party but he was still a freshman senator. We had a four-person office: Frank, Sally Stapleton (his newly hired secretary), Tom Feeley (student intern from Portland State College), and me (Frank's legislative assistant) ; the office space was cramped, but we soon had a close-knit, working team. We all shared research needs on issues where Frank needed supporting information. We all sat in on hearings and took notes for Frank while he participated in the hearings for his own three committees. We became familiar with Frank's twenty-nine Senate colleagues, their staff, and many of their spouses who worked in the Senate as well. It was accepted, in fact it was common practice at that time in Oregon, for wives of legislators to serve on their husbands' staff.

The combination of experienced, knowledgeable senators and enthusiastic, ready-to-go freshman members made for a results-driven Senate. I was totally enthusiastic to have a front-row seat, observing the in-depth policy work and first-class debates on legislation. Every day was an educational adventure for me. Day after day I sat beside Frank at his floor desk listening to legislative debates, noting the skilled speakers and the not-so-articulate ones. Frank was definitely the finest orator in the Senate, then and for the rest of his years in that body. I began to appreciate the advantage that a fine public speaker has in the world of politics. I was determined to become one of those skilled public communicators.

In the Oregon Senate in 1975, roll call votes were taken by voice vote rather than the electronic voting system used today. The reading clerk rapidly read each senator's last name from the front desk and the senator shouted out his aye or nay vote. When the vote count reached the "R" section of the alphabet and the reading clerk quickly read, "Roberts, B., Roberts, F., Roberts, M.," you could often hear a quiet giggle go through the upstairs Visitors' Gallery. Several married couples had served as Oregon legislators simultaneously over the years, and a father and son served together in the 1970s. The other clan in the Oregon Legislature were three brothers named Bunn (Stan, Jim, and Tom, all Republicans). Yet the Frank Roberts, Betty Roberts, Mary Wendy Roberts combination was unusual even by Oregon standards. It was confusing to reporters, voters, and even some political insiders. Mary Wendy was Frank's daughter by his first marriage. Betty was Frank's second wife. Betty and Mary were not related. When I "joined" the "family," I further confused the situation.

The best private Roberts story to come out of the 1975 session was the day Frank and I were standing side by side at his desk as the minister-of-the-day prepared to begin the opening prayer. Betty, arriving just as the prayer began, realized she didn't have time to reach her own desk, stopped right beside me and bowed her head. Mary Wendy, also running late, entered the Senate chambers, saw the prayer in progress and respectfully stopped at Frank's desk and stood beside Betty. As the prayer ended Betty leaned over, smiling, and whispered, "The family that prays together, stays together."

Frank and Betty had been divorced since 1966 after five and a half years of marriage. They seldom seemed to show any sign of that former relationship as they worked together in the political atmosphere of the state Senate. There were a few rare exceptions. During one Senate session, Betty was the main carrier on a life insurance bill. SB145, introduced at the request of the Oregon State Bar, was legislation related to employer-provided insurance policies where the spouse is usually named as the full beneficiary. When a couple divorces it is not uncommon for a husband, for instance, to forget to remove his ex-wife from those legal documents. He may remarry, may even have additional children, but those death benefits would go to his former spouse rather than his current family. The bill Betty presented to the Senate that day terminated such beneficiary status upon divorce and the senators gave it a strong passage. When the vote was done, Frank walked over to Betty's desk, congratulated her, and then thanked her for reminding him he had an old insurance policy at Portland State on which she was still the named beneficiary.

On the weekends, back in Portland, it was catch-up time: mail, laundry, vacuuming, grocery shopping, and time with Mike and Mark. I was always so happy to see my sons and to find out how both of them were getting along. Mike and I were already ordering his graduation needs—cap and gown, announcements, the works. I was so excited to think of him finally accomplishing this educational landmark. He had already called his father in California to remind his dad of his graduation date. Mike was so hopeful his dad would come back to Oregon for the ceremony.

On the other hand, Mark's focus seemed to be more on his car and his friends than his classes and studies. He was talking about dropping out of high school and going to work full time. Frank and I both tried to explain what a bad life decision that would be for him.

We couldn't tell if we were getting through to him at all. His ongoing anger toward his father seemed to color so much of his thinking. I wondered how Mark would react if his dad came back to Portland for Mike's graduation. Would he be glad to see Neal or would his bottled-up anger turn into an emotional explosion? I was hopeful that the chance to see his father again would diminish some of his fury. I wanted so much for Mark to be a happier person. I wished that some of my own happiness could rub off on him.

Finally we heard from Neal. He would be here for the June 7 graduation ceremony. As the date approached, Mike grew quite excited and somewhat restless. As chair of the school board I would actually be presenting Mike with his diploma. For me, it would be both an emotional personal moment and the culmination of the work and leadership I had taken on to create public school opportunities for children with disabilities. I remembered the excitement and emotion of Mike returning to public school with the added services and support that made education possible for my older son. It hadn't always been easy. Mike had been harassed by students who knew he couldn't, or wouldn't, defend himself. He had felt fear and non-acceptance so many times over the years. Yet my work for his educational opportunity had made me a political activist, an advocate for special-needs children, and moved me into a political arena that would change my life forever. What a pair we had become: two unlikely successes!

This event would be the first time my sons had seen their father since he left Oregon three years earlier. My own feelings about his return to Oregon, even temporarily, were definitely spiraling off in all directions: happiness for Mike that his dad would be here for the big moment; worry about Mark's reaction to seeing his dad again; a sense of intrusion that Neal would be back in my life even for this short time; anger that Neal was here for the happy times with no commitment to his sons any other time; frustration that Frank's role as "parent" to my boys for the past few years would somehow be overshadowed by Neal temporarily usurping that role. I wanted to be happy and proud. Parts of me felt frustrated and tense.

As Neal arrived at the auditorium for the ceremony, he looked somewhat uncomfortable in his suit and tie. He looked equally uneasy around his sons. Even I felt a little sad for him. My own worry about Neal stepping back into "my world" began to fade as I recognized I basically *owned* this setting: *my* school board, *my* sons, *my* husband, *my* parents, *my* city, *my* life. Neal needed to be here. I deserved to be here.

On graduation night, Frank brought his camera to the auditorium (he was a fine photographer) to capture the moment when Mike would accept his diploma from me. Mike's fellow students gave him a huge ovation as he crossed the stage. I was so touched I was nearly in tears. It would be wonderful to make copies of this special photo and frame it for all our family members. A few days later, Frank went to pick up the prints; he discovered that, in error, he had used an already exposed roll of film. Every photo was ruined. Frank felt so sad about his mistake. Mike and I were terribly disappointed. There were other pictures with family members before and after the ceremony. But the historic shot of the two of us at Mike's moment of triumph was lost forever, never to be recaptured.

My boys' father left Oregon within less than two days and didn't return for another thirteen years, when he came back for Mark's 1988 wedding. I came to understand that I had been the "winner" as a parent. Parenting is not about being there

Mike and me, following his high school graduation, June 1975.

for the highlights. It's about sharing your life and theirs day after day, month after month. It's about watching your boys grow into men and knowing who they are. I had that privilege, that honor, an experience that enhanced my life and expanded my heart. I had my reward.

With Mike's graduation behind us, I refocused my attention on my staff work for Frank as the end of the 1975 legislative session approached. End-of-session was a new experience for me. Everything moved faster. Committee hearings tabled bills if compromise didn't come quickly. Committees began closing down. Night sessions and Saturday sessions were added to the work schedule. Everyone was tired. Tempers were short. I was ready to see adjournment *sine die* at 10 p.m. on the night of June 14, 1975.

We approached the rest of that summer with plans for sailing and also with the wonderful reality that Frank wouldn't have an election race the next year. What a relief that was! Four-year Senate terms were a big improvement over every-two-year elections in the House. I still felt like a bride even after more than a year of marriage. We were now starting to talk about next steps for Mike. I was still enjoying my role as a member of the school board. Frank would return to his position as a professor at Portland State University after a nine-month break from the classroom. Our life was so fulfilled and happy. There was only one major worry troubling me. Mark was growing more insistent about quitting high school and getting a job. He only had one more year before graduation. It seemed so foolish, but it was also clear he was gaining little from the forced attendance. We talked about a GED certificate, about moving to the community college, about working for a while and then going back to school. It felt like an endless, unsatisfying discussion. However, I understood I was losing the battle. He was so smart and so able. It saddened me to have him miss the opportunity for a good education and a higher education degree. Frank was more than willing to help Mark financially if he wanted to go to college. Even that didn't persuade Mark at that point. Maybe later, he argued. In January 1977, Mark quit high school and found a job. The conflict now ended, he was soon enjoying his work, and even the manual labor. He bought a car and a leather jacket and seemed to be a much happier person. My one sense of maternal comfort was that Mark continued to live at home, where I hoped he would feel a sense of family and support.

In early 1977, Frank and I found a comfortable apartment in Salem as we prepared for the next session. The boys were both living in our house in Portland but at almost twenty-one and nineteen they certainly didn't need the "babysitter" this session that we had arranged in 1975. I was glad to have the house occupied while we were in Salem.

The first big change we found at the Capitol was the two new wings added to the building, one on the Senate side, one on the House side. We moved into Frank's beautiful new office space, with new furnishings, new office equipment, even a new bright purple sofa! Frank's new secretary, Kathi Foisie, was another great addition to our office. This remodeling also added impressive new hearing rooms to the building with plenty of seating for citizens, a well-microphoned desk for those testifying, and a raised seating and desk area for the legislative committee members.

The Senate had three newly elected members, all Democrats. Dell Isham from the coast and Jan Wyers, an attorney from Portland, were real "newbies" in the legislative process. Stephen Kafoury from Portland had been an active member of the House in the 1973 and 1975 sessions.The 1977 Oregon Senate again had a strong Democratic majority with only six Republicans in the thirty-member body. However, it is well to remember that numbers are not the whole equation. Of those six Republicans, for example, Victor Atiyeh would later be elected Governor, Wally Carson would become Chief Justice of the Oregon Supreme Court, Tony Meeker would be elevated to Oregon Treasurer, and Bob Smith would be elected to Congress. There were jokes in the Capitol that the Senate Republican Caucus was so small they could meet in a telephone booth! But wherever they met, they were able to fill a room with political potential.

The 1977 legislative session was long and frustrating, with some internal strife in the House. The session began with major calls from the press and public for school finance reform, resulting in a school-funding protection measure on the May 17 ballot, which failed when the voters had their say. However, on the final day of the session a local-option tax base election measure lurched through, with no small amount of controversy. Sen. Frank Roberts said the measure might be a "good idea" but "I deplore a legislative process that attempts to pass a major bill, from start to finish, on the last day of the session." Frank always had a huge respect for an open process with citizen input. But on that last session day, process came in second to politics.

Three of the big winners in the 1977 session were Governor Straub, the senior citizen lobby, and organized labor.

Governor Straub's number one priority, the Domestic & Rural Power Authority, passed at the very end of the session. Straub also won legislation on community corrections, field-burning levels, economic development, and land use.

The Oregonian of July 6, 1977, reported that no single lobbying group in the session "could claim a better record than Oregon's senior citizens." The well-organized senior lobby won utility-rate relief, $4 million worth of home weatherproofing for seniors, and the passage of the major Homeowners and Renters Property Tax Relief Program, HB2040.

Organized labor was able to prevent any attacks on unemployment benefits. They enhanced benefits under workers' compensation laws for permanently disabled workers and gained tax credits for child care for working mothers. Another win for labor was the establishment of a Labor Center at the University of Oregon. Finally, labor played a defining role in retaining Oregon's election day voter registration, which had been under constant attack from legislative Republicans.

If the Democratic Governor, senior citizens, and organized labor were big winners, the Democratically controlled Legislature would chalk the session up as pretty successful. All that, and the budget part of the process ended with a $40 million unspent "emergency fund."

I observed this session from beginning to end and gained a broad education in policy issues, politics, well-organized lobbying efforts, and the power that rested in the leadership of the President of the Senate. The House Speaker had been stripped of much of his power that session, and the difference in the two chambers was evident. Frank was a wonderful mentor as I raised questions on policy and politics during that session. I was no longer the neophyte who had lobbied in the 1971 session. I was a serious student of the potential that was possible in this arena with careful preparation, diligent research, continual observation, and a love of the process.

When the 1977 Legislature adjourned on July 5, Sen. Betty Browne, one of the Senate's three women members, announced her immediate resignation. In August, Representative Ted Kulongoski was appointed to fill the vacancy. In September, Sen. Betty Roberts announced her resignation to accept Governor Straub's appointment to the Oregon Court of Appeals. She would become the first female member of that court in state history. Betty's Portland Senate seat was filled with the appointment of Raul Soto-Seelig, a Cuban immigrant. The following month Sen. Wally Carson, who had earlier announced he would not be seeking reelection, resigned from the Senate to accept Governor Straub's appointment to the Marion County Circuit Court bench, filling the vacancy caused by the death of Judge Jena Schlegel. Wally's replacement in the Senate, L. B. Day, would become a strong, vocal, and sometimes unpredictable, member of the Senate. Now, Frank's daughter Mary Wendy would become the only remaining woman in the Oregon Senate from September 1, 1977, until she took statewide office in January of 1979 as the newly elected Oregon Labor Commissioner, another Oregon "first" for women.

Women in Oregon worked so hard to be elected to local government, legislative, and especially statewide offices; these public positions were treasured by activists in the women's movement. But as women advanced politically it was critical that we "build the bench" for women ready to step up and fill vacancies created by these early women's succession to higher office. In 1979 it was more than obvious that the women's movement had failed this test. The 1979 legislative session would convene without a single woman member on the floor of the Senate in Oregon.

Just think how different the state Senate in Oregon might have been long-term if we hadn't had to start back at square one in 1980. If Betty Browne's departure from the Senate had been replaced with a strong new woman from her district; if Betty Roberts had been able to see a talented, prepared woman fill her state Senate shoes; if we had raised the question in Salem of seeing a Republican woman appointed to the Oregon Senate seat to replace Wally Carson, it would have created a much different political picture. Our case should have been easy to make with the Carson vacancy since a Republican woman had not served in the Oregon Senate since 1943 when Dorothy McCullough Lee left the chamber.

The women's movement was only doing *part* of the work when we helped elect women. We needed to prepare *more* women, mentor them, put them in line before a vacancy presented itself. It was not likely someone else would think of us if we were standing in the shadows. Our visibility and electability was up to us. We couldn't flinch at the idea of self-promotion for our female leaders, our potential women candidates. Viewing the make-up of the 1979 Oregon Senate should have been an obvious lesson for the Oregon women's movement.

Over in the Oregon House, female legislators were a little more in evidence. Nine of the sixty House members were women, both Democrats and Republicans. Five of the women were from the Portland metro area, two from Lane County, one from Salem, and one from Albany. It was apparent we also had much work to do in encouraging women candidates from the more rural areas of our state. In time, I believed that would happen. And it did.

CHAPTER TEN

County Commissioner Roberts

After the 1977 legislative session ended I found I was struggling with some medical challenges, not serious ones, not new for me, but challenges none the less. My physician felt the time had come for major female surgery. She scheduled a hysterectomy for early February of 1978, after the Christmas holiday season. My sons were both in their early twenties, so permanently ending my childbearing years was not an emotional adjustment for me. Once the surgery was completed, I returned home for a period of recuperation. I had lots of time for reading and resting and talking with friends and family. Every day I read the newspaper from cover to cover, digesting national, state, and local news. Political articles were of growing interest to me, and I read those stories down to the last paragraph.

In mid-February, a story hit the local papers and also the television news: the appointment of Multnomah County Commissioner Mel Gordon to a federal agency position as chair of the Pacific Northwest River Basins Commission. A new County Commissioner would be appointed to fill the vacancy. As local government went, this was a big political announcement ... a paid political office in the state's most populous county — my home county.

Over the next few days I scoured the newspaper for the small stories containing the names of those candidates who were seeking the appointment. One evening, I complained to Frank about the list of names; I had expected stronger, more prominent applicants for the job. Frank turned to me and said, "If you don't like the list, add your name to it." I laughed out loud. Here I was, recuperating from major surgery, a school board member, with no thought of ever running for higher office ... ever. Plus, I was already on the spring ballot, running for the board at Mt. Hood Community College. Two offices ought to be enough for me.

Frank made his case about my elected and community credentials, my potential support base, and my speaking and people skills. But I still laughed at the idea. We went off to bed. Frank fell asleep. I lay in bed with my thoughts racing and my eyes wide open. As the night hours passed I watched headlights from the freeway just below our back yard as the lights crawled up the wall, across the ceiling, and disappeared. In the quiet of the night I weighed the "silly" idea, rejected it several times, and finally fell asleep as dawn approached.

When I opened my eyes the next morning, Frank lay next to me, face to face, and smiling. "Well, Commissioner," he chortled, "what can I do to help with the campaign?"

Frank had planted the seed. I had nurtured it through a long, restless night. By morning it had definitely taken root. I was feeling amazed, but Frank didn't seemed at all surprised. My husband, lover, and best friend was also a skilled and experienced mentor. He knew I was ready for this next step even when I couldn't yet see it myself. How fortunate I was to have him in my life.

My decision to seek the appointment to board position number five on the Multnomah County Commission might send me down a challenging path. The four current board members had determined that whoever they appointed would have to agree not to file for election to the full four-year term. The closing deadline for that filing was still days away and that would have been possible. Looking back, I am not certain that the board could have *legally* prevented the newly appointed commissioner from filing, but this was an understood "gentlemen's agreement." The side effect of that policy was that the already-announced candidates for the full-term vacancy would not be involved in the short-term appointment process. They would certainly not be willing to give up a four-year opportunity for a nine-month appointment.

I was still recuperating from my recent surgery, so some of my efforts to gain support for the appointment would be done from my home telephone. The first important call, however, was made by Frank, who called his old Portland State teaching colleague and friend, Ben Padrow, who was now chief of staff to County Chairman Don Clark. Frank informed Ben that I had decided to seek the appointment and then inquired about the status of other potential appointees. Ben was very hesitant. He finally told Frank there was a likely front-runner already working quietly behind the scenes and shared the man's name with Frank. The other candidate had acted as the campaign treasurer for the county chairman in the last election. Frank thought that his "inside track" would not sit well with the local press and told Ben so. The conversation ended on a quite formal note considering these two were close friends and had taught together in the PSU speech department for over twenty years.

I thought I had a fair shot at the job and decided to employ serious planning and strategy toward making this effort a successful one. Working from home, I notified the county Democratic Party that I was seeking the appointment and said I planned to attend the endorsement meeting to ask for my party's support. I composed a strong letter asking for that backing and mailed my request to every Democratic precinct committeeperson who was qualified to vote at the upcoming meeting. I worked by phone, usually attired in my nice warm bathrobe.

My next step was to secure the endorsement of the local chapter of the Oregon Women's Political Caucus. Women's rights activities were in full swing across the country and this particular endorsement would carry some weight with at least three of the voting commissioners. I felt fairly confident about my chances of success with the OWPC since I was an active member of the organization and a recognized feminist. I was also making a real effort to line up endorsements from prominent Democrats, elected officials, and community leaders. This super-short campaign was pressured and tiring but I was having a grand time. Win or lose, it felt like a growing experience for me.

By late February there were a dozen of us in the race. The four people who were crucial were, of course, the four County Commissioners who would make the appointment decision. The chairman, Don Clark, was a progressive, hard-working, good guy. Dan Mosee was a local appliance-store owner, conservative and often described as negative and temperamental. Alice Corbett was in her last year of a four-year term and seemed somewhat detached from the whole process. Dennis Buchanan, a former newsman and stock-market enthusiast, filled out the remaining fourth position on the commission. I would need to have the votes of three of the four commissioners to secure the coveted appointment. Over the next ten days I gained the endorsements of the Oregon Women's Political Caucus and the Multnomah County Democratic Party. Every day I added new endorsers to my support group. I was slowly regaining my pre-surgery strength and part of my usual energy level.

Finally the big day, March 27, arrived. The County Commission chambers were packed with press and visitors. As the meeting began, the chairman read a request from the behind-the-scenes "front-runner" asking that his name be removed from consideration. I felt a slight elation at this news. Each of the remaining candidates was allowed to make a five-minute statement and then fielded questions from the four commissioners. Finally, the time had come for the big vote. I was tense and not at all confident. In less than five minutes it was all over. By three votes and Dan Mosee's abstention, I became a Multnomah County Commissioner for the next nine months of 1978. Now I was going to be paid a nice salary ($28,000 annually) for doing the public policy work of Oregon's most populous county. I would have a big office and a county car, and would be able to select three staff people for my office. While school board work brought little public attention, being a County Commissioner in this particular county put me in the public eye on issues and actions in a way that I had never yet experienced. Television and newspaper coverage were an expected part of almost every action on the part of the commission.

With my three new staff immediately on board, we were ready to tackle our upcoming responsibilities. John Hankee had previous county staff experience, and I felt fortunate to have him on my team. Tanya Collier and Genevieve Hansen, both friends, were newcomers to the county, but I knew I could trust them to be hard working and dedicated. The four of us were excited and ready to go to work.

From day one there were big decisions to face … land use, mass transit, juvenile corrections, and the list went on. However, there would be some smaller, more unusual decisions first.

I moved into an office full of large, dark brown leather furniture and big pedestal ashtrays. It looked like a scene from an old men's fancy smoking club! This setting had worked for Commissioner Mel Gordon, but it didn't feel like an office I could live with … even for nine months. Yet I didn't want the county to spend tax dollars to refurnish my office for such a limited period of time. So I set out on a scavenger hunt in various county offices and buildings all over town. I selected a desk, sofa, chairs, tables, and lamps. I brought framed art from home and potted plants from a local nursery. With some personal photos and a few political artifacts, it now felt like *my* office.

Next came the issue of the car furnished to each commissioner at county expense. My predecessor had had a very large impressive car. The flashy Chevrolet Caprice with plush red interior, a stereo tape player, and air conditioning was very "high-end" for 1978. There was certainly no way I was going to drive that car around the county. The press soon caught wind of the car issue and requested permission to take my photograph sitting behind the wheel of the big car as the county prepared to trade it in on a more compact model that better suited my needs and, perhaps, my image. The press seemed to be having great fun with the story. This kind of media attention was new and somewhat surprising to me.

In my first few days in office I decided and then publicly declared I was going to visit every county department, facility, and building over my first two months in office. As a new commissioner, I had envisioned only the courthouse, the county jail, the county juvenile facility, and the Elections Department. I soon learned, to my dismay, that the county also had cemeteries, parks, storage facilities, printing operations, road maintenance buildings, alcohol and drug programs, a fairgrounds operation; in all, there were thirty-nine county facilities. Yet I had made the commitment to see it all and I kept my word. Some county employees told me they had never met a real live County Commissioner. Now I knew why! That experience taught me to be better informed before I made big public commitments and promises.

As I settled into my new role as County Commissioner, I added another success to my political resume with my election to the board of Mt. Hood Community College. With my election and that of Gladys Brooks, MHCC now had the first community college board in Oregon with a majority of women board members, five women and two men. We met only one Wednesday a month, but even that schedule would add some extra preparation and work to what I was now doing on the Parkrose School Board and my busy schedule on the County Commission. Maintaining the details of my calendar became a challenge for my staff and for me.

Looking back now, I realize that my short time as a Multnomah County Commissioner took place at a particularly opportune time with regard to state and local public policy choices.

The first big decision would be determined by the County Commission in conjunction with the Gresham City Council (just east of Portland), the Tri-Met Board (our three-county transit agency), and the Portland City Council. The majority vote of all four boards was required to begin the massive funding and reconstruction of the east-west I-84 freeway and the building of a fifteen-mile light rail system between Gresham and Portland. Governor Bob Straub was supporting the project. Portland Mayor Neil Goldschmidt was an enthusiastic promoter. County Chairman Don Clark was openly and actively in favor. However, this project would cancel a freeway long in the planning stage, intended to go east through the city and past Gresham, and replace it with the light rail "trolley" (as it was referred to in that area). The further east one traveled in the county, the more controversial the big plan became. I lived east, outside the Portland City limits. My neighbors wanted more freeway and less mass transit. Plus, the majority of the five-year construction disruption would be borne by drivers coming in and out of the eastern part of the county.

Yet, in spite of those conflicts and the controversy, I soon became an advocate for the project, even taking on television debates. I was feeling considerable heat in my own neighborhood but the light rail concept made sense to me, and it was crucial that leaders moved on it while large federal monies were still available. By the time voting by the four boards began in early October, I was a recognized and expected "yes" vote. I was publicly yelled at during a high school athletic event, at my local hardware store, and even a couple of times on the street but I still consider my vote in favor of that light rail project one of the best decisions of my public career.

For the next five years of the seemingly endless construction phase, I was sometimes taunted or teased by doubters and opponents of the project. Yet finally, when the rail line opened in September of 1986, I was there for the celebration and the first rides. Many years later, after my time as Governor, one of the light rail cars was named in my honor. The plaque is still mounted in the rail car, and it gives me real pleasure to see both the plaque and the many riders who use this great transit system every day. That initial fifteen-mile light rail system is, today, forty-six miles of track and rail system going in all four directions, plus a link to the Portland International Airport. New southbound expansions are in the works including a line that will reach my current neighborhood in the next few years. Almost 30 percent of week-day transit in the metropolitan Portland area is by our light rail system, fondly called the MAX. Visitors, including transportation designers and government officials, come to Portland from across the nation and the world to see the quality and design of our system. Opponents may continue to holler all they like about the dollars and the disruption, but this metropolitan area is a more livable place because of the 1978 decision we made for this region's

Commissioner Roberts in her office.

future and the transit decisions that have followed over the next three decades. As a County Commissioner I was proud to second the motion of support for light rail on October 5, 1978.

The other big decision that occurred during my County Commission service, and that had lasting effects on our county's future and its livability, was the Commission's thoughtful and visionary work on the urban growth boundary under Oregon's statewide comprehensive land-use laws. As our state and its city, regional, and county governments set the boundaries in each jurisdiction for development, growth, and preservation, they required vision, thoughtfulness, technical knowledge, and no small amount of political courage. There were a hundred variables and a thousand opinions regarding every element of the UGB. But before I finished my short-term stay on the Commission, we had defined the UGB for Multnomah County that would determine residential housing policy, stimulate dozens of new high-rise condominium buildings, create neighborhood in-fill, turn old warehouses into living and retail space, eventually expand green space in the region, and still preserve productive farmland and forest areas and prevent urban sprawl. The timing was perfect. Had the State of Oregon and its municipal jurisdictions waited another decade, the opportunity to save our fertile farmland, our forest acreage, and green space would have been missed. Between that decision year of 1978 and the time I left the Governor's seat in early 1995, Oregon's population had grown from just under 2.5 million residents to 3.1 million people and is now over 3.8 million. The majority of that growth has been in the Portland metro area. Once you lay concrete there is no turning back. Our timing was perfect.

Most of the work that took place during my term as County Commissioner was much less exciting and controversial than the milestone decisions on light rail and land use. There were routine matters regarding noise issues, animal control, road repair work, and employee negotiations. There were more complex matters on crime and corrections, potential airport expansion, bridges, the closing of the old county "poor farm," and budget cuts.

Yet even the most mundane decisions can take on a new interest when they are set in the climate of cultural change and political controversy. In Oregon and across America, 1978 was one of those times. As the national battle over the Equal Rights Amendment faced the reality of less than the two-thirds required ratification from the fifty states, political activities were building to put pressure, particularly economic pressure, on the states that had not yet ratified. Groups and organizations all over the country were curtailing purchases from and travel into those states as a way of showing displeasure. I determined that Multnomah County should make such a statement. I introduced a board resolution that prevented Multnomah County employees from traveling on county business or at county expense to any of the unratified states except where law-enforcement movement of inmates or similar travel needs had to take place. That translated into no conferences, no government conventions, no workshops, no paid professional trips into any of the fifteen states that were saying "no" to women's equality. As you might expect, the story of this proposed action made the news for several weeks and filled letters to the editor columns with emotional words from both sides. I became a hero to the Oregon Women's Political Caucus and the Democratic Party. I was, however, a demon with horns in right-wing circles. Oregon's Legislature had already ratified and then reaffirmed their position on the ERA in two separate legislative years. I was simply asking Multnomah County government to show some "muscle" in support of Oregon's official position.

On December 21, 1978 (my forty-second birthday), the County Commission voted in support of my resolution. Looking back now I recognize that the impact of that effort was hardly earth-shaking, but it offered an opportunity for me to understand that even symbolic acts can be important in times of cultural change and social controversy. Eventually the ERA would fail in this country but not without first energizing and politicizing hundreds of thousands of American women. I was definitely one of those women!

As 1978 was nearing its end, I was preparing to go back to Salem as Frank's leading staff person. Frank had just won reelection to the Senate. We were both looking forward to working closely together again. Yet I looked back on what a great nine months I had experienced as a hard-working County Commissioner. I had taken on the extra assignments of sitting on the Multnomah County Library Board and chairing the County Board of Equalization, which heard appeals on property-tax evaluations. I had been very visible in the community and had seemed to get more than my share of positive press and media coverage. I had enjoyed my tenure as a Commissioner and begun to wish it could continue. I was an improved policymaker, a better public speaker, and a more confident official. How fortunate I was to have had this opportunity. Thank goodness I had been brave enough to put myself into the public selection process. Frank had been correct in encouraging me. This had been my time to stand up and be counted, personally and politically. How different my future would have been if Frank hadn't encouraged me to step forward. In those years, too many capable women hadn't yet recognized their own skills and potential. Frank's loving push had opened my eyes to my many talents.

By now, most people in my state have forgotten I was ever a Multnomah County Commissioner. My tenure was short. Yet I have never forgotten the opportunity I was given to demonstrate my abilities, stand up for solid public policy, and to make long-term positive choices for my community. A final Stan Federman *Oregonian* story on December 31 stated, "The popular Mrs. Roberts continues to win verbal bouquets from the public and politicians for a job well done."

As the 1979 biennial legislative session approached, Frank reached out to find a new secretary for his Senate staff. He received several strong resumes and set up personal interviews at our Portland home. The earliest applicant arrived, and she and Frank headed for the living room to get acquainted. Her name was Patricia McCaig and she would become not only Frank's secretary for the '79 session, but a large part of our personal and political life for the next fifteen years. Patricia used to love to tell the story of that interview morning. While Frank was discussing the duties of the position with her, I had just finished my shower, put on my rose-colored bathrobe, and walked into the room carrying our black cat. She later recalled that I looked like the "mistress of the manor" rather than a hard-working legislative wife. She almost turned down the job when she knew she would be working with me in Frank's office! The image was almost too much for her.

It was our good fortune that Patricia decided to join Frank's staff. She turned out to have wonderful political instincts, a deep passion for many policy issues, a wild sense of humor, and a strong commitment to Frank. She was a great asset to Frank in 1979 and by the end of that session she was like part of our family.

Four new senators joined the body for the 1979 session, two Republicans and two Democrats, a loss of one Democrat. One of the new senators was Frank's fairly new son-in-law, Richard Bullock, Mary Wendy's husband. His entrance into the Senate was somewhat controversial. On filing day in March of 1978, Mary Wendy had made a surprising and very last-minute filing for Oregon Labor Commissioner. This left her Senate seat vacated, and her husband filed for her seat. That last-minute switch prevented anyone else from having an opportunity to run for Wendy's vacated seat. Considered a "set-up" for Bullock, it was not a popular political move. Frank and I were caught completely off guard, unaware of the plan.

The other new Democratic senator was Jim Gardner, also from Portland. Frank and I had mentored Jim through this first election, writing his campaign brochures, doing campaign photos, and sharing lots of policy and political advice. The two new Senate Republicans, Tom Hartung and Mike Ragsdale, had previous experience in the House. Jason Boe began his fourth term as President of the Oregon Senate. His tenure was beginning to wear on a number of Democratic senators. There was a week-long political squabble in the House of Representatives over the election of the Speaker of the House and the appointment of members of the Ways & Means Committee. Finally Representative Hardy Myers was elected House Speaker. The Senate appeared well organized and ready for business when compared with the week of conflict and maneuvering being reported daily on the other end of the Capitol building. Not a great beginning for the 1979 session.

Frank's committee assignments were, as usual, heavy-duty and multiple. He would find the Elections Committee assignment particularly interesting as the 1980 census approached and discussions began about the redistricting of the House and Senate seats. This process is always a huge area of conflict in legislative bodies, and Oregon is no exception. The actual redistricting, the drawing of House and Senate district boundaries, would not happen until the 1981 legislative session, but the pre-planning left lots of room for conflict and disagreement about how the work would take place and who would hold the power strings in the legislative committee structure. Frank would also be serving on the Health and Welfare Committee, which covered so many areas where he had strong interests and had amassed a great deal of expertise over the years. It was an area of legislative work where he felt he could make a strong difference to citizens in need ... and he did. Frank would also chair the Senate Local Government Committee, where he had extensive historical and technical knowledge.

With the House and Senate in comfortable Democratic control (at least, in terms of numbers) both houses now faced several tough legislative challenges in 1979. Phil Cogswell of *The Oregonian* summed it up after the Legislature adjourned. "The long shadow of last year's property tax revolt dominated the 1979 legislative session, producing the largest tax relief package in state history, an emphasis on tight state budgets, and an unwillingness to launch any major new programs." The development of the tax-relief legislation dominated most of the 1979 session and caused a series of conflicts and disagreements between newly elected Governor Victor Atiyeh (R) and both houses of the Legislature. The Governor, unhappy with the final product, allowed it to become law without his signature, a sure sign of his disapproval.

Other major conflicts included House and Senate battles over whether or not legislators should receive any salary increase on their $654 monthly salary, a moratorium on the development of any new nuclear power plants in Oregon until studies were complete on the nuclear accident at Pennsylvania's Three Mile Island, debate over field-burning acreage increases, and a proposal to use lethal injections in Oregon's newly reinstated death-penalty law. In the end, legislative salaries were raised to $700 monthly, the nuclear power moratorium was quite short term, field burning increased from 180,000 to 250,000 acres, and the lethal injection bill died, leaving Oregon with no facility or means to apply the state's 1978 passage of a new death-penalty law. I personally would have been elated if the law had never been applied at all.

In the end, 903 bills passed the 1979 session and Governor Atiyeh vetoed nineteen of them. Finally, at 11:22 p.m. on July 4, after 178 days, the session ended. Happy Independence Day!!

CHAPTER ELEVEN

"A Woman's Place Is in the House"

After three legislative sessions on Frank's Senate staff plus almost a year as Multnomah County Commissioner, I began to actually see myself as a future voting member of the Legislature. I desperately wanted to run in 1980 but I had two serious hurdles, or more accurately, *roadblocks*. My husband was my senator, and I obviously could not, would not, run against Frank. My state representative was George Starr, a very dear friend. I would never challenge his reelection to a legislative seat he had won over huge odds six years earlier, a seat he had earned and served with hard work and dignity. My time as County Commissioner had enhanced my public political reputation. More importantly, it had whetted my appetite for decision making on broader policy issues that I knew the Legislature dealt with. For the time being I would just have to be content with my board positions at Mt. Hood Community College and the Parkrose School District. However, I could dream of more exciting political adventures in my future. The question was: "Would my opportunity come?"

For the six years I had worked on Frank's Senate staff I had been exposed to a wide variety of state issues. I had once thought that tax matters were totally boring, but as I followed Frank's work on the Revenue Committee and learned the details of property, corporate, personal, and timber taxation, I discovered a new area of interest — taxation. The Senate also became involved with early efforts to increase international trade for Oregon products. Additionally, there were heated debates on costs vs. safety vs. waste storage regarding nuclear power generation. Environmental concerns were gaining priority status under Senate Democratic control plus the leadership positions that had been voiced by former Governor Straub, who was a strong conservationist. Air quality, water quality, river protection, land use, and coastal safeguards were debated each legislative session with increasing support for protections. The list of legislative policy matters was broad: highway construction, juvenile delinquency issues, higher education funding, insurance debates, teacher tenure, school funding distribution, and prisons. My knowledge base on state government issues grew with each week I spent on Frank's staff. I truly had six years of broad-based preparation to become a legislator. Now, if only there would come a time and a place that would allow me to become an actual legislative candidate ... if only!

After the 1979 legislative session adjourned in July, Frank and I prepared for a sailing trip to the San Juan Islands in Washington State. Mark was working full time for the Pepsi Company, and Mike was in the food service training program at Portland Community College. As a parent of two young men in their early twenties, my life had changed over the past four years. With our sailboat docked in Friday Harbor, Washington, year-round, we were able to drive home every couple of weeks to check the house, our mail, and the kids. Mike and Frank would get the lawn mowed and the yard in shape while I did laundry, wrote checks, and made a major grocery store run. After almost four years of being a single mother it was now a true bonus to have a partner who shared the chores, the responsibilities, the fun, and the finances. How had I been so lucky? I had found a special soul mate. Our fifth wedding anniversary had just passed, and it was always a reminder for both of us to celebrate our good fortune.

In late August we made our final summer trip of 1979 to the San Juan Islands, preparing to close the boat for the season in advance of the Labor Day crowds. We used that trip to sail our favorite San Juan waters, anchor in our familiar and special small scenic coves, dine in the historic inn at Roche Harbor, and lift a few glasses in the local pubs. We read quietly on the deck each day with our morning coffee. At anchor, we marveled at crimson sunsets. We thrilled as the orca pods (killer whales) shared outer water passages with us. We made love in our cabin bunk as the waves slapped the hull of the boat and the halyards rang musically against the mast. Never in my adult life had I known such contentment.

With our return to Portland, I was handed the true gift of friendship. George Starr had decided not to seek reelection and so had given me the chance to run for the Oregon House of Representatives. To this day I remain grateful for his decision. I know he could have won again. He knew it, too. Yet George also understood I was patiently warming up, waiting for my chance at bat. Today George is in his nineties and still the loyal, caring Democrat and friend he was in 1979 when he stepped aside and gave me a great political opportunity.

I didn't waste any time announcing my candidacy for the 1980 election. I hoped an early declaration might discourage other political hopefuls from entering the race. The state filing deadline wasn't until the following March, so I wouldn't know for six months if this strategy had actually worked. I entered the race with what I believed were several possible assets, some earned, some acquired. The number one "acquired" asset was my married last name. Frank Roberts was well known as the district's state senator and a former long-time Mt. Hood Community College board member. Betty Roberts, Frank's second wife, had held public office for a number of years in our county and had also been a statewide candidate for both governor and U.S. senator in the mid-1970s. Frank's daughter Mary Wendy Roberts had been elected statewide as Labor Commissioner in 1978. It was a very solid, well-recognized political name in our part of the state. I laughingly compared the Robertses of Oregon to the Kennedys of Massachusetts ... without the money! My own service on both the MHCC and the Parkrose education boards provided elected credentials that voters tended to feel positive about. Plus it had only been a year since I completed my appointment in the very visible position of Multnomah County Commissioner. I had the longtime asset of being a successful legislative advocate for children with disabilities. At the time I had also spent almost two years chairing the board of the Multnomah County Juvenile Services Commission. Both on paper and in person I felt I offered strong credentials to the voters of my district.

As the months passed I watched the newspaper every day for an announcement of my first challenger in the race. November, December, January, February ... no one had yet filed. However, in the Oregon tradition, at least in those days, it was not unusual to see last-minute entries on the mid-March filing deadline. On that deadline date, Frank and I drove to Salem for the big political gathering that occurred every two years in the House chambers. Large reader boards were installed on the chamber walls listing every statewide, congressional, and legislative seat that would appear on the May primary ballots across the state. Democrats and Republicans mingled, talked, laughed, kidded each other, and waited as new filings were added to the big boards. I kept my eyes glued to the "State Representative, District #17" listing. So far, I was the only name on the board, the only Democrat for the position, and no Republican had entered the race by mid-afternoon.

As the final hour for filing began, the chamber was packed, shoulder-to-shoulder with politicians, family, press, staff, lobbyists, and even some just plain hangers-on. As was the case every filing day, the noise level was very high and all eyes were on the big boards *plus* the Secretary of State's filing line at the House Speaker's podium at the front of the chamber. Every time someone approached that podium line no less than a hundred politicians held their breath.

Filing day was all about a great deal of political speculation, and it was also about dreams and about taking chances. Nothing puts you "out there" quite like choosing to place your name on an election ballot. I scanned my name constantly on the big board as the 5 p.m. deadline neared. As the last minutes passed, everyone watched the line, the boards, and the clock. As the clock's hands reached the 5 p.m. deadline, a staff person closed off the line and Secretary of State Norma Paulus dropped the big gavel and declared the filing complete for the 1980 Oregon elections. I had absolutely no opponent! No Democrat in the primary, no Republican in the general election. Frank threw his arms around me, gave me a big kiss, and congratulated me on a "hard-fought race"! I could barely believe my good fortune! A lot of hand shaking and hugs began from fellow Democrats, legislative spouses of both parties, and lobbyists (some of whom had already contributed to me, others who would).

My parents, my sister, my sons, all seemed elated at my great political "coup." Mother and Dad were already planning for my swearing-in ceremony in January of 1981, over nine months away. My sons thought Frank and I would be a "dynamic duo." The way it was looking, my actual election would be anti-climatic. As the House chambers began to empty and the room quieted, I looked again at the big boards. With no real race I would be able to help other Democratic House candidates with tough challengers.

Under Oregon election law, in partisan races, a candidate may actually secure the nomination of *both* parties. Since I was the only Democrat in my primary race, Democratic voters were likely to give me an overwhelming vote. With no candidate opposing me on the Republican ticket, I needed to secure that nomination as well, to be certain the Republican Party did not put forward a last-minute write-in candidate. I sent a letter to several hundred registered Republicans in my district who had active voting records, asking them to write in my name on their Republican nomination ballot. To my amazement, in the May primary, sixty-eight Republicans in my district did exactly that. I would now go into the fall election carrying both major party nominations. This is as close to a "sure thing" as one can have in the political arena.

I was half-way there! Primary election done; general election six months away. Tonight's parties and even tomorrow's post-election events would be a time for celebration. In the Portland area a post-election tradition had started two years earlier. On the day following the election, Democratic women candidates, women office holders, and their supporters would gather for a big potluck lunch and a little wine. It was privately and laughingly referred to as the "Wednesday Winos." We cheered the winners, gave sympathy and support to those who had lost the night before, and planned for the fall campaigns. The 1980 event was held at the home of State Representative Gretchen Kafoury, and I was thrilled to be part of the celebration. There was so much to feel good about with the success of this year's women candidates in Oregon.

Partway through the afternoon festivities, a telephone call came for me at Gretchen's home. One of my neighbors had tracked me down. Frank had taught his usual Wednesday classes at Portland State and returned to our neighborhood on the bus. Less than a block from the bus stop, he had been hit in the crosswalk by a pickup truck, knocked unconscious, and taken to the hospital by ambulance. The neighbor had no idea *which* hospital. I was so scared I could hardly breathe. The party atmosphere stopped as we began calling local hospitals to see if Frank had been checked in to their emergency room. Each hospital told me Frank was not there. I began to panic. Maybe he had been killed and not simply injured. My fear escalated with each phone call. I was so frightened. Someone even made a quiet suggestion that we call the county morgue! Then Gretchen took charge and said we had to call back through the hospital list again. Maybe there had been a mistake or maybe we had actually reached the hospital before Frank's ambulance had arrived. Maybe. On the second hospital call, we found Frank. He was injured but he was alive. I was so relieved I broke down crying and had a hard time calming down enough to drive. That day it was clear that political success is exciting and certainly important, but it doesn't define one's happiness, nor should it.

Frank had a severely damaged shoulder, a large ugly head laceration, and a body covered with mean-looking bruises. He spent a week in the hospital and missed his classes for three weeks, but with the exception of some permanent scars, he was soon back to normal. I would never put my hand in his hair again without feeling the bump under his scalp from that head wound. I would see his shoulder surgical scars each time he removed his shirt. Yet, he was alive and I was grateful, enormously thankful. I had felt the fear of believing he had been killed that day in the crosswalk. Frank was alive and I now began each day acknowledging that I had again been given the gift of my life's soul mate.

So we had weathered the frightening crisis of Frank's accident, but 1980 offered us another ongoing family challenge. In the years following Mike's high school graduation, we took a number of approaches to making him employable. He spent some time at an agency called Portland Habilitation Center, where young people with various disabilities did contract work for companies such as the commercial airlines. They did pre-packaging, sorting, labeling, and other repetitive chores for minimum wage. In most cases this was a first job experience for these young adults. Mike attempted to apply himself but was quickly bored by the work. It was not a good match for him. The center finally suggested Mike might do better at the state employment office. Unfortunately, in the mid- to late seventies, employment agencies including state-operated programs generally placed persons with disabilities into one of three job categories: food services, janitorial work, or yard work. I felt quite certain that janitorial and yard work were not skill areas Mike could perfect. After much discussion, Mike and I determined that food services training was well worth looking into.

Mike enrolled as a full-time student in the food services program at Portland Community College. He learned dishwashing, serving, bussing, waiting tables, and a variety of skills necessary to work in most restaurants and fast-food establishments. It was a year-long program. Mike traveled to the campus by bus and seemed to enjoy the experience and training. When he finished the program, he began applying for jobs in our neighborhood. Over several months, he landed three different jobs and lost each of them within a few days. Autistic people generally respond poorly to pressure, to being rushed. That exact atmosphere is the work environment where food service takes place. It became clear this was not Mike's forte. Frank and I racked our brains for some kind of work situation that would be a match for Mike's cheerful demeanor, his ability to follow a routine, a position that would be more about doing something correctly than speedily. We were getting desperate.

It had now, in 1980, been over five years since Mike's graduation from high school. He was almost twenty-four. We finally decided we would do something we had always avoided — ask a favor of a public agency friend or associate. So we approached the president of Mt. Hood Community College about any potential jobs that Mike might qualify for on that campus. We made it clear that Mike would consider part-time work if they had anything where he could prove his worth as an employee.

That summer Mike started his new job on the campus, working a twenty-four-hour-a-week position. Thirty years later, he is still delivering the mail for MHCC. His job is his life. He works hard, never missing a day. He is loyal to the college and looks forward to every day on his job. It turned out to be the perfect match of duties and responsibilities for Mike. I have been grateful for that opportunity for Mike for thirty years. It has given real meaning to my older son's life.

As the 1980 fall election approached, I felt I needed some visibility even though the outcome of my election was pretty much a done deal. Frank and I designed a small, unpretentious campaign brochure with a recap of my background, several photos, and a handwritten note to the voters of my district (for once I was grateful for my hours of practice on penmanship as a grade school student!). The crux of the note was, "Even though I am running unopposed, you have a right to know who I am." A number of citizens from my district actually wrote and thanked me for caring enough to send the flyer. It had been a good decision.

When the ballots were counted that November, I had 9,412 votes and there were 109 write-in votes for miscellaneous candidates including Mickey Mouse. Quite a few voters do not like going to the polls and finding only one name on the ballot for any office. Often times those miscellaneous write-in votes represent a protest vote. That has always seemed understandable to me. Yet, protest votes or not, I would soon receive a certificate of election as State Representative, District #17. I was one happy politician. *Politician?* Even though I had been elected three times before and appointed to an important local office, I had never before thought of myself as a politician. Now it felt like the correct title and not a label I found at all uncomfortable wearing. "Politician." It felt just fine.

Frank and I now became a small piece of Oregon history. We were another married couple serving simultaneously as legislators in our state. It was a fun piece of history. It would be exciting to work with Frank in this new way. We shared so many views, so many political positions. I couldn't wait until January.

Nineteen women members would be serving in the sixty-member Oregon House of Representatives during the 1981 legislative session. This was the largest number of women to ever serve in our House. The twelve Democratic and seven Republican women included nine brand-new female representatives ... another piece of Oregon history. The Oregon Senate had only one female, newly elected member Ruth McFarland, a Democrat.

Some of the women House members were starting to ask whether we would be given a realistic share of the committee chairmanships and vice-chair positions. Our returning Speaker, Representative Hardy Myers, was respected for his fairness, and there were high expectations he would recognize the nearly one-third female membership. However, we also understood that with nine freshmen women and the fact that seven of the women were in the minority party, we could not expect one-third of the committee leadership slots. Yet, with seventeen House committees and therefore thirty-four leadership opportunities, somewhere around eight to ten slots would feel like leadership equality. When the committee assignments were announced, the women members had reason to feel satisfied. Women members would be chairing five committees and would hold vice-chair spots on four. Women were now becoming a solid part of the committee leadership of the Oregon House of Representatives.

I was thrilled about my own committee assignments. I had received my first-choice committee — Revenue. Additionally I was placed on the Business and Consumer Affairs Committee. It did, however, seem pretty clear that this second committee was not exactly a plum assignment. With the exception of the chair and vice-chair, the remaining five members of the committee were all first-term legislators. However, the Revenue Committee slot was such an important opportunity, I wasn't particularly concerned about the status of my second assignment. Frank's committee assignments on the Senate side were outstanding: Ways & Means, chair of Local Government, the Urban Affairs and Housing Committee, plus the

Rules Committee and the Human Resources and Aging Committee. Frank's days would be packed full once the 1981 session began.

My assignments would obviously keep me busy as well, particularly the Revenue Committee, which met every morning at 8 a.m. Few committees in the Oregon Legislature met on a daily basis. Plus, I would still be returning to Portland for board meetings for both the school district and the community college. Oregon law allows a person to serve in more than one elected office at the same time as long as only one of the positions is a paid office; neither of my education board roles paid a salary. Ten years before, I had entered the state Capitol building as a citizen advocate for disabled children: young, divorced, inexperienced, and scared. What a difference a decade had made in my life.

At age forty-four I was now a freshman member of the Oregon House, though, in truth, I was never treated as a freshman legislator. After three legislative sessions on Frank's staff and time as a lobbyist, I began my first session with other legislators, lobbyists, and staff treating me as if I were an experienced lawmaker. That was especially true in the Democratic caucus where there were a number of longer-term incumbents plus new members whom I had assisted with their campaigns. I was never given the leeway afforded many newcomers. Yet those higher expectations very likely played to my advantage. When the ten newly elected Democrats voted to select a member to sit on the Speaker's Leadership Council, my "classmates" selected me on the first ballot. So I started out as a leadership insider from the opening days of the 1981 session. My job would be to apply myself to my legislative work in such a way as to do credit to the confidence my Democratic colleagues had shown in me.

On January 12, 1981, the House session began with thirty-three Democrats, twenty-seven Republicans. The party breakdown in the Senate was still pretty lopsided: twenty-two Democrats and eight Republicans. The six men from both houses who held leadership posts were all experienced, long-term legislators. There were real challenges ahead for them, for all of us, as we faced growing budget problems associated with the increasing economic recession in Oregon. Economic experts always asserted that, in nationwide recessions, Oregon was usually one of the first states to feel the impacts and one of the late states in terms of recovery: In early. Out late. The major reason was Oregon's heavy economic dependence on the timber industry and that equally strong connection to the housing market nationwide. A national recession meant housing starts headed to the cellar and Oregon's economy followed closely behind.

Since Oregon was one of only five states in the nation without a state sales tax, we were left with a huge impact on our state budget, which was almost totally dependent on the state's personal and corporate income taxes. When a downturn in the economy occurred, we knew our state government budget was in for a battering. I thought how strange it was that I always seemed to arrive in a government position just as the money slipped away. I had seen it in Multnomah County, in the Parkrose School District, and now in state government.

My newly hired two-person legislative staff included my friend and fellow board member from the Parkrose Board of Education, Donnella Slayton, and David Gomberg, who would be my Legislative Assistant. I would be earning the "princely" salary of $700 monthly as a member of the House. During the legislative session there was an added benefit of $44 per day to help pay for temporary housing, travel, and other expenses. That *per diem* made it possible for many members to serve once they left other employment for the usual six-month session every odd-numbered year. During non-session months, Oregon legislative members continued to receive their $700 monthly salary plus $300 monthly for expenses, replacing the $44 *per diem* payment that ended at *sine die*. There was certainly no chance of getting wealthy as an Oregon legislator.

After three legislative sessions on Frank's Senate staff, I knew how I wanted the office organized. Since I was in the Revenue Committee every morning by 8 a.m., I depended on my staff to get the needed morning organizational chores done without my supervision. When the morning House session began around 10 a.m., I would have already read all the legislative bills on the morning calendar as part of my previous night's homework. Anything related to the morning session that had come in late would be ready and waiting for me when I returned to my office from Revenue. We developed an effective and efficient office team.

Before long, even as a freshman member, I was being assigned the responsibility as a "bill carrier" for legislation coming from both my Revenue Committee and the Business and Consumer Affairs Committee. That duty required explaining the bill in detail before the entire House and the visitors' galleries. It also meant answering technical and political questions about the proposed new law, sometimes from legislators opposing the bill. I worked diligently to be 100 percent prepared for these assignments. My success rate for the passage of bills I carried became impressive. Of course, the better job I did, the more and bigger the responsibilities that were handed to me. This increased preparation took more and more time but brought me increased attention from my colleagues, the lobby, and the press.

As I neared the end of my first legislative session as a member of the Oregon House of Representatives, I looked back with satisfaction on my personal accomplishments and growth and had many fond memories of that period of public service. I found serving as a state legislator an energizing, stimulating, and strategic role. In every day's work you touched the lives of your state's citizens from dozens of angles. You worked on and debated over and voted up or down on laws regarding adoption, land use, fishing licenses, marriage laws, taxation, voter registration, minimum wage levels, abortion, speed limits, high school graduation requirements, air and water standards, health insurance coverage, higher education, and budgets for state police, economic development, mental health, and senior services. I found my legislative service was far more about people than about politics. It was seldom boring and often emotional. On a five-member school board or county commission you have only the views and experiences of four other colleagues. In the House, I had fifty-nine colleagues from every corner and county of the state with vastly different experiences and multifaceted views of the world. I loved every aspect of my time in the House — issues, politics, fellow members, rules of order, speaking, vote counting, committee work, *all* of it.

When the rankings came out from Portland's two newspapers at the end of the 1981 legislative session, I had fared well. *The Willamette Week* commented, "A healthy majority of the people we interviewed regard Barbara Roberts as the top freshman of the seven in this year's metropolitan delegation. Some even think that she and Bill Bradbury are the finest new members in the Legislature." *The Oregonian* reported, "In a class of 19 freshman House legislators in the 1981 session, Roberts was among the top five in terms of effectiveness, ability, diligence and peer-group respect. She is ruled by logic, with an ability to sway others to support her positions."

Looking back twenty-five-plus years on that session, it is now difficult to remember many of the details about that first session's legislation. However, a few issues are still in my memory bank.

The 1981 legislative session added new bonding authority to keep Oregon's Veterans' Home Loan program alive. I voted "aye," clearly remembering the asset the program had been when my first husband and I purchased our very first home under that program. It had given us a tremendous opportunity to be part of the American dream. That session also created the Senior Services Division to help older citizens receive the support needed to remain in their own homes. It became a vital state department in aiding and informing Oregon's aging population about services and options available to them.

The Business and Consumer Affairs Committee on which I served worked successfully to place an amendment into Oregon's health insurance laws regarding alcohol treatment coverage. It did not require health insurance companies to cover such treatment but did require that when a policy covered in-patient alcohol treatment it must give equal dollar coverage benefits for out-patient treatment. My view was that the in-patient treatment was basically an "executive" provision for those with position and economic wherewithal to be confined for treatment for three to six weeks without risking their job or serious financial damage. Out-patient alcohol treatment meant that equally successful help would be available to Oregonians who could not leave their jobs or young children. However, in 1981 there were no insurance benefits to help pay for those out-patient services.

In the end, successful passage of the bill required limiting the new coverage to state employees only for a two-year test of costs and outcomes. It was less than I wanted but still an important first step. I fought like mad for the amendment, becoming its chief advocate in and out of my committee setting, plus testifying when the bill was being heard in the Senate Labor Committee. Insurance lobbyists fought back. That lobby tried to make the case that out-patient treatment was ineffective and success was short term, at best. Alcohol-treatment professionals shared examples of recovering alcoholics with years of sobriety to counter those erroneous arguments.

Finally I won the battle. The bill, House Bill 2080, passed the House on a 43-17 vote and in the Senate with every senator present voting "aye." I believed I had started a process whereby thousands of Oregonians with substance addictions could recover their lives and their sobriety. However, that important work went down the drain when Governor Atiyeh vetoed HB 2080. It would be several years until the coverage was put in place for Oregonians. Years later I would watch my only sister take advantage of that insurance provision. When Pat died in 2001 of a heart attack, she had been sober for eighteen years.

The 1981 legislative session in Oregon lasted into the month of August for the first time in state history. It was described in an *Oregonian* headline as a "woeful session." Just over twenty-four hundred bills were introduced in the session. Nearly one-third of those bills became law. With serious revenue shortfalls, the most significant legislation was a package of temporary tax measures that would raise $167 million over the biennium. In spite of the session's length, the revenue crisis, and bitter fights over the size and make-up of the tax-increase package, there were some positive outcomes.

The Legislature was able to redraw its political boundaries as is required following each decade's national census—no small accomplishment. In fact, *The Oregonian* reported it was "the first time in at least seventy years" the Legislature had accomplished reapportionment without that legal chore being passed on to Oregon's Secretary of State. Plus the two houses were also able to redraw the state's congressional boundaries, including a new fifth congressional district.

The legislative session made sweeping changes in the state's court systems with the state gradually assuming more and more of the cost of administering the circuit and district courts in each county. The Legislature did major work in furthering Oregon's statewide land-use system, expanding community corrections options, creating a statewide safe drinking-water program, requiring kindergarten programs in all Oregon school districts by 1989, and finally adjourned with the rare and highly unusual situation of a Democratically controlled Legislature passing a tax package that the Republican Governor felt was too small!

In a record-length, 203-day session that stumbled to a final adjournment at 6:30 a.m., Oregon's ninety part-time legislators brought their energies, opinions, experience, and even their families to Salem to do the public's work of representative government. I had been part of that small segment of Oregon history. I looked forward with excitement and anticipation to playing an even larger role in 1983 when the Legislature returned to Salem. I did not anticipate in

August 1981 that our return would be only weeks away. In fact, four special sessions of the Legislature would occur before the regular session reconvened in January of 1983. Special sessions were held in October 1981, January through March of 1982, June 1982, and finally, September of 1982. So much for the concept of a part-time citizen Legislature!

The October 24, 1981, special session was the result of Governor Victor Atiyeh's veto of two bills passed in the regular session that streamlined Oregon's court system. The Governor vetoed the court reform package because it allowed the justices of the Supreme Court to choose the chief justice from among their number. Governor Atiyeh believed that the appointment should be made by the Governor. He called the Legislature into special session to repass the original two bills plus a referral to the voters in the May 1982 primary election that would give the Governor the authority he wanted. The special session lasted only eight hours and forty minutes, setting an Oregon record as the shortest special session. In May, the voters overwhelmingly rejected the Governor's expanded authority—Yes: 129, 811. No: 453,415.

The next special session was a completely different story. It lasted from January 18 to March 1, 1982—thirty-seven miserable days of conflict and disagreement. Governor Atiyeh called the session to erase a projected state budget deficit of $240 million. Besides the expectation of major cuts in most state agency budgets, Atiyeh brought forward ideas to remodel the Economic Development Department and the Land Conservation and Development Commission. He announced his further plan to appoint a committee to examine questions of negative economic impacts due to Oregon's tax code. This long session was wearing, combative, cranky, and frustrating. On the House Revenue Committee, we considered several elements of Governor Atiyeh's package, including a speeded-up schedule for employers' payments of withholding taxes to raise $72 million. Our committee had a tough work schedule and no shortage of either critics or "creative thinkers" as the special session trudged through revenue-raising possibilities.

When that longest-ever special session finally adjourned, we had seen bitter disagreements, not just between Democrats and Republicans but between the Senate and House, plus strong debates created in arguments between local government advocates and school fund protectors both in and out of the Legislature. Upon adjournment the session had raised cigarette taxes by 3 cents a pack, cut the state property-tax relief maximum payment from $355 to $287, and cut state agency budgets by $87 million. The Legislature also approved $2 million to finance part of the Governor's economic recovery agenda.

Then the Legislature went back into special session on June 14, 1982, to once again rebalance the state budget. A pre-session compromise ended up passing in final form after only a fourteen-hour session. The major elements of the budget cuts included another $30 million from the state Property Tax Relief Program, $13 million from the Basic School Support Fund, $10 million from state agency budgets, and $20 million in cuts to state employees' salaries, including legislative members and state elected officials. Not only were the budget deficits and special sessions wearing thin, but now we took a salary cut from our already-meager paychecks.

Well—one more time around! Two months later—on September 3—we were back in Salem. This time we needed to fill an additional $87 million hole. The newest budget-saving plan was an $81 million special assessment against the State Accident Insurance Fund Corporation's surplus account. The proposal was attacked from the right and from the left. The Attorney General said it was legal. Sen. Ted Kulongoski, an announced Democratic candidate for governor, said the SAIF "raid" was illegal. SAIF officials aggressively lobbied against the "plot." The twelve-hour session felt like a ride in an automatic washing machine. In the end, the measure passed.

After what had been the longest regular legislative session in state history, I had now served in four special sessions as well. I longingly remembered the summers of sailing I had experienced with Frank between legislative sessions. Not much sailing took place that summer and fall.

When Hardy Myers announced he would not seek a third term as Speaker of the House, Majority Leader Grattan Kerans became an early candidate for the position. At that point I began planning to become the next House Majority Leader. Of course, others also had their eye on that same political prize. I believed I carried a solid reputation from my work in the 1981 session, plus my ability as a constantly improving public speaker, and my demonstrated skills in taking on complex issues like revenue and taxation. But just as importantly, my caucus understood I was a committed Democrat with a record of helping our candidates during each campaign season. That was a big component of the work and responsibility expected of a Majority Leader.

Although the Democrats had a 33-27 majority in the House, we all knew that majority didn't hold solid on a number of issues. It took thirty-one votes to pass legislation and we had several conservative Democrats who often "went South" on environmental, labor, and social issues and voted with the Republicans. Adding additional Democrats to our caucus would give us the extra margin we needed on those tougher policy votes. If I wanted to be Majority Leader I had to help recruit skilled new candidates, actively raise funds for their campaign expenses, and mentor our first-time candidates. I also needed to be sure our returning incumbents were reelected. Yet anyone who wanted to be Majority Leader could figure that out! I just had to work harder and do better at each of those efforts.

Finally, there was one other small matter. In the history of the Oregon House of Representatives, a *woman* had never before held the post. Damn! How often and for how long would I have to confront those historical challenges? With three or four members likely to compete for Majority Leader, I certainly did not need any extra hurdles. Plus several of our women Democratic members were considering leaving the House to run for state Senate or local government positions. I definitely did not need fewer women in the Democratic caucus if I was going to take on this competition.

Once I made the decision to run for Majority Leader, I decided I should resign from the Mt. Hood Community College Board a few months in advance of the end of my elected term. I needed to be totally focused on this new political challenge. I had chaired the college board for a year. I had been honored to present the certificates at the college's first-ever graduation ceremony for successful GED students. I had been an active campus advocate for women and disabled students in both policy areas and programs. I had helped create the MHCC Jazz Festival, even over the objection of the faculty union representative. I had been active on budget matters and represented the college at meetings and public forums. I had fully enjoyed my tenure on the board, but now it was time to take that same kind of active leadership in my role as a state representative.

In the end, the Majority Leader hopefuls worked closely together to recruit candidates, raise funds, and strategize to expand the size of the Democratic majority in the House. Our commitment to the

Democratic agenda was stronger than our need to compete for the title. We even made some recruiting trips together, traveling in the same car and "ganging up" on the potential candidates we were encouraging to run in the 1982 election. And, boy, were we convincing! We soon had first-time candidates running from all over the state ... lawyers, business leaders, teachers, a newspaper editor, a mill worker, two college instructors, a consultant, a longshoreman, an electrician, and a contractor. They were a fine group of candidates, and we had high expectations for their political success. And bottom line, *our* success depended on *their* success. As we worked toward a larger Democratic majority in the House, we each also had to protect our own legislative district seat during the upcoming 1982 election season. I had watched a decade before as Frank worked to expand his caucus and neglected his own reelection, losing his House seat. I didn't plan to make that same error.

During the interim between the '81 and '83 legislative sessions, the Speaker of the House appointed me to two committees in addition to my standing appointment to the Revenue Committee. One of these was actually a one-time-only Task Force on Election Law Revision. We examined in detail Oregon's voter registration laws, our election hours, polling place rules, the state's voters' pamphlet uses and costs, and even special election dates. Oregon had a high voter-registration percentage and was also a high turnout state at both primary and general elections. As we looked at ways to increase these numbers even further, there were long committee discussions and debates on changing the voter registration deadline to ten days, five days, one day. The work I did on that task force proved to be a solid foundation for important political and policy work I did over the next decade.

One story from that interim period was unforgettable for me personally plus a perfect example of arriving *unprepared* as a legislative committee witness. The chair of the Revenue Committee called an open hearing on the subject of funding Oregon's public school system. He indicated the discussions and testimony could include taxes and revenue proposals or ideas for savings or cuts in the cost arena of Oregon's schools. The hearing room was filled to capacity ... citizens, lobbyists, legislators, agency personnel, prospective future candidates, and press. The daylong hearing included thoughtful ideas, policy statements, anti-tax rhetoric, thoughts on redistribution formulas, and pleas for increased taxation to better support our public schools in Oregon.

In the early afternoon a superintendent of one of Oregon's most populous county educational service districts sat down at the witness table. Rumor had it that he was expected to be a legislative candidate on the Republican ticket in 1982. What followed was a dictionary definition of "unprepared" and "uninformed." He proceeded to describe the multimillion-dollar educational cuts he was advocating in order to free up dollars for the general education of Oregon school children. First he pushed the idea of no more special education classes for what were then labeled "mentally retarded" children. He felt financial costs were way too high for very little gain. He then went on to firmly advocate for removing all autistic children from Oregon's public school classrooms. He was clear: this schooling was a complete waste of educational funds for young people who would never be productive.

The room was absolutely silent when he finished his remarks. It was almost as if the entire audience was holding its collective breath. Almost every person in the hearing room, except for the superintendent, knew that the chair, Bill Grannell, had a "mentally retarded" son and that I had an autistic son. Rep. Grannell waited for the superintendent to gather up his notes and then looked at the committee members, cast his eyes across the entire room, turned to me and said, "Rep. Roberts, would you like to go first?" I shook my head and responded, "Mr. Chairman, be my guest."

What followed was a slicing and dicing of an unprepared, misinformed, insensitive school official who very quickly became an unelectable candidate for public office. The lesson: know your audience!

Unlike my unopposed primary and general election races in 1980, I faced both a Democrat *and* a Republican rival in the two elections in 1982. Due to the legislative redistricting that happens after each decade's national census, my district now had some minor boundary changes and even a new district number. District #17 became Representative District #16. That meant that no materials were re-usable—not lawn signs, buttons, or brochures. It meant I had to reach out to the new voters recently added to my district and I needed to do this extra campaign work interspersed between the constant disruption of special legislative sessions.

My primary race was a quiet one. My opponent had only one financial contribution—from himself. I easily won the May primary.

However, my upcoming November race appeared much more competitive. My Republican challenger, Jim Walker, was a practicing attorney, was active in his church, and worked with a local Seniors United group. I took the race seriously. During the campaign, I emphasized my record in the community, my strong rating from the 1981 session, my work on the Revenue Committee, and the fact that I was the parent of two adult sons; I also focused on several votes I had cast in 1981 (for veterans, senior services, education, and necessary state budget cuts). My voters' pamphlet page and all campaign literature used the slogan: "Barbara Roberts — A Representative you can be proud of." In the end, it was a good solid win.

Frank was also up for reelection in '82. He had been unopposed in the primary but had a solid Republican contender in the fall campaign. By the end of that race Frank had another win in his extensive legislative career.

When the dust settled from the 1982 House elections, we had elected thirteen new Democrats (twelve men, one woman). The partisan balance for the 1983 session would be thirty-six Democrats and twenty-four Republicans, a gain of three Democratic seats. Our hard work and serious recruiting had paid off.

By this time, Bill Bradbury from the southern Oregon coast and I were the only viable Democrats left in the competition for Majority Leader. The Democratic caucus elected me on the first ballot. Bill and I had come to the Oregon House as freshmen together in 1981. We had competed actively for the position. I knew then and have witnessed in the years since that Bill is a genuine leader. He would later become Majority Leader of the state Senate, President of the Senate, and a two-term statewide elected Secretary of State. We have remained friends over all these years.

Representative Barbara Roberts, House Majority Leader. That certainly had a nice ring to it. The press failed to comment on the fact that I had made a little Oregon history as the first woman in the post. However, members of the Oregon Women's Political Caucus considered it a real high-water mark for women in the Oregon Legislature. Over the years since then, I have watched as Oregon women have become Speakers of the House, Majority and Minority Leaders in both houses, and chairs of every major committee in the Legislature. At this writing my state has yet to select a woman as President of the Senate. There are still some notches to be carved.

CHAPTER TWELVE

Jumping Off the High Board

Well, here I was moving into the office of the House Majority Leader! Instead of my former legislative office with dividers outside my private office door that allowed desk space for each of my two-member staff, I was excitedly moving into my big private office with an outer office for four or five staff plus a reception area for those waiting for appointments. After what I was accustomed to, this felt darned impressive—or would have been if the décor and clutter hadn't reminded me of a makeshift campaign office. My new office was certainly ready for a woman's touch. Donnella Slayton moved with me to the majority office but the rest of my staff was new. The head of my staff was Chris Dorval, who was from the East Coast. Chris and Donnella were joined by Michael Morrisey, Alma Hill, Shirley Aker, and Patrick Wolf. My staff and I created an atmosphere that looked professional and organized. When the legislative session began on January 10, 1983, I was proud to show off my new office to family and friends and the thirty-six Democratic members of my caucus. Yes, indeed, I felt ready for business. The House of Representatives was equally ready. With Grattan Kerans as our new Speaker and a 36-24 majority, we had high expectations for the session.

The Senate organized after a delay of four days following a bitter debate over the election of a President. Frank was the leading candidate with twelve of the sixteen Democratic votes needed. However, he lost the position due to a couple of compromises by fellow Democratic members (or perhaps more correctly, capitulations). It was a sad disappointment to Frank. Having once been so close to becoming Speaker of the House, this felt like (and would be) Frank's last shot at being the presiding officer. He felt hurt and discouraged. He had given so much to the legislative process and to his party for so long. This political rejection was a very personal loss for him. The 1983 session was soon in full swing but it was several weeks before Frank's usual enthusiasm for the process returned, although he was serving on four important committees: Ways & Means, Rules, Energy and Environment, and finally, Local Government and Elections.

As the legislative session began, Republican Governor Victor Atiyeh had just won reelection by the largest margin of any gubernatorial race in thirty-two years in our state. He had trounced Democratic State Senator Ted Kulongoski, an attorney and well-liked legislator, and strong friend of labor unions in Oregon, who had come through as a strong winner in an eight-man Democratic primary race. Atiyeh caught him unprepared as the general election campaign opened. Governor Atiyeh hit Kulongoski with radio and television ads that very early in the election season discredited Senator Kulongoski as "dangerous." Ted's fall campaign wasn't even off the ground. It was a swift and successful political strategy. The results of that coup were clear in November. In spite of Democratic majorities in the House and Senate, Governor Atiyeh could pretty well claim a "mandate" with his almost twofold margin of victory over Kulongoski. Additionally, the Republicans held the offices of Secretary of State, State Treasurer, Attorney General, and Superintendent of Schools. Mary Wendy Roberts, Labor Commissioner, was the sole statewide elected Democrat. We began to speculate if our party would ever gain such an impressive-sized list of statewide office holders. We were fielding good candidates but continued to come in second in election after election. (At this writing, the Democrats hold all six of these state offices and have since 2002.)

In addition to my responsibilities as House Majority Leader, I returned to my role as a member of the Revenue Committee and also became chair of the Legislative Operations and Rules Committee. This committee was informally referred to as "the Speaker's Committee." It was rumored that the Speaker could pretty much guarantee that any bill assigned to the Rules Committee would either pass or be killed, whichever the Speaker wanted. That is rather an exaggeration but the Speaker's priorities did get close attention.

Serving in the 1983 legislative session was one challenge after another. We worked through a difficult regular legislative session of 187 days, the second-longest session (to that point) in Oregon history, and two special sessions. It was reminiscent of the previous lengthy legislative session, followed by four special sessions. Most observers of the 1983 session would have agreed that the Legislature had two major responsibilities—to balance a state budget more than $600 million in deficit and the political need to do something significant about property-tax relief. With great struggles, the session made $180 million in cuts from the Governor's budget. There were huge battles about the state's responsibility to both schools and local governments, which caused active conflicts over each member's priorities in the Democratic caucus. After the cuts, the remainder of the deficit was met with a continuation of the "one-time" tax measures passed in the previous sessions.

The House finally passed a property-tax relief measure: a sales-tax/expenditure-limitation package to be referred to the voters. The package died in the Senate without a vote of that body. Many House members were furious at the Senate leadership. We had taken a huge political risk to cast our vote for a sales-tax package in a state famous for its long record of no sales tax. Without the House package, the Legislature was unable to offer voters a tax-reform measure to cut their property taxes, though the outcry for property-tax relief was strong and vocal in 1983. Unfortunately, from the beginning to the end of that session, the House and Senate never seemed to be in sync.

That said, the session finally produced 871 bills. Governor Atiyeh, proving that not all conflicts were between the House and the Senate, vetoed forty of them. It was the largest number of gubernatorial vetoes in the state's history.

House Majority Leader Barbara Roberts strategizes with Democratic colleagues (from left) Wayne Fawbush, Carl Hosticka, and Grattan Kerans (1983). From Oregon Archives Collection.

My role as a Revenue Committee member brought me a good deal of attention. The Oregon Constitution requires that all revenue measures must originate in the House. That meant that the discussions on property-tax relief, sales-tax packages, income tax and corporate tax changes were all before the Revenue Committee. Our committee hearing room was packed every morning with lobbyists, citizens, stakeholders, and even visiting legislators from other committees. Our committee chair, Tom Throop, a Bend child-development specialist, ran a great committee. He was well organized, thoroughly prepared each day, and kept debates under control. The members of the committee worked well together, exchanging points of view and usually debating with an air of civility. Jane Cease (D), Carl Hosticka (D), John Schoon (R), and George Trahern (R) exemplified that respectfulness across party and policy divides. The exception to that rule of civility and polite discourse was the most left-wing member of the Legislature, Wally Priestly (D) of Portland. It certainly wasn't that Wally was rude as much as it was that he saw the world and its political issues from only one unique perspective—his. He added frequent "color" to the black-and-white world of tax policy.

I explained tax measures to my Democratic caucus members, carried the bills on the House floor, and voted on them, working for a balanced budget and some form of property-tax relief. I took a full leadership role as we trudged through that session's biggest challenges. I believed then and still do that leaders must lead by example.

One piece of legislation that I worked on diligently in 1983 was a bill that I had introduced at the request of the Oregon Architectural Barrier Council. House Bill 2004 established a Commission for the Handicapped of fifteen members appointed by the Governor and allowed for the hiring of an executive director. I pointed out to members of both houses that Oregon had over two hundred thousand people who met the definition of "handicapped." Services for that large community needed to be coordinated, plus there was a strong need for advocacy, evaluation, and support. HB 2004 passed the House without a dissenting vote and passed the Senate on a 23-to-2 vote with five members excused for legislative business. This legislative success took me back to my memories of the passage of Senate Bill 699 way back in 1971 and what that legislation had meant to children with disabilities. I began to recognize how often leadership was about the coming together of heart and head.

Holding the position of House Majority Leader, at times, felt a little like being a camp counselor. I dealt with members going through divorces, undergoing health issues, and with every political question and challenge you can imagine. The most trying matter I recall was a member struggling with an alcohol problem that was interfering with her work and even her daytime sobriety. On several occasions, I had to quietly remove her from committee or the House floor. I finally confronted a couple of lobbyists who were reportedly supplying her with multiple bottles of liquor every evening. The liquor deliveries stopped immediately, and without that enablement, she got back control of her life and her reputation.

Majority leaders deal with policy issues, political concerns, vote counts, and press coverage. While all of that is vitally important, I think now, looking back, my role as "camp counselor" may have mattered even more. The Legislature can be pressured, hectic, time consuming and even life changing. For some members, there is the additional stress of living in Salem almost full time, perhaps two hundred miles from home and family. I knew my political role but I gained understanding that offering myself as a listening post and a confidential adviser may have enhanced the success of some of my members and the output of our caucus as a whole. It is hard to take care of business if you fail to care for your members. Some of our caucus members became local government leaders, lobbyists, moved on and ran successfully for the state Senate, statewide offices, and Congress., A few became successful in out-of-state positions, labor union leadership, and business. At least seven are now deceased. I remember every face, every name, and the many sacrifices they made. I know the risks they took to deliver positive results in tough times for the people of Oregon.

I served with, respected, and liked many of my Republican colleagues as well. My favorite Republican from my years in the House was definitely Nancy Ryles. Nancy and I served together in the 1981-82 House. and later she served in the Senate with Frank. In 1990, Nancy was in the hospital dying of brain cancer at the same time Frank was being treated for both cancer and a fractured hip. Since they were in the same hospital, we put Frank in a wheelchair so he could go visit Nancy and, realistically, say goodbye. We visited her room, told some political stories, laughed together, and then hugged and parted. When we got out in the hall, Frank and I fell into each other's arms, both of us weeping. Suddenly, we heard a soft voice from the hospital room. Nancy called out, "You two stop that. It's really okay. I'm ready to go." Brave soul. Nancy died while I was campaigning for governor. And, as per her specific orders, I did not attend her memorial service. She had instructed me to keep on campaigning, to skip her services, so Oregon could finally have a woman governor.

Nancy and Frank both have scholarship programs named in their honor at Portland State University. I love that Nancy's scholarship is dedicated to returning women students. She designed it while she was terminally ill. An amazing woman.

The work didn't stop as the session adjourned. We were still on a mission and already busy recruiting new Democratic House candidates for the 1984 elections. All summer long and into the early fall we made lists of potential new candidates and found some weak spots among the Republican incumbents. We were raising campaign money for our caucus members and our new recruits. Things were looking good.

Yet my head was also full of thoughts about my *next* political step. I knew that I could be chosen, again, by my Democratic colleagues as the House Majority Leader. I had worked diligently, and the Democratic Caucus was in great shape. However, I knew the Democratic Speaker of the House was not likely to seek reelection to the House; he was considering a statewide race for Treasurer. My chances of becoming Oregon's first woman Speaker of the House looked very positive. The idea of becoming Speaker stirred my blood. I imagined appointing committee chairs and members. I thought about having much more input on the state budget priorities. I visualized the role model I could be to female schoolchildren who watched me on the podium. It was exciting to imagine. Yet out of respect to my caucus members, I needed to make my political choices sooner, rather than later, to prevent our caucus from losing any political momentum.

However, in truth, I knew that Majority Leader or Speaker were not my only options. The current Secretary of State, Republican Norma Paulus, was constitutionally limited to two four-year terms and could not seek reelection. No Democrat had yet stepped forward to announce a run for the opening. At first glance, this might sound like a perfect political opportunity. But in Oregon, the Secretary of State is considered the stepping-stone to Governor. No Democrat had held the office for one hundred and ten years! The Republican

Party had no intention of allowing their "ownership" of that office to come to an end after more than a century.

I faced a *career-altering* decision! My reelection to the House was pretty much a sure thing. My selection as Majority Leader could also be labeled as a certainty. And, as I saw it, my chances of becoming Speaker of the House seemed better than 80 percent. Those are the kind of political odds I like!

On the other hand, running for Secretary of State was truly a long shot. It meant a full year of campaigning statewide. I would have to raise more campaign money than at any time in my political experience. I assumed the Republicans would field a strong candidate. There was also the potential of facing a Democratic primary opponent for such a coveted office. A campaign is always seen as an easier race without an incumbent in place.

In Oregon the political party system was not a strong one. I had no expectation my party would be able to aid my campaign, financially or organizationally. In many senses, I'd be on my own. I quietly kicked around my three options for several weeks. Frank helped me weigh and balance all the aspects of my choices. We talked about it almost daily. We kept our discussions in–house until pretty late in the decision-making process. It finally came down to what seemed either a sure thing or a very long shot.

Every time I thought about the "long-shot option" I would find myself *tempering* that description with some of the assets I felt I brought to the race.

I knew community leaders from every part of Oregon: school board members, community college board members, Democratic Party activists, legislators, and county elected officials. I had worked with disability advocates, environmentalists, women's rights leaders, and human and civil rights organizations all over Oregon.

Secondly, I knew I was a solid public speaker, able to make my case to most audiences, sway listeners with well-organized facts and information and even stir emotions on many subjects. Those skills would be critical as a statewide candidate.

Another thing I considered an unusual asset would probably have caused my more sophisticated political friends to laugh out loud *if* I had actually shared it with them. I felt my Oregon Trail ancestors were a winning addition to my campaign, especially in rural Oregon. My pioneer family had settled in two separate Oregon counties. My grandmother was born in yet another small rural community in the far eastern part of the state. I had family members in nearly half of Oregon's thirty-six counties. I was born in Corvallis, grew up in Sheridan, and now lived in Portland. I had deep roots in Oregon and I believed that fact would add positively to how Oregon voters saw me and felt about me.

Another positive point was the fact that for the past eight years the public had become accustomed to seeing a woman in the office of Secretary of State. Norma Paulus was Oregon's *first* female Secretary of State and eight years can define political expectations. I had been making public decisions for almost fifteen years: policy choices, budgets, long-term planning, handling tough, controversial issues. I was experienced, prepared, and confident. Additionally, I was certain no other candidate could outwork me!

Each time I reweighed the "sure thing" vs. the "long shot" the gap seemed to shrink! But was it just wishful thinking? Should I be satisfied with what I had already gained politically? Who did I think I was anyway, reaching so high? But the statewide race was in my head and I couldn't shake it. Plus, I couldn't see anyone else in my party waiting in line who was better prepared to take on this statewide challenge. Other Democrats were certainly ready and able to become Speaker of the House and Majority Leader. They would step forward and do a fine job. There were strong, capable leaders in my caucus.

I imagined what I could do for my party's future if I demonstrated that a Democrat could triumph in an office where we had been shut out for over one hundred years. The last Democratic Secretary of State, Stephen F. Chadwick, had been elected for a second term in 1874. However, as I looked at the possibility of a statewide race as a Democrat, I didn't need to look back one hundred-plus years to get a reality check. The only statewide elected Democrat was my husband's older daughter, Mary Wendy Roberts, who was the elected Commissioner of Labor and Industries. However, I understood that her office was one the Republican Party put little stock in. The battle for that office was almost always a Democratic primary election contest. That left the federal statewide offices, and *both* of Oregon's current U.S. senators were Republicans. The political odds were daunting, but as hockey player and philosopher Wayne Gretzky once observed; "You miss 100 percent of the shots you don't take." Perhaps it was a long shot but it was, in fact, a shot.

As I privately considered the possibility of a statewide race for Secretary of State, I doubled my speaking schedule, particularly opportunities beyond the Portland and Salem areas. Wherever I traveled, I scheduled time to visit with the local newspaper and the radio and television stations in each community. I contacted the local Democratic Party leaders to let them know I would be in their county. I leaned closer toward a run with each public speech and every interview. During my visit to the small town of Redmond in Central Oregon (a three-hour drive from Portland), an editorial appeared in the local weekly newspaper, the *Redmond Spokesman*. The September 1983 editorial entitled "Rising Star" said, in part,

Following in the shadow of Secretary of State Norma Paulus isn't a task most rising political stars are up to. State Rep. Barbara Roberts is. ... Intelligent, dynamic and honest only partly describe Barbara Roberts. Her history is one of effective leadership, as school board member, Multnomah County commissioner and legislator. She has the ability to understand issues; the intelligence and political savvy to effect change. She cares about people and she cares about Oregon. It's a little too early to tell who the contestants in the Secretary of State's race will be in 1984. It won't be easy to find one more capable or qualified than Roberts.

Talk about a "heady" piece of press, particularly coming from a more rural and Republican part of the state. If I was indeed still on the fence, this glowing editorial may have been the nudge (or even shove) to push me into the "statewide candidate" column. The race for Secretary of State was no longer simply in my head ... it was in my gut. I felt like a race horse, pawing at the ground. Never before, in all the races I had entered, had my adrenaline level been higher. I truly wanted to run. I felt I could survive a defeat statewide. What I couldn't handle was standing aside and missing this opportunity.

By the end of September my decision was made, and plans began quietly for an official announcement "kick-off" day and the statewide campaign that would follow.

There were not yet funds available for hiring a staff or printing classy campaign brochures and certainly not for renting office space. This was a "bare-bones" campaign start, and it would be largely about hard work, a grueling travel schedule, and volunteers who would help get the campaign off the ground. Frank and I gave up two rooms in our Portland home and turned them into temporary office space. We hung large statewide maps on the walls and added charts showing county populations and voter registration numbers in Oregon's thirty-six counties. We started lists of every person I knew in Oregon. At first, there were hundreds of names, then a few thousand. That growing list would become the basis for some of our earliest fundraising efforts.

I talked my sister's oldest son, Craig Turley, into moving into our home and becoming my campaign driver. At twenty-five Craig had already worked for a couple of years as a long-haul truck driver. I could trust his driving. I could trust him. He accepted our offer for room, board, on-the-road meals, and a small amount of spending money. For Craig, it was the best and cheapest political education available. And I do mean *cheap!*

Prominent Portland attorney Cliff Alterman became my campaign treasurer (an unpaid position), and Norma Jean Germond, former state president of the Oregon League of Women Voters, joined us as campaign coordinator. As we planned toward my announcement day, we hit a serious delay. The Legislature went into special session to try once again to craft a property-tax relief measure. We went into session on September 14, and adjournment did not come until October 4, after twenty-one fractious days. The session produced a referral measure that included a 4 percent sales tax with the proceeds dedicated to property-tax relief. The constitutional amendment measure also placed a limit on state and local government spending and a cap on property-tax rates. A final provision of the complex measure required the approval of a majority of local government bodies in the state. This "ratification" amendment was insisted on by Senate President Ed Fadeley. Legislative observers believed Fadeley had added the provision to sink the 4 percent sales tax. In the end, the Oregon Supreme Court found the local government ratification process to be unconstitutional. Once again the Legislature had failed in yet another attempt to create property-tax relief for Oregon citizens.

With the special session behind me, we set my campaign announcement day for November 10, 1983, with plans for a three-city kick-off tour. We printed our first piece of campaign literature. We compiled a listing of my early endorsers, including quotes regarding my skills, experience, and integrity. We made dozens of copies of the "Rising Star" editorial from the Redmond newspaper. We updated and "spiffed up" my resume. We settled on a temporary campaign slogan: "Barbara Roberts has earned your trust!"

Every day we banked checks from individual donors. They were small checks and weren't even impressive in their accumulated amount … but by the time the primary campaign was over, we had over $45,000 in contributions under $100. Those small contributions, early on, were essential in laying the foundation for success.

As my announcement day neared, it became more and more clear that I would be heavily challenged in the Democratic primary election. State Senator Jim Gardner, an attorney from Portland whom Frank and I had mentored in his first election campaign six years earlier, was ready to announce. He was already lining up support and financial pledges. He was quite open that if he won the race for Secretary of State, he planned to run for governor in two years. He was raising contributions for one race based on the higher office he would seek two years beyond. I immediately made my position clear. I informed the press and every audience I addressed that they had my pledge I would serve the full four-year term for which I was campaigning. My pledge turned out to be important throughout the rest of the primary campaign.

On November 10 I officially joined the race for Secretary of State. I held press conferences in Portland, Salem, and Eugene, the three highest-population cities in Oregon. Our press packet looked impressive. I delivered my carefully prepared remarks in each city. My early supporters were there to cheer me on. The press coverage went very well, with newspapers, radio stations, and TV channels represented at each stop. We closed out the hectic day with a fundraiser in Eugene—my first as a formal statewide candidate. I was pooped but pumped as the long day ended.

Now the campaign was ready for the "grown-up" fundraising. I needed labor union endorsements and the financial support that went with them. It was also critical that I capture the coveted endorsement of the Oregon Education Association. That success would mean not only a large campaign contribution but grassroots help in every part of the state. I could not afford to lose these important endorsements. Not only were they financially advantageous, but they were also the public indication of campaign momentum. The state filing deadline was in early March. We needed to work individual labor unions, the Oregon AFL-CIO's state leadership, and the Oregon Education Association, both state and local. I had to hit the road.

The Oregon Education Association's political endorsement process was as grassroots oriented as anything I've experienced in campaigning. It was participatory democracy with a bottom-up slant. In almost three hundred school districts in Oregon there are OEA local associations with decision-making leadership boards. Local teachers and these Uniserve boards use various local processes to select their choice for teacher endorsements. Once the state filing deadline has passed, the OEA locals from across the state meet in convention to make their state organization's public endorsements in statewide and congressional races. The OEA endorsement convention was at the time the only event of its kind, not only in Oregon but also within the entire National Education Association.

My challenge was to meet with as many of these three hundred Uniserve boards as possible and make the case for endorsement. I faced more than ninety-seven thousand square miles of Oregon, and every day counted. I acquired the list of names for each

Campaigning in Eastern Oregon, 1984. From Oregon Archives Collection.

teacher on every local OEA board, and these teachers received my personally signed letter. Next we followed those letters with my face-to-face appearance at local meetings of Uniserve boards all over Oregon. My nephew Craig and I traveled six days a week, sunup to late night, Portland to Pendleton, Salem to Sisters, Ashland to Astoria, Corvallis to Coos Bay. Nonstop meetings. Nonstop travel. But it felt like I was making progress. We talked school funding at these meetings, plus special education, class size, collective bargaining, kindergartens, and school transportation. My ten years on the Parkrose School Board, four years on the community college board, and two terms on the House Revenue Committee gave me a solid foundation on school policy matters.

As the filing deadline for candidates grew closer, two other Democratic candidates entered the primary contest: Steve Anderson, a Salem attorney and perennial candidate, plus Jack Reynolds, a small-business owner with the campaign slogan "Do not delay. Trust Jesus today." Clearly Jim Gardner remained my chief opponent on the Democratic side. Jim was also working the OEA local boards every place he traveled. The OEA endorsement race between us began attracting some press attention and was being closely watched by political observers. On filing day, the race turned out to be competitive in both parties. We had four Democrats in the race; the Republican primary race was a three-way battle. Now the OEA state endorsement convention was only days away.

At this critical time, a group of twenty-eight faculty members from the Parkrose School District, including five former Parkrose Faculty Association presidents, released a strong letter of endorsement on my behalf. Knowing I had spent ten years on the Parkrose School Board caused some teachers from other districts to be hesitant about my commitment to teachers—a concern from the labor-management perspective. This strong letter should have erased their doubts. The closing paragraph of the letter read, "We believe Barbara is an excellent philosophical and political choice for Secretary of State. We believe that in the state's second highest position, she will continue her work on behalf of education and educators." That letter had an impact on the hundreds of teachers who read it. It had an impact on me. It was one thing to have the endorsement of a teacher who had recently met me and had been impressed with my presentation or positions. It was quite another thing to have the active support and endorsement of faculty leaders who had observed and followed my board service for a decade. They had also watched me as the parent of two sons in their classrooms and an activist for special education in our school district and statewide. That endorsement touched me personally.

On Friday, March 30, we arrived early at the hotel to make certain everything was ready to go for the convention. I had the speech I would deliver to the teachers the next day. The speech had to stand out since all the candidates for statewide office and for Congress would be delivering remarks over the two days. This was no time for a B or C effort. I needed to turn in an A-plus presentation. My material was very good, but delivery was equally important. Then I thought back to my high school speech teacher, Fern Eberhardt, and one of her pieces of advice at every speech competition: "Content counts, presentation is crucial, but, in the end, they have to *like* you." My assignment was clear.

I felt I had hit a bull's-eye with my speech but only the balloting would give me the answer. After all, this was not an academy awards ceremony. This was the powerful OEA endorsement for the second-highest state office in Oregon. This was not an Oscar for performance. This was the *vote* based on trust and leadership in the eyes of Oregon's professional educators. Each district stood ready to vote. The roll call began in alphabetical order. Patricia McCaig, Frank's long-time staffer, was tabulating the count as each district spokesperson delivered the votes from the delegates representing the faculty in their home district. *Albany, Ashland, Astoria, Baker City, ...* The tension mounted. Some districts gave all their votes to me. Other districts were 100 percent for Jim Gardner. Some districts submitted a split ballot. As each vote was announced, we tallied the new totals. ... *Lake Oswego, McMinnville, Medford, Newberg ...*

As we reached the middle of the alphabet it appeared that Jim was pulling ahead at a fairly steady pace. My stomach was in a knot. I was trying to appear calm on the outside but my worst political nightmare was taking shape and the count was only half-way complete. After months of work and thousands of miles on the road, I might lose this tough-fought endorsement battle. My staff and I began steeling ourselves to publicly face a loss as the balloting continued.

We were so busy adding numbers that we missed the fact that the second half of the alphabet included some of Oregon's largest districts and many of my strongest supporters. ... *North Clackamas, Oregon City, Parkrose, Philomath ...* There was some small hope beginning to come through as those later districts' votes were announced. But it was too early to analyze the impact yet. ... *Portland, Redmond, Roseburg, Salem ...* It was looking better. ... *Seaside, Springfield, Tigard ...* The numbers were definitely trending in my favor. ... *Tillamook, Willamina, West Linn.* The tide had turned. We had done it. The OEA endorsement was mine. Roberts: 21,710. Gardner: 15,053.

I was proud of the endorsement and grateful for the teachers' financial support. I was excited about such a visible political success. Yet, there was little time for celebrating. With two months left until the May election, Craig and I were back on the road. I was speaking to Rotary clubs, labor union meetings, Democratic fundraisers, and newspaper editorial boards. I did radio shows, television interviews, and so-called candidate fairs, where there were frequently more candidates and spouses than interested public citizens.

After more than six months of statewide campaigning, the pattern of my life became clear. Six days a week on the road. One day a week to do my laundry, read my mail, hug my family, and plan the strategy for the upcoming week. I read press clippings and signed thank-you letters, while Craig picked up new supplies of campaign literature, bumper strips, volunteer cards, and "county notebooks."

Each of these thirty-six loose-leaf notebooks included pages listing the size and population of the county; the voter registration breakdown numbers; the outcomes of recent major elections; the county elected officeholders; legislators who resided in or represented all or part of that county; the cities within that county and their elected local leaders; and Democratic Party officers and their contact information. There was also a listing of major industries and crops grown in each of the thirty-six counties. Some also had notations of major tourist attractions, special physical features, and important historical information. The final notebook pages listed every radio station, newspaper, television station, and college campus within the county and the lists of my supporters, contributors, friends, and even relatives living in each county.

By the time we left on our week's travels, we had a detailed schedule of every appointment for the week, every speech I was delivering, and the contact persons and locations. Craig had the trip mapped out, and I began studying my county notebooks. I often read the county information aloud so that Craig became equally informed about our destinations. It was not simply a matter of memorizing facts and figures. It was about becoming knowledgeable regarding the people and places in every community we visited. Sometimes when we traveled we added new information to these notebooks. Imagine the difference this knowledge could make in a press interview, during a debate, or while taking questions at the local Chamber of Commerce luncheon. Sometimes I had more details about a county than the folks who lived there!

These trips were challenging, fun, exhausting, educational, and very effective politics. I came fully prepared, shared ideas and positions with voters, listened and learned, and added supporters to my notebook pages. As the May primary race reached its last six weeks, it became clear that the campaign needed more strategic help on fundraising, and a more creative free media plan. I needed to have Patricia McCaig step in and manage the last weeks of the campaign. Patricia agreed to manage the closing period of the primary campaign. She was more than up to the job.

In April the 1984 Primary Election State Voters' Pamphlet arrived by mail at every household in the state. Statewide candidates were entitled to a full page, with photo, for only $300, the best political bargain in an Oregon election season. Published by the Secretary of State's Election Division and predominantly financed with taxpayers' money, this pamphlet features every statewide candidate, judicial candidates, legislators of both parties, and the complete text of statewide ballot measures plus the paid pro and con measure arguments. It is the most useful tool Oregon voters receive and the best "sales" opportunity afforded to candidates in our state. Every household in Oregon could read my political offering. What an opportunity! However they could *also* read the pages of my Democratic opponents.

My voters' pamphlet page focused on my role as a citizen, leader, and administrator and then listed my qualifications for the major responsibilities of the office. My page included quotes from four Oregon newspapers from diverse parts of the state, each commenting positively on a different aspect of my qualifications. I felt very satisfied with the message I had delivered on my page and its comparison with my three opponents' pages.

My campaign staff and I looked critically at Jim Gardner's submission, since we considered him my only serious rival. His statement said: "Oregon's Secretary of State is, for all practical purposes, our Lieutenant Governor. We need a proven leader as Secretary of State. We need Jim Gardner's breadth of experience, strength of character and mature judgment. We need the skills of a Governor, if the need should arise." Jim's message was clear. The Secretary of State's position was only an "oasis" on the way to becoming governor. He ended his page with these words, "Right for the job. Right for the times." The question, from my perspective was "Which job?" and "Which times?"

So … on to the next, and maybe final, challenge in this 1984 primary race: the battle for newspaper endorsements. There were twenty daily newspapers in Oregon, and my focus would be on those. I had visited most of the dailies at least once but I needed to reinforce those visits. Obviously I would also be courting the weekly papers at the same time. Finally the first endorsements appeared. I held my breath awaiting their editorial evaluations, which appeared throughout late April and the first ten days in May. I had soon gathered an impressive number of editorial endorsements, some expected, some surprising.

The *East Oregonian* from Pendleton (in the eastern part of the state) gave me the Democratic primary nod. The show-stopper line in that editorial column read, "We favor Rep. Roberts basically because we think she is more straightforward than Sen. Gardner." They added, "He is more of an opportunist." The *Bend Bulletin* in Central Oregon, not known for its support of Democrats, said this, "Four Democratic hopefuls seek this nomination for Secretary of State. Three can be disposed of quickly. Barbara Roberts is the best of the lot."

Finally, after nine challenging campaign months, on May 15, 1984, at our election night party in Portland, we truly had something to celebrate. Jim Gardner had doubled my fundraising efforts. But I had doubled his vote count (208,013 to 103,989; neither of the other two candidates received 30,000 votes). I had little question which outcome was the more impressive. Some press stories called my win a "surprising margin." The press was almost always surprised with my political wins. They just never seemed to see me coming! Perhaps I was too short to be a leader (five foot two and a half). Perhaps I wasn't smooth enough. I suppose being a divorced mother only a few years back, plus not having a college degree, may have colored their view of my abilities and leadership. Whatever their evaluation was based on, they continued to be surprised at each of my victories. I was now planning a "surprise party" for the November election.

Representative Donna Zajonc had clearly won the Republican nomination. This was the first time in Oregon history that two women had won their major party's nominations for the same statewide office. Rep. Barbara Roberts (D) and Rep. Donna Zajonc (R) would be challenging each other in the November race. It appeared that Oregon's next Secretary of State would indeed be a woman. Yet it was certainly too early to carve anything in stone.

CHAPTER THIRTEEN

110 Years

In the summer of 1984, the Oregon press was definitely interested in a two-woman general election race for Secretary of State. It was the first time in Oregon history that the two major party candidates for a statewide race were both female. So often competitions between two women were focused on the choice of a Rose Festival Princess or homecoming queen. In fact, Donna Zajonc and I were running in the only statewide race in the *nation* with two women nominees facing off against each other. However, the election picture shifted in May when Independent Don Clark from Eugene qualified for the November ballot. Don was a television newscaster, well known by his viewers in the Lane County area. He was handsome, carefully groomed, and well spoken. To complicate the political landscape, there was another well-known Don Clark from the Portland area. That Don had been County Sheriff, the elected Multnomah County Commission Executive, and an unsuccessful candidate for governor in an eight-way Democratic primary race in the 1982 election, only two years earlier. The name confusion was clearly not a positive from my perspective. I needed every vote possible from Lane and Multnomah counties, both strong Democratic areas. The television viewers in Eugene would recognize and likely trust their local newscaster. In the Portland area voters might think their old political friend Don Clark was running again. The other potential role Clark filled was to hand a male option to voters who didn't feel positive about a woman of either party holding major office. In a close contest, this factor could be decisive.

Yet, in truth, there was little logic in worrying about those things that couldn't be changed. My job was to deal with the things that *could* be changed in my favor—minds, hearts, opinions, and votes. Over one hundred fifty thousand Democrats had cast their primary election vote for one of the three other candidates. I needed to put those voters in my camp and try to persuade Republicans who had voted for Donna Zajonc in the primary to vote for me in the November election.

While Patricia McCaig now managed the thousands of details and decisions required for a successful general election, Craig and I again hit the now-familiar campaign trail. It is amazing what you can learn to do in the car when, most often, six days of every week require you to be on the road. For six months, from June to November, I wrote the checks for our personal household bills, stamped them, mailed them, plus balanced our personal checking account … in the car. In our ten years of marriage, I had always paid our first-of-the-month bills. I couldn't see any reason to shirk that job now. The younger generation calls this "multitasking." I had always done it. Now I had a label for it.

Every morning as Craig put our luggage and campaign papers in the car I jumped into the front seat and began putting on my makeup. No sense wasting road time by waiting around to do that job in the motel. After all, there was a perfectly good mirror on the passenger side of the front seat. I always warned Craig before I applied lipstick or mascara. He avoided a sudden stop or jerk while I accomplished this more "dangerous" part of cosmetic application. I wrote speeches in the car. I prepared for debates in the car. I read issue papers, news clips, and the morning newspapers — all in the car.

I navigated for Craig as we traversed the state, reminding him of turnoffs and coffee and gasoline stops in rural areas where gas stations and cafés were often miles and miles apart, as were restrooms! However, my skills on the road didn't end there. I made and served sandwiches and drinks, avoiding the need to stop and eat on tightly scheduled trips. Plus I learned to change clothes, when necessary, *between* semi-trucks. This is a specialized skill I could not have perfected if Craig had simply been hired staff and not a family member! I could not arrive at a luncheon event with ink or mayonnaise on my blouse, and frequently there was no time to make a stop. Blouse off. Clean blouse on. No entertainment for the truck drivers on our route. A wonderful skill!

My nephew Craig was only five months younger than my younger son, Mark. Many years ago, after my sister's tragic car accident, Craig and I had formed a special bond. Yet it was these months on the road that really cemented our relationship. We talked for hundreds of hours: about family, about relationships, my future, his future, and life in general. At twenty-five, Craig was now becoming a skilled political assistant, gaining knowledge about statewide public policy matters, and meeting dozens of state and local officeholders and candidates. Craig was receiving a crash course in practical political science. Plus he was a fun and enthusiastic traveling companion.

One of the real challenges during the general election campaign was the three candidates' decision to accept a large number of invitations to debate in communities around the state. We wanted to be accessible and we all three wanted press exposure. However, we may have overshot our goals on the accessibility side. We suddenly had sixteen debates on our political calendar: League of Women Voters' forums, City Clubs, Rotary engagements — we had accepted them all. The three of us debated so frequently and listened to each other's political spiels so often that Donna and I began to joke privately that we could actually trade places and deliver each other's remarks. Later in my political career I was exceedingly grateful for the debating experience and skills I acquired during that 1984 race.

As Craig and I drove throughout the state, we were touching base with so many people we had met in the primary campaign. I didn't feel as if I was a stranger now, even in the most outlying parts of the state. Some friends we had made in the primary season now offered to host us in their homes as we continued to travel. They usually spoiled us with wonderful meals, good wine, and lots of interesting conversation. The only liability was the fact that the late-night visits kept us from getting our much-needed sleep quota. Our hosts were interested in political analysis and campaign tidbits. Craig and I were interested in the beds they had offered us. We had to carefully find middle ground with our generous hosts.

It was summer, and there were county fairs and celebrations in almost every community. We not only visited potential voters but saw plenty of cows and pigs and chickens and rabbits. We admired canning exhibits, gave kudos to the local art displays, and had our pictures taken with restored antique cars. We consumed hot dogs, buffalo sausage, and homemade apple cider. I visited both the Democratic and Republican fair booths and did dozens of on-site radio interviews as I toured the fairgrounds of Oregon.

Summer was also parade time, and we made arrangements to ride or walk in dozens of community parades. In some locations my local supporters would march with me, carrying campaign placards and balloons, and distributing my election materials and stickers to the parade viewers. On that Fourth of July, I actually rode in three parades, in three different parts of the state, traveling over two hundred miles to meet that holiday schedule. At the end of every parade I would be hoarse from shouting greetings to folks on the sidelines. That summer felt a little like a three-month party, or it would have if I didn't count the fundraising, the debate schedule, and being away from Frank and my two sons. I missed my family every day I was on the road.

On the positive side, I soon had the AFL-CIO endorsement, the ongoing endorsement of the Oregon Education Association, and the public endorsement of environmental groups, women's organizations, pro-choice groups, and dozens of prominent citizens statewide.

Once again on July 31, my campaign hit a short delay when the Legislature was called into special session to pass a repeal of Oregon's unitary taxing method for multinational corporations. The bill, proposed by Governor Atiyeh, passed handily in both houses, and the session ended in a mere thirteen hours. It was a huge relief not to find myself back in Salem for another several weeks when I needed to be campaigning statewide.

In mid-September the first major poll on the race was released by *The Oregonian*; it gave my campaign a huge boost. Although 27 percent of those polled were still undecided, the outcome of the race was certainly taking shape. I captured 36 percent of the "decided" and "leaning" voters. Don Clark's numbers were 19 percent and Donna Zajonc had 18 percent favoring her. I basically had a 2-to-1 lead over *both* of my opponents. Among women voters, I carried a 21 percent lead over Donna. The poll also demonstrated I had an extremely strong following from Democratic voters while 30 percent of registered Republicans were still undecided.

Those polling numbers also added to my fundraising momentum, although I was still trailing Donna in campaign contributions. Yet a 2-to-1 lead in a three-way race gives contributors a great deal of confidence in picking a winner. It seemed now the only chance Donna had was a major television blitz. Television time is expensive. It costs big bucks. And as a political consultant was quoted as saying in the Salem *Statesman-Journal*, "I'd hate to be in Donna's shoes trying to raise money after the release of that ... poll." I crossed my fingers and just kept plugging away.

A Secretary of State's election race is not very "sexy" by campaign and press standards. However, in 1984 Oregon had an election issue that was attracting both statewide and national attention and was definitely heated and controversial. It was soon a factor in our race.

The controversy related to a religious order with an East Indian leader, a guru named Bhagwan Shree Rajneesh. The Rajneeshees moved their world headquarters to a very rural part of our state, east of the Cascade Mountains, on sixty-four thousand acres of rangeland, far removed from almost all populated Oregon communities. They had notable financial resources, were recruiting new followers, and began building a community, a new town to be called Rajneeshpuram. They also began visiting and then inhabiting a very small rural community named Antelope, twenty miles away by dirt road.

One of the first acts that raised eyebrows was the Rajneesh Foundation International's purchase of the Antelope General Store. The store housed a café and the town's post office, and was considered the community's business center. Near that same time, several of the new religious order members purchased six houses in the tiny town. Six houses may not seem intrusive unless it is weighed against the most recent official census — a total city population of forty people.

A proposal by the Rajneeshees to incorporate their ranch, making it the City of Rajneeshpuram, was being challenged under Oregon's comprehensive land-use laws. The outcome of the legal challenge was not considered hopeful for the Rajneeshees. They needed municipal rights to create water and sewer systems. They needed a city.

Antelope did not intend to become that city. In March of 1982 the Antelope City Council voted unanimously to schedule an election to *disincorporate* their city. Mayor Margaret Hill explained the decision: "They want our city charter, and this is the only way we have to prevent that." The election was set for April 15th and the battle was under way. The longtime settlers would go to the sole voting precinct in a month to kill Antelope's corporate status rather than see legal control of their community go to what they considered a religious cult with a transplanted guru from India. The political and cultural conflict was evident. The followers of the guru often wore long sari-type garments and the only colors they were permitted to wear were on the orange-red-maroon segment of the rainbow. The guru rode only in Rolls-Royce limousines. Many things about this group seemed strange to Oregon citizens in more rural areas. Out of this uneasiness and unfamiliarity, a series of voting issues arose. Were these new people all American citizens? Were they residents of Oregon? Could you transplant street people from downtown Portland, register them to vote, and take over the government of a small town? Could *opponents* of the Rajneeshees move their RVs from other parts of the state, create an encampment in Antelope, and offset the votes of the new religious order?

With Secretary of State Norma Paulus and Wasco County Clerk Sue Proffitt setting clear standards for valid voter registration, challenged ballots, and residency requirements, the life-or-death battle for the tiny community of Antelope would be decided at a closely observed ballot box.

Antelope's community expanded dramatically as five hundred or so national reporters, photographers, and commentators flooded the small town. In an almost festive atmosphere reminiscent of a county fair, local women prepared and sold sandwiches, pie, and coffee to the media horde. However, the festive mood disappeared quickly on April 15, 1982, when a vote of 55 to 42 turned down the effort to disincorporate Antelope. On June 1, Oregon Circuit Judge John Jelderks upheld the outcome of the challenged election results. In November of that same year, on votes of 69 to 27, Rajneesh followers won the mayor's race and three of the six city council seats. The majority of Antelope's council votes now rested with the Rajneeshees.

During the Secretary of State's race, perhaps for lack of any other public issue of interest, this ongoing and lengthy controversy reared its head. Both my opponents began to comment on the issue. Meanwhile, over in Wasco County, where the controversy was local and very heated, there began to be concerns about a potential outbreak of violence. Both local residents and the guru's followers had adequate weapons to create a tragedy.

It could have been tempting to use the Rajneesh conflict as an easy target, stirring fear and anger. Throughout the state, ugly words and ugly rumors circulated about these "strangers in our midst." Yet, the bottom line for me was to apply the same legal standard to this religious group as I would to a group of Catholics or Methodists or Mormons entering Oregon. I believed strongly this was one of those ethical furors where statesmanship must override political gamesmanship. As the election season continued, my handling of the matter proved to be the correct choice. An editorial from the Eugene *Register Guard* was an example of the press's reaction: "Unlike her two opponents, Roberts has impressed us during the campaign by resisting the temptation to capitalize on the volatile Rajneesh dispute with demagogic oratory."

I was exposed firsthand to the level of animosity in Wasco County with regard to the guru's followers. Craig and I, still on the road, dropped into a small coffee shop in the county one morning for our usual coffee and handshakes. I was already dressed in my suit and heels, prepared for a professional day's work. As we stepped into the front door, all smiles on *our* part, the place went dead silent. No one returned our smiles! It was as if everyone were frozen in place. This was a reaction I had *never* experienced on the campaign trail. Yet I understood the reaction … completely. I may have been professionally attired but I had dressed in my best red wool suit. At that point in time in Wasco County, *nobody* wore red or orange — nobody except the Rajneeshees! Craig admonished me that I better not plan to stop anywhere wearing that outfit. I replied, "No group owns any part of the rainbow, Craig. I intend to show that today." And I did, including a noon speech before a local service club wearing my red suit.

The 1984 general election in Oregon featured more women for major public office than ever before in our state's history. Margie Hendrickson, a state senator, gained the Democratic nomination for U.S. senator against Republican incumbent Mark Hatfield. The Democratic nominees for two congressional seats were women, and Geraldine Ferraro was the vice presidential candidate on the Democratic slate. It was fun and exciting out there on the campaign trail with so many bright, talented women running alongside. I was proud to be a part of this political "revolution."

I was excited to be selected as a delegate to the 1984 Democratic National Convention in San Francisco in July. It was my second national political convention, and this gathering of over five thousand Democratic delegates held two very special moments. First, a vote by the fifty Oregon convention delegates gave me the honor of announcing the Oregon delegation's votes for President. Thousands of Oregon voters would see me on national television. In the tradition of convention hyperbole, I announced our delegation's vote: "Madam Secretary, the beautiful State of Oregon, still demonstrating the pioneer spirit that brought Americans westward from every corner of this nation, the state of clean air, clean water, and clean politics, casts thirty-one votes for Sen. Gary Hart, sixteen

Presidential candidate Walter Mondale and his running mate, Geraldine Ferraro, kept relatively dry under an umbrella. I had to wipe my wet glasses. Associated Press photo by Jack Smith.

votes for Vice President Walter Mondale, and two votes for Rev. Jesse Jackson." What a rush I felt. I knew back home my parents were smiling from ear to ear. As a matter of fact, so was I.

Still, the greatest thrill of the convention was yet to unfold. *This* memory is seared in my brain, never to be forgotten. It is the moment in history when Congresswoman Geraldine Ferraro of New York was nominated for Vice President of the United States. When she stepped to the microphone, the convention went wild. Hundreds of male delegates had given up their seats on the convention floor so that female alternate delegates could be part of that historic event. At that moment, more women were seated on the convention floor than ever before at a party nominating convention in America's history. They waved flags, stood on chairs, and cheered, and cheered, and cheered. I stood on my chair, marveling at the reaction, slowly turning 360 degrees, taking in the scene. Women were embracing, singing, weeping, celebrating. On the huge podium at the front of the hall, national male political leaders were beginning to look slightly stunned. What had they unleashed?

Yet for most women in that convention hall, Gerry Ferraro's nomination represented political adulthood, at last, for the women of our party and our country. As long as I live, that scene will be with me. Even today, I can close my eyes and bring that moment back into view. Still, after twenty-five years, I get choked up in trying to re-tell the story. I may or may not live to see a woman President or Vice President, but I will always have the memory of the night Rep. Geraldine Ferraro accepted the Democratic nomination for Vice President of the United States of America. Always.

Meanwhile back in Oregon the race continued. I had raised over $100,000, but the rumor mill reported that Donna Zajonc might have raised twice as much. The financial reporting would not be filed in the state elections division for several more weeks, so we couldn't yet verify those numbers. The polling had looked good a few weeks before, but we still feared a late media blitz. We put our heads together and decided we needed to put some statesman-like ads on television. You know the kind: hard working, serious, experienced, honest. The "experienced" element of the ads was particularly important for voters still becoming accustomed to female candidates. Yet to meet the deadline for submitting ads to our media buyer, we needed the money right away. Now! This was no time to err on the side of caution.

We lined up several co-signers and went to the U.S. National Bank and borrowed $27,500 for television buys. If I won, we hoped we could raise the money fairly easily to pay off the loan. If I lost, Frank and I would be repaying the loan for years. This doesn't sound like much money today, but only a few years before we had purchased a five-bedroom home for $38,000. In 1984, $27,500 was a huge risk. Plus, we already had a $2,000 campaign loan owed to my parents. It was indeed a risky choice both for the campaign and for us personally, not to count my oh-so-generous co-signers. I had to be careful not to let it keep me awake nights once the decision *and* the loan were made.

As the final weeks of the campaign approached, our political debates were down to the last few. We awaited the editorial endorsements from daily newspapers across the state. It was unlikely there would be any late polling numbers in the race. Our campaign certainly wasn't going to spend precious and scarce dollars on polling this late in the election cycle. The campaign was wildly busy, but there was still a sense, for me, of winding down.

My campaign staff had done so much with so little. As a team they made the campaign more professional than our size and finances should ever have dictated. FDR Services, a two-year-old political consulting firm out of the State of Washington, had delivered the full package. Blair Butterworth and Tom Hujar had taken us on as their first statewide race and also their first campaign outside of Washington State. They had been a superb find! Everyone, including our outstanding campaign staff and volunteers and my financial contributors, played a necessary part in moving toward potential success. Plus, Frank remained my advocate, my number one fan, my advisor, and my source of strength during the long months of campaigning. If I had, hopefully, done *my* part well enough, success was within reach.

On October 26, 1984, we prepared for one of the last debates. This one was a big one! The Portland City Club debate would attract a standing-room-only crowd plus radio, television, and newspaper reporters. I was excited and feeling good but was searching for one final "zinger" that would demonstrate the winning trend of my campaign. It was handed to me late that morning … times three!

We were checking the morning editorial endorsements across the state and also had campaign supporters standing by to get copies of the earliest of the afternoon editions. Since this was long before the Internet, such on-site newspaper checking was the only option we had to gain the information quickly. The news was very good. I entered the debate with hot-off-the-press information.

I took the podium at the Portland City Club to debate, once again, my two general election opponents. I came armed with strong polling numbers, more finely tuned debating skills, and three brand-new newspaper endorsements. When the time was right, I shared with the audience my growing statewide editorial support. I told them of the previous endorsements from newspapers on the coast, in central Oregon, and in the Willamette Valley. And then I told the debate watchers that on this very day I had been honored with the added editorial support of three daily Oregon newspapers … the Corvallis *Gazette-Times*, the *East Oregonian* in Pendleton, and the Salem *Statesman-Journal* (Donna Zajonc's hometown paper!). Donna's face visibly fell. I felt sad seeing Donna's apparent disappointment, but we had competed fairly and actively for those endorsements and I had used them for maximum impact. The election outcome looked more and more favorable for me. However, polling wasn't looking quite so good for a number of my Democratic colleagues running in statewide and congressional races. I was watching those races and cared, but my number one priority was to stay focused on my own campaign.

I was also keeping a close eye on some ballot measures. Measure 2, a property-tax limitation measure, seemed to be a close call as the election neared. I had publicly opposed it and had my fingers crossed for its defeat. I fully expected Measure 5, creating a state lottery, to win, even though I felt it was bad public policy. Measure 7, which would reinstate Oregon's death penalty law, was very likely to pass, but I was opposed to the measure and said so during the campaign. I felt the death penalty sent all the wrong messages. If murder was so terrible, how could the state justify murdering someone, taking their life? I wanted my state to be more humane than that, but I knew my feelings represented a minority position in Oregon and across the nation as well.

Then—finally—the campaign debates were done, the fundraising and speeches were winding down, and the candidate and staff were threadbare in terms of energy! When I had started this campaign almost eighteen months before, I could never have imagined how long and grueling—and educational—it would be. I had covered thousands of miles, spoken with hundreds and hundreds of Oregon citizens, marched or ridden in dozens of parades, been interviewed more times than I could count, and participated in sixteen general election debates. I could close my eyes and visualize a complete map of Oregon with every town, river, highway number, and county boundary in the proper place.

On the evening of November 6, 1984, we stood in our election headquarters watching the television screens and waiting for results. Some outcomes were decided early. Attorney General Dave Frohnmeyer (R) was reelected. The state lottery measure and the death penalty measure were both passing strongly. Three Democratic congressmen would be returning to the House, but the other two congressional seats went Republican. Senator Mark Hatfield (R) won another strong victory. Some Republican victories meant that Margie Hendrickson, Larryann Willis, and Ruth McFarland had been defeated—not a good night for major women candidates in Oregon.

We held our breath and waited for definitive numbers in the Secretary of State's race. Patricia paced.

It appeared the state House of Representatives and state Senate would remain in Democratic control for the next two years. In a much closer race, it looked as if Measure 2, the property-tax limitation initiative, would be defeated by a narrow margin. Walter Mondale was losing badly to Ronald Reagan in the Presidential race, even in Oregon, and with Mondale's defeat Geraldine Ferraro would not become VP.

We waited.

Finally the local television stations began declaring my victory. Staff suddenly began appearing with T-shirts that simply read, "110 Years!" One hundred and ten years since a Democrat had held the office of Secretary of State in Oregon — an historic victory.

When the numbers were completely tabulated from all thirty-six counties in Oregon, my victory, by a plurality, was clear:

Barbara Roberts (D) 518,145
Donna Zajonc (R) 439,865
Don Clark (I) 241,995
Misc. 2,035

My parents, Frank, my sons, my sister, my entire staff celebrated. It was wonderful! Balloons and champagne and hugs and cheers filled the headquarters. I did interviews. Patricia did interviews. It was a great evening.

A couple of times that night I paused and remembered the difficult decision I had made at the close of the 1983 legislative session. The race had seemed a long shot then. It was a big political risk for me. Looking back, that leap of faith — faith in myself — had felt right from the beginning. I felt elated enough to dance on the table … but that would hardly be appropriate behavior for Oregon's new Secretary of State. But in my head, I was dancing like crazy!

CHAPTER FOURTEEN

Secretary of State

Election night is all about waiting, watching, nail biting, pacing, and moving between frowns and smiles. It is about early returns, political speculation, wine and cheese, hugs and hope. On November 6, 1984, for me, election night was about winning.

Our campaign headquarters was decked out with streamers and balloons, posters and lawn signs. Even today, I can still recall looking across the room, watching the expressions of pride and excitement on the faces of my parents. I almost felt their pleasure more strongly than my own. I sensed I had given them a gift of parental bragging rights. They hugged my staff and shook hands with my supporters. It was a scene I treasured then and recalling it, even today, makes me a little misty.

Frank was moving around the room, the senior politician and proud spouse. His familiar, strong laugh could occasionally be heard over the din of voices, television commentary, and telephones. Even understanding the risk of this run for higher office, Frank had encouraged me to jump. He had been right. Frank had accepted having a wife on the campaign trail, tolerated my hectic travel schedule and my many campaign distractions with good humor. My arrivals back home often resulted in honeymoon-like reunions. Now I couldn't wait to return to being a full-time wife. On election night, Frank reconnected with me every ten or fifteen minutes, hugged me, and then continued to circulate. I sensed that he, too, was looking forward to again having a full-time partner.

Election night ended with radio and television interviews, champagne toasts, a short thank-you speech to my staff and supporters, and finally an exhausted campaign crew locked the headquarters door and left clean-up chores until the next morning. That night, once I finally calmed down, I slept without worries about tomorrow's debates, road trips, endorsement battles, or vote counts. The next morning, Frank, Dad, and I headed to the campaign headquarters. A telling image met us as we walked in. The dozens and dozens of blue and white balloons that had decorated the ceilings and walls just the night before now lay deflated, limp and inanimate, on the campaign floor. The party was definitely over! The work of Secretary of State was about to begin.

The campaign office would be closed. Final fundraising would take place to pay off our bank loan, late expenses, and staff salaries. And we would start planning my swearing-in ceremony. The first time I said "swearing-in ceremony" aloud I felt like a kid at Christmas.

I chose the State Capitol Rotunda for the ceremony. The acoustics were difficult but the setting was impressive. Two huge staircases from the House and Senate chamber areas lead to the rotunda floor. Four beautiful historical murals adorn the walls. Overhead the ceiling dome rises to 106 feet. On the rotunda floor, directly below the dome, a large glittering gold replica of the Oregon state seal makes clear the authority of this place.

Choosing a judge to administer the official oath of office could have been complicated. I had a number of friends on the bench. My clear choice, however, was State Supreme Court Justice Berkley "Bud" Lent, the judge who had performed our wedding ceremony ten years earlier. When I selected someone to fill the role of emcee for the ceremony, I called on my former legislative colleague Grattan Kerans. He was in the last days of his term as Speaker of the House and had, unfortunately, just lost his race for State Treasurer. He was a skilled speaker, well known to the political community, and I considered him a friend and ally.

Although I would not officially take office until January 1, we scheduled the ceremony on Sunday afternoon, December 16, to avoid overlap with the opening of the 1985 legislative session. I felt after Democrats had waited one hundred and ten years to elect a member of their party to the office, we deserved some focused attention for this particular moment in Oregon history.

Well, I need not have worried about press attention. I had selected the Portland Gay Men's Chorus to perform the musical selections for the day's events. I chose them for two reasons. Number one, they were the most outstanding chorus in Oregon. The second reason was much more personal. I had been a strong advocate for gay rights for a number of years, but in 1984 this was not yet a mainstream position. I recognized this selection for what it was—a statement. I determined that if I took a position of personal principle on my very first day in statewide office, I would never be afraid to stand up for what I believed as my political future unfolded.

The story of my inaugural ceremony appeared in every daily and weekly newspaper in Oregon. And, without exception, every story included the fact that the Portland Gay Men's Chorus had performed as part of the ceremony. This story also hit some papers outside of Oregon, notably most gay publications across the country. It was believed to be the first time in America that a gay chorus had performed in a state Capitol ceremony. However, it would not be the last time this chorus sang in Oregon's Capitol building. My intention was not to politicize or sensationalize but rather to make clear to Oregon citizens that I was

Judge Berkley Lent swearing me into office in December 1984 in front of the Portland Gay Men's Chorus.

not afraid to stand up for people or policies, even those that garnered controversy. Some political friends predicted that my choice of the chorus on this important day would kill my chances of ever being reelected to statewide office again. Interestingly, four years later, I would be reelected, winning every county in Oregon.

Today, I am still involved with the Portland Gay Men's Chorus, attending their concerts, supporting their music and their work for equality, even acting as moderator at their initial concert of "Brave Souls and Dreamers," a musical work promoting peace. At the post-concert event, I reminded them that the real "controversy" of 1984 was when the chorus came attired in bright red vests and I stood in front of them in my beautiful magenta wool suit. Boy, did we clash!

Hundreds of Oregonians from every part of the state were in the Capitol that day as I took the oath of office. It is strange to struggle so hard for something and then have the accomplishment affect you as if it were a complete surprise. All those people, the press and cameras, the level of excitement and celebration … I felt a little out of focus, a little hazy. Perhaps this is what people mean when they speak of a "dream-like state." There was so much to react to, to observe, take in, save for future memories. There had never been a day quite like this one in my life. How could I have predicted then that such a day would come again?

After the beautiful choral music, the entire rotunda was silent as Judge Lent and I stepped forward for the official oath of office. I raised my right hand and repeated the words of the oath. When I had finished, the whole Capitol seemed to erupt in cheers and applause. As the crowd quieted, Judge Lent reminded me, "The last time I united you for a lifetime. This is only guaranteed for four years!" I kissed Frank and stepped to the microphone. Here is a portion of the remarks I delivered on that special day:

As a fourth-generation Oregonian, I have always known our state was unique among the fifty states. But this past year, having traveled to every corner of Oregon, I know and appreciate the beauty of Oregon more than ever. And I know Oregonians better. I've walked in your towns, I've ridden in your parades, I've joined in your celebrations and I've listened to you – your ideas, your concerns, your hopes and your plans.

Oregon is at a crossroads. Every decision we make now as citizens and as office holders will shape Oregon for decades to come. We must not be afraid to be pathbreakers.

Standing in our Capitol rotunda, surrounded by the pictorial history of Oregon, makes it apparent that the Oregon story was written by risk takers, by those willing to start new things and try new courses. That's the Oregon tradition.

So, today, as your first Democratic Secretary of State in over a century, I pledge to you my commitment and energies to the duties of this office.

I finished my address and then publicly thanked my wonderful, hard-working campaign staff and introduced my family. I was particularly pleased to introduce my parents with the words, "They had the foresight to make me a native Oregonian. Their example of people concern, integrity, humor, love and Democratic principles (with a big D) shaped my life." It is not often one has the opportunity to publicly thank their parents before hundreds of witnesses. I was grateful for that chance.

With the ceremonial aspect of my new role complete, it was time for the real deal! I had four personal staff people to hire including my Deputy Secretary of State. I needed to take the out-going Secretary of State's budget and decide what changes were required to make the office's spending and budget priorities my own. And — since Oregon's Constitution required the Secretary of State to reside in the same county as the state Capitol building — I had to immediately find a Salem home for the next four to eight years. This was a strange constitutional provision left over from the early days of Oregon's statehood when the Secretary of State's daily responsibilities meant "he" couldn't live more than a day's horseback ride away. But as a state senator, Frank had to maintain residency in his Portland legislative district. When Frank was ready to run for another Senate term in 1986, he would file his candidacy with my office. I certainly couldn't accept his filing if I knew he was living pretty much full-time in Salem ... with me! This would be a new personal and political complication for us! So much for believing that the end of the campaign season meant Frank and I could resume our normal married living situation. It made little sense for me to rent a place in Salem when my tenure would be at least four years. I needed to purchase.

I bought a nice little condo only blocks from the Capitol with a big open deck facing the local mill stream. I spent most weekends in Portland. Frank spent a couple nights a week in Salem. And we were apart two nights a week. It wasn't perfect, but we each used those two nights to catch up on reading and work. It was certainly an improvement over the recent campaign schedule of six out of seven nights on the road.

By this time, Frank was serving in the state Senate with Glenn Otto, the man who had defeated him for his 1972 House reelection. Glenn was aware of how hard Frank and I had worked to adhere to the letter and spirit of the state constitutional residency requirements demanded of each of our offices. Without consulting us, in 1985 Senator Otto introduced a constitutional amendment to remove the outdated provision of one-county residency for the statewide position of Secretary of State. The bill easily passed the Senate and House, headed for the next year's ballot. In 1986, voters passed the constitutional amendment, 771,959 to 265,999. Otto labeled it the only truly "pro-family" legislation on the November 1986 ballot!

In looking back at the six years I served as Secretary of State, I would like to tell you the stories of the accomplishments of which I am most proud and the people who worked with me to make them happen. These are successes that came only after years of hard work and administrative, legislative, and public leadership. As you will note when I detail these stories of political accomplishment, no leader reaches big goals without the commitment, energy, dedication, and loyalty of a very strong and skilled staff.

I brought some real talent with me to the agency in January of 1985. My Deputy Secretary of State, Felicia Trader, was a skilled manager with broad administrative experience, experience that had caused me to ask Felicia to serve on the selection committee for the new hiring. Yet before the committee actually met, it occurred to me that Felicia might be interested in the position herself. She was! She resigned from the committee and became a star applicant for the job. She was solid and highly organized with a BS in business and an MBA. She would take the lead on the agency budget, plus our plans for changes in both the Audits and Archives divisions. I knew I could put my full trust in Felicia as the administrative leader for the office.

Patricia McCaig made the switch from my general election campaign manager to executive assistant in the new office. We had worked closely together, and she understood where policy and politics came together in my new role. She was skilled with handling press and media and had extensive interest in the way the Elections Division was managed. As an environmental advocate, she also coveted the work that was part of my responsibility as one of the three members of the State Land Board, which managed over two million acres of state lands and waterways.

Donnella Slayton once again moved with me as I took my first statewide office. She had served on my staff for all of my four legislative years and worked on the campaign staff, plus we had served together as board members for eight years on the Parkrose School Board. I was happy to have her on my team. Donnella was totally dependable. The final member of our front-office staff was Susan Gomberg. Her husband, Dave, had worked on my 1981 legislative staff. Susan was warm, friendly, and excited about her new position. I knew she would do a good job.

The remainder of my administrative staff was, for the most part, "inherited." Bill Miles, the Director of the Audits Division, had been part of the Audits staff since 1960. He had been appointed to his current position two years earlier. He was a real professional in every sense of the word, and I looked forward to working with him.

The Election and Public Records Division was directed by Ray Phelps, who was well known in his position, particularly around the Capitol building. He was often considered the voice of the office among legislators. Ray had managed the division for several years. I did have some concerns about his administrative style, but I wanted to observe that close up for long enough to evaluate how he worked and how well we worked together. Time would tell.

The final major administrative position was a new hire that would turn out to be a crucial choice. The new Director of the Archives Division, Dr. Roy Turnbaugh, came to Oregon from the Illinois State Archives program to start his new role from the very start of my term in January 1985.

An Archives Building for Oregon

When I became Oregon's brand-new Secretary of State, I had an old problem to deal with … a very old problem. I was now responsible for Oregon's Archives Division, meaning the storage and preservation of the state's original provisional government documents, our territorial papers, the state constitution, and all of the permanent papers of state government, the legislative records, and judicial papers. The problem was that the state had no archives building for the safe and permanent storage of these records. All of Oregon's paper heritage was housed in one-half of an old 1930s hops warehouse leased by state government. The opposite end of the building was occupied by a discount carpet operation.

For years there had been off-and-on discussions about the need for a proper archives facility, yet here we were in 1985 with more than one hundred fifty years of historical documents crammed into an old warehouse without proper humidity controls, without necessary security protection—a building that could easily and accurately be described as a "fire trap." Except I was highly uncomfortable to speak *publicly* of this threat of fire for fear that some vandal would take my words as a challenge.

So I set out in 1985 to give Oregon's historical records a permanent home. With the strong support of our new professional archivist, Dr. Roy Turnbaugh, and my deputy, Felicia Trader, and my own belief that I had an ethical and public obligation to protect Oregon's documented history, we began the process to gain legislative and financial support for Oregon's very first state archives building.

After a year of planning and initial research, on February 14, 1986, Oregon's 127th birthday, I announced plans at a press conference to seek support from the 1987 legislative session for an Oregon Archives Building. That same day I released a large poster with a historic photo from our archives collection. The bold type on the top read: "Forty Years of Service." Across the bottom the words read: "Oregon State Archives 1946-1986 — Looking for a Home." Every one of Oregon's ninety legislators received a copy of the poster.

We were launched!

In July, the Department of General Services submitted its capital construction requests for the 1987-89 biennium to the Capitol Planning Commission, including $122,175 for the initial planning for our Archives Building and Records Center. The commission recommended approval. It was a big and thrilling step — and I do mean "step," for this would become an arduous trek from that decision point until the archives program moved into its new building in early December 1991. I certainly could not have envisioned the number and variety of the controversies that would arise at every point in the next six years.

Secretary of State Roberts shows off Archives poster as the campaign begins for an Archives Building.
From Oregon Archives Collection

During the 1987 legislative session, the first request for funding went quite smoothly. I gained approval for the $122,175 for the initial planning work. Portland architectural firm Zimmer, Gunsul, Frasca was active in the process, through much of 1988, of designing the building, considering site needs, and developing cost estimates. This was not an ordinary state office building; this was a specialized building with a number of technical requirements. This building was expected to have a significant presence as both a powerful symbol of government and our commitment to an open democratic society and its records. I hoped for the building to be beautiful, functional, and an asset to state government and to our citizens.

Well, 1988 proved to be a year in this process that demonstrated that beauty is in the eye of the beholder. The controversy was not regarding the design of the building itself but rather with the *siting* of the Archives Building.

Oregon's Capitol Mall is bordered on the south end by our modern Greek Capitol building, built in 1938, after two earlier capitols had been destroyed by fire. The exterior of our four-story Capitol is faced with beautiful white Danby Vermont marble. The building is topped by a bronze statue of the Oregon Pioneer weighing 8.5 tons and finished with gold leaf. The mall stretches north for six blocks, bordered on both the east and west with large state buildings. On the far north end at this time, on state-owned land, were thirty-five homes the state rented to local citizens. There had long been expectations of eventually using that acreage for a significant state structure, including perhaps a governor's residence, a new state library, or a cluster of natural resource agency buildings. The Capitol Mall Plan had last been updated in 1976 with no real clarification about the use of the north end site.

As plans advanced on the design of our new building, it became apparent that the structure, if faced with marble rather than brick and placed on the north end site, could become the matching "book end" to the state Capitol building. It was a significant and potentially historical idea!

The Department of General Services, in charge of construction of state facilities, began to move forward on the proposal to site our new building as the Capitol Mall's north end anchor building. Well, talk about you-know-what hitting the fan! The renters of the houses located on the north mall raised the first objections. Many of them were long-term renters—five, ten, twelve years. They were shocked that their homes could disappear. The proposed site also bordered a residential neighborhood and those homeowners were concerned about traffic and parking and increased congestion. The Salem *Statesman Journal* editorialized against the siting. The eight-member Capitol Planning Commission was facing a controversial decision and lots of heat. Questions soon included the wisdom of destroying both affordable housing plus a few historical homes on the state property. Finally in June of 1988 the commission held its decision-making hearing. Under the leadership of Chair Jean Tate of Eugene, the commission took testimony. Salem Mayor Sue Miller, a member of the commission, finally pointed out that the site could easily be chosen by the state for a five- or six-story office complex that would far overshadow the height and square footage of the Archives Building. The hearing ended with a unanimous vote to allow the Archives Building to be constructed on the property. We agreed to work to find a site where the viable houses could be relocated rather than razed, and succeeded in saving almost all of the homes plus donating three of them to the city as historic properties.

We returned to the 1989 Legislature with our architectural designs, our site selection decisions, and the budget figure for the building and furnishings. The one change that had occurred over the previous two years was the separation of the Archives Building from the Records Center. The records storage facility would be housed elsewhere in less-expensive square footage. Senate Bill 5570, the budget bill for capital construction projects, did not have its first Ways & Means hearing until June 30, six months into the legislative session. Yet, once that step was taken, the process moved swiftly. On July 2, the bill received a successful vote of 18 to 8 in the Senate. The next day, it passed in the House by a vote of 36 to 24.

Well, one more hurdle behind me. Next year, in 1990, there would be several big steps: final approval of the design by the Capitol Planning Commission, our ceremonial groundbreaking, and the public bidding process and selection of a general contractor. It had taken us more than four years to reach this point. I had begun this dream as a newly elected Secretary of State. I was now serving in my second four-year term and we hadn't yet turned our first shovel of dirt!

Speaking of *dirt*—once the rental houses had been removed, it was very soon discovered that the soil beneath most of the home sites was deeply contaminated with heating oil residue from years of leakage from heating oil tanks. All construction preparation was halted while experts cleared the site of contaminated soil, resulting in an extended delay of the beginning of site preparation. Although the ceremonial groundbreaking took place on May 2, 1990, it was summer before work began in earnest. Sometimes it seemed as if nothing would come easily for this "dream."

Yet the next few steps were quite orderly, and I began to feel our big project might finally be in for some smooth sailing. The Capitol

Planning Commission granted its final approval. The project was publicly bid, and a contract was awarded. We were moving forward. It was September of 1990. Just over a year later, the Archives Building was complete and ready for occupancy! As the Archives staff began the move, the first boxes of state historical records crossed town from the old hops warehouse to the shiny new Archives Building. Over the next two weeks more than twenty thousand boxes of records were relocated.

The building came in on time and nearly $500,000 under budget. We kept our promises to the neighbors and the City of Salem. We saved the houses that were removed from the site, and they were converted, almost entirely, to affordable housing for Salem residents. We had placed Oregon's historical documents in a place of security and long-term preservation. I was so proud of the leadership I had taken to make this archives facility a reality for Oregon.

In a December 10, 1991, *Oregonian* article, Archivist Roy Turnbaugh said, "I really like government records. I like them because they are records of everybody, rather than just the distinguished, the prominent, or the wealthy. There's a very democratic quality to these records." Well, that was about the only positive thing you would see in the press about this beautiful and important new building for the entire next year! We saw nothing but negative press accounts of the cost of the furnishings, right down to the cost of the carpeting in the building's public areas. I am not sure how it began, but the press fed on it for months and months. Finally, the Legislature got into the game, demanding an accounting, pushing for an audit of the project. The glow of this wonderful accomplishment began to fade quickly. Questions were raised about the cost of the stone flooring, wood paneling, light fixtures, and reference tables. All of the items in question were in public areas of the building. The materials had been selected way back in the design phase by interior professionals trying to provide a warm, inviting atmosphere within the context of the building. They were also selected for durability and easy maintenance. All of these interior furnishings were part of a lump-sum bid, traditional for these kinds of projects. But in the feeding frenzy of negative press it was difficult to make any of these explanations heard. And truthfully, it was really not the marble exterior, the stone flooring, the paneling, or the light fixtures that made this such a controversy. It was a carpeting decision that became the "poster child" for this year of negative press stories.

Three different grades of carpeting were selected for three separate areas of the building. The staff and office work area carpet was $18 per square yard. The archivist's office carpeting was $36 per square yard. The carpet for the reading room and two small display rooms was reported to be $54 per square yard when the high-grade wool carpet was chosen. However, the architect's staff misstated the cost, and the actual installed cost was a shocking $127 per square yard! It was this story that broke first and was replayed over and over. We had never been informed of the error and we should have been told and a corrective adjustment should have been credited to the state.

What I had expected to be a proud and celebratory opening for this wonderful building turned into a negative, finger-pointing period for newspaper columnists, some legislators, and many members of the public. The criticism was partially valid but lost more and more perspective as it overshadowed the long-term and positive asset that had been created for Oregon's history and generations of our citizens.

As I worked on the manuscript for this book, I made a large number of trips to the Oregon Archives Building to do research. Each trip reminded me of the value of our collected history that is housed under its roof. The Archives Building was designed to last one hundred years. With that perspective, I have accepted the year of controversy when the building and furnishing were new and under harsh scrutiny, knowing that for the ninety-nine remaining years Oregon's documented history has a home!

I will always consider Oregon's beautiful Archives Building one of my successes as a public official.

Performance Auditing

My second success story as Secretary of State is one that has the overtone of a technical and administrative saga. It relates to my strong efforts to gain legislative authority for my office to conduct performance audits. Oregon's Secretary of State is also the state's Auditor. Since statehood, the constitutional authority for fiscal auditing had rested in that office. Across the nation, more and more governments were beginning to step beyond the dollars-and-cents auditing role to examine the effectiveness and efficiency of government agencies in the delivery of their prescribed duties. I believed it was time for Oregon's government to make use of this expanded audit tool. Much like the bumpy path to create an archives building, performance auditing faced a large share of hurdles and pitfalls. What seemed to me to be a "good government" effort became a contest between my good intentions, the Legislature's competitive nature, and the seated Governor's sense of executive ownership.

I had vocally supported performance auditing during my campaign, but an opinion from the Attorney General's office concluded that the Legislature would have to authorize my office to take it on. I moved for the introduction of Senate Bill 769 to clarify that authority, and it was submitted to the 1985 legislative session. I also understood that, if performance auditing authority was granted, the Audits Division would need to hire professionals to implement the program. My first budget reflected that need.

An editorial in *The Oregonian* supported SB769 and the appropriateness of that authority being housed in my office, citing examples of the important successes of this audit practice now taking place in King County, Washington, and under the new authority of Portland City Auditor Jewel Lansing. Governor Atiyeh, however, objected to my gaining this new authority. Senate Bill 769 passed the Senate Government Operations Committee unanimously, easily passed the Senate, and when it reached the House, was referred to the Ways & Means Committee, where it hit the first major roadblock. Concerns about the new authority raised by members of the House forced the committee to make major amendments in order to gain House passage, reducing the budget number and authorizing my office to conduct only two performance audits: one at the Highway Division and the second at the Department of Transportation. I wasn't happy, but I felt forced to support the changes, believing these pilot projects would prove themselves to be solid demonstrations of the service they would offer to legislative decision makers and the significant tax dollars that would be captured in the outcomes of the audits.

On June 6 the amended version of SB 769 passed the House on a 33-25 vote. Twenty-four of the twenty-five "no" votes were from Republican members. The bill repassed as amended in the Senate on June 11 by a 26-2 vote.

On July 9, 1985, Governor Atiyeh, who had objected to the idea from the first, vetoed the amended version of SB769! That veto meant that, since Oregon's legislative sessions only convene biennially, unless some crisis caused a special session, any chance of a veto override would not occur until January of 1987. For eighteen months not even our pilot performance audits could move forward. I was disappointed and frustrated. The day following the Governor's veto, I put out a detailed press release criticizing Governor Atiyeh's action. One of the last sentences made my future intentions clear: "We need a governor who wants the results produced by performance audits."

In the 1986 campaign season I actively supported the Democratic candidate for governor, Neil Goldschmidt. Governor Atiyeh had always been respectful of me, even including me in his weekly cabinet meetings. But I was enthusiastic about working with a strong Democratic governor. I was there with Goldschmidt when he celebrated the opening of our light rail line. I was there with him on election night. And he was there with me in support of my performance audit efforts. As the 1987 Legislature prepared to convene, *The Oregonian* editorialized in support of the veto override of SB769 from the 1985 session, and the veto override was successful! I had then gained the authority to do the two pilot performance audits, on Highway and on Transportation. Only two, no more.

On June 30, 1988, I released the initial performance audit covering the Transportation Department's maintenance program. The audit identified $3 million that could be saved in the program every year. On December 5, the second performance audit was released covering the ownership and maintenance of Highway Division equipment. The audit found a potential annual savings of $3.8 million. The division was spending twice as much to maintain its existing fleet, where more than one-half of the trucks and vehicles were beyond their useful life, than the cost of replacement with new equipment.

Two successful performance audits. Millions of dollars in savings identified. Yet here I was again—back at square one! No authority or budget ability to move forward. I had a supportive governor, a Legislature with, hopefully, growing respect for the new auditing process, but the earlier opinion from the Attorney General limited my next step. My staff and I took a new tack on the Attorney General's opinion of 1985. My new Deputy Secretary of State, Marilynne Keyser, a CPA, who began her position in October of 1987, Audits Director Bill Miles, and I determined that a major legal change had occurred in the past four years, one that could very well affect the legal questions we had earlier submitted to the AG's office. The recent passage of the federal Single Audit Act required the Secretary of State to audit the entire state government every year. This audit of the consolidated financial statements meant that our auditors were now continually performing a fiscal audit of Oregon's state government. With this new perspective, we revised our questions to the AG and received an updated opinion: the new way of looking at our complete audit responsibilities made it possible to broaden our audit duties as long as the results "remained limited to fiscal affairs." The opinion ended up validating the full audit authority of the Oregon Secretary of State.

In 1990, with this authority clarification, our Audits Division established a performance auditing group with interdisciplinary staff composed of professionals with backgrounds in public administration, finance, economics, industrial engineering, law, and information technology. The work of this professional team has saved million of dollars and improved the service levels and program outcomes in every arm of Oregon's agencies and departments. I remain very proud of the outcome of this policy initiative.

Openness in the Election Division

The most visible department in the Secretary of State's office to Oregon citizens is the Elections Division. When candidates for statewide office or the Legislature or judicial positions file for public office, they do so with the state Elections Division. This same department handles candidates' required financial reports, including releasing numbers to the Oregon media. Citizen initiative petitions are handled, processed, verified, and counted by this department. The Elections Division works with the state's thirty-six county clerks to conduct every election, count every ballot, handle recounts in close elections, and certify election winners.

During my years as Secretary of State, I placed high priority on assuring that every Oregon polling location was handicapped accessible. A change in federal law started this effort in states across America. It was common at this time to find polling locations in church basements, on the second floor of local government buildings and schools ... all with stairways as the only access. Obviously many eligible citizens were cut out of the opportunity to be part of our democracy. I set out to put Oregon's election sites in the 100 percent accessible category. Thirty-six county clerks joined me in that huge effort. Within only three years, more than a majority of Oregon's counties had achieved that 100 percent mark. I was so proud of the amazing efforts and commitment to bring voting equality to every Oregon voter.

I also introduced legislation to add an hour to Oregon's voting day, opening the polls at 7 a.m. to help workers cast their votes before they started their morning work shift. That expanded thirteen-hour voting day increased Oregon's turnout all across the state.

Patricia McCaig took on the leadership for creating a detailed matrix for determining fines and penalties for late and inaccurate information on campaign financial reports. Previously, these fines had been applied with little consistency and were frequently so minor as to have almost no deterrent to late and inaccurate filers. Well, Patricia and I fixed that! Once the detailed matrix was completed and publicly released, all new financial reports were subject to the fines and penalties. Unfortunately, at least from the perspective of my own political party, the first major fine assessed under the new system was against the House Democratic Caucus office. Their report was riddled with errors, was not financially balanced, and did not match the contribution figures reported by candidates who had received Democratic Caucus support. When error after error accumulated and the matrix was applied, the Elections Division billed the House Democratic Caucus $61,234, the largest election fine in the state's history! This policy change proved quite valuable in turning the state political financial reports into highly accurate and timely documents. Citizens deserve that accuracy and openness.

A New State Motto

This next success may appear to be a small one, but it was one that brought me a great deal of pleasure.

The state of Oregon had had two state mottoes in its history. Its territorial motto was in Latin: *Alis Volat Propitis*. Later Oregon changed its motto to "The Union," and that motto appeared on our state seal over all the decades thereafter. Each time I read the words, "The Union" on the state seal, it seemed to have little to do with the state I knew and loved. In asking for the translation, from Latin to English, of the original territorial motto, I had my answer. I introduced a bill into the 1987 legislative session that would return Oregon to its original state motto but this time in English. At the end of that legislative session, Oregon had a new state motto: "She Flies With Her Own Wings." The beauty of the words, the image of soaring and independence, described my state of Oregon. It was an unusual accomplishment, but each time I repeat the words, they give me pleasure.

In 1999 a conservative Republican legislator, Kevin Mannix of Salem, tried to return to the state motto, "The Union." I was thrilled to find that, without my active leadership in Salem, the House of Representatives, under Republican control, had defeated the proposed legislation on a 30-30 vote with five Republican men joining every House Democrat to kill the Mannix effort. I guess one could say of this action, "She Flies With Her Own Wings."

Leadership Work beyond Elected Duties

In my years as Secretary of State I focused on the many responsibilities of my office: elections, audits, archives, Uniform Commercial Code filings, corporations, the state seal, public records, the regulation of notaries, the publication of the *Oregon Blue Book*, and the work of the State Land Board. I had over two hundred thirty employees and an overall budget of $15.6 million. It was a full platter! In addition to this list of agency and department responsibilities, I had a heavy public-speaking schedule throughout the entire state. I volunteered actively in advising and helping candidates during election season. I was also studying at Marylhurst, a small private university, writing academic challenge papers.

I also took on several other responsibilities tackling policy issues unrelated to my own office obligations. The two most demanding and complex of these assignments were both done at the request of Governor Goldschmidt. The first was as the chair of the Governor's Policy Advisory Group on Workers' Compensation that was formed even before Goldschmidt took office in January 1987. The second obligation was a four-year term I accepted in April of 1988 to become the vice-chair and the governor's representative on the newly created Hanford Nuclear Waste Board. Both of these assignments were highly technical and complex, and had the potential for serious controversy. They also represented new subject-matter areas for me. I needed to learn quickly. It would require some serious cramming to get prepared for these new responsibilities.

Oregon had one of the most expensive workers' compensation systems in the nation at that time. All previous discussions relating to reforming the system caused immediate head-to-head combat among labor members, business organizations, insurance companies, and trial lawyer groups. Middle ground may as well have been on

Mars! Governor Goldschmidt believed our best chance of developing any realistic reform was to assemble a broad-based, knowledgeable group, have them meet and work privately to avoid outside pressure, and, if we were successful, to use our recommendations as the first steps toward long-term reform. Crazily, the Governor wanted our report available for his review by the end of February, with the possibility it might lead to legislative action during the 1987 session. We were talking about a six- to eight-week turnaround on a subject that had eluded every other attempt at reform!

My committee included Senator Larry Hill from the Eugene area and Representative Bob Shiprack from Clackamas County, both well-placed pro-labor Democratic legislators. Karl Frederick, Vice-President and Director of Legislation for the powerful statewide Associated Oregon Industries, Jim Francesconi, successful Portland attorney, Steve Socotch, Secretary-Treasurer of the Oregon AFL-CIO, and Ted Kulongoski, newly appointed State Insurance Commissioner, made up the rest of the team.

The task force held its meetings in my office. Each committee member gave more than fifty hours of intensive, thoughtful, open-minded time to these meetings, and most spent extra time reading background research, workers' comp. reports, legal cases, and cost reports. We worked, thought aloud, compared reports, debated, and analyzed. We sought consensus on each of our recommendations to the Governor.

I presented the committee's initial report to Governor Goldschmidt the last week in February, and we made final recommendations on April 1, 1987. Once the Governor had examined our work, he sent a letter indicating his strong approval, stating, "You and your fellow task force members have accomplished what some thought was impossible. For the first time, representatives of the major interest groups involved in the workers' compensation issue have reached a consensus on what must be done to create a fair and affordable system. I congratulate you and wholeheartedly accept your recommendations. The task force has completed an historic accomplishment."

Our recommended amendments and changes progressed successfully through the 1987 legislative session. Oregon's workers' compensation costs dropped from the nation's third highest to the eighth highest in the country within just two years. The Governor later assembled a second committee to take the next reform steps, building on our committee's successful results. Oregon's strong new emphasis on workplace safety added support to the process and policy amendments of our committee and put our workers' compensation system on a road to improvement in terms of both cost containment and support to injured workers. I felt a real sense of success regarding my leadership on these improvements.

The second obligation I assumed was on the Hanford Nuclear Waste Board created by the 1987 Legislature. Fifty years of nuclear weapons waste and radioactive materials were stored at the Hanford "dump" on the Washington side of the Columbia River. The first meeting of the board was convened in the Capitol building on May 2, 1988. I made clear at the first meeting the Governor's priorities as well as my own strong views on the Hanford issue: "We must help the Oregon and Washington congressional delegations convince Congress to do three things: increase funding for the Hanford clean-up; direct the U.S. Department of Energy to adopt a work schedule to finish the clean-up in thirty years or less; and last, direct USDOE to provide and pay for our two states' oversight and involvement in nuclear weapons waste clean-up, transport, and disposal."

At a meeting of the U.S. Department of Energy held in Kennewick, Washington, in November, I said: "Oregonians are not amused that we may spend billions on Star Wars to protect us against nuclear warheads from the sky while a very real threat seeps toward the Columbia River. If you want a Hanford message from Oregon, hear this: Clean up the nuclear weapons waste at Hanford. Get that stuff away from the Columbia River, away from the local groundwater, and away from our people."

The more I learned, the more I understood about Hanford, the more frightening the information became. It seemed to be a silent nightmare putting the Northwest, its people, and its environment at growing risk. It would take decades and billions of dollars to make it safe—if indeed, we actually have the science to reach any realistic level of safety. Then—and now—I am not convinced that such a scientific level has been achieved. Sometimes humans become their own worst enemy.

New Responsibilities

As a new governor, Neil Goldschmidt proposed a number of changes as part of his "100 Day Agenda." He set out to reorganize several areas of state government. One of his early efforts was the complete dismantling of the Commerce Department; some of the "spill-over" from that redesign landed in my office — the Corporations Division, the State Board of Accountancy, and the State Board of Tax Examiners. I felt this 1987 action by Governor Goldschmidt, and the strong approval by the legislative assembly for these changes, indicated obvious approval regarding the professional level of administrative leadership being shown by my agency. These new responsibilities, now standing beside the approval of the new Archives Building and my expanded auditing authority, made it clear that I had earned the trust of the Legislature and the new governor. There was satisfaction in that knowledge.

Administration Reform

This final "success" story that I want to share is really not *my* success but rather the result of the leadership of my second Deputy Secretary of State, Marilynne Keyser (who had taken over in 1987 when Felicia Trader was offered a position with the City of Portland as Director of Transportation), and the cooperation and collaboration of the two-hundred-plus employees of my state agency.

Marilynne set out to analyze the divisions, departments, and boards under the agency's authority. From that point on, the agency would never be the same! Marilynne found that employees and even directors saw their roles *only* as they related to their own divisions. She found no sense that they were part of a cohesive organization with a common mission. There was no forum for interaction among the division directors. She felt the agency was lacking in innovation and creativity and was without a positive performance-appraisal process.

Within the first two years of Marilynne's tenure as deputy, the agency gained a highly functional new information technology system, a mission statement developed with the active participation of every single agency employee, a first-time management council with every division actively participating, a two-way (employee and supervisor) performance-evaluation system, and a new supervisory training program. Marilynne also worked closely with the management council to develop a centralized support services arm for the entire agency that was soon formally recognized as the Administrative Division of the Secretary of State's office.

Over the time of Marilynne's tenure as deputy, a number of employee task forces were created that addressed concerns in some complicated areas, including wellness, smoking, cultural diversity, and child care. Yet of all the issues and changes my office dealt with in those years, one of the most interesting and inspiring for me was the result of making several new employees feel at home in our agency. The new hires were recent alumni of the Oregon School for the Deaf. In addition to their hearing disability, they were also new to the work world. These young people were highly skilled at computer entry, an area where my agency had a heavy workload. Shortly before these new employees joined our agency ranks, we hired a faculty member from the state deaf school to teach signing to any agency employee who wished to participate in the classes. The response was thrilling to me. I joined my employees as a student, and together we began to learn the basics of sign language. Several of my agency employees became proficient at signing and were able to communicate easily with our new employees. After years of nonuse most of my own signing knowledge has slipped away. Yet my appreciation for the art of this special language remains with me today.

Change is so often difficult to create and even more difficult to accept. However, it was stimulating and satisfying to see the changes my administrative staff brought to this agency and the willingness of so many staff members to participate actively and to accept new roads for reaching our work destinations. It was gratifying then and remains so even today when I think back on these years and the people who made the agency a model of administrative success.

Professional Organizations

In the early months of my service as Secretary of State I received an invitation to become a member of an organization called Women Executives in State Government. In order to become a member, a woman must be either a statewide elected official, the chief of staff to a governor, or a cabinet member reporting directly to the governor. WESG was a group of very high-powered women with heavy responsibilities and broad-based political skills. They were Democrats, Republicans, and nonpartisans from almost every state in the nation, and I was being offered the opportunity to become part of this extraordinary group of women. I joined immediately.

You've certainly heard reference to the "Old Boys' Network." Well, WESG was the "NEW GIRLS' NETWORK" — in capital letters! I can't believe there was any other women's political or governmental organization in the nation at that time that could hold a candle to WESG. In 1985 there were only two seated women governors:

Martha Layne Collins, Democrat of Kentucky, and Madeleine Kunin, Democrat of Vermont. Just a handful of women, five, served in the Lieutenant Governors Association, eleven in the National Association of Secretary of States, eleven in the State Treasurers' Association, and a single female Attorney General served in that organization. There were, in fact, only forty-three statewide female "electeds" out of 323 positions nationwide. Women played a minor role in most of their respective national groups.

At the federal level in 1985 only two women were United States senators, Nancy Kassebaum of Kansas and Paula Hawkins of Florida, both Republicans. Out of 435 members of the U.S. House of Representatives, only twenty-three were women. Male domination of these national elected groups was quite obvious. WESG was definitely the exception.

Over the next years, I never attended a national meeting of WESG without coming away inspired, better informed, feeling supported, encouraged, and overstimulated! It was like having a whole conference full of mentors. We shared. We offered advice. We learned new skills from each other. These were some of the most powerful women in America, and their willingness to help each other crossed political party lines and state borders. I found it thrilling.

I made some wonderful friends in the years I was active in WESG. I had never, in my almost fifty years, been exposed to a group of women with more brains, more drive, more skill, and more fire-power! However, over the next ten years I certainly learned these same women were about more than power and politics. When Frank was first diagnosed with cancer, a number of these women called and wrote frequently, offering support and encouragement. I received their notes of congratulations when my granddaughter was born and flowers when Frank suffered a heart attack. Even when many of us eventually left WESG, we managed to stay connected for years. WESG was a magical link for an incredible group of women in a time of social and political transition in America.

In addition to this extraordinary network of women, WESG gave me another opportunity, a gift really, that positively influenced my life and my future. Every year the organization awarded three fellowships to prestigious leadership programs, including two at Harvard's Kennedy School of Government. In the early spring of 1989, as I began my second term as Secretary of State, I applied for one of those fellowships. They were valued at more than $6,000 and covered tuition, classes, and housing for an intensive three-week campus leadership experience. The competition for the awards was always highly active, but I felt I had a fair chance of securing one of them. Time would prove that supposition to be accurate. As you will read later, that fellowship and the Kennedy School experience changed my life.

Most of America's Secretaries of State have a number of responsibilities and departments in common, but this state office is also considered the one where duties and responsibilities vary the most from state to state. Thirty-nine states elect their Secretary of State, nine are appointed, three are chosen by the Legislature, and three states do not have the position.

Oregon's Secretary of State uniquely holds what would be considered *two* statewide offices simultaneously: Secretary of State and Lieutenant Governor. He or she serves next in succession to the governor should the governor die, leave office, or be unable to perform the duties of office. Because of this unusual state constitutional provision, Oregon's Secretary of State is eligible to become a member of the National Lieutenant Governors Association. So once I took office, I began attending the twice-annual meetings of both this organization and the National Association of Secretaries of State.

There is a *third* major role in Oregon's state constitution for our Secretary of State, who is also in charge of the State Audits Division. That combination makes the position in Oregon much more powerful than it is in most other states in the nation. In the state of Washington, for example, the voters elect their Secretary of State *and* their Lieutenant Governor *and* their State Auditor, three separate officials. Oregon gets three state positions for the price of one.

When I began attending the NLGA meetings, I found their membership's duties were all over the map. Some lieutenant governors worked as a team with their state's governor, since they were elected together on a ticket and had a shared political agenda. Other lieutenant governors might even belong to a different political party than their governor. A number were focused on economic development work. The lieutenant governor of Alaska was in charge of his state's Elections Department, duties usually performed by the Secretary of State. Some of them had no legally assigned duties or responsibilities and created a work agenda of their own choosing. My role was only that of "next in succession," so I had little reason to create an agenda beyond my full-time job responsibilities as Secretary of State.

When I was preparing to attend my first NLGA conference, one of my friends joked that I was going to spend two days learning how to take the governor's pulse! Pretty sick humor it seemed, but I must say, I met few lieutenant governors who didn't plan to "grow up" to be a governor. Interestingly, two research projects done by the NLGA, going all the way back to 1900, showed a consistent pattern: only 25 percent of governors had previously held the position of lieutenant governor in their state. For 75 percent of these, the "Lt." title was as close as most of these officeholders would ever come to being a governor. Yet, where there is a dream, there is always hope.

Attending two meetings annually of these three groups gave me six opportunities each year to meet statewide political leaders from every state in the nation. The conference speakers and programs were informational, stimulating, diverse, and often included senior members of each organization as presenters. I recognize that we have all heard negative remarks that such conferences are nothing more than "boondoggles," but I returned from these meetings with new information, with ideas to help me better manage my agency, and with a list of colleagues I could and did confer with from throughout the country. It was taxpayers' money well spent.

However in addition to learning, I was sometimes teaching in the election arena. I was frequently asked to share information related to the details of the Oregon experience with our state's first-in-the-nation vote by mail experiment. Our increased voter participation was a big positive, but a number of NASS members were concerned about potential election fraud if they duplicated Oregon's process. My detailed updates to the national membership certainly increased my visibility in the organization. It was that professional give and take from issue to issue at these national meetings that made them so valuable, so worthwhile.

When I arrived in Boston, Massachusetts, for the 1987 summer meeting of NASS, I had come with an agenda. I was prepared to make a presentation encouraging the group to come to Oregon for their 1988 summer meeting. I had scenic brochures showing the glory of our beaches, our forests, our wine country, and the city of Portland on the Willamette River. I had already secured Governor Goldschmidt's invitation to come to the governor's residence in

Salem for an outdoor dinner on the verandas and lawns of that lovely home. Even in a tough competitive situation, the Oregon proposal won a solid vote at that NASS meeting.

A year later I was excited to play host. The opening dinner at the governor's residence, Mahonia Hall, was a wonderful success. The weather was perfect, the food and Oregon wines were enthusiastically received, and the governor and his wife, Margie, were warm and charming. The one hundred fifty guests were unaware they were attending the first official function at Oregon's newly purchased governor's residence. I was thrilled to be able to give them that special treat. The rest of the meetings, workshops, and speakers took place in Portland. A number of people stayed after the conference to visit the Oregon coast, the Columbia River Gorge, and Oregon's vineyards and wineries. My sales work had evidently been successful, adding to the state's tourism business.

As mid-1988 approached, two big events were on my calendar. It was the year of my reelection and I could face both a primary and general election race. The second big event was the upcoming wedding of my son Mark and his fiancée, Susan.

Their wedding date was set for August 13. It was the perfect date for my family—my parents' fifty-third wedding anniversary. Mother and Dad were thrilled. The wedding was held in Susan's family church in the Southern Oregon town of Klamath Falls. I was planning a second reception in Portland for the next weekend because many friends and family were unable to attend the Klamath Falls ceremony nearly three hundred miles south of Portland.

Two wedding guests came all the way from California—Mark's dad and his wife, Karen. The wedding party and many of our family members were spending the three celebration days staying in a local motel. Neal and Karen were also staying at the same facility. I had worried about having the two of them come to the wedding, knowing I would be thrown into close proximity with them at rehearsals, meals, parties, and evening gatherings. I had dreaded finding myself in such uncomfortable situations. Yet I hadn't fully considered how different things were from when our marriage ended in 1971. I was feeling so successful and self-confident. I was happily remarried. I had a great hairstyle, had lost fifteen pounds, and had a classy wardrobe. I had a close, warm relationship with our two sons. *Plus,* I was Oregon's Secretary of State and was recognized every time we entered a restaurant, or store, or reception location. I wasn't the brokenhearted young wife he had left behind. I was an assured fifty-year-old woman with a wonderful husband and a promising political career. I could afford to be charming and warm, even forgiving. How sweet it was!

I relaxed and enjoyed the rest of the wedding activities. This weekend would start a new part of Mark's life. It also finally closed a once-painful chapter of my life. I believed, and hoped, each of these changes would be for the better.

As we moved into the late fall season, I thought back over my first four-year term as Secretary of State. So many memories, so many successes. I felt proud of my record and the performance of my entire agency. That record mattered. This was an election year for me, but I had no primary election opponent. In the general election my Republican opponent, John Shepard, was relatively unknown politically. During the fall campaign season, we appeared at several of the same venues, meetings, and debates. Honestly, he was such a nice man that I would rather have shared lunch with him than to have faced him as an election competitor. The final outcome of my reelection as Oregon Secretary of State was an impressive margin of victory, more than 2-to-1. In fact, I won a majority in every one of Oregon's thirty-six counties, a pretty unusual record for a Democrat in Oregon's more rural and conservative counties. I had worked hard to serve and connect with Oregonians statewide, and it had obviously paid off.

I was excited and ready for my second term. This could, in fact, be my last four years in public office, and I planned to work diligently and enjoy every day of serving the people of Oregon. What a privilege it had been and would continue to be for me.

CHAPTER FIFTEEN

Transitions: Public and Private

On the early afternoon of March 9, 1989, I received an excited call from my son Mark. He was taking his wife to Woodland Park Hospital with increasing labor pains. They had asked me to be present in the birth center room with them for the birth of their first child. I was excited and very nervous. I had only witnessed two births before— that of my two sons. This was definitely a much different perspective and experience.

I called my parents and my sister in Salem. They drove the fifty miles and took up residency in the more traditional waiting room with lots of coffee and pacing. My daughter-in-law was a real trooper during labor and the birth. I thought about the women of the past who had endured this process of pain and birth and understood I was privileged to witness the intimate experience of the birth of my first grandchild—especially as a mother-in-law of the birthing mother. I shed a few quiet tears as the birth grew closer.

Finally, at 9:11 p.m., the baby was here! Much to everyone's surprise, since our family usually produced boys, the baby was a little girl. Mark sent me to the waiting room to share the news with our family members. I started out excited and happy, but by the time I reached the waiting room I was bawling so hard I could barely deliver my wonderful message. "It's a girl! I have a granddaughter," I shouted while trying to gulp back tears. "She's beautiful," I added, "and everyone's fine." Suddenly my whole family was crying. These were tears of joy, but they were also a recognition that a new baby girl had not arrived in our family for a generation, not since my sister's daughter Kimberly Kay was born in 1962. That baby had died in a car accident at age two months. I knew some of the weeping was about that memory. I walked over and cradled my sister in my arms, delivering a message we both understood.

Then Mark arrived in the waiting room, accepting hugs and congratulations on the birth of his daughter, Kaitlin Rochelle. He was one proud papa!

As I noted in the previous chapter, early in 1989 I applied for the Women Executives in State Government fellowship to the Kennedy School of Government at Harvard University. The Harvard program was costly, and I knew that without the fellowship support I would be hesitant to apply. Once my application was mailed, I would have to wait about two months regarding the decision on the fellowship. Next there would follow another month or so to see if the Kennedy School accepted me to their state and local government summer program.

By May of 1989 I had received both acceptances! I was thrilled. I was going to Harvard! Frank was almost as excited as I was. He knew this would be a stimulating experience for me: three weeks in campus housing at the Harvard Business School; three weeks of Harvard professors pushing leadership concepts and policy. It was an academic opportunity unlike any in my life.

In early July, I stepped onto a flight to Boston. I had read, more than once, my Harvard cases for the first two days of classes. I had scanned the biographical sketches for the sixty-plus fellow members of my upcoming class. They were legislators, mayors, state agency directors, county department heads, a small number of statewide elected officials, and even one nonprofit president. The first week's schedule was included in my materials. It was stunning in terms of expectations, from early morning through the dinner period. It included Saturday classes and hours of reading every night. I took my seat on the plane feeling some anxiety about the next three weeks. I hoped I was up to this academic challenge.

Well, truthfully, I need not have worried about my classroom skills and ability. I did well. However, much more important, I found the Harvard faculty stimulating, brilliant, challenging, thought-provoking. I was having a truly remarkable experience. It was far more than I had anticipated. As the first week of classes drew to a close, I became aware of a subtle change in the classroom. Out of more than sixty class members, five or six began to be treated as leaders by their fellow students. I was one of that select group. When the Harvard professors pushed the class for answers, the class turned to us for leadership. It happened again and again. I finally began to understand. In this room full of leaders from across the nation, I had risen to leadership among my peers. I would take the risk of challenging a professor. I could analyze quickly and articulate ideas. I could move others to my position in a debate. I had spent years developing these skills, and now they were apparent in this academic setting.

This may sound strange in telling it now, but I was fifty-three years old, twice elected statewide as Secretary of State, and I did not understand I was a leader. Oh, I recognized my hard work and skills plus the importance of the office I held; however, that is not the same as seeing oneself as a leader. The State and Local Government Program changed my understanding about who I had become and how others saw me. It was a life-changing revelation!

By the time I finished the three-week program at Harvard, I had gained several important assets. First was this newfound understanding of my leadership. Second was a set of tools for governing that are an amazing product of the Kennedy School of Government. I also had a new collection of academic heroes who taught at the Kennedy School: Faculty Chair Mark Roberts, Dutch Leonard, former Massachusetts legislator Marty Linsky, Jan Shubert, Chris Letts, Dan Fenn, formerly with the Kennedy White House, and Robert Reich, who would later serve as Secretary of Labor in the Clinton Administration. And finally, I gained two lifelong friends. Amy Dienesch Coen, who was the executive director of the huge Chicago-area Planned Parenthood, was a tall, vivacious, and gregarious redhead who always seemed to live life fully. She was my roommate in the dorm and one of the other class leaders. We bonded almost immediately and remain close friends to this day.

My second new friend was a member of the program staff, Persis Whitehouse. She was in charge of making certain that housing, meals, materials, and scheduling worked flawlessly for the entire three weeks. It is no easy chore to keep over sixty executive types happy and working for such an extended time. She was a master at the role. Persis was a person I didn't want to lose track of. Six years later our friendship would become much more important in my life in a role I could not yet imagine.

What I am about to say here sounds like a commercial on television for a sleep-number bed or a magic diet supplement, but, in fact, the Kennedy School program changed my self-image, my life goals, and my future.

I returned home with the first truly serious thoughts about running for governor. My second term as Secretary of State would end at the close of 1992, and the state constitution would not permit me to seek the office again. I began a quiet self-conversation about a run for governor in 1994.

I was working toward finishing my bachelor's degree as a communications major. For the past two years, I had been in a program at Marylhurst College that permitted me to earn college credits by limited classroom attendance and the writing of academic papers that demonstrated my knowledge base in a variety of academic areas. These papers basically challenged college courses; if my writing proved my strong knowledge and experience in the given area, I was awarded the credits by my advisers and related faculty. My plan was to continue my work on these academic challenge papers until my term in office ended in three years. By that time, combining these new credits with my old but still transferable Portland State credits, I should need about a final year in the classroom to complete my degree. That done, I would be ready to run for governor. It seemed a fine plan. My time at Harvard made it seem slightly less crazy!

I finally shared my thinking with Frank. He had listened to all my wonderful Harvard stories and had clearly witnessed my excitement plus my expanded thinking on leadership. He was not really surprised when I confessed my new political goal. I understood it was a long time from 1989 until a potential race for governor in 1994. For now, it would be more a dream than a plan. Maybe once the excitement generated by my time at Harvard had settled down, I would reevaluate this dream and find it less plausible. Realistically, only a handful of women had been elected governor in the nation's entire history.

In the meantime, the work at my agency continued. With the 1989 Legislature's approval of the funding for the new Archives Building, the architects had begun the next phase of construction-design development. It would be a complex but exciting period as we moved toward construction in 1990. Preparations for our next performance audit were in the works, and we were making plans to establish a permanent performance auditing group with interdisciplinary skills. 1990 was an election year, and that always meant hundreds of decisions and details. My speaking schedule continued to be heavy and kept me traveling across the state. I certainly had more than enough responsibilities to fill my professional life.

Plus, I was also having a fun time as a new grandmother. Katie was almost six months old when I returned from Harvard at summer's end. She was so darling and bright-eyed. After raising two sons, it was an extra treat to buy frilly little pink outfits. I was discovering this grandparenting gig was as special as I had always heard. My life, professional and personal, was totally satisfying.

However, I would also like to share with you a seldom-discussed matter that affects many of us who serve in public office. It is a complex dichotomy between our public life and our private challenges. It is not unique to elected officials but may be exacerbated in our case.

During the six years I served as Secretary of State I experienced, like many Americans in their fifties, the challenges of what is often labeled as the "Sandwich Generation." I was sandwiched between my children, who were in their twenties and struggling to make their way in the adult world as many young people do, and parents in their seventies with some health issues, retired and living on social security.

However, my personal life was further complicated by two other factors. My older son, Mike, still required both financial and personal support from me. Although he was settled into his part-time position at Mt. Hood Community College, being autistic meant Mike needed some supervision and help. The second was one that did not come as a complete surprise, in one sense, but was nonetheless emotional and challenging. I understood when Frank and I married that choosing a husband who was twenty-one years my senior might mean I could one day become his caregiver. My father raised this question with me privately when Frank and I announced our engagement. I remember replying to him, "Daddy, I understand that risk but I would rather have one good decade with Frank than a lifetime with someone else." I would recall those words many times once that "healthy" decade ended and Frank's serious medical issues surfaced. Those first challenging years coincided with my term as Secretary of State.

On December 21 of 1984, just before I began that term, I celebrated my forty-eighth birthday. A week later, Frank turned sixty-nine. As far as we knew, we were both in good health, full of energy, and looking forward to our public office responsibilities. But before my six years as Secretary of State came to a close, Frank had twice been diagnosed with cancer, had major back surgery, experienced a heart attack, undergone a quadruple heart bypass, lost the use of both legs, and been confined to a wheelchair. Believe me, this kind of worry and stress is not recommended for the graceful aging process for either patient or caregiver.

Frank's first cancer diagnosis in 1987 was advanced prostate cancer. It was summertime and he was sailing in the San Juan Islands. I was in Boston attending the summer conference of the National Association of Secretaries of State when I got Frank's call. He had spoken to his doctor by phone earlier in the day to get the results of tests and a physical exam from the prior week. Frank was calm when he called, and I tried hard to follow his lead. He would simply sail for a few more days then moor the boat and drive back to Portland. I would fly home and be there to do the next medical appointment with him. His calmness and confidence made it unthinkable to believe he wouldn't survive the cancer. At that point, neither of us would have accepted the thought that Frank would never again be well enough to be the captain of his sailboat. But the unthinkable happened.

Frank started a lengthy series of radiation treatments that summer, and grew very weak. He lost his appetite and consequently lost a great deal of weight. His color turned ashen. He was aging right before my eyes. Once the treatment ended, Frank came to Salem to stay with me in the small condo I had purchased after my election. He was still feeling pretty frail, and I didn't want him staying alone in our Portland home.

We were all expecting Frank to regain his strength and return to his normal activities. However, he did not get better. He began to experience pain in both legs and the pain intensified as the days passed. It was finally determined that he had a pinched nerve in his back. He underwent back surgery to relieve the pressure on the nerve. The surgery did not help. The pain grew worse. The non-technical way to describe what happened to Frank went like this: A nerve center in his lower spine had been damaged by the extensive radiation treatments. The nerves in both legs were "dying." It was like a toothache when a cavity exposes a nerve; each of the nerves in Frank's legs and feet was "exposed" and dying. The pain was constant and intense. There was no relief for the pain. We consulted two pain specialists. We talked about surgical options. The pain experts were helpful. The surgical options were far too extreme. The pain grew worse, as did Frank's depression.

As Frank began to lose further control of the muscles in his legs, I didn't feel he could be alone during the time I was at the office. He went to stay, during the daytime hours, at my sister's home across town. She installed a hospital bed in her living room right in front of the large picture window. She cooked for Frank, helped him to the bathroom, and kept him company. After each work day I would pick Frank up and transport him back to the condo. I was exhausted. So was my sister. Frank's depression became a growing concern for me.

One Saturday I returned home to the condo from a very brief grocery store run. At this point I never left pain medications, kitchen knives, or razors within Frank's now-limited reach when I left him alone. Yet, regardless of those precautions, I always grew anxious to get home and be sure he was safe. As I walked into the condo I found Frank seated on the sofa rather than in his usual sleeping position. His

Frank and me on our sailboat, the Ship of State.

hair was brushed, and he had on a clean shirt. I couldn't believe it!

Suddenly both of us were in tears. I was so relieved to see this change, and he had a big decision to share with me. "Honey," Frank began, with tears streaming down his cheeks, "I don't want to die. I can't stop the pain but I finally recognized today that I want to live. I hurt no matter what I do so I may as well be doing something I like."

I was on my knees, kneeling before him, holding his face in my hands and trying not to bump his pain-sensitive legs. As I wiped his tears away and cried my own tears of joy, I made him a promise. "If you'll make this painful commitment to live, I will do everything possible to bring your life back to a place of quality. We will remodel the condo to make it accessible and easy for you. We will buy one of those motorized carts to give you as much flexibility and mobility as possible. We'll go to work every day together in the Capitol even on days you don't have to work. We can go out to dinner together again.

We can learn how to handle the changes in our life. I want you to live as long and as well as you can. I need you and love you. Don't leave me when we have a choice about our future together."

Frank's earlier heart attack and by-pass surgery had been difficult. Yet that surgery had been about getting better, getting well. Frank's cancer ordeal had, by this time, become about getting worse, about long-term pain and deterioration, about losing hope. Now we had both rediscovered hope, mixed with big changes, but hope nonetheless.

Let me now put this in context with my *public* life. When you are a public officeholder, particularly on the statewide level, there are expectations. You show up where you are scheduled. You deliver speeches you have committed to. You are properly dressed and well groomed. You are friendly, attentive, prepared. You do press interviews and attend meetings. You read reports and take public positions on state issues. No one asks how your older parents are getting along or if your children are meeting all their bills. No one offers to do your grocery shopping, get your clothes to the cleaners, make your dental appointments, or take your car in for servicing. Folks assume you have staff—or at least a wife—to do all those things. That said, my years as Secretary of State came with challenges far beyond those easy chores.

Certainly no one ever asked if my husband's health was so horrible that he was suicidal and how was I handling that. No one asked what a motorized wheelchair cost and how much it weighed every time I lifted it in or out of the car trunk. No one really thought about why Frank had to eventually rent an apartment in his legislative district to seek reelection when we had a big house only ten blocks from the apartment. (Residency in the district was required but our Portland house had only upstairs bedrooms and steps at every entrance.) No one asked if having a house payment, an apartment lease, and a condo payment might be stretching finances a little tight. No one wondered how many times I cried privately as I adjusted to my healthy strong husband giving up sailing for life in a wheelchair. No one wondered what else we both gave up.

Each of us, in our life, must make adjustments, face changes. Some of them are done privately, some are more public. You often hear people comment that running for public office means giving up your privacy. While there is some truth to that, there is a flip side to that old adage. You present yourself to the public by trying to put your best foot forward or maybe, more accurately, putting your best face forward. Yet sometimes a public person has a private life so challenging that holding it private is done at real personal cost. I certainly learned that in my tenure as Secretary of State. We survived it, both Frank and I, and felt we came through it stronger, more compassionate, with a new view of life, and an even more committed marriage.

I look back on those years with an understanding of the importance of good health that I had never appreciated before. Frank's heart bypass taught me what it means to bring medical science, skilled surgical ability, and highly professional post-surgical care together to return a patient to health. I came to understand that pain can be more debilitating than most other medical losses. I learned what the term "major medical care" meant in terms of coverage and choices. Frank's Medicare coverage and his being a Kaiser patient offered him medical support and options not available to millions of Americans in today's health care crisis situation. Finally, I learned that in times of medical crisis, people who care can mean everything. My sister, Pat, stepped up to offer help and care at a time when Frank and I both needed support. The medical professionals who worked with us were wonderful. But I couldn't have personally begun to get Frank to every medical appointment he had over those years. I called on and depended upon our friends, family, and Frank's staff for dozens and dozens of those appointments. It would have been impossible otherwise.

So the next time you see one of those so-called public figures at a luncheon or a meeting or even on television, take a good look at that public face and wonder if the private life you don't see may include some personal challenges met with some highly perfected coping skills. Just in case, give them an inch and send a little compassion their way. It just can't hurt.

CHAPTER SIXTEEN

Short Notice, Tall Order

One of my most remarkable life changes came as a brief telephone call on a Sunday evening. It was February 4, 1990. Frank and I were home at our Salem condo. We had an overnight houseguest visiting. The three of us had just finished dinner and were savoring a glass of wine and stimulating conversation. When the telephone rang I reluctantly left the room and took the call in the bedroom. I wanted to avoid interrupting the animated discussion. It turned out to be fortunate that I was in a separate room where no one could see the expression on my face as the caller spoke.

"Barbara, this is Neil Goldschmidt," he began. "I have something important I need to share with you." When your Governor begins a conversation with such demanding words, you are immediately on the alert. The Governor continued, "I want you to know there is a very strong likelihood that I will not be running for reelection. I will announce my decision in the next couple of days. I wanted to give you a heads-up." I slowly sat down on the edge of the bed, trying to formulate a response. Hardly pausing, the Governor went on. "This is obviously confidential. I just wanted you to know right away what my likely plans are. Hey, I've got to run. It's half-time of the Blazers game and I don't want to miss the beginning of the third quarter. I'll be in touch with your office tomorrow."

I stammered a sentence or two of regret and surprise and then he was gone. The whole telephone conversation had lasted less than two minutes. I stayed seated on the bed trying to catch my breath. "Inhale, exhale," I told myself. Another few seconds passed and then I stood and headed for the living room to drop a bombshell on Frank and our houseguest. Talk about stimulating after-dinner conversation! I swore them to secrecy, and then we proceeded to talk rapid-fire for the next two hours. I just kept shaking my head in disbelief. I had been catapulted onto a roller coaster of instant tough choices, list making, secrecy, and excitement.

The Governor's tone left little question in my mind that his decision to drop out of the race was all but made. I didn't believe he would have made the call to me otherwise. I wondered if he had called any other potential candidates. My sense was that this might have been his only such call.

Truthfully, most other Oregon Democrats were not looking at this election year as an opportunity to become governor. As the March filing deadline neared, Neil was unopposed by other Democrats for several reasons: He was the incumbent governor of our own party. He was a highly respected political mover and shaker with the ability to raise big political funds. Any Democrat who challenged him was likely to lose. However, if by some miracle they defeated Goldschmidt, they would still face Republican Attorney General Dave Frohnmayer in the fall election … not very appealing political odds for any Democratic challenger.

Dave Frohnmayer had been Attorney General for ten years. He was a well-respected, moderate Republican from a prominent Oregon family. He was well educated, pleasant, with an attractive wife and children and few political enemies. He had already been in the race for a year and was rumored to have raised a million dollars this early in the campaign. Not very fertile territory for a Democratic challenger. Dave was expected to be a formidable opponent for Goldschmidt.

Yet I also knew an opportunity like this rarely comes along. I was mid-term in my current position as Secretary of State. If I ran and lost, I would still hold that office for two more years. If I ran a creditable race and made a decent showing, such added visibility would greatly enhance my political position and public image for the future. On the other hand, I had little interest in making this huge effort with the expectation of losing. If I ran, I wanted to win.

I slept restlessly that night, but in spite of the lack of a good night's sleep, I awoke energized and ready for action. Between that Monday and Thursday, believe me, *action* was the name of the game!

I knew I needed to call my trusted staffer, Patricia McCaig, first thing. Her political reaction and advice felt essential. Unfortunately, she was out of the office for a week of moving, painting, unpacking. I understood I was about to throw a major kink into her carefully organized week's schedule. But she stopped her moving activities and arranged emergency meetings with longtime supporters and friends to discuss next possible choices and steps. Donnella helped me rearrange my entire calendar and clear all the pending work on my desk. The Governor's office called asking for my next four days' schedule.

Tuesday my support team from my last two elections met with Patricia to hear the confidential surprise news about Governor Goldschmidt and my possible run. The meeting resulted in strong support for me to make the run if Neil withdrew. I was already 95 percent certain I would enter the race, but the confidence of my "kitchen cabinet" pushed me over the 100 percent mark.

At a press conference on Wednesday, February 7, Governor Neil Goldschmidt shocked Oregon by announcing he would not seek reelection. The public, the press, politicians, and pundits were all caught totally off guard. He told Oregonians that a trial separation after twenty-five years of marriage meant he needed to focus on his children and private life, not on a reelection campaign. At the time, I privately speculated that the polling numbers released by *The Oregonian* in late 1989 showing Frohnmayer slightly ahead of the Governor may have played a larger than acknowledged role in his decision to leave the race. Little could I have imagined that almost fifteen years later, a sex scandal from the past would emerge regarding Goldschmidt and a fourteen-year-old girl. That long-held secret could well trace back to his *actual* reason for withdrawing from the campaign.

When that sex abuse scandal hit the press on May 7, 2004, Oregon was stunned. The entire state learned that Goldschmidt had had an illicit sexual relationship with a fourteen-year-old neighborhood girl while he was mayor of Portland in the 1970s. Once Goldschmidt met with *The Oregonian* editorial board and delivered his emotional confession, newspapers and media statewide retold the details for days. Goldschmidt acknowledged that the threat of exposure of that long-held secret was "certainly a factor" in his 1990 decision to drop out of his reelection bid.

Yet, whatever the actual reason or reasons for his surprising 1990 political decision, Governor Goldschmidt was no longer a candidate for reelection.

Twenty-four hours later, on Thursday, we capped off a remarkable four days with a press conference announcing my candidacy for Governor of Oregon. In the Secretary of State's office, surrounded by my entire family and many close friends and supporters, I delivered my prepared remarks to a full turnout of press and media.

I began, "Today, I am announcing my candidacy for Governor of Oregon. This was a statement I had hoped to make in 1994.

My press conference to announce my candidacy for Governor. From Portland State University Collection.

Governor Goldschmidt's announcement yesterday has not changed my goal ... it has simply changed my timetable." I went on to note my experience and qualifications and my goal—" the same one that brought me into government twenty years ago ... my belief that I can make a difference for people." When I finished speaking, the assembled audience applauded enthusiastically. I felt satisfied with the prepared remarks and elated by my strong delivery. It was a first important step in my brand-new campaign. Hopefully, all the steps that would follow would be equally effective.

When Patricia opened the press conference for questions from the press and media, I awaited inquiries about major state policy matters. (After all, I was running for governor.) However, the first press question came from a completely different direction. "Secretary Roberts, you are often described as a liberal. Is that an accurate label?"

Well, there is a lot to say about being well prepared for the unexpected. *This* was my answer to the question: "The dictionary defines liberal as tolerant and open-minded, a person favoring progress and reform. If you are asking me if that describes my philosophy and leadership, the answer is, yes." I was never asked that particular question again in the entire campaign. If I was going to be labeled, I was definitely going to define the label!

When the press conference ended, it was hugs and smiles all around from my assembled supporters. Mother and Dad were beaming, although my father had tears in his eyes every time I looked his way. Frank and I shared a kiss several times as I circulated in my office. He seemed so proud and happy. My sister, Pat, looking extra beautiful that day, said as I embraced her, "Here we go again, Sis." My two sons and my daughter-in-law, Frank's family, all of them were excited. My friend Terry Bean gave me a big supportive wink each time I caught his eye. Yet in spite of all those smiles and the obvious enthusiasm, the words "tough" and "challenging" arose often in the passing conversations. Even my most ardent supporters had little illusion regarding the mountain I would struggle to climb in the next nine months.

Later in the day, I met one of the Governor's longtime Portland supporters in the Capitol corridor. I will never forget her remark as she *glowered* in my direction: "You could have at least waited until the body was cold!" I was shocked at both the remark and the venom in her reaction. Perhaps she felt I had not been respectful enough of the Governor. Likely, she was in mourning for a promising leadership career that seemed to be coming to an end. However, for me, the Governor's private call on Sunday meant he had some expectation for me to act—hence the "heads-up." So, without comment, I walked on down the Capitol corridor headed for a yet-uncertain destination.

Within the next few hours, Oregonians began choosing up sides in the race for Oregon governor. Three of my earliest supporters were members of Oregon's federal delegation: Congressmen Les AuCoin, Peter DeFazio, and Ron Wyden. Governor Goldschmidt publicly called me "the best Democratic candidate" and made clear that day that he would support me. State Representative Peter Courtney of Salem, who would one day serve several terms as Oregon Senate President, added one of my favorite lines of support: "I think there will be a tendency to underestimate Barbara. Her smile and personality mask her toughness."

However, on the other side of the aisle, U.S. Senator Bob Packwood of Oregon said, "I think it means that Dave Frohnmayer wins the governorship." Other Republicans agreed that Frohnmayer had now emerged as the clear favorite. The Republican leadership began immediately trying to cast doubts on my "hasty" announcement. State GOP Chairman Craig Berkman said he thought I was "doing it more for political reasons rather than thinking through the ramifications of the job." Berkman went on to add, "I'm surprised how quickly she made such an important decision. It almost seems a little crass." Funny how I could have served next-in-succession to two governors for over five years without thinking through the ramifications of that job! *The Oregonian* in its coverage of my announcement made several interesting observations. They referred to my family and supporters surrounding me at the press conference as "a hurriedly assembled group." It sounded as if I might have collected strangers from the Capitol parking lot!

On the same day as my big announcement, Patricia took a leave of absence from my Secretary of State's staff and assumed the role of campaign director for my new race. With this very late entry into the governor's race and only a little over $11,000 in my campaign coffers, several matters became instantly clear. We had to put fundraising on the top of our priority list; we didn't yet have the resources to rent a campaign headquarters facility; we definitely needed to reach out to long-term supporters, friends, and family, to find volunteers, the up-front cash, and some borrowed office space until we had our campaign act together. By the following Monday we were temporarily housed in two rooms in the law offices of Frank's daughter Leslie Roberts and her two partners, Frank Josselson and Irv Potter. We had our very first campaign volunteer, Bob Weil, ready to help with early staffing needs. And a stranger walked into our temporary office with a $1,000 check on that Monday morning, our first *official* campaign contribution.

It was February 12, and I was a candidate for Governor! In just over a month I would know if I had a Democratic challenger. I had nine months to put an entire campaign together, raise the huge funding necessary to support a statewide race, convince hundreds of Oregonians across the state to volunteer in my campaign efforts, and win debates, editorial endorsements, the support of unions, businesses, educational organizations, environmentalists, and national political groups. Plus I had to win a majority of votes from Oregon's almost 1.5 million registered voters. And those were just the *obvious* challenges!

Policy papers. Television ads. Polling. Strategic planning. Printed materials. Speeches. Statewide travel. Press conferences. Radio interviews. Staffing. Issue development. This would have been a tough job even in a two-year time-frame. In a mere nine months, it would be like running a marathon at a one hundred-yard-dash pace. So — we put on our running shoes and stepped onto the track!

I wasn't given much of a chance of winning that 1990 election. Entering the race so late against a strong, popular opponent who had been organizing for months — this was not likely to produce a victory for me. Becoming Oregon's first woman governor, knowing that both Betty Roberts (D) in 1974 and Norma Paulus (R) in 1986 had lost in their attempts to become Oregon Governor — this was not promising. Understanding that only five women in the United States had ever been elected governor "in their own right" in the country's history — these were pretty poor odds.

I have, over the years, described this as a race that only my dad and my husband *really* believed I would win. Not my mother, my sons, not even my campaign manager believed it was a winnable race. They weren't saying this out loud, but I knew. And the truth was, it wasn't far from reality in early 1990. Democrats thanked me for stepping forward and carrying the party banner into the governor's race. Often their tone made it sound as if I was carrying a white flag rather than the Democrats' pennant.

Yet, I'd been underestimated before ... by the press, by my opponents, by the good old boys. I was far more than a good sport for taking on this race. I was a good candidate! I felt no one in Oregon could outwork me on the campaign trail. I have always been high energy and that's a valuable commodity in a political campaign. I love people and am stimulated by meeting and talking with all kinds of citizens. Another asset: I knew Oregon well and was familiar with state government and its issues, budgets, and controversies. Of course, it would be a tough race, but I wasn't starting at ground zero. I was an energetic, skilled public leader, and I intended to make that clear over the next nine months. I thought back to my time at Harvard's Kennedy School, only the previous summer, and recalled my leadership "awakening." Now I would fully test that new confidence, drive, and self-image. I would also learn, soon enough, if that leadership self-identification was mine alone or was reflected in the eyes and attitudes of Oregon citizens.

The campaign started short on the money end and the staffing level, and without a campaign plan. Yet those were challenges where we would work diligently and constantly to close the gap. However, there was another huge gap that we identified early in the race. In a head-to-head political poll commissioned by my campaign, Dave

Frohnmayer was 22 percentage points ahead of me. A 22-point lead is a "Grand Canyon gap" in a major race! This was clearly a number we did not want in the press or even in the rumor mill. We held those numbers so close to our chest that they began to feel like a tattoo!

We had to *move* those numbers as early as possible. It was not simply important to get a turnaround by the election date on November 6th, though that was, of course, essential. We also knew that *The Oregonian* would conduct a poll and release polling numbers on the Labor Day weekend for all the high-profile races and ballot measures. If we could not close that gap in a meaningful way by Labor Day, our support and fundraising would quickly dry up, leaving us out in the cold, politically.

With that understanding, Patricia made a major policy decision: of every dollar that came into the campaign, fifty cents would go into the media account and could not be spent for any other campaign expenses. Fifty cents of every dollar. Without a viable and visible television and media purchase, I could not compete in the race for governor. Fifty cents of every dollar was held for that purchase. Every dollar! No exceptions! It would turn out to be *one-half* of a brilliant Patricia McCaig strategy.

On filing day in March, I did not have a single Democratic challenger. One could surmise that I was either that strong or that popular in my party — or reflect that every other Democrat in the state saw the 1990 race as a futile run against an unbeatable Republican candidate. I like to think that my move to announce immediately on the heels of Governor Goldschmidt's withdrawal kept other candidates from taking a stab at the race simply to gain name familiarity or have a podium for a single issue that they felt needed airing. Whichever the case, I could immediately focus on the November race with few distractions regarding the May primary election. The one exception was that Frank had to fight a primary campaign, but *The Oregonian* had named Frank the area's most diligent senator at the close of the 1989 session, and we both felt confident of his reelection. I just hoped my run for governor would not cause any problems or confusing press stories for Frank in his campaign.

Interestingly, Attorney General Frohnmayer found himself in a Republican field of *seven* candidates running for governor. With the exception of locally prominent businessman John Lim, from Gresham, the other five challengers were considered "also-ran" opponents. Yet these six Republican men would use up some time and resources until Dave, as expected, would win the May Republican primary.

Patricia continued pulling together a strong staff for our now-expanding campaign efforts. The campaign was fortunate to grab Kevin Smith, who was just leaving Congressman Les AuCoin's Washington D.C. staff, as Legislative Director. Kevin wanted to move back home to Oregon and Patricia and I jumped at the chance to bring his expertise into our newly forming staff. I was dividing my time between fundraising, travel, speeches, keeping tabs on my Secretary of State responsibilities.

Several months before I even entered the race, the issue that would dominate the campaign was already brewing. In fact, this was a political, policy, and economic issue that would be paramount on the Oregon scene for at least the next decade. Battles in Congress and the courts were mounted to seriously curtail logging in old-growth forests in the Northwest. Legislation to stop or tax international log exports was pushed hard in an attempt to create domestic processing in Oregon and Washington lumber mills and discourage harvest and clear-cutting in the millions of acres of federal forest lands in the region.

The likely upcoming listing of the Northern Spotted Owl as a threatened species under the federal Endangered Species Act (ESA) brought these issues into sharp and controversial focus. This was not an ESA listing that might close a small lake in some state. This listing had the potential to economically devastate Oregon's largest industry. Oregon political leaders were looking for answers, short-cuts, alternatives ... and cover!

U.S. Senator Bob Packwood became a vocal spokesman against the listing of the spotted owl and any curtailing of timber harvest levels; he also started working on a federal waiver process (referred to as the God Squad) to obtain a possible but rarely allowed exception under the ESA provisions. Packwood took the lead for a huge timber rally in downtown Portland in mid-April where as many as ten thousand demonstrators from timber communities gathered to protest the spotted owl listing. In many timber communities, schools were closed for the day and employers closed mills and furnished buses to allow workers and their families to attend the rally. My opponent in the governor's race, Frohnmayer, spoke before the huge rally calling for legal hearings to "test the science" of the federal spotted owl report. The crowd cheered his remarks. Protests signs reading "Kiss My Axe" and "I love spotted owls … fried!" were shown on television stations at 6 p.m., 8 p.m., and the 11 o'clock evening news. The tone for the issue was definitely set on high volume!

As if this issue weren't already heated enough, the Northwest Forestry Association invited the two major candidates for governor to speak at their April conference in Portland. These were the first major speeches on timber policy delivered by Frohnmayer and myself. They were scheduled for the day following the release of the federal report on the spotted owl and its required habitat. That scientific panel had recommended creating 8.4 million acres of spotted owl reserve in Oregon, Washington, and California, where logging would be banned. In that climate, I stepped to the podium to deliver my timber policy presentation to the timber industry leaders of my state.

I attempted to set a historical and factual background for how we had reached this crisis stage. I cited a 1936 research study done by Oregon State College that indicated that decades of over-harvesting without replanting Oregon forests meant we were moving toward a crisis in our forests. The 1936 report concluded that if major reductions in harvesting, followed by replanting, did not begin soon, within fifty years the Oregon timber industry would be devastated. "Well, here we are fifty-four years later." Obviously, that study was shelved and the industry chose to favor more immediate profits over long-term asset conservation.

I pointed out that the spotted owl was not the culprit but rather the indicator species relating to the long-term choices made by the industry. Now that the federal government had listed the Northern Spotted Owl, I felt the industry in Oregon had the best chance of influencing our state's harvest plans by working with the federal scientists and agencies rather than attempting legal challenges that would put us in court for years without a resolution or a species recovery plan. Tough as it was for our timber communities, our workers, and the industry, I felt we had to face reality. I added the sentence, "We must play the hand we've been dealt." That one sentence would plague me for the next several years as the spotted owl controversy remained front and center. However, one of my strong positive lines from that speech made the press and media for several days. When Frohnmayer called for an "evidentiary hearing" on the scientific committee's report, and Sen. Mark Hatfield (R) and

Congressman Les AuCoin (D) rejected that route as impractical and even counterproductive, Dave looked indecisive and overly cautious. I countered, pointing out the dangers of additional delay, "My God, the patient is bleeding to death and he wants a second opinion!"

It was quite clear that the timber/spotted owl controversy would have a major impact on the 1990 governor's race. I tried not to focus on the historical fact that for about a hundred years no Oregon Governor had been elected without the support of our state's timber industry. I kept trying to bring the facts to light and show that the anti-owl rhetoric would get us nowhere. I criticized Frohnmayer for trying to exploit the timber crisis for political gain while he clearly knew that this crisis went "deeper than the spotted owl."

On April 18th, Willamette Week newspaper released a new poll with the headline "Frohnmayer Increases Lead Over Roberts." The numbers were 43 to 34 percent. Two weeks later, on May 3, an *Oregonian* story had Dave at 50 percent, me at 38 percent. The poll numbers were discouraging, yet I knew Dave was running a $300,000 ad campaign and doing extensive direct mail since he was in a seven-person May primary race. My campaign was still husbanding our limited resources to focus on the November race.

When the voters' pamphlet arrived for the May primary election at every Oregon home, we quickly compared my page with the entry of my major Republican opponent, Dave Frohnmayer. My full page looked very good. I was happy with the smiling photo we had chosen. The final bold-type statement read: "Barbara Roberts — A Governor for All Oregonians." Dave's photo was pleasant but quite unanimated. No bold-type headlines stood out. His page was well written but with so much type and very little white space, it was not terribly inviting. I felt we had done a superior planning job of presenting my message to Oregon voters. Even small wins feel good in a tough political campaign!

A few days before the primary election, *The Oregonian* ran the first major story on the fundraising totals in the governor's race. Dave had raised, by then, $1.6 million. I had raised $472,000. I had been in the race for three months. Frohnmayer had been fundraising for over a year. The story pointed out, however, that Frohnmayer had $504,000 cash left in the bank while my bank balance was $281,000. That felt a lot closer. Yet — it's a long way from May to November!

That sounded like a song title, but I didn't yet feel like humming along!

Our campaign was working twenty-four/seven on fundraising. We had been quite successful with a number of labor unions and with the women's community. By the final primary election report, we had contributions of $596,000. We now faced the final five months until the November election and had to more than match our primary fundraising rate.

When the primary election votes were counted, I had won my uncontested Democratic nomination for governor, and Frank had also won his contested primary, more than doubling the votes of his nearest challenger. Frohnmayer had won the Republican nomination in spite of over sixty thousand votes being split among his six challengers. Frank's daughter Mary Wendy Roberts had won both the Democratic and Republican nomination for State Commissioner of Labor. The stage was set for the general election in November.

It was way more than apparent that the timber controversy would quickly transition from the May primary election to the fall campaign. A June 21 *Oregonian* story quoted a recent statement of mine: "We had a timber problem long before anyone other than a few biologists had even heard of the spotted owl. Mill jobs had been declining for several years. The state needs to end raw log exports and retool its mills to handle second-growth trees and also to manufacture more finished products. We need to use higher timber taxes to help retrain workers and provide grants for sawmills to retool." I was also quoted as criticizing Frohnmayer for taking an estimated $225,000 in campaign money from timber interests. Dave then called job retraining "a cruel hoax." It was clear this spotted owl issue and its impact on the timber industry was the never-ending debate of our political race.

In late July Dave and I were invited to the Sunriver resort in Central Oregon for our first joint appearance. The invitation came from the Oregon Newspaper Publishers Association, a well-informed, influential, statewide audience. This was not a debate format but rather an opportunity to hear the opinions of both gubernatorial candidates on a number of issues of interest to Oregon citizens. Patricia accompanied me on the three-hour road trip, and we used the travel time to go over a variety of issues that might be asked by the newspaper publishers and editors at the conference. I was a little anxious about appearing on the podium with Dave for the first time. He was, after all, a skilled attorney with extensive courtroom experience plus a former Oxford debater. Although I had known Dave since he was a state legislator, I was unsure of what to expect from him in this new political relationship.

Patricia assured me that I would do just fine. She pointed out that I knew Oregon issues inside-out and had survived sixteen general election debates in my 1984 race for Secretary of State. "You'll do great," she said, "but just in case they ask one of those questions that causes you to say 'Oh, shit' under your breath, just go for it." The implication may well have been, "What do you have to lose?" We laughed and then drove on down the road toward Bend, Sunriver, a roomful of publishers, and that *one* question that would set the tone for the rest of the campaign.

The exchange between Dave and me was actually pretty tame. We took turns answering questions and the audience soon recognized we had similar views on most Oregon matters. The moderator was about to wrap up the program and announced there was time for one more question. A hand shot up from the audience, the moderator pointed at the person, and the question followed. "How are you going to vote on Measure 4?" Measure 4 was an initiative petition ballot measure that would close Trojan Nuclear Power Plant until it met standards for earthquake safety, waste disposal, and safe storage. This was definitely an "Oh, shit" question! I looked at Patricia, she smiled, shrugged her shoulders, and waited for what she knew would be my answer.

I prefaced my response with a few short comments about my experience as the governor's representative on the Hanford Nuclear Waste Advisory. I spoke about the huge dangers we were facing at Hanford with leaking storage tanks, threats to the water table, and the fact that we were putting the entire Columbia River at risk with the nuclear wastes being stored at the Hanford site. Then I said clearly, "Unless we can meet safety standards at Trojan, I intend to vote in favor of Measure 4."

The audience was shocked! The publishers, editors, and reporters were writing feverishly in their notebooks! They had not expected that direct answer. Dave followed up with a reasoned response about the need for Oregon's only commercial nuclear plant, which generated energy to create jobs, run factories, light homes, offices, and schools. He was clearly against Measure 4. He added, "I don't think the case has been made for a shut-down." Obviously

Dave's people would use this new controversial issue to their full advantage.

After the ONPA event ended, Frohnmayer and his campaign aides chortled over the "major issue I had handed them." Frohnmayer pollster, Bob Moore, contended that "Roberts' stand reinforces the impression that she takes environmental stands instead of protecting jobs."

During the time it took Patricia and me to drive back to Portland, two members of my campaign finance committee had resigned! We prepared a press release on the three-hour drive home, but it was likely a waste of energy and time. Before we could drive back across the Cascade Mountains the story had hit every corner of Oregon: radio and TV stations, Associated Press, and UPI. The general election campaign was only days old, yet, that day, dozens and dozens of politically active and aware citizens and pundits wrote the race off as "over, done, finished." I understood the moment the question was asked and the instant I delivered my answer that this could well be a *fatal* political blow. If the Sunriver question had been phrased asking, "What do you think about the issue?" or "Are there legitimate concerns about safety?" or "How do you think Oregonians will vote on Measure 4?" the result might have been less shocking. But asking how I intended to *vote* left little room for nuance. I knew my answer, and I felt I had to be honest.

Well—do you know what I love? I love Oregonians! I love when they surprise you. I love when they reinforce my moments of personal courage. And they did exactly that. On the Monday after the Saturday Sunriver event, a dozen new volunteers showed up at the campaign office. The next day twenty more volunteers arrived, and the mail contained a small stack of envelopes with checks and thank-you notes for the stand I had taken. For the next couple of weeks support arrived in every day's mail delivery. We even received a few checks from citizens who disagreed with my position on Trojan but respected my honesty and clarity.

Two days later, I further escalated this issue. "For the safety of all Oregonians, our children and our environment, I support closing the Trojan Nuclear Power Plant," I said. "Dave Frohnmayer may be willing to risk our environment and our economic future—and our safety—but quite frankly, I am not."

The campaign took on a new tone. Now folks were saying, "You may not always agree with Barbara Roberts, but you sure as the dickens will know where she stands." What had, for a short time, felt like a political disaster, had emerged as a campaign "energizer bunny." We had lost two businessmen from our finance committee and gained a headquarters full of volunteers and dozens and dozens of envelopes containing checks from $10 to $500. And the press and media coverage was worth its weight in gold! It was certainly way too early to count me out. I was a contender!

Patricia and Kevin continued to assemble an amazing campaign staff. Roger Auerbach, a labor union leader from AFSCME, came to us "on loan." Gwenn Baldwin was a second "loaned staff" arriving from Oregon Congressman Ron Wyden's office. Another great addition to the staff was Thalia Zapatos, a talented writer and organizer with ties to the feminist and LGBT communities. Carole Morse came to us from the business sector, and she was definitely the fashion plate of the staff. With her long association on staff for Oregon Congressman Les AuCoin, Barbara Allen was a walking card file! Marc Overbeck was added to the staff as one of our younger recruits. Terry Surgine came to the campaign with a list of political activism that impressed the entire staff. We watched somewhat wide-eyed as he created a complete statewide field organization out of whole cloth!

In addition to our remarkable staff and dedicated volunteers, no major campaign can be successful without the professional consultants who add special skills and expertise to the operation. Even with our squeaky-tight budget, we had some of the best: Dan Payne from Boston, Mandy Grunwald with ties to Emily's List, and D.C. pollster Mark Mellman. The polling helped us sharpen our message and served to develop a greater message discipline. I might add here, a comment, perhaps even a warning, about campaign consultants. No matter how much expertise and experience they bring to a campaign, a strong candidate must have the last word about commercials, ads, and printed materials that go out in the candidate's name. Wins and losses are obviously important to consultants that make their living in this field. Yet it is wise to be wary of win-at-any-cost professionals. The candidate must set that standard of approval with both staff and consultants from the very beginning. Obviously a candidate campaigning at full steam does not have the time to review every little detail. But on policy matters and political ads, there is always time for a thumbs up or down on the part of the candidate. This is a consultant's business; this is *your life*. Make that difference clear as you move into this high-level political arena.

As our fundraising work continued, our staff handled hundreds of campaign details. With a newly enhanced focus on the race, my telephone calls and endorsement contacts were meeting with growing success. Everyone was working at maximum efficiency. My race for governor was clearly coming into its own.

Then in early summer the race took an interesting change of direction with the entry of two new candidates into the field. Under Oregon law, once the primary election has ended, nonpartisan or minor party candidates can earn a place on the November ballot through a convention nomination process. That is how Libertarian candidate Fred Oerther and nonpartisan candidate Al Mobley qualified as candidates for governor in 1990. It was suddenly a four-person race. Pundits and the press speculated about how these new entries would affect the outcome in November. Would three male candidates and only one female challenger mean the men would split the vote and give me an advantage? Or would the more conservative Mobley and Oerther take votes away from Republican Frohnmayer? Or, if voters did not want a woman governor, would the three men all take votes away from my total? Whatever the impact, it looked as if it would be unlikely for any of the four of us to secure a *majority*. The winner was much more likely to take office with a *plurality* win in November.

During the summer months, the challenges, political issues, fundraising, statewide travel, and speeches seemed endless. Frohnmayer began running a radio ad that strongly criticized my stand on protection of the Northern Spotted Owl. He ran the thirty-second spot on radio stations in rural communities throughout Oregon. Part of the radio ad stated, "[B]efore the spotted owl decision was even final, Barbara Roberts had already given up. She thinks Oregon should just play the hand it's dealt, no matter how bad it is for Oregon." The radio ad ran for several weeks but avoided Portland stations and other urban areas of the state. Dave's political strategy seemed pretty obvious: hurt me in rural areas where timber workers lived and voted and avoid losing his own votes in the city areas where the environmental vote was stronger. He was dumping big money into those radio ads.

Over the last weekend of June, the National Organization for Women held its annual convention in San Francisco. Two thousand delegates strong, they arrived in California, representing the 270,000 NOW members across America. They were there to discuss the new legal and legislative attacks on a woman's right to choose, to consider the possibility of forming a national third political party, and to strongly push efforts to elect more women to high public office. The convention received national press.

The delegates were furious about President Bush's two recent vetoes—the Family and Medical Leave Act and the Child Care Bill. These two issues were further stirring NOW's discussions of a national third party.

Late on Saturday morning, backstage at the convention, an unusual group of women gathered for box lunches. Seated around the table were Dianne Feinstein, the former mayor of San Francisco and current candidate for governor; Molly Yard, national president of NOW; Evelyn Murphy, candidate for Governor of Massachusetts; Josie Heath, running for U.S. Senate from Colorado; Patricia Ireland, vice-president of NOW; and myself, running for Governor of Oregon. We talked excitedly about the ten women running for governor nationwide, seven female candidates in U.S. Senate races, and a historic fifty-four women in contests for the U.S. House. We laughed together, plotted together, and dreamed together. Then, one by one, we stepped through the curtains, up to the podium, and delivered our remarks to a totally supportive audience. When we had each spoken, Molly Yard called us together at the front of the stage and two thousand women delegates became cheerleaders for women in elected leadership! What a moment and what a shot in the arm to send me home to Oregon reenergized and re-inspired. It was an additional bonus to read my name in the *New York Times* with a quote from my remarks: "It sounds great to say you're in favor of the family, but if you don't want to talk about family leave or about child care, what makes you pro-family?"

In July my campaign people and Dave's people were in touchy negotiations about the number, location, and format for political debates in the fall campaign months. Dave stated firmly, "I'm not going to debate anybody but the Democratic candidate for governor." Dave did not want to see Al Mobley and Fred Oerther in any of the debates. My side was pushing for ten debates, two of which would include all four candidates. While some of my opponent's advisors believed Dave would lose votes if Mobley was given any extra exposure, others believed that Mobley would self-destruct if given broader visibility.

After all the negotiations and strategizing, we were only able to get four debates, including one with all four candidates. Dave was still ahead in the polls and didn't want to give me any more press coverage than was necessary. The four debates were in Eugene (home of the University of Oregon and Dave's current hometown), Forest Grove, Medford (in the heart of the timber country and the place Dave was raised), and Pendleton (in eastern Oregon and strongly Republican territory). The Portland City Club's invitation was, as always, extended for one of the debates. This was a traditional governor's debate setting in Oregon. Dave, however, would not agree to a debate in Portland, the state's largest city. I would appear on that podium alone. I thought back to the sixteen candidate debates I had participated in for the 1984 Secretary of State's race. In 1990 that exposure and opportunity for policy exchange would be limited to just four debates. I wasn't happy, but the negotiations had come to an end.

As the campaign continued to heat up, we were pushing the image of the Attorney General as cautious, careful, overly legalistic, and somewhat indecisive. In July at a speech to the Portland Oregon Visitors' Association, I took a couple of jabs at Dave's leadership style. "Dave's approach is a little more lawyerly and academic. But Oregon needs a governor who leads not only with brains, but also with guts." Later in the speech I commented, "You will find me to be a governor bold enough to move forward and who will not just circle the wagons in times of change and uncertainty."

My campaign staff and I began to feel that this message was being heard. It was time for a brief television ad that would not notably deplete our "sacred" media account but would reinforce our message on Dave as careful, overcautious, and indecisive. We ran the television ad only for a few days, but everyone who saw it remembered it. The spot showed a tall man wearing an old-fashioned striped swim garment standing on the beach at water's edge. He cautiously brought his toes close to the water, hesitating twice to dip them into the surf. We did not mention my opponent's name in the ad. The announcer simply delivered a short message on the need for leadership in Oregon. It was actually a somewhat humorous spot. Through no intention on our part, many viewers thought the swimmer in the antique swim suit looked exactly like

Dave Frohnmayer! In a few short days with a limited TV buy, we had made our point. Media expert Dan Payne had definitely done his job with this creative ad!

Now it was time for the serious media strategy. We had to move the polling numbers in our direction, and time was not our friend as August approached. If we couldn't make some notable gains in the polls *soon*, our fundraising would be irreparably affected and the political perception of Frohnmayer as the obvious winner would begin to solidify. Patricia now introduced the second half of a very risky but strategic media plan. The first half of the plan had been fifty cents of every dollar going into our media account starting in the earliest part of the campaign. It was now time to make a bold decision on the second phase of our media plan.

In Oregon, political television buys in August are almost unheard of. Everyone in Oregon is outdoors—hiking, camping, biking, at the beach, in the mountains. We had always been told by the "experts" that nobody watched television in August in Oregon. Now Patricia was proposing to spend our *entire* media account on a major August television buy. I repeat, the *entire media account.* We knew our TV spots, already taped, were well-designed, professional messages. We knew they would be effective. What we couldn't predict accurately was who would see them if they only ran in August. Patricia made the case that if we took this action in August and our numbers began to move, our fundraising would pick up sufficiently to fund the rest of the campaign and a later media schedule. Obviously if this August strategy *failed,* we would be unable to compete in September and October. It was an all-or-nothing plan. My campaign team weighed the risks against our sagging poll numbers, and we made the August television purchase.

CHAPTER SEVENTEEN

Strategizing Toward Victory

In the summer of 1990, while we secretly waited for our August television buys to go on the air, policy issues and campaign matters were bouncing off every surface. It reminded me of the movie title, *The Good, the Bad, and the Ugly.*

In the "good" category, I had just won the solid endorsement of Oregon's AFL-CIO delegates. Their summer labor convention gave Attorney General Dave Frohnmayer only polite applause during his speech. I received four standing ovations from the delegates and an $8,000 check from AFL-CIO President Irv Fletcher when my speech concluded. The next day the AFL-CIO state endorsement became official, and a number of new checks from individual unions were added to my campaign totals. I also received the overwhelming political endorsement of the Oregon Public Employees Union by a greater than two-to-one vote of the full membership plus the unanimous reaffirmation of the OPEU Board of Directors. The fifteen-thousand-member union stood prepared to make a significant volunteer commitment to my campaign plus strong financial support.

Then on top of the ongoing environmental and economic challenges of the timber/spotted owl controversy, that summer brought yet another environmental crisis to the forefront. In southern Oregon's Klamath County a battle had been brewing for several years over the proposed construction of a hydroelectric facility on the Klamath River. Two years earlier the voters of Oregon had cast their vote statewide to designate several miles of the Klamath River as a State Scenic Waterway, a designation that would likely put an end to the plan to build a dam on the last free-flowing, pristine segment of the Klamath River, a stretch used extensively for fishing and rafting.

Yet, unbelievably, that summer of 1990 the Federal Energy Regulatory Commission recommended granting a license for a dam on this stretch of the river, labeled as the Salt Caves Hydroelectric Project—in spite of the earlier decision by Oregon voters and the support of state regulatory agencies to protect that waterway. I immediately held a press conference, adamantly criticizing the federal government's action. "I'm outraged that the federal government wants to turn this beautiful Oregon river into a pond, ignoring our state agencies and our voters." I reminded the press and our citizens that three of our Oregon congressional members were actively supporting HB 4728 to designate the last free-flowing stretch of the Klamath River as a National Wild and Scenic River, halting this damaging construction project forever. I strongly supported the legislation. Little could I have guessed at that point in 1990 that I would be dealing with this issue for the next four years plus.

Meanwhile, two late July news items hit the press. The first related to my job as Secretary of State. My office had just qualified six more state initiative petitions for the November ballot, bringing the total to eleven. I knew these six new measures would now rear their heads in my public appearances, at press conferences, and once our scheduled governor's debates began in September. Two of the measures fell into the category of anti-abortion laws: one prohibited abortion except in cases of incest, rape, or to save a mother's life. The second was a parental-notification measure. There were also measures requiring seat belts, a work-replacing-welfare bill, a recyclable packing measure, and a tax credit for children going to private schools. These new measures would certainly supply lots of fodder for disagreement and controversy during the rest of the campaign season.

On the timber front a good piece of news came out of Congress that, for a change, almost all sides could agree on. First, Congress passed a new trade bill to ban the export of logs from most state lands in Oregon and Washington. The legislation also created a permanent ban on the export of logs cut on federal lands in the West. It was a first step toward preventing job loss caused by the environmental measures to protect the spotted owl. Banning these exports would help supply timber to the mills and keep more workers on the job. However, logs harvested from *private* forestlands would remain available for international export. The export ban would cover only about one-sixth of the raw logs harvested from the Northwest each year. The remaining millions of board feet would continue to be exported. It was helpful but, in reality, only a baby-step.

Just as my August television ads hit the airwaves, an unexpected, nonpolitical crisis put the brakes on any positive lift in my spirits. On August 9, Frank was tooling down the sidewalk in downtown Portland in his motorized cart, took a corner too fast, and his cart tipped over. Frank's left hip was broken and he was rushed to the hospital. Luckily, I was close to Portland and not campaigning in some far-off corner of the state. At the hospital, as they prepared Frank for surgery to replace the ball joint in his hip, the only thing *he* was worried about was that he was diverting my focus from the campaign. I was upset about the accident, the pain Frank was experiencing, and not totally comfortable having him go under general anesthetic at seventy-four. I called his two daughters, my parents, and my younger son to let them know Frank was on his way to surgery. In the heat of a governor's race, this is not exactly the call your family members are expecting to receive. When you take on a major campaign, your family members often get pulled into the fray. Suddenly I had a hospital waiting room full of family members (and volunteers! — Frank's accident took more than the candidate away from the campaign).

Frank came through the surgery well and was expected to be home in about a week or ten days. However, the partial paralysis Frank already suffered in his legs complicated his recovery and his healing slowed dramatically. Usually hip-replacement patients are put back on their feet in a very short time to rebuild their strength and the use of the replacement joint. Since Frank was unable to walk *before* the surgery, that type of rehab wasn't possible for him. The ongoing pain in his legs made hands-on physical therapy hard to tolerate as well.

I thought of the many magical Augusts in the past that we had spent sailing, wind in the hair, sun on the face, savoring the sounds and smells of the sea. This August was focused on healing, hospital rooms, and adjusting my campaign schedule to allow me time with Frank in between meetings, speeches, and fundraising calls. Thank goodness our campaign team had opted for the risky August television buy. I had great visibility statewide even at the same time I was spending extra hours with Frank! Well — I had visibility *if* Oregon voters were actually watching television during our beautiful summer season. That remained to be tested.

As contributions mounted, Democratic organizations all over the state were pitching in with whatever they could send to help with my campaign. But we would soon learn that Dave's Republican Party contributions far overshadowed my party's support. One of the more interesting contributions I received was from the Re-Elect Neil Goldschmidt Committee. When Neil's check arrived, I was not only pleased to get the donation Neil had promised, but I had to smile just a little about the newspaper story from way back in February where Neil's campaign manager had made it publicly clear that no part of Neil's large campaign fund would be shared to assist with my election. Apparently Governor Goldschmidt did not agree with her view.

The next good news came after almost a month-long run of my television ads. On Sunday, September 2, *The Oregonian* headline read, "Poll Shows Frohnmayer Lead Shrinks." It was the Labor Day headline we had hoped for. I had gained 3 percentage points in the polls in one month and the numbers now showed 45 percent to 38 percent with 10 percent undecided and a 4 percent margin of error. This was definitely a race within my grasp if these new numbers brought in additional contributions and if this trend continued in my direction.

Mark Mellman, our campaign pollster, put the new polling numbers in national perspective. "The Roberts-Frohnmayer race is now one of the handful of close governors' races in the country." The Frohnmayer camp contended the new polling numbers meant little since his staff speculated my campaign had gained that new bump by draining the last of my hard-to-come-by money. They predicted I would be "swept away" by the massive Frohnmayer advertising campaign in the fall without any financial ability to respond. Dave's campaign implied that it had far outpaced my fundraising, although neither candidate had been required to report their finances for almost three months. The truth was, we *had* emptied our media account but we certainly weren't going to advertise that fact. However, in six months I had gained 15 percentage points on a candidate with a year's head start and a million-dollar advantage when I had entered the race. The truth was that we didn't know what Dave's money actually looked like; plus the Independent candidate, Mobley, was siphoning votes from Frohnmayer's numbers, *not mine.*

I began preparing for the first of the four scheduled gubernatorial debates on September 12. This first debate would be held in the university city of Eugene where Dave Frohnmayer and his family lived. Sponsored by the local League of Women Voters, the noon debate would be televised by the local station, rerun in prime time that evening on one of the Portland TV stations, and aired live on several radio stations, including public radio. All four candidates would be included in this debate; in the three debates that would follow, only Dave and I would appear. Responses in the Eugene debate were limited to one minute.

As I studied and rehearsed for the debate, I could anticipate several subjects that would likely arise: timber and the spotted owl crisis, my stand on four or five of the more controversial ballot measures, my tax-reform positions, land-use matters, education funding, and my background and experience to serve as governor. I focused my preparation on developing clear, concise, honest answers to that series of tough issues.

A few days before I headed to Eugene for the debate, Frank was transferred to a different hospital to receive some new method of therapy for his hip. Recovery was not going well, and he was experiencing far more pain than was normal this long after surgery. I was growing more and more concerned. The afternoon before the debate I headed to the hospital to again check on Frank; I was planning to drive the two hours to Eugene late that afternoon and stay overnight. When I reached the hospital Frank was looking quite tired and haggard. He could not get comfortable in his hospital bed, and hadn't eaten his breakfast or lunch. I was used to dealing with his pain, but that afternoon his eyes reflected a more severe pain. I knew the look. I consulted with the nursing staff and insisted that the doctor examine Frank that evening. I said I could call back the first thing the next morning.

At 7:30 a.m., I called the hospital to get the doctor's report and to speak to Frank. Frank was no longer at the hospital! He had left by ambulance very early that morning to transfer back to his regular hospital in preparation for a second surgery on his hip. They would be operating at 11:30, just before the scheduled debate. The ball joint on the hip replacement had slipped out of place and created a puncture wound that had finally pierced Frank's tissue and skin from the inside out. The reason for his pain was clearly visible by the time his surgeon examined him the previous evening. Frank had refused to let them contact me in Eugene about his pending surgery. I felt overcome with guilt. I called the second hospital and reached the surgical ward. Frank was already under heavy sedation, and they were prepping him for the operation.

I would just have to go ahead with the debate, call the hospital as soon as I finished, and then drive directly back to be there when he got out of recovery. This is definitely not the frame of mind one needs to face a tough campaign debate! I wanted to cry like a baby. I wanted to be at Frank's side. But I pulled myself together, focused on my debate materials, and waited to go downstairs to the hotel dining room for the first big debate in my race for governor. This would have been a tough moment under the best of circumstances. This, however, was *not* the best of times!

This first debate would produce, for me, one good quote I would use for the rest of the campaign plus a unique question and a very lucky opportunity that I could never have predicted or prepared for.

In a criticism of Frohnmayer, I attacked him for a legal opinion he made as Attorney General that kept Oregon from banning log exports when the Legislature had passed such a law several years earlier. When Dave meekly defended his earlier legal opinion, I delivered the line, "Don't look for leadership in the governor's office if you don't see courage in the campaign." It turned out to be such a quotable and useful line that I repeated it several times when Dave sidestepped a tough question or issue for the rest of the campaign.

For a highly pressured hour, we exchanged jabs and answers on land use, abortion, the death penalty, taxes, timber, and even the debate schedule. Finally, the last question was posed by radio reporter Bob Valdez, a question that the *Eugene Register-Guard* described as the "most telling" question and answer of the entire debate: "If you were not running for this office, who among the other candidates here today would you vote for and why? And ... *none* is not an answer."

We had been rotating our order on all previous questions and on this amazing question I would be the final responder. Both Mobley and Oerther ignored the reporter's instructions and said they would cast their vote for themselves. When Dave's turn came, I expected better of him. I was disappointed! Dave indicated that he was the *only* candidate on the stage prepared to be Oregon's Governor and he would have to vote for himself. Now it was my turn. I felt obligated to follow the instructions the radio announcer had laid out. "Unlike the three men on this stage, I will answer the question we were all asked. If I were not in this race, I would vote for the only *other* person on this platform qualified to be the Governor of Oregon. I would cast my vote for Dave Frohnmayer." The crowd applauded loudly and approvingly.

The Oregonian said the three male candidates had "ducked the question." The *Eugene Register Guard* said I had delivered "the perfect answer—exactly what Frohnmayer should have said about Roberts." The Eugene paper declared me the winner of the first debate. Debate outcome? "Round One for Roberts."

As worried as I was about Frank's surgery, I never imagined I would be able to do well in that debate. However I just steeled myself, faced what I could not change, and did my job. Now it was done! I talked with reporters, audience members, and even the debate sponsors at the close of the event. Now I needed to get back to my hotel room and call the hospital about Frank. The nurse said he was out of surgery and everything had gone well. He was still in recovery, but they reported he appeared to be resting comfortably. I was relieved and grateful.

That evening I watched the rerun of the Eugene debate with Frank in his Portland hospital room. My speech-professor husband gave me a "very good grade." He celebrated the answer I delivered on the final question. He thought it was brilliant. Frank believed that Dave had damaged himself when he "wimped out" on that particular question. Frank, even on pain meds, could discern that the voters knew when one avoided the truth. A number of the newscasts that night and the next day, showed the segment with all four of the candidates answering. Those news clips were decidedly more helpful than most candidates' paid commercials.

Our next debate was scheduled for just over two weeks later, on September 30. After the Eugene experience, I would certainly approach it with much more confidence, feeling more at ease. Dave's campaign materials noted his background as a debater at Oxford University, and he had argued before the U.S. Supreme Court. Yet perhaps these more formal experiences don't easily translate into the realm of political debating. I was hopeful that my command of Oregon issues plus my ability to articulate opinions and my warmth and quick wit would be assets on the future debate platforms. This sounds rather egotistical but, as a candidate, one should be able to recognize both one's own assets and one's shortcomings.

During the next two weeks I was able to get in some additional statewide travel. My field staff members had every area visit planned to the last detail. Radio interviews, plant tours, main street visits, fundraisers, Chamber of Commerce luncheons, harvest festivals, Democratic Party meetings, wall-to-wall, nonstop opportunity for community exposure. It was a treadmill existence, but I was getting more positive reception with each passing day. Several citizens commented on my final response at the Eugene debate. It had really grabbed people. It was interesting to hear chuckles when the discussion was raised. It seemed like such a minor and simple exchange, yet it stayed with people and they appeared to enjoy retelling the story. I wasn't about to discourage the repeating of what had become a political asset. I suspected it was having a positive impact on my polling numbers.

With Frank clearly on the mend, new campaign contributions coming in, and a growing "buzz" about the governor's race, I was feeling very positive. Frohnmayer was running a heavy-duty series of TV ads attacking me for my timber/spotted owl position and what he felt was an anti-law-enforcement attitude. This latter criticism was built on a shaky foundation. He may have raised it simply to find a hook on which to hang his recent endorsements by the Oregon District Attorneys Association and the support of the state's sheriffs and police chiefs. I knew perfectly well that after ten years as Oregon's Attorney General, he would expect to get the support of these law-enforcement groups. That fact hardly made me "anti-law enforcement." Interestingly, with Dave's TV ads running regularly, no one was asking me about my positions on crime, law enforcement, or corrections. I sensed that Oregonians weren't being fooled by these negative commercials. As I prepared for our next debate in the small college town of Forest Grove, I planned to confront Dave about the ads. I knew he could find some ground to stand on with regards to the timber issue. I could find absolutely no legitimacy in the law enforcement attack, and I planned to say that clearly on the debate platform.

When I arrived at Pacific University's campus (Frank's alma mater) for the debate, I immediately spotted Mother and Dad. My parents were so supportive of my candidacy and of me. It gave me a real lift to know they would be in the audience. Independent Al Mobley and a large group of his supporters were also there, carrying anti-abortion placards and protesting the fact that he had not been invited to participate in the debate. Mobley contended, "There is no debate here. It is a farce." He felt Dave and I had such similar views that no debate was really possible.

Well, I might have agreed *before* that debate. *After* the debate, I definitely disagreed! The newspapers the next day told the story:

The Oregonian: "Sparks Fly in Governor's Debate"

The (Forest Grove) *News-Times*: "Gubernatorial Candidates Trade Blows"

Corvallis *Gazette Times*: "Frohnmayer, Roberts Spar on Spending"

The Daily Astorian: "Candidates Clash"

Frohnmayer's campaign had apparently decided the negative television ads weren't doing enough damage. It was time to use the more traditional Republican fallacy about "tax-and-spend Democrats." Dave came after me for what he labeled my "automatic reflex to want to spend." He added he would never vote for me unless there were "chains, locks, and pit bulls guarding the state treasury." Wow! I guess Dave had missed my four years of service in the state Legislature where I voted to *cut* state budgets through two regular sessions and six special sessions. He kept hitting me as a big spender. He talked about my proposals for affordable housing, increasing school support, and for job-training programs as "vastly exceeding any resources presently available to the state." Dave several times throughout the afternoon offered the threat that I would raise taxes.

I took Dave on regarding the issue of crime. "You've been AG for ten years. I've been burglarized three times in the last eighteen months in two Oregon cities. Why can't you do something about this?"

We fought over land-use protections, the hiring of minorities, a willingness to veto legislation restricting abortion rights, and school funding. Mobley may have felt that Dave and I had no debatable issues. He was certainly wrong on that count. I ended that exchange feeling slightly drained but more than ready to take on my next battle with Dave. His comment about the "pit bulls" raised my ire. He would think PIT BULL the next time we debated! Yet, as the debate ended, we met in the middle of the stage, shook hands, and smiled for the cameras and the audience. Suddenly, as people were just beginning to disperse, my dad jumped on the stage, took me in his arms, and gave me a huge hug. It was just what I needed! I felt a little like when I was a kid and someone picked on me. I could always depend on a comforting hug from Dad. That Sunday, the embrace was not only welcome, it was needed. He always knew.

Three days later I received another very "warm embrace." *The Oregonian* released a poll with the headline "Roberts Closes Gap." I had drawn even with Frohnmayer; the story said: "[T]he governor's race is a virtual dead heat. Attorney General Frohnmayer has 44 percent to 43 percent for Secretary of State Roberts, well within the poll's 4 percent margin of error. One month ago Roberts was seven points back."

They quoted my campaign director, Patricia McCaig, saying, "Roberts is steadily pulling in the undecided voters." That's what

I had been *feeling* out there on the campaign trail. Now I had solid verification. So I headed to Pendleton for the third debate with brand-new polling numbers, an added sense of confidence, and an awareness that the November 6 election was only a month away and I could not, I must not, lose my momentum. The October 4 debate, held at Pendleton's Blue Mountain Community College, covered many of the same subjects we had argued over in Forest Grove, although the tone was just *slightly* more civil. An editorial published three days later in the *East Oregonian* out of Pendleton noted: "We think Roberts scored points by offering a confident, polished performance. This debate should add to her campaign momentum. Frohnmayer is an intelligent, thoughtful public servant ... yet his campaign staff has managed to present him as shrill and petty. They have lost the high ground."

The day after the Pendleton debate, I was back in Portland for what should have been the major debate of the campaign. The Portland City Club has traditionally been the site of political debates for races for governor, U.S. senator, secretary of state, and other major offices. It is a respected and tested format that always plays to a standing-room-only crowd and full press coverage. Well, the crowd was there. The cameras were there. I was there. Dave was not! He had turned down this debate. I had been willing to debate in *his* home town. He was unwilling to debate in *mine*. The Portland City Club was clearly miffed. Members and guests were exceedingly warm and supportive, including a standing ovation when I was introduced. I made my opening statement and then took a number of questions. *The Oregonian* reported, "Members served up a few softball questions that Roberts obligingly knocked out of the ballroom of the Hilton Hotel."

There would be two more debates before the election. The final debate with Dave was scheduled for October 10 in Medford in the southern part of the state. I had also agreed to a debate on October 23 in Portland with Independent Al Mobley and Libertarian Fred Oerther sponsored by the League of Women Voters. Dave had been asked to participate but had bluntly refused.

With my ever-improving polling numbers, contributions were notably on the rise. It is, without question, easier to raise money in a neck-and-neck race than when you are trailing by 7, 10, or 15 percent. My campaign staff was working overtime on research, press releases, telephone banks, securing new radio buys, and the unending chore of raising contributions. Then on the morning of October 9, another very encouraging news story hit the press statewide. In the four months between June 5 and September 27, new financial reports filed by gubernatorial candidates showed I had actually raised more money than Frohnmayer. According to *The Oregonian*, almost half of Dave's new money had come from the timber industry. Obviously, those were four-month numbers only; from the beginning of our races Frohnmayer had amassed $2.3 million while my totals came to $1.3 million. Yet the story clearly demonstrated the results of both my growing political support and the outcome of having a first-class staff behind me.

Perhaps the place for me to prove my momentum was that very evening at the debate in Medford. We were, after all, debating in the town where Dave grew up and where his prominent and respected parents still lived. I knew my own parents would again be in the audience, driving three hours to attend the debate and also joining me for a planned reception of my supporters that would follow. I had some new research materials prepared for this exchange. I recognized that all my recent press on new poll numbers, on the debates, on fundraising, had been quite positive. I suspected Frohnmayer might be a little edgy. I hoped my positive press would not push him into an even stronger attack mode. Instead Dave and his campaign began the evening with two surprise statements. Minutes before the start of the debate, Frohnmayer aides released the news that Dave had fired his California advertising agency because of concerns that his campaign had turned too negative. Then as the debate began, Dave opened with an amazing request for an *additional* debate. Both of these actions felt to me like desperation moves.

Dave said he regretted that none of the debates had been televised statewide. I knew and he knew that he had turned away from just such an opportunity at the Portland City Club only four days before plus he had turned down the upcoming League of Women Voters' venue in Portland on October 23. I felt Dave was trying to turn this debate question into a "wedge" issue. Amazingly, here we were debating in the community of his youth, in Republican-leaning territory, *and* at South Medford High School from the stage of the very high school Dave had attended. I certainly didn't feel I had avoided any tough debate venues.

From that rather strange debate beginning, Dave and I found a stack of issues to disagree on. I confronted him for a vote he had cast, while a state legislator, a vote *against* a marital rape bill. "How can you reconcile that vote with your claim that you have been acting on behalf of women's rights?" Dave admitted he regretted that vote and would vote differently now. "I voted at the time because I believed it would be difficult to find a prosecution under it." I clearly felt that I had won a point or two on that round.

While Dave again came after me for my programs and their budget impacts, I fought back. I cited his promise to raise higher-education salaries and create an environmental research institute as examples of spending without budget matches. I added that the Attorney General's office budget had gone up 140 percent since he took office ten years earlier. I had no intention of accepting Frohnmayer labeling me as the "big spender," so I added another little fact from his elected past. "In three legislative sessions you voted for sixty-eight tax increases." *Two* could definitely play this game.

We again clashed on an issue that had received considerable attention three months before—Ballot Measure 4, requiring the closure of Trojan Nuclear Power Plant. Frohnmayer indicated that the state Revenue Department estimated the plant closure would cost taxpayers over $500 million. I came back at him saying, "The issue of Trojan is a *safety* issue, and it shouldn't be anything else." Irritated at Dave trying to turn this huge environmental risk into a taxpayer concern I added, "The most immediate of all power sources is called conservation, and we can all learn to conserve for the good of Oregon." The audience broke into applause. Welcome home, Dave! Perhaps he didn't own this venue.

When our appearance ended, the press went straight for the additional debate issue. I had always wanted more debates. But Dave was still insisting he would not agree to a debate that included all four of the candidates. He wanted television coverage. He was asking for another debate. Yet he wanted to set the rules. The solution seemed pretty obvious to me. We already had another debate scheduled for three of the gubernatorial candidates on October 23. One of the major Portland television stations offered to cover the debate live if Frohnmayer joined the venue. Dave refused.

The statewide Oregon Voters' Pamphlet would soon be arriving at every home in the state, at libraries, local post offices, and county election offices. October also saw the publication of the earliest endorsements in the governor's race. The first endorsement went to Dave from the *Springfield News*. The next endorsement was mine from the Washington County *Valley Times*. There were many more editorials to come from every corner of the state. I just hoped I had held my own with these editorial boards, publishers, and writers. I certainly wasn't going to earn the majority of these endorsements, particularly those from the more conservative parts of the state, but there were only a couple of papers where I expected to both lose the endorsement and get highly negative remarks from the editors: The *Bend Bulletin* and the *Coos Bay World*. Those anticipated problems had more to do with the editors personally than the communities where they were published.

On Saturday, October 13, I had a full day's schedule centered in Salem. One of the most pleasant stops during that day was at the Salem Senior Citizen Center where my father had been a Meals on Wheels volunteer for two or three years. Dad was there when I arrived, wearing two versions of my campaign button and looking very proud. I took the opportunity to talk about what a wonderful and loving and supportive parent my Dad had been throughout my life. I told the gathered crowd that his Meals on Wheels volunteer time was just one example of the many kindnesses he did for others. I also told them he was my best campaign volunteer and most loyal supporter. I could see tears glistening in his eyes from four or five rows away! I was grateful to have an opportunity to thank him in such a public way, surrounded by his fellow senior citizens. As I left the center we stopped for a big hug. Dad looked thin and seemed almost frail in my arms. That thought felt strange for the father who had always felt like a tower of strength to me.

As I left Salem, I was feeling a little tired and even tense, but I knew my campaign staff was completely on top of every item we needed to complete in the last three weeks before election day. In fact, things were in such good shape my staff had given me the next day off from any campaign duties. I couldn't remember the last totally free day I had experienced. Frank and I were going to stay overnight in his Portland apartment on Saturday night, sleep in on Sunday, and then see our kids and grandkids. I also couldn't remember the last time Frank's pain was under control to the degree that we could actually sleep next to each other. That night I experienced a renewed taste of simply being a real person again. I fell asleep feeling contented and happy.

The next morning the telephone rang, earlier than I wanted to be awakened. I reached for the phone, smiling at Frank as I put the receiver to my ear. My smile immediately faded. My sister was on the line, crying, saying Dad had been taken to the hospital in an ambulance; he was still in emergency but they didn't think he would make it. I needed to come immediately! I was crying as I helped

Frank out of bed and into his wheelchair. We both began dressing as fast as possible. I reminded Frank to take his pain pills and to bring them with him, since I couldn't predict when we would be back. I grabbed my overnight bag and my purse and we headed to the car.

That one-hour drive was one of the longest in my life. I had just seen Dad yesterday. I had hugged him, laughed with him, left him to go out with a crew of folks to put up the last of my Salem-area lawn signs. Maybe my sister was just emotional and overstating his condition. Maybe.

As I drove into the hospital's parking lot I saw my Uncle Orv standing outside, smoking. He looked up, recognized my car, and lowered his head. I jumped out of the car. My stomach turned. My uncle shook his head sadly and took me in his arms. "He's gone, honey. About forty-five minutes ago. Go in and see your mother and sister. They need you. I'll help Frank out of the car and into his cart."

As I walked through the automatic glass doors into the Emergency Department, I saw Pat and Mother sitting close to each other, hand in hand. I burst into tears as they saw me and stood. The three of us bonded in a sad and tear-filled embrace. He was gone. My mother had lost the love of her life after fifty-five years of marriage. Pat and I faced life without the man who had been there for us every day, the father, the supporter, the hero.

Once we began to calm down enough to speak, I asked where Dad was. A nurse walked me down the curtained corridor. I stepped into the half-lit area behind the curtain and saw him on the bed-like cart. A sheet covered him up to his shoulders. I looked at his face, eyes closed, as if in slumber. I gently touched his cheek. It felt cool. "My Daddy is dead!" Yesterday's embrace, the sense of fragility, had been a message, one I had not understood. Today, the message was very clear. I said good-bye to my father in a sterile hospital room, with curtains for walls, with an "I love you" that seemed to drift away, felt but unheard. My Dad was dead. I kissed him one last time. I caressed his familiar, rough, worker's hands, hands that represented my blue-collar background but also recalled his gentleness and warmth. What a gift he and his love had been in my life.

The next few days were a blur. I suspended my campaign for a few days. Some engagements were cancelled, some rescheduled, supporters stood in for me at other events. I took charge of the plans for Dad's memorial service and other necessary arrangements. I was the eldest child, and I felt it was my place to carry the load for my family. I found a location that was perfect for his service:

a glass-walled building right in the middle of a pretty little park, bright with fall color. Friends helped with food arrangements, setting up chairs, program printing, and flowers. My dad had been a Mason and the lodge would do a piece of the service. I prepared his obituary for the newspaper, made arrangements for speakers and music, notified far-flung family members and close friends, and then I wrote a eulogy for Dad.

My dad, Bob Hughey

The memorial service was simple, genuine, and warm—just like the man it honored. I knew when I wrote my dad's eulogy that I would never be able to read it aloud. My friend Grattan Kerans did that special favor for me. After Dad's memorial service ended, I was emotionally and physically drained. Yet the next day I would return to the campaign. Dad would expect that. Friends reported to me that, during the previous two days, statewide television had been running stories of my dad's death accompanied by video footage of Dad hugging me at the end of the Forest Grove and Medford debates. My friends said the footage of the two of us embracing and laughing together had been very warm and quite emotional to view. I thought, "Thanks, Dad, for one final piece of positive press." I knew he would have applauded that. I, however, have never been able to watch those news clips, not even today.

On my first day back to the campaign I was feeling edgy and tired. I tried hard to be at my best, but I was remarkably relieved when the day's schedule came to an end. As I tried to catch up on all that had happened during the four days I was out of touch with the world, I found that several newspapers had made endorsements in the governor's race. On the day Dad died, *The Dalles Chronicle* had given me their clear endorsement. A few days later, Dave won the endorsement of the *Keizer Times*. It wasn't a strong endorsement but in the end, Dave got the nod. The next day, *The Daily Astorian* gave me a positive, outspoken endorsement. "Unlike too many politicians these days, Roberts knows who she is and what she believes in. There is nothing artificial about this woman and she is tough. Frohnmayer has been greatly outclassed by Barbara Roberts. She has exhibited more self-possession. She has demonstrated superior toughness. Roberts has the guts, moxie and intelligence to lead Oregon where it needs to go."

The day after that *super* editorial, the Oregon Voters' Pamphlets started arriving in mailboxes. We compared my pages with Dave's. We felt we had clearly done better, in content, verbiage, clarity, and even a little "pizzazz." My favorite section of the material we had submitted was an opening paragraph headed, "Barbara Roberts: Not a Typical Politician." The section stated, "Barbara is not like any politician you've ever met. She's a lot better. She listens. She talks straight. And she gets the job done." The final paragraph on my page read, "No other candidate has the background in business, local government, or community service. Barbara's proven that hard work and high office don't mean less caring ... and less courage. She's been tested. And she's ready."

I certainly hoped so!

I now called my mother and my sister, Pat, every day, no matter how hectic my campaign schedule became. I was preparing for another debate in Portland on October 23, only a few days away. My sister felt I needed family support at the event. My Uncle Orv, Mother, Pat, and Frank would all be there. I was relieved to know they were coming. I didn't want to find myself searching the debate audience, looking for Dad's familiar face. I was grateful my family was making this extra effort for me. I knew it wasn't easy for Mother or Pat. It wasn't easy for me.

Frohnmayer had *finally* decided to participate in this debate. Channel 2 in Portland was now planning to televise it live across the state. Dave called this change of heart "part of a thirty-day plan to be as flexible as possible." He added, "It's not a sign of panic, it's a sign of ability to adapt." Very interesting!

An exciting new poll was released that week that gave me my *first* polling lead in the race: Roberts 44 percent, Frohnmayer 40 percent, Mobley 11 percent. Oerther didn't even reach a 1 percent showing. I arrived at the Hilton Hotel for the last debate of this 1990 campaign—ahead in the polls, holding my own in the fundraising department, breaking even (so far) on the newspaper endorsements, with, in my opinion, a superior voters' pamphlet page, and with my ads still running on television. Not bad for a small-town girl without an Oxford degree!

All four candidates were present. The television cameras were there, and the press was in attendance. My family was seated near the front. I could almost *feel* their vibes of support. However, that was about the only supportive activity I was involved in that afternoon! The four candidates argued over our campaign slogans. We debated over debates. We pointed fingers about negative ads. Then, to everyone's surprise, we eventually hit a topic that had not been discussed at any of our previous debates ... gay rights. I said I would support going back to the ballot and allowing Oregonians to vote again on the 1988 measure that reversed Governor Goldschmidt's executive order banning discrimination against gays and lesbians. I thought we could clarify and redefine the debate between "special rights" and "civil rights" and reach a different election outcome. I hoped so. Frohnmayer thought it was harmful for the state to again take up the gay-rights issue. The debate ended with Oerther getting the most laughs, Mobley calling Frohnmayer a liar, and Dave and me sniping at each other on any and all issues that arose *except* our final agreement in favor of increasing the gasoline tax for highway construction and even mass transit.

No more debates! Less than two weeks until election day. More quick road trips ahead for me. New newspaper endorsements now coming, fast and furious. Polling numbers holding steady. Candidate: tired and sad. Yet, as good as the race looked, I knew that two weeks could be a lifetime in a major campaign. One error, one attack commercial, one slip of the tongue, and the whole outcome could be up for grabs. It was too early to give in to being tired or even sad. I had to buck up, get a grip, as they say. Rest and grief, as badly as I needed *both,* had to be moved to the back burner for the last two weeks.

That day, I received the endorsement of the Oregon Women's Political Caucus, the Black Leadership Conference, and the Rainbow Coalition, obviously liberal groups. But liberal votes count the same as moderate votes and conservatives at the election polling place. The next day *The Skanner,* Oregon's major African American newspaper, gave me its endorsement, and the following day Portland's *Willamette Week* joined in endorsing my candidacy. *The Skanner* said, "Roberts' record shows she is willing to exert leadership on difficult issues." *Willamette Week* stated strongly, "Don't even hesitate on this one. Barbara Roberts is, without question, the superior candidate in this race." My next two endorsements came from major daily newspapers, one from each side of the Cascade Mountains, *The*

Oregonian and the *East Oregonian*. These were papers that carried both respect and influence in huge areas of the state. The statewide endorsement of *The Oregonian* was considered a great coup for my campaign. *The Oregonian* criticized Dave saying, "Frohnmayer has failed in his campaign to deal effectively with conflict and pressure. He squandered a big lead, and left us truly worried that he is soft at the core and squishy around the edges." The endorsement went on to say, "Roberts is a feisty liberal, but also a highly practical, results-oriented politician. ... Roberts was miles ahead of her opponent in suggesting the proper way to deal with Oregon's timber crisis; she would bring to the governor's office a much more resolute defense of state land-use policy than Frohnmayer; and she is both more knowledgeable on urban issues and gives higher priority to the state's role in growth management." The state's largest newspaper ended its endorsement with these words: "in the matter of leadership, Roberts is the clear choice."

On the east side of the mountains, the *East Oregonian* stated, "The question is leadership ability. ... We need a governor who leads instead of follows." In those same few days, Dave received several newspaper endorsements of his own. None came as a surprise to me, but Dave was gaining in the newspaper endorsement competition. As I had predicted, the *Bend Bulletin,* which had a long history of Republican support both locally and statewide, endorsed Dave. The publisher-editor of the *Bulletin,* Bob Chandler, was very clear about his partisan position. The first time I ever walked into his office as I began my race for secretary of state, he had made his personal position even more clear. "I've never met a Roberts I liked or endorsed." I remember responding, "Well, Mr. Chandler, you haven't met me yet." So, not only did Dave get Chandler's strong endorsement, the *Bend Bulletin* editorial used consistently negative comments about me throughout their writing: "Dave Frohnmayer is the only candidate qualified for the job." "Roberts has done a bum job as Secretary of State." This was an editorial that required a thick skin as a candidate!

Also, just to make certain I didn't get too confident as the last week of the campaign began, the local chapter of the IBEW (the electrical workers union) who had given me a $1,000 contribution early in the campaign, reversed their endorsement, due to their anger over my support of Measure 4, to close the Trojan Nuclear Power Plant. This might well be a very tough final week. Who could guess what was coming next?

On October 30, Oregonians in Action, well known for their opposition to land-use regulation, endorsed Frohnmayer, who claimed he didn't know what OIA's exact platform or objectives were. The president of the group claimed he had met with Dave and given him their detailed platform. I attacked Dave for accepting the OIA endorsement. I thought if I could get enough attention to this endorsement it would raise controversy, backfiring on Dave and harming his support in the Portland metropolitan area and in the wine country. The press picked up the story and gave it broad coverage. All endorsements are not necessarily helpful.

As Secretary of State, as is the Oregon custom, I announced my prediction for voter turnout in the upcoming November 6 election — a high prediction: 73 percent. With eleven ballot measures, many of them controversial, I felt the turnout would be strong. With the close governor's race and a number of other very active, competitive races, this seemed a pretty accurate calculation. Time would tell.

Of the eleven statewide measures, my greatest concern was Ballot Measure 5. This citizen initiative would have potentially devastating long- and short-term impacts on Oregon. A property-tax limitation measure, it would decrease property-tax support for schools, community colleges, and local governments. The measure's additional requirement that the local public school cuts must be replaced from the state's general fund put the budgets for state human-services programs, state police, corrections, and higher education in direct competition for the same scarce dollars. In an editorial feature in *The Oregonian* just days before the election, Associate Editor David Sarasohn labeled Measure 5 "Oregon's next governor," pointing out, correctly, that if Measure 5 passed it would immediately cost the state budget $626 million. In the next full two-year budget (for 1993-95), the state would be obligated for an additional $1.7 billion. In 1995-97 that number would explode into a $2.9 billion financial burden for Oregon's state government. Oregon's general fund budget was barely $7 billion at that point.

In addition to the ballot measures and candidates in Oregon, I was also keenly aware of some of the major women's political contests around the nation. Dianne Feinstein (D) was in a tight race for the governorship of California. In Texas, State Treasurer Ann Richards (D) was in a neck-and-neck race for governor; it had been a major mud-slinging fest. In Colorado, Josie Heath (D) was trailing in a race for the U.S. Senate, but Colorado voters had a way of surprising the experts. Joan Finney, also a state treasurer, was making a strong run for governor in the state of Kansas. She was an anti-choice Democrat with long experience in state government.

The last week before the election was an absolute whirlwind. I was going to every venue where I could shake hands, get press, and recruit volunteers for our get-out-the-vote efforts. Frohnmayer was likely doing the same thing. Two new polls were released in that week. Channel 2, the ABC television affiliate in Portland, released a poll showing me at 44 percent, Frohnmayer at 40 percent, and Mobley at 11 percent. An interesting side issue in that survey: voters were asked, if Mobley were not in the race, would they select Roberts or Frohnmayer. Surprisingly Dave only received half of the support from those conservative voters. An *Oregonian* poll two days later showed me leading Frohnmayer by 8 points, my biggest lead in the entire campaign.

On Friday, November 2, as the final weekend of the governor's race began, my campaign held a noon-time rally in Pioneer Square, right in the heart of downtown Portland. The square is often referred

Hugging a supporter at the Pioneer Square rally. Photo by Mike Lloyd from The Oregonian.

to as "Portland's front porch," and five hundred supporters showed up to cheer me on. The Salem *Statesman-Journal* reported our big noon rally, including photos, calling me "exuberant." If I *seemed* that energized, I deserved an Academy Award! I shook hundreds of hands, posed for photographs with supporters, and smiled for the TV cameras. While I traveled the state campaigning, another financial report was released. Most of my major contributions were from labor unions and employee groups, and a major donation from Right to Privacy, an Oregon gay rights organization plus another big check from the Democratic Governors Association. This new report also showed contributions from Emily's List that now totaled $97,000 from its members. The majority of Dave's new money came from businesses, including a number of additional contributions from the timber industry. Dave had raised more funds than I had, but my campaign still had a substantial balance while Frohnmayer's report showed a deficit, despite his having raised almost twice as much over the entire course of the campaign. One more financial story would become available in a few days, since all contributions over $1,000 received in the week before the election must immediately be reported to the Oregon Elections Division. During the last days before the election Frohnmayer was focused on what *The Oregonian* termed a "desperate struggle to win back conservatives who had defected to Independent Al Mobley." Yet, a day later Dave was quoted in the Salem *Statesman Journal* saying, "By the end I expect Mobley will not be a factor in the race. When push comes to shove, people want to vote for a candidate who can win."

In the midst of this last tiring and crazy week, I was allowed an afternoon off for two essential chores: to get my hair cut and to buy a new suit for the election night gathering. I needed to look sharp and professional on Tuesday night—win or lose. My hairdresser, Sue, always gave me a big personal lift. She had been doing my hair for about fifteen years. She knew me well—and she knew my hair. She could always tell when I was under real stress because my hair began to fall out. *This* was one of those times. What a treat to lie back at the shampoo bowl and get the pleasure that comes with nimble fingers, warm water, and caring attention. After months of stress and pressure plus the recent death of my dad, this was a wonderful break. She knew me and knew my family, and, like the proverbial bartender, a hairdresser hears it all. She was not only my hairdresser, she had become my friend and confidante. She was just what I needed in that final week of the campaign.

Looking fresh and styled, I headed off to find the perfect suit for election night. I ended up choosing a beautiful emerald green wool suit with black trim highlights. I opted not to buy a new pair of stunning black shoes, deciding I couldn't risk breaking in new shoes on election night. I needed comfortable feet for the hours I would be standing on Tuesday evening. It was now time to go home and begin the work of preparing my election night remarks—two speeches: one for victory, one for defeat!

In the last week of the campaign, my staff decided to run a television spot that criticized Frohnmayer on the log-export issue. We had prepared the spot earlier but didn't plan to use it unless we felt Dave's people were again turning negative. Frohnmayer claimed he was staying positive, no longer running negative ads against me. That was true. Yet I was being hit with Republican Party radio ads across the state, and Frohnmayer's campaign was sending out letters strongly criticizing my record. Patricia, Kevin, and I felt that "negative" meant "negative." So we ran the spot for several days at the end of the race. Dave complained loudly. I wished his campaign had felt that way earlier when they were spending thousands and thousands of dollars on radio and television attack ads against me.

On Monday, November 5, the day before the election, an interesting and somewhat unusual story broke about a newspaper ad published in the Corvallis *Gazette-Times*. The ad led off with the phrase: "We're Voting for Dave." That was followed by a list of 697 people purporting to be Frohnmayer supporters. However, the list immediately raised the ire of more than twenty-five people — some of them Democratic Party activists — who said they did not endorse the Republican candidate and had not given permission for the use of their name. *The Oregonian* stated that the list included three couples living outside the U.S., people who had moved from Corvallis years before, and three who were dead! Among those listed in the ad was the head of the county's "Hispanics for Roberts Committee," Rudy Asunsolo.

The Frohnmayer campaign apologized, calling it an "unfortunate accident." The city attorney for Corvallis, a well-respected local citizen, had prepared the ad for publication. He said he had received permission from the campaign office to use the list of former supporters and volunteers from Dave's races for attorney general in 1984 and 1988 and some additional Republican Party lists. Some of the people on the list declared themselves strong Democrats who had never supported Republican candidates. The whole incident was over in a few hours.

That same Monday, the state Elections Division released its final pre-election financial numbers. I had raised $110,300 over the final week. Dave had raised $83,850. A contest — right down to the wire.

I was feeling good on Monday — good but cautious. I told *The Oregonian*, "Our numbers have grown progressively stronger. I think it's clear that if everything goes well for the next twenty-four hours,

I have reason to feel good today." I added, however, "In the last twenty-four hours of a campaign, *everything* makes you nervous." I quickly avoided any discussion of filling my Secretary of State's seat once I had won the governorship. I was just superstitious enough to find it bad luck to discuss that topic.

My *two* election night speeches were written, approved by my campaign leadership, and ready for delivery. My suit was pressed and hanging. My staff assured me that all the details were ready and waiting for tomorrow's election night party. I was anxious and a little nervous about the election results, but other than the hundreds of statewide volunteers who would make our carefully organized get-out-the-vote efforts happen, we had done all we could do. The rest was up to the voters.

As I headed to meet Frank for a quiet dinner, I grabbed a stack of recent newspaper clippings to see how we had been doing in terms of late press coverage. It would help keep my mind off the next day's voting. Frank and I relaxed over dinner, even treated ourselves to dessert. I had lost more than ten pounds during the campaign. The heavy travel schedule, tension and pressure, and skipping some meals, certainly gave me extra leeway for dessert on the evening before the election! What an unreal, amazing nine months this had been. Frank and I laughed and joked as we anticipated my very possible win, only twenty-four hours away. He had always believed in me, in my ability to win this race. He had started out as my mentor and become my best fan, my cheerleader, and my haven.

After dinner we relaxed, and both of us read through the newspaper clippings. My favorite news clip was a photo of one of my Labor Advisory Committee members, Steelworker Union President Ernie Tibbits, holding two Roberts yard signs and smiling broadly. He was my statewide lawn sign coordinator. Over twenty thousand signs had been distributed and placed in every one of Oregon' thirty-six counties. The story reminded me of how much effort and how many supporters are required to put a candidate in the winner's column. I felt I had been a strong, skilled candidate, but I had no illusion that I had traveled this far on my own.

CHAPTER EIGHTEEN

The Win

As I opened my eyes on Tuesday morning, the reality hit me. Election Day! November 6, 1990! This was potentially a day that would change my life. And, three hours later, as if to put that possibility into CAPITAL LETTERS, two Oregon State Police officers pulled into the driveway. I had been informed that this security unit would be with me for the entire day and evening. Dave Frohnmayer would receive that same protection for the day. Tonight, one of us would lose that special state police detail.

The big election night gathering for my supporters was held at a large Portland conference building called Montgomery Park. We had not only rented the entire main floor for the election night party, but we had also secured space in the office floor upstairs for my staff, family, and close friends to await the updating of the early returns and the posting of the county-by-county results on the big white marking boards. As hundreds of people began to gather on the main floor, our campaign staff began analyzing the early voting reports.

We understood that those small first numbers were likely to be absentee ballots that had been waiting for the 8 p.m. cutoff time to be counted. We knew Dave's campaign strategy had included an outreach to Oregonians who had applied for absentee ballots, including military members stationed out of state or on international duty. Our budget had not been large enough to do the same. We expected these earliest returns to lean in Dave's favor ... and they did.

All around me, staff, family, and friends were clearly anxious and nervous. Strangely enough, I wasn't experiencing that same edginess. I had the sense that I had given my all, done everything I could, and the votes were definitely cast. The results would be what they would be. Two friends recently related almost exactly the same memories of the early part of that election evening: they recalled me walking around carrying my nineteen-month-old granddaughter, Katie, seemingly without a worry in the world. Even remembering back twenty years, they were still amazed at my total calmness while all around me folks were pacing and wringing their hands.

The county-by-county vote totals were being posted on the large white boards. Around 10 p.m. a big cheer burst from one of the rooms. I was winning Washington County! This heavily populated county, part of the metropolitan tri-county area, was definitely not a jurisdiction where we could have predicted victory. As far as any of us could remember, a Democratic candidate for governor had never won in that county. My votes in the other two metro-area counties were looking equally strong. I was ahead in Clackamas County and hitting it out of the park in Multnomah County, where Portland was located. My votes were also looking strong in most of the coastal counties and I was forging ahead in Lane County, where Frohnmayer lived. I smiled each time I looked at the numbers in Yamhill County, my hometown county. It was traditionally a Republican county, with a large number of citizens connected to the timber industry, so my growing vote totals there were unusual but, for me, heartwarming.

By 10:30 p.m. I was ahead in eleven counties, running close in another seven, and behind in the remaining eighteen. The notable difference was *my* winning counties were Oregon's most populous. Many of those that Dave was winning were small, sparsely populated, rural counties. Dave would win more counties; I would win more votes … hopefully.

We were waiting for just a little more assurance that I was, indeed, winning the race for governor. My staff and I wanted to go down to the main floor and greet the hundreds of supporters who had been waiting for two hours or more. It appeared I was holding at about 45-46 percent of the vote with Dave at 39-40 percent. Mobley was polling between 12 and 13 percent. We would wait another fifteen minutes or so to be certain that no last-minute shift was taking place. In the meantime, in anticipation of my arrival downstairs, we began directing family and friends and my staff to use the elevators, so they would be less noticed, and take their places on or near the stage. Now I was feeling some tension — but tension laced with excitement.

As the ballot measure votes came in, the most disappointing result, from my perspective, was what appeared now to be the passage of Measure 5 by a squeaker vote. This severe property-tax limitation had failed across most of the state, particularly in the counties east of the Cascade Mountains. However, voters in the Willamette Valley and the Portland metro area appeared to be supplying the votes for passage. What a disaster this would be for school budgets and state government finances. And even after all my risky political positioning on Measure 4, the Trojan Nuclear Power Plant would remain operational. Additionally the anti-welfare measure, Measure

7, would clearly pass by a solid vote. A lot of bad news for the new governor!

State legislative results usually came in more slowly but early returns gave me much to be concerned about. Democratic incumbents were behind in several contests around the state. With all I had on my platter if I won, I certainly didn't need the extra challenge of the Oregon House returning to Republican control after twenty years. I thought of the old line, "Be careful what you wish for." If I won the governorship but was faced with the passage of Measure 5 and the potential loss of Democratic control in the House, it could tie my hands both in terms of the state budget and my policy agenda. Now I was feeling some real tension as I prepared to come face to face with my future.

With my staff and personal support group all headed downstairs, I checked my hair and makeup in the mirror, pulled out my "winner" speech and quietly reread it aloud one more time, and waited for the cue to head downstairs to the cameras and the crowds. This would be a moment in Oregon history. I wanted to savor it. I wanted the gathered crowd to be excited *with* me and to retain this memory for future storytelling. "I was there on the night Oregon elected our first woman governor." This wasn't just my own personal moment of glory. This was a night to experience what it feels like to help make history happen.

Patricia checked the numbers one more time. My percentage showed 46 percent; Frohnmayer was holding at 40 percent; Mobley was at 12 percent. Almost 80 percent of the vote was in. Portland's four major TV stations had declared me the winner. It was 10:45 p.m. It was time to give me—and my supporters—what we had worked toward for nine come-from-behind months. It was time to declare victory!

The offices in the Montgomery Park building are two stories above the main floor. So, when I stepped onto the long, slow-moving escalator, I was high above the crowd. They looked up, saw me, and the place went wild! As I floated down the moving stairs, it felt like the ultimate "grand entrance." People were waving, applauding, cheering. Flashbulbs lit up across the huge room. It was an amazing scene. My emotions were bouncing off the walls. This was a moment I would hold close forever.

When I reached the lobby level, I rushed onto the stage, kissed Frank, hugged Mother, walked toward the microphone, and embraced my friend Congressman Les AuCoin; and then Governor Neil Goldschmidt hugged me, swung me around, and actually lifted me off the ground! Then Les and Neil each grabbed one of my hands and we raised our arms high in the air in a strong show of victory! The crowd cheered even more loudly.

Just before I stepped to the microphone I turned and looked at my two sons. They were all smiles. I winked at my sister and looked toward my mother standing at Pat's side. That was almost a major mistake. Mother had tears running down both cheeks. These were more than tears of joy. My mother was grieving the absence of my dad on this special night. He should have been here! This should have been his night, too. I had to look away from Mother before I lost control of myself.

Then I stepped to the podium, waved at the assembled crowd, and delivered my first "official" words as Oregon's Governor-Elect. "When I entered the race for governor in February, I told Oregonians that they were looking at the hardest-working candidate they had ever seen. Tonight I'd like to tell you, you're looking at the happiest candidate you've ever seen!" And they laughed and cheered, and applauded.

After thanking all my volunteers and staff and the Oregon voters, I acknowledged that the likely passage of Measure 5 and Democratic losses in the Oregon House meant I had some tough new issues to deal with. "I have never been intimidated by adversity and I have never backed away from a challenge. I will not let you down. I'm proud that I've run this campaign as the real Barbara Roberts and not some creation of a political strategist. I am honored that Oregon voters found the real Barbara Roberts to be worthy to be their governor. And now, the really hard work begins. I hope you'll stay with me in the tough years ahead."

Once I stepped from the podium, I did live television interviews for all the major affiliates, then the radio reporters and the newspapers. As I moved from interview to interview I stopped to shake hands and accept embraces from dozens and dozens of supporters. I also found that as I completed the first few interviews I began to react to reporters using the term "Governor" as they spoke with me. This would take some getting used to!

It was almost 11:30 p.m. when I completed the last interview. The media had just reported that Frohnmayer had gone to bed without a concession speech or any acknowledgment of my win. In fact, he was quoted as saying I had declared victory prematurely. "There are still votes of many Oregonians to be counted," he said. "We don't think it's over yet. It's going to be a long night." And then, he reportedly went to bed.

When I was speaking on the podium, my campaign received a call from one of the national television networks. They wanted to put me on the air live at 7:30 a.m. — East Coast time. That's 4:30 a.m. in Oregon! The network was planning to interview Governor-Elect Ann Richards of Texas, Governor-Elect Joan Finney of Kansas, and me, Governor-Elect Barbara Roberts of Oregon, on a three-way split screen to show three women elected governor on the same night for the first time in the nation's history. Can you imagine going on national television with less than four hours of sleep at the end of a grueling campaign? Can you imagine looking put-together and sounding articulate and gubernatorial at 4:30 a.m.? Welcome to grown-up politics!

Celebrating with my mother. Photo by Dean Guernsey from The Skanner.

During the course of this hectic but magical night I would occasionally become aware of the two, and sometimes three, state police officers following my movements in the crowd. I would smile at them and they would nod in my direction. This would definitely be a new life experience, both personally and politically. I had watched officers with Governor Atiyeh and Governor Goldschmidt, standing near, watching, observing, while the governor went about his activities. I had never really contemplated the complexity of their roles and responsibilities … until now.

Frank came to say good-bye. He was tired, and headed home. Even as weary as I knew he was, he was still smiling, ear to ear. His own reelection had been successful; his daughter Mary Wendy had again been returned as Oregon's Labor Commissioner; and his wife had been elected Governor. The Robertses had hit a grand slam on this election night! Since I had to be up so early to go to the television station for the network broadcast the next morning, my sister, Pat, and I were staying in a downtown Portland hotel on this unusual night. Mark would drive Frank home tonight, and Frank and I would meet tomorrow at the state Capitol for lunch.

Pat and I headed for the hotel with our overnight bags and my change of clothes for my network TV appearance. The state police were with us. They checked us into our rooms. Pat and I were sharing a room, just like when we were kids. We were both very tired but also finding this hotel situation a little bit of an adventure. We had shared a room for hundreds and hundreds of nights but never one like this! My two officers checked into the room right next door to ours. It was past midnight. We were leaving for the TV studio at 4 a.m. We were still giggling as we drifted off. Pat said sleepily, "Goodnight, Governor."

As we left the hotel the next morning, I was carrying a huge bouquet of yellow roses that Frank had sent to the hotel the night before. I felt like a bride! The two state police officers helped Pat and me get everything into the car and we headed to Channel 2 for my very first live network television experience. I was tired and a little nervous but what an exciting interview! Three brand-new women governors—making history and capable of making a few waves. It was the first of many wonderful opportunities I would have with the amazing Ann Richards. Ann, Joan Finney, and I would help change the face of the National Governors Association.

As we left Portland, headed to the state Capitol, we stopped to pick up the early morning street edition of *The Oregonian*. It was the first headline I had seen on the previous night's election results. "Roberts, Hatfield, Measure 5 Win." I saw that Dianne Feinstein and Josie Heath had lost their respective Senate races in California and Colorado. *The Oregonian* also pointed out two facts about *my* win that I was unaware of. I was the first Democrat to succeed another Democrat in the Oregon Governor's office since 1878. I would also become the first Oregon Governor elected with less than a majority since Democrat Charles Martin won a six-way race in 1934 with just over 38 percent of the vote. My 46 percent now looked strong in comparison.

The Oregonian also had a column on the defeat of the two anti-abortion measures: "Activists on both sides of the abortion issues watched Tuesday as Oregonians crushed a measure that would have banned most abortions and narrowly rejected another that would have required doctors to notify a parent before a minor could have an abortion. That Oregon vote caused reaction all the way to Washington, D.C., where Kate Michelman, executive director of the National Abortion Rights Action League showed her strong excitement. 'The national pro-choice community is really ecstatic. The news in Oregon is very gratifying.'" I thought of my attendance at the NOW conference in San Francisco in early July and knew that over two hundred thousand members of that group would also be thrilled with the Oregon vote.

The news coverage that was definitely *not* thrilling for me was the outcome of the contests for the Oregon House of Representatives. Although three new Democrats would enter the House, we were losing several important incumbent seats. In addition, the Democratic House Caucus lost two races where our incumbents had not sought reelection and those two open seats became gains for the Republicans. If those numbers held, the Republicans would control the House by a majority of thirty-two to twenty-eight, an exact reversal of last session's numbers, an added detriment for me as a Democratic governor.

By the time we reached the Capitol and walked into my Secretary of State's office, the whole place was abuzz. Telephone messages were already stacking up. More flowers had been delivered. Several Oregon newspapers were on my desk with headlines to cheer about. The other interesting news clip in the stack indicated that my prediction for 73 percent voter turnout had been low; the actual turn-out had been 77.3 percent, the highest Oregon turn-out on record for a nonpresidential year. Final numbers in the governor's race: Roberts, 46 percent; Frohnmayer, 39 percent; Mobley, 13 percent. The *Statesman Journal* reported that I had won 81 percent of those voters who identified themselves as feminists and 56 percent of the women's overall vote compared with 29 percent who voted for Frohnmayer. Interesting numbers; encouraging trend.

One of the most prophetic press pieces on my desk that morning was an editorial from the Medford *Mail Tribune* under the headline, "Roberts takes charge." One short paragraph from that editorial would be repeated, at least in theme, over the next four years:, "Voters who elected Oregon's first woman governor have handed her the most difficult assignment ever given to a governor." As I said earlier, be careful what you wish for!

Before lunch, I made my first official announcement, sharing the name of the chair of my Transition Team, John Keyser, President of Clackamas Community College. I had known John Keyser since he was a faculty member and dean at Mt. Hood Community College while I was a member of the college board.

When Frank arrived for our lunch date, I had already put in an eight-hour day! We decided to simply go downstairs to the Capitol coffee shop for a quick bite. Every time our eyes met, he gave me a huge smile. He seemed thrilled with my election success. Between my office on the east end of the first floor and the coffee shop on the west side of the basement floor, we were stopped about fifty times by well-wishers. To my complete surprise, when we walked into the Capitol café, the other customers all broke into applause. I had never seen this happen before in all my years in the Capitol building! I had been coming here for twenty years since I was a "newbie" lobbyist back in 1971. The previous night in Portland over a thousand people had cheered my victory, but Capitol insiders giving me this unusual acknowledgment was a special honor. I was truly touched.

Back in my office, I contemplated a growing list of high-priority items. Yet I realized that everything can't be high priority! Some responsibilities and actions must rise to the top of the list. I needed to create a process for the selection of a new Secretary of State when I left that office to become Governor. I had to make an informational appointment to begin understanding the exact magnitude of Measure 5 on the state budget. I needed to make calls to the Democratic legislators who had lost their elections and calls of congratulations to the new legislative winners. I was especially pleased to see Tricia Smith win the highly competitive state Senate seat in Salem, bringing the Senate women's numbers up to eight. This had been a very successful decade for women in our Senate. Women's membership also appeared to make a gain in the Oregon House from eleven last term to fourteen in the upcoming session. If only the House Democrats had made the same level of gains as the women candidates.

My Transition Team had been assigned office space on the third floor of the Capitol building in what *The Oregonian* described as "spartan" quarters. However, this space would be assigned to my team for less than two months. We didn't need fancy; we needed results, vision, and just a taste of good luck. In the next few days the wrap-up work for my campaign office went forward, and a number of my campaign staff began plans to move from politics to policy. Patricia would be working closely with the Transition Team. Kevin Smith would supervise the closing down of the campaign office. As the weekend approached, I realized I could not remember any other three days of my life where I had made so many decisions, delegated such a long list of important chores, set in motion so much action, and had such a wonderful time! I knew the fun would likely be short lived, considering the budget crisis and my heavy responsibilities, but these first days after the election had been stimulating and hopeful. I so wanted those two words to translate to the work of my administration — "stimulating and hopeful." I was realistic enough to understand that was a very tall order. Yet this past year had allowed me to grasp what it meant to set seemingly impossible goals; to reach for the stars; to claim the gold ring. I would remain hopeful.

CHAPTER NINETEEN

Preparing for Inauguration

On Monday, November 12, as the new week began, my first full week as Governor-Elect, I was reminded of a quote I had once read by Governor Bob Straub of Oregon (1975-79): "The governor's job is so big because it involves thousands of state employees, a large number of state agencies, an innumerable number of problems and it takes time to feel like you are really running the ship." On that Monday I was hit with the reality of the magnitude of items that grew by the hour on my *Needs Immediate Attention* list. *Delegation* would soon become one of my very best friends!

Appearing early in the *delegation* column was the name of Dr. John Keyser, who had accepted the massive responsibility of chairing my Transition Team. That team would help define my first legislative agenda, have strong input on the huge Measure 5 program cuts that would be necessary in my initial two-year budget, and would also advise and assist in evaluating some of the personnel choices for my staff positions. Nine working groups would be meeting under Keyser's leadership, and each would additionally be looking at proposed budgets in their subject arena, with instructions to recommend a 10 percent cut. The range of issues these teams handled will demonstrate the complex and elaborate responsibility that lands on the shoulders of a new governor.

While these dozens of Oregon leaders, working under a six-week deadline, volunteered both time and talent to their government and my new administration, I made some early but important decisions. My first was to retain the skilled, experienced, and knowledgeable director of the Oregon Executive Department, Fred Miller. Fred had over fifteen years of leadership experience in state government, and his willingness to turn down other offers and continue in his current role felt like a gift to me. My decision to replace the administrator of the state Budget and Management Division raised a little controversy. Jon Yunker had held the position for ten years but I replaced him with Mike Marsh, who had been with the division for eight years and had a great reputation. I knew I would be more comfortable working with Marsh. I had had past conflicts with Yunker, and I believed a change of leadership style and attitude would build a stronger team.

The Transition Team committees
• Economic Development, Rural Development, and Transportation, chaired by Ed Whitelaw
• Education and Workforce Training, chaired by my friend Roger Bassett
• Natural Resources and Environment, chaired by Pam Wiley, deputy director of the Division of State Lands, had an especially tough issue agenda with the spotted owl/timber crisis facing my administration
• Human Resources, Housing, and Health Care team, subdivided into three subcommittees. Terry Rogers, with Legal Aid, Representative Bev Stein, and Rey Ramsey, director of the Oregon Housing Agency handled many tough issues and choices
• Peter Ozanne chaired Public Safety
• Mark Gardiner chaired the Intergovernmental Relations group
• Timber Communities, chaired by Catherine Mater
• Insurance and Workers' Compensation, chaired by Michael Dotten
• High Performance Organizations, chaired by Chemeketa Community College President Bill Segura

Over the previous weekend the House Republican Caucus had designated Larry Campbell from the Eugene area as the next Speaker. Campbell had served as Minority Leader of the House during the two years I was Majority Leader. You could say we had a little history! I didn't think this was going to be good news for me when my legislative bills began to reach the House. Although we knew each other and had worked together, some of our interactions had definitely been adversarial. After waiting twenty years to regain control of the Oregon House, Campbell and his Republican Caucus could well be into a show of muscle flexing! If that attitude surfaced or even prevailed, my agenda could be in for a very bumpy ride in the House.

I certainly wasn't short of challenges, but some of that difficulty was offset by the large dedicated pool of talent available to me everywhere I turned … public officials, business leaders, educators, government administrators, community organizations, current and former legislators, and my newly forming staff … so many citizens who cared about our state and the success of my administration.

With my Transition Team in full operation, planning under way for the inaugural ceremonies, the first outline of my inaugural speech partially drafted, with a growing list of possibilities for my appointment of a new Secretary of State on December 7, plus a professional seamstress now in possession of the beautiful royal blue wool fabric and the designer pattern for the dress I would wear when I was sworn in, it was time for the next big step. I was leaving mid-week for Lexington, Kentucky, for my first meeting with the National Governors Association at the seminar for new governors. Frank was attending the seminar with me, since several segments of the program were designed for governors' spouses. I honestly believe Frank was anticipating the meeting as much as I was. I also looked forward to the week's vacation Frank and I were taking once the seminar adjourned. We hadn't spent this much time together, just the two of us, since the campaign began in February, nine months before. I had assured my state police security team that I would be completely safe on a one-week car trip far from Oregon where no one would know or recognize me. I promised them, once this road outing was over, I would accept my full-time security detail without complaint.

On Wednesday, I left, *with security,* for a brief overnight in Washington, D.C. I attended the winter meeting and dinner for the members of Women Executives in State Government, a group I had belonged to for six years. This meeting had been on my calendar for months. I knew when I scheduled it that I would be there either to receive the accolades of the group or to seek sympathy and support if I had been defeated. Little could this organization have guessed, or even hoped, that we would all have so much to celebrate: three women winning governorships on one election night for the first time in American history!

The next morning my two security officers and I left Washington for our flight to Lexington, where I would meet Frank. The NGA program listed eighteen governors-elect, nearly equally divided between Democrats and Republicans (with two Independents) and pretty closely split between large and small states. Where the balance ended was on the gender scale—fifteen men and three women. Yet during those three days it became quite evident to me that every male governor, newly elected or part of the twelve seated governors acting as our faculty, was constantly aware of female presence in the group and in every room. I had the feeling that the NGA would never be quite the same again!

The other fun gender issue of this seminar was the first gathering of the group of new governors' spouses. Spencer Finney from Kansas and Frank Roberts from Oregon received no shortage of attention from the twenty-three women in the spouses' group. When Frank returned to Oregon and a reporter asked him what he had learned about being a governor's spouse, Frank smiled and quipped, "Well, I certainly did not learn how to correctly serve tea!"

By the time the seminar ended I felt I had made some strong connections with several of the seated governors, particularly from the western states. Among the new governors, it is no surprise that Ann Richards of Texas stood out. She was bright, funny, tough, and yet friendly. She had earned some political scars from a bitter race for governor, but I felt she was very capable of delivering some bruises in return.

The agenda for the weekend had encompassed major matters for preparing to establish a new administration: strategic scheduling, setting agendas, executive-legislative relations, press and media, agency management, and staffing. We also heard in-depth presentations of state and federal relationships, budgeting, working in the international arena, and managing time and staff. Finally, the tough subjects of personal stress management, living in the public eye, impacts on family and close relationships, and managing to stay healthy under all of these other challenges.

By the time I had digested the last part of that program, I knew the upcoming vacation week we had scheduled was even more essential than I had recognized earlier. I was ready for the break. I was certainly ready for the time with Frank. Our rented car was now parked in front of the conference hotel and our luggage was packed. We were ready to hit the road. Like the old Nat King Cole song, we were about to "get our kicks on Route 66." I had almost no work with me with the exception of a briefcase full of press clips that I hoped to read during the week. Pretty light duty! With our luggage in the car, Frank settled into the passenger seat, his motorized cart in the trunk, I slipped into the driver's seat for the first time since the day before the election, two weeks before. Little did I recognize that day that this road trip would be my last driving experience for the next four years.

That first day, as we left Kentucky, driving across southern Indiana and southern Illinois, Frank and I talked about the seminar, the people we'd met and heard, our impressions, plus the wonderful Kentucky hospitality. I shared with Frank one of the funniest lines I had heard from one of the governors' staff leaders. She thought every governor should be required to carry a business card that simply said, "The Governor Cannot Schedule Himself." It got a huge laugh, especially from the experienced governors. I shared with Frank that my six years as Secretary of State had taught me that particular calendar lesson years ago. I was somewhat prepared for such calendar realities … but only somewhat.

As we headed west into Texas, I found myself thinking about the fact that this would be my first time back in Texas since I left to move home to Oregon for my son Mark's birth. The young woman who had left Texas in December of 1957 in her grandparents' car was now returning to that state in 1990 as Oregon's Governor-Elect. This scenario wouldn't even make a very believable B-grade movie.

Frank and I had a wonderful week together, nothing fancy, just moving across the country. I felt relaxed and happy. Frank and I had caught up on nine months of conversations plus starting to anticipate what the next months and years would be like for us. This trip had not been about fancy hotels and exotic resorts. With Frank's physical limitations he could no longer sail or play golf. Long airline flights were almost impossible for him. We could no longer take long walks on a beautiful tropical beach. We now found contentment just being together. And the past week had given us an amazing opportunity to fully reconnect. We both understood that as soon as we arrived back in Oregon we would face a life of calendars, schedules, pressures, and intrusions into our time together. We understood and we accepted that reality — at least, as we imagined it would be. Yet, as I would learn later, you can't actually understand what it will be like to be governor until you've experienced it. Maybe every former governor should be issued a T-shirt emblazoned, "Been there, done that, have the scar tissue to prove it!"

I returned to my Salem office knowing the month of December would be packed wall to wall. In my absence, Patricia McCaig, John Keyser, and the Transition Team had been hard at work. Patricia was also working through the office budget, preparing for both our personnel decisions and the budget cuts the office would take along with every other state agency. I believed strongly I couldn't ask others to sacrifice while I, as Governor, was held harmless. My office budget would reflect that philosophy.

One of the other matters that was garnering some press interest and occupying a fair amount of my thinking was the appointment of a new secretary of state. According to Oregon law, the appointee had to be a member of my political party and would serve out my term until the end of 1992. This was a plum of a political opportunity, and the interest in the position expanded by the day. Several state legislators had made their interest public, and others had supporters who were advocating for them when they felt uncomfortable tooting their own horn.

In the earlier part of December, I was also spending time with Geoff Sugarman, who would soon be named as part of my communications staff. Geoff was helping me with the organization and writing of my inaugural speech. Few speeches one delivers in a political lifetime rise to the significance of a gubernatorial inaugural address. There was so much I wanted to say, so much I *needed* to say to the citizens of my state, to the members of the Legislature and ... to the future. Geoff and I worked well together as we outlined content, ideas, historical information, and the hoped-for quotable lines of the speech. I wanted to set the speech in historical context. I also felt I must include the fiscal realities of Measure 5. I was excited to share my ideas and plans on livable communities, on preparing Oregon's workforce, and on overhauling our state's tax system. We constantly revised the outline, perfected language, and detailed the policy sections.

On December 7, just before the weekend, I announced the first major appointments for my staff. Naming Patricia as my chief of staff was not a surprise in most Oregon political circles. Her management of my come-from-behind governor's race, her years of service on my secretary of state's staff, her recognized political contacts and skills ... my quotation in *The Oregonian* the next day said it all. "Patricia met all the criteria I had outlined for chief of staff ... she is a person who knows me. The ability to work together closely is a critical element in choosing a chief of staff." On that same day I announced several other appointments, feeling confident that they represented the quality of the personnel I hoped to be able to recruit to this level of public service.

We were also planning the details for my inaugural ceremony. In Oregon, a governor's swearing-in and first speech as governor take place in the chamber of the House of Representatives. The chamber is packed wall to wall that day with sixty House members, thirty state senators, the members of the Oregon Supreme Court and the Court of Appeals, the other five statewide elected officers, and ticket-holding guests including former governors, former Speakers of the House, other dignitaries, press, and family members of legislators and the new governor. The galleries overlooking the House chamber are equally filled with visitors, staff, and lobbyists.

Although the Speaker of the House and the President of the Senate must approve the activities in the House chamber on this first day of the new legislative session, it is customary to allow the new governor to select musical entertainment and other ceremonial aspects of this special morning. We wanted to set a tone for the ceremony that would reflect some of my personal leanings and priorities. I wanted the ceremony to be warm, simple, and uncluttered and to include a somewhat different cast of players from past inaugural programs. Planning was also under way for an evening reception in the Capitol Rotunda that would be open to the public, to offer Oregon citizens a chance to celebrate with me, an opportunity to meet their new governor, to mingle, relax, and just enjoy the moment.

I found time to squeeze in my Christmas shopping and plans for our family holidays. I also was able to host a nice luncheon that was a tradition for me and three other special women in my life. Every year my sister, Pat, our dear family friend Arlene Fall, my mother, and I gathered together to celebrate our four winter birthdays. This year, however, there were mixed emotions as we came together. Both Mother and Arlene had become widows that fall and Pat and I were still grieving the loss of Dad. Yet all of us felt we needed to be together, to keep our tradition, and also to celebrate my election victory. Our closeness was even more important after this difficult year.

Following that birthday luncheon, I came to Frank with an important idea. Oregon's governor's residence (formally called Mahonia Hall), now only three years in service to the state, was a beautiful older home, purchased and remodeled with private funds. However, with the exception of the grounds keepers and the security officer on duty, there was no staff to this large three-story, seven-bedroom home. It was expected that the governor's wife would manage the home. However, I did not have a wife! Plus the residence had no elevator at that time, and Frank was unable to get his motorized cart onto the second floor. I needed more help in caring for the residence but with the Measure 5 budget crisis I didn't feel I could ask for household support. I suggested to Frank that we hire Arlene, personally pay her a small salary, and have her move into the residence and be part of our household. She was now alone following her husband's recent death and the necessity of selling her home after his long, costly illness. Moving in with us would mean she had no housing expenses or utility costs or food bills. She would be in a place where she felt quite safe, and I hoped our company would help her face the loneliness after so many years of marriage. We, on the other hand, would have the help we needed in managing the house, plus we both liked her very much. It felt like a perfect match. Frank thought it was a great idea. Thank goodness, Arlene agreed. Oregon's governor's salary at that time was one of the lower ones in the country, but it would still permit me to make this arrangement that seemed to be to the advantage of all concerned. When we moved into this lovely home in January, Arlene would move with us. One more decision made ... a very good choice.

Under, over, and around all other activity of this transition period was the constant matter of the state budget crisis. The Transition Team was looking closely at potential cuts as they examined policy issues. Every dollar was going to matter as we faced the multi-million-dollar hole created by the passage of this anti-tax, anti-government initiative. To make matters even worse, the first $600 million cut in the 1991-93 budget would grow to $2.9 billion by the 1995-97 budget once the measure had been fully implemented. Over those five years, Measure 5 would slice a huge percentage of the state's resources out of what was, in 1991, a $6 billion general fund budget. State agencies had earlier taken a 1-2 percent cut as they prepared their new budgets. Then following the passage of Measure 5, Fred Miller, director of the Executive Department, had ordered them to show an additional 10 percent cut level in all general fund areas. On December 1 a new state revenue forecast for the next two-year period showed an additional loss of $211 million. Oregon moved from a period of slow growth to an actual decline, with timber jobs and construction leading the way in what could well be described as a mild recession. Miller began encouraging state agencies to institute hiring freezes and asked them to make cuts in their budgets for the remaining six months of the current 1989-90 budget period to hopefully create a larger carryover into the new biennium.

As I contemplated these cuts, I thought back over the last decade of America's so-called tax revolution. From the 1978 passage of the trend-setting Proposition 13 in California that immediately cut $6-$7 billion out of local tax revenues, through a nine-state set of tax-chopping ballot measures in 1980 (four of which passed), to what the *New York Times* described in November of 1980 as "Massachusetts' biggest tax rebellion since the Boston Tea Party," which had passed by a 60 percent vote, until Oregon's passage of Measure 5 in 1990, tax revolt was part of the nation's political lexicon. On September 28, 1989, the *Christian Science Monitor* stated, "The tax revolt movement ... has fizzled in recent years." They were *almost* correct. Of the eleven measures on state ballots in 1990 that sought to repeal, roll back, or cap taxes, only the Oregon measure passed — after citizens had rejected several versions in five earlier Oregon elections.

Every state agency was now feeling the impact of the new ballot measure with some real immediacy. Then, a survey released by *The Oregonian* showed that 84 percent of citizens interviewed believed the Legislature should cut the state's budget. The story went on to say, "But strong majorities *oppose* cuts in funding for the four programs that take almost all of the state budget: elementary and secondary education, corrections, social services, and higher education." Russ Dondero, political scientist from Pacific University, described it this way, "The psychologists call it cognitive dissonance. We want our cake and eat it too."

The *Oregonian* article went on to say that, although three-fifths of those polled agreed that Oregonians pay more in taxes than people in most other states, the reality was that Oregon currently ranked twenty-seventh (before Measure 5) in per capita state and local taxes. So we were moving from the middle of the national tax rankings to a number of steps below that average. Between the budget realities that state agencies, local governments, and schools would be facing right away and the erroneous perception of a majority of Oregon citizens about being overtaxed lay a huge canyon of miscommunication, mistrust, and need for education. My job, on that score, was becoming more clear.

Since the passage of Measure 5 almost two months before, I had spoken openly to the press and Oregon citizens about my intent to create a replacement revenue measure to fill the huge hole created in critical state budgets. I believed strongly that a small, well-designed, constitutionally protected sales tax was the best answer for that replacement package. Oregon political reality and current polls showed that a sales tax was a tough challenge. In a state with a long history of adamant opposition to a sales tax and voters looking for bigger cuts in state government, it would test my creativity, my political skills, and perhaps my policy acumen to find an answer to this huge challenge. Yet with each cut I made in basic school support, mental health programs, higher education, community college programs, alcohol treatment, AIDs services, state police, and state park services, I was reminded of the importance of my leadership and advocacy to bring these efforts to success for Oregon.

In the midst of all this December budgeting, planning, and preparation, an interesting story appeared in the Sunday *Oregonian*, reporting a newly released survey that showed that 60 percent of Oregonians thought that I would do an excellent or good job in my first year as the state's new governor. Considering that I was elected with only 46 percent of the vote in a four-way race, that 60 percent looked pretty good to me. Geographic breakdowns of the poll numbers indicated 67 percent support in the Portland metro area and 55 percent in the rest of the state.

On December 24, I finally announced my appointment of State Representative Phil Keisling, who was just completing his first term in the House, as Secretary of State. Keisling went on to win election to the post in 1992 and was reelected in 1996. In a surprising, and many thought unwise, decision, in 1999, Keisling announced he planned to resign from the office to seek private-sector experience. His decision was assumed by most political observers to be an attempt to add business credentials to his resume in hopes of running successfully for the governorship in the future. With few exceptions, political pundits considered the resignation a questionable political choice. Phil's decision came as a complete surprise to me. I still shake my head every time I think of the opportunity I handed to Keisling and his resignation from the state's second-highest office.

There is one more quiet, behind-the-scenes story about that 1990 appointment. One name that was never discussed in any press stories but should have surfaced was Oregon's Commissioner of Labor and Industries, Mary Wendy Roberts. She had the political experience, the intelligence, the wish to hold the office, but she had the handicap of being my stepdaughter. I could not even consider her for the appointment. It wasn't fair, but it was both a political and public reality. This reasoning on my part created a conflict between us that I was not able to resolve. In 1992 when Mary Wendy ran against Keisling for Secretary of State, I felt obligated, as I informed her, to support my appointee. The personal damage between us was understandable and painful and long-term. Frank, as he should have, supported his daughter's election. I was quiet during this difficult campaign but was unwilling to abandon my appointee in his election bid. Politics can be exciting and stimulating. It can also be hurtful and divisive. It still makes me sad to recognize the personal cost of that election contest.

As inauguration day approached, two large processes reached completion: the reports from my Transition Team were completed and my 1991-1992 state budget was made public.

The Transition Team report, in printed version, was a four- to five-inch-thick document, printed on both sides, with hundreds of ideas, concepts, plans, budget suggestions, and policy analysis papers. Some of the concepts in the thick blue notebook were already encompassed in new legislative proposals while others were longer-term ideas, savings suggestions, staffing concepts, and task force plans. Its value was priceless for my new administration—a road map for the future of state government policy and management.

On Thursday, January 10, four days before inauguration, I released my first state budget. Included were payroll reductions of 1,570 positions reached through layoffs, a hiring freeze, and early retirements. The single biggest hit came in the Department of Human Resources, which was facing $137 million in cuts. Basic school support lost $80 million, higher education's cut was a proposed $74 million. *The Oregonian* said, "Roberts responded to the passage of Measure 5 by chopping about $570 million from the current spending programs of state agencies. She made up the rest of the $841 million shortfall caused by the property-tax limit and the economic slowdown by increasing government fees and by proposing to keep surplus income-tax money that is now returned to taxpayers through the so-called 'kicker program.'" The same story went on to report my comments: "I think you're going to see we tightened our belts … but we made cuts that are probably not good for Oregon in the long term … or the short term. There is no question that the public is going to see some pain." Yet I also insisted that I did not try to target popular programs to build support for a sales tax. The article went on to say, "The governor-elect's basic budget strategy seemed to pass muster with legislators from both sides of the aisle." Generally speaking, the reaction to this very harsh budget had been positive. Knowing that you can't please all the people all the time, I thought I had survived the budget release with as much positive reaction about fairness, good faith, intent, and process as a budget such as this one could ever garner. Now, it was the Legislature's job to act. They had six months, or more if needed, to do what I had done in two months. I wished them well.

In the late afternoon of the day of the formal release of my new budget, while the press and media were full of stories about cuts, levels of reduction, pink slips, and school support, I headed to central Oregon to a meeting at the invitation of a citizen group labeled the Sagebrush Coalition. The coalition was made up of educators, business owners, private citizens, community leaders, and social service providers who lived and worked on the east side of the Cascade Mountains. Their major concern was the negative impact of Measure 5. Sagebrush Coalition members pointed out that only one of the eighteen counties east of the mountains had given a majority vote to the measure. The metropolitan areas of the state had provided the winning votes on the close election outcome yet these more rural counties would suffer the impacts on the budgets of their small cities, their county government services, and their schools.

As I entered the auditorium and saw the size of the huge crowd, I was quite grateful for my active position against Measure 5. I may have been on the losing side of the ballot issue, but I was clearly in a majority position at this particular gathering.

Dennis Maloney, director of the Deschutes County Juvenile Department and a member of my Transition Team, emphasized that the meeting was not going to be a "bureaucratic whining session" but rather concerned citizens talking about possible solutions to the toll Measure 5 would take on all kinds of programs at every level. Maloney said the gathering had been promoted under the title: "Making Measure 5 Work: A Sagebrush Response." In the spirit of solidarity I was asked, and agreed, to wave a sagebrush branch at the opening of the meeting, a symbol of the eastern part of my state. That wave caused a huge cheer from the hundreds of people gathered for the meeting.

As I listened to the panel and then to citizens from some of the most rural parts of my state, I could already feel the negative impacts that Measure 5 and my budget would have on their communities, their services, and their lives. I hadn't even taken the oath of office yet, but the mantle of leadership already weighed heavily on my shoulders — and my heart.

On Sunday, January 13, 1991, the day before my inauguration, I experienced one of the most amazing parts of the preparation for taking office. Frank and I, with the help of friends and family, moved into what many Oregon citizens now referred to as the governor's mansion. We moved our clothing, personal possessions, a small amount of furniture, a few plants, two television sets, books, and groceries. The rest of the very large house was completely and beautifully furnished. A large part of the furniture had been selected when an interior designer decorated and furnished the house three years ago. A number of other pieces in the residence were on loan from the Oregon Historical Society. Never had I imagined living in a home like this.

When everything was in the house and placed in the correct rooms, one of our volunteer movers returned with hamburgers, fries, and drinks. Arlene put out the napkins and place mats on the lovely, long, formal dining-room table and we ate our very first meal in Mahonia Hall. Everyone was tired but a lot of giggling went on about the menu for the first gubernatorial meal.

When my alarm rang early on the morning of January 14, 1991, I reached over and turned it off. There was no danger I would drift back off to sleep … not on *this day.* For this was the day I would become Oregon's Governor. Keeping my eyes closed, I prepared for the sense of surprise when I gazed upon my new surroundings. I smiled to myself and opened my eyes. Even at age fifty-four, I felt a little like a princess. Yet, I also sensed that such whimsy would be short lived!

I grabbed my robe and headed all the way down two flights of stairs to the basement level where we had created bedroom space for Frank until the installation of an elevator would allow him to reach the bedroom level of the house. I wanted to make certain he was awake and preparing for his day. The Senate would begin at 9:30 a.m., swearing in newly elected members and casting the organizing votes for the sixty-sixth legislative session. The House and Senate would then recess and reconvene jointly at 11 a.m. for the inaugural ceremonies. Frank was already showered and dressing and was full of smiles. What a day this would be! Frank would be sworn in for a new Senate term and I would be inaugurated as Governor. I kissed Frank soundly and headed to the kitchen. No matter how stimulating this day would be, I still needed my morning coffee. And what did I find in the kitchen? Arlene. The coffee was brewed; the breakfast nook table was set; orange juice was poured; our expanded household was going to work out wonderfully.

With breakfast over, I rushed upstairs to get dressed. My new royal blue dress with the long shoulder drape hung pressed and ready. The matching blue leather three-inch heels stood on the floor. My jewelry was on the dresser. I applied my makeup with special care and checked my hair from every angle three or four times. I knew my security officers would be there early to make certain my day was flawless. I had made certain all of my immediate family had transportation and they all had VIP seating tickets in the center of the House chambers. Frank would arrive with the senators when they were escorted into the House. I felt confident about the details and planning for the ceremony and reception, all arranged by a highly capable, dedicated staff.

As is the tradition in Oregon, about an hour prior to the opening of a new legislative session, statewide officers, past governors, and members of our two state courts meet in the public rooms of the governor's office for group photographs, coffee, and conversation. This is also the time to get all these participants prepared for their formal introduction and entrance into the chamber of the House of Representatives. You've heard the term "herding cats" and, believe me, this accurately describes this pre-ceremonial event. With around forty statewide judicial and political leaders gathered together in two adjoining rooms, the longtime coordinator from the attorney general's staff patiently gives instructions, order of line-up, and the lists of legislative escort members to the gregarious leaders, who seem more intent on conversation than on ceremony. Yet, somehow, it always seems to come together with appropriate pomp and historical seriousness. I made mental note of Supreme Court Justice Susan Graber and Associate Judge of the Court of Appeals Mary Deits, currently the only women serving on those two courts, which had a total of eighteen members. "Change comes slowly," I thought. I clearly understood that on this monumental day in my life.

With the House and Senate in joint session, the roll call complete for both houses, the official processional would now begin. Governor Neil Goldschmidt, only minutes from the end of his term, was escorted into the House to loud and appreciative applause. In an unusual decision, he had chosen to forgo the usual final address delivered by an outgoing governor.

It was now my moment. I was escorted by Senators Bill Bradbury and Jim Hill and Representatives Bev Stein and Peter Courtney. As I entered the House the crowd rose to their feet and the applause seemed to rise to the ceiling of the chamber. I had three times before been escorted down this center aisle as Secretary of State but that in no way compared to this walk into state history. I felt elation, emotion, wonder, and the sense of lineage that comes with such a historical passing of the guard. I could see Frank as I approached the front of the chamber, smiling and applauding. My very best fan.

As I was seated, Senator Kitzhaber, the presiding officer for the day's ceremonies, announced the posting of the colors. This was a moment where my personal ceremonial choices would become really evident for the first time in the ceremony. Traditionally, the colors are posted by members of the Oregon National Guard. I had instead chosen to have a group of Girl Scouts representing four councils from across the state, perform this ritual. I felt, as Oregon's first female governor, that I would like to share this moment with girls who would be able to tell of their inclusion as they became women, mothers, grandmothers, and perhaps future Oregon leaders. After all, I was the first former Girl Scout to ever be the Governor of Oregon!

Following the posting of the colors, "America the Beautiful" was sung by twelve-year-old vocalist Hannah Johnson of the Portland Symphonic Girls Choir, accompanied on the guitar by Ceeva Riskin, age eighteen, a skilled musician and recent immigrant from Eastern Europe. It was a moving rendition by two amazing young talents. Next on the program was Oregon author Barry Lopez, who did an inspirational reading that called for compassion and grace from us, as citizens and as leaders.

And then, at last, the official moment arrived. Rather than being sworn in on the accustomed House elevated podium, I had chosen to move this part of the ceremony to the floor level of the chamber so Frank could be by my side. Former Oregon Supreme Court Justice Berkeley Lent, who had performed our wedding ceremony in 1974 and had sworn me in as Secretary of State in 1984, would now administer my oath of office as Oregon's new Governor. As I raised my right hand to take the oath, my left hand rested on Dad's Masonic Bible, which Frank held. Exactly three months ago to this day, my father had died. My choice of his bible helped me feel that he was part of the ceremony. I repeated the oath, kissed Frank, looked at my sons and my mother a few rows away, and then grew amazed at the lighter-than-air feelings as I took the podium steps one by one.

As I stepped to the podium and lowered the microphone, I looked over the chamber and up to the galleries. I waited for the applause to subside, waited to deliver my first words as Oregon's new Governor. I took a deep breath, tamped down my emotions enough to begin speaking, and called on all my personal strength as I now cemented my place in Oregon history.

I began with the words from the diary of a thirteen-year-old girl who had recorded her own history as she traveled the Oregon Trail. At the end of her moving words I added this statement honoring those who made the grueling trip westward: "Their dream is my dream: that as governor of this state, when my term is complete, we will have traveled along *this* generation's Oregon Trail and come to a better home." Then I asked, "One hundred fifty years from now, as future generations look back on *our* journey, how will they see us? ... Will they speak of our courage, our creativity, our care and stewardship of the future? Or will they see us as short-sighted, self-centered, greedy, timid?" I then delivered the line I would use year after year: "For each generation has but one chance to be judged by future generations, and this is our time."

I closed my inaugural address saying, "You are looking at a woman who raised two children — one of them autistic — by herself. You are looking at a person who struggled for years to make ends meet. You are looking at a part-time student still working on and committed to earning my college degree. And you are looking at a woman who got actively involved because she saw a wrong that needed to be corrected. And today, you are looking at the governor of the greatest state in the union.

"Am I proud? You bet I am.

Frank holds Dad's Bible as Judge Berkley Lent administers the oath. Photo by Mike Lloyd, from The Oregonian.

"Will I make a difference for Oregon? I've never wished more for anything."

And then I added my earlier words: "For each generation has but once chance to be judged by future generations, and this is our time."

I now acknowledged the tremendous applause following my words while one of America's most talented African American vocalists, Linda Hornbuckle, accompanied by the Concord Choir from the gay community, began an exciting rendition of "Great Day/Brand New Day." I was then escorted from the House to the sounds of both applause and the "March and Fanfare" played by the David Douglas

High School Herald Trumpeters. These beautiful horns were a great final touch for an amazing ceremony.

At the informal reception following the inauguration there were hundreds of handshakes, hugs, laughs, greetings, and even a few surprise guests. I was greeted by three former high school teachers and about fifteen classmates from my four years at Sheridan High School, which really warmed my heart. My former roommate from the Harvard Program in 1989, Amy Coen, came all the way from Chicago. I had a dozen first cousins in attendance plus two aunts, two uncles, four nephews, a sister, two sons, a granddaughter, two stepdaughters, and my mother ... for starters! A number of legislators and three Oregon congressional members came by to extend congratulations. Guests ate oatmeal cookies and chocolate kisses, and mingled.

The next day's *Oregonian* commented, "Some pomp and circumstance attended the inaugural celebration of Governor Barbara Roberts but mostly it was a simple affair, more a gathering than a crowning." I smiled to myself when I read those words. That was exactly what I was aiming for.

That evening a large celebration reception was held in the Oregon Capitol building. Friends and supporters filled the first floor, sipping wine, snacking, talking politics. The event began at 5 p.m. and within an hour the rotunda was filled with hundreds of Oregonians. At 6 p.m. I made a grand entrance. Spotlights focused on the wide marble staircase from the front of the House chambers to the floor of the rotunda. I stepped into the spotlight and walked slowly down the staircase. I walked while they cheered and waved and applauded. I silently hoped I wouldn't trip wearing three-inch heels on those slick marble steps. I silently hoped I wouldn't disappoint them, wouldn't fail to meet their expectations. At the bottom of the steps, Frank was waiting. He was always there for me. This new journey might be a rough trip. I was grateful to have him at my side. We would make it together. Tonight we were celebrating. Tomorrow we would work.

CHAPTER TWENTY
An Agenda of Change

On my first official morning in the office as Oregon's new Governor, I met with Senate President John Kitzhaber (D) and Speaker of the House Larry Campbell (R) at 8 a.m. for our first of many joint briefings and discussions about the budget and legislative priorities. By 10 a.m. I was on a ninety-minute tour of the Salem offices of Oregon Adult and Family Services. I spent a good share of that first afternoon doing back-to-back radio interviews. By the end of that first week, I had attended the ceremony and reception for newly appointed Secretary of State Phil Keisling, had survived my first two-hour television interview at the Portland studios of KATU-TV, met with the Oregon Business Council, had meetings and courtesy calls with several Portland-area officials, called a crucial meeting with two members of the State Accident Insurance Fund for a lengthy briefing, toured the state's largest mental health institution for three hours, and read reams of briefings on newly introduced legislation—just for openers. This was the first glimpse into my new world.

I closed out that first week with three important new staff appointments. My administration was extremely fortunate to secure the leadership of Jeanette Pai as the state's affirmative action officer, and I named Kevin Smith and Victor Vasquez as my intergovernmental and community relations officers. Victor brought a highly unusual background to my staff. He had come to rural Oregon with his parents who were migrant farmworkers. He remembered clearly his time in the agricultural fields of Eastern Oregon. The other significant happening in my first week as Governor was a national and international crisis. International negotiations had failed to drive Iraqi forces out of Kuwait as a midnight Tuesday United Nations deadline passed. President Bush stood ready for war, including deployment of 415,000 U.S. troops. Within hours of the deadline U.S. Tomahawk missiles hit Baghdad. Operation Desert Storm had begun. Oregon National Guard troops would be affected immediately. I was their Commander in Chief. Oil supplies were at risk. Television stories speculated about the potential for terrorist attacks. Five hundred anti-war protesters marched throughout Wednesday on the Oregon Capitol steps.

On Wednesday night, January 16, I informed Oregon citizens that we had taken steps to protect sensitive Oregon sites. Extra security was placed around military installations, airports, and Trojan Nuclear Power Plant. I urged Oregonians to conserve oil and to avoid topping-off gasoline tanks. In spite of predictions by the President that this military operation would be swift and sure, many experts were making early comparisons between Iraq and the quagmire of Viet Nam.

As the 1991 legislative session began to settle into place, my office was following a large package of bills including legislation developed by my Transition Team, ideas I had advocated for during my campaign, my proposals as part of the state lottery budget, and high-priority agency bills. We were also keeping a very close eye on the Ways & Means subcommittee hearings to make certain state agency directors and leadership personnel were not second-guessing the 10 percent agency cuts that had been a necessary part of the budget-balancing package. We got the loyalty we required — almost to a person. There were only three exceptions: the Corrections Department, the Public Utility Commission, and, surprisingly, from the National Guard budget officer. The instant and harsh feedback those three managers experienced kept everyone else on-script for the rest of that painful budget process.

I met weekly with legislative leaders: the Senate President, the House Speaker, Minority and Majority leaders, Ways & Means Committee co-chairs, plus legislators working closely on the big policy proposals regarding land use, the Oregon Health Plan, and natural resources issues. Also high on my legislative priority list were the creation of the Oregon Housing Trust, our important new plans for the Workforce Quality Council, and the work of the Oregon Progress Board. I was also fully engaged with the welfare-reform implementation agenda affected by the unwelcome passage of Measure 7 on the November 1990 ballot. I was leading the effort to give broad new funding to teen health centers in many Oregon high schools. It was a large and very ambitious agenda that my administration brought to the 1991 session, particularly in light of the monetary atmosphere of Measure 5.

As we took on the challenge of this heavy legislative agenda, I was reminded of my campaign slogan: "The Change Will Do Us

Good." Yet, truthfully, my push to innovate was motivated by four major factors that were not of my making.

At the top of this list was Measure 5. This property-tax limitation measure required a massive dismantling of Oregon's public finance system and pushed the need to protect essential services at the state and local levels of government and education, now in a crisis mode. Close behind Measure 5 was the Northwest timber crisis. The federal listing of the Northern Spotted Owl as an endangered species created a further decline in Oregon's timber harvests and seriously began to hurt the state's largest industry. Rural timber communities would be particularly hard hit.

Oregon was also experiencing a period of population growth. The influx of new residents to the state surged steeply upward during this period, placing a major strain on Oregon's schools, land-use planning, affordable housing, public services, and our environment. And, much as I wished it otherwise, Oregon was not able to escape the *national* anti-government mood that hit America in the 1980s and the early 1990s. Across the country economic and social changes created anger, pessimism, and frustration. Voter turnouts dropped. Incumbents lost more elections. Anti-tax ballot measures blossomed. The idea of term limits for elected officials gained great popularity. Oregon felt the heat generated by that unrest and anger.

These complex factors demanded new approaches, new thinking, better communication with citizens, and proven outcome results from government programs and expenditures. No matter how these changes are labeled — redesigning, reinventing, or reengineering government — it is pure hard work. It requires collaboration, creativity, and constant vigilance to push such improved public policy intentions toward realistic outcomes. Even early in the 1991 session I began to understand that my mission was broader than simply being a successful state CEO. I needed to help my state and its people through this economic, social, and environmental transition. It felt as if I needed a cape and magic powers!

Several years later, after I had left office, I read a book entitled *Leadership without Easy Answers* by Harvard professor Ron Heifetz. A single sentence in its text described perfectly my sense of that period of change and adjustment that confronted my state and me as a new Governor: "Leadership is a razor's edge because one has to oversee a sustained period of social disequilibrium during which people confront the contradictions in their lives and communities and adjust their values and behavior to accommodate new realities." The follow-up book Heifetz co-authored with Harvard professor Marty Linsky, *Leadership on the Line*, added two more profound ideas that reflected the challenges of leadership I faced at that time.

People do not resist change per se. People resist loss. You place yourself on the line when you tell people what they need to hear rather than what they want to hear. ... The hope of leadership lies in the capacity to deliver upsetting news and raise difficult questions in a way that people can absorb, prodding them to accept the message rather than ignore it – or kill the messenger.

People don't want questions; they want answers. They don't want to be told that they will have to sustain losses; they want to know how you're going to protect them from the pains of change.

One of the most revealing sentences in the same chapter reads, "Leadership requires disturbing people – but at a rate they can absorb." I couldn't engineer the impacts of Measure 5 cuts to take place *gradually*. I couldn't slow down the population increases or the new diversity this increase brought to Oregon. I couldn't effectively, legally, or ethically delay the economic and social disruption of the spotted owl habitat requirements.

Bottom line: I didn't have a cape or super powers. What I did have was a set of ideas and the guts and determination to actively promote them.

We could create new jobs and a more diverse economy. We could make state government more effective and economical. We could communicate better. We could restructure Oregon's tax system for more equity and more stability. I couldn't turn back the clock, but perhaps I could turn back the forces of doubt, inflexibility, rigid thinking, and being cemented only to the past. We had to make changes if Oregon was to avoid becoming an economic backwater. We had to work for and believe in a healthy, vital new Oregon economy in every part of the state.

On Saturday, February 2, I left for Washington, D.C., for the winter conference of the National Governors' Association. I quickly found out how much of the frustration and detail of travel seems to disappear when one is escorted by two Oregon State Police officers! No luggage juggling. No check-in lines. No seating issues. I thought back to the last time Frank and I had flown. His motorized wheelchair; a luggage cart piled with both our suitcases; getting Frank through security and on the plane; and then reversing that process on the other end of the trip. This time I took my seat on the plane feeling relaxed, calm, put together ... and safe.

The next three days were meticulously planned by the NGA. Everything ran like clockwork. The first meeting was on subject matter that I was deeply involved with in my new administration: workforce education and training. The discussion was focused around the newly released report by the Commission on the Skills of the American Workforce. This meeting, alone, made my trip to D.C. worth the time away. That same morning I did two press interviews that were a step up from my familiar press and media contacts in Oregon. The first was an interview with David Broder and Gwen Ifill of the *Washington Post*. The second was with the ABC affiliate in Washington, for a program called "Working Woman." That morning I began to understand that the three new women governors were going to get more than their share of press and media attention during the conference.

At noon a governors-only working lunch discussed the fiscal condition of the states, I was called on to give an explanation in detail of the impact of Measure 5 on Oregon's state budget. That Oregon measure had followed the earlier passage of tax-limitation initiatives in California and Massachusetts. Governors without initiative processes in their states expressed gratitude for not having that potential citizen burden added to the current economic slowdown.

On that Sunday evening, the governors and their spouses were invited to the White House to dine with President George H. W. Bush and Barbara Bush. This formal dinner was an annual tradition for the NGA at their winter meeting; for most of the new governors this was a "first." It was certainly a first for me! The grandeur of the White House, the striking floral arrangements, the elegant dinner settings, the tuxedos, gowns, and the music of a string quartet, all made me aware that this was a rare opportunity. I made mental notes so I could share the experience with my mother and sister, with Frank and Arlene, and with my staff, when I returned home. For this small-town kid from Oregon, it was definitely a night to treasure. I still have my photo with George and Barbara Bush among my special keepsakes. The fact that he was a Republican was incidental to me. I had dined with the President of the United States!

Monday, February 4, was book-ended with my first meeting of the Democratic Governors Association at breakfast and a formal fundraising DGA dinner in the evening. The power evidenced at the evening event was impressive. It was my first exposure to the political weight of the DGA in Washington, D.C. The breakfast meeting gave me firsthand experience with two other power sources: Governor Bill Clinton of Arkansas and Governor Howard Dean of Vermont. All I can say on that subject is "Wow."

On that same Monday the governors returned to the White House for a working lunch on education with President Bush, followed by a press conference on the White House lawn. How many times have we all watched those press events on the White House lawn? This time I had a brand-new perspective from the other side of the bank of cameras. The view was great.

My Monday afternoon schedule allowed me to spend two hours as part of a discussion group sponsored by Emily's List (Early Money Is Like Yeast, which provides early support to pro-choice Democratic women candidates). I had received tens of thousands of dollars of support from Emily's List contributors in my governor's race. This discussion was part debriefing and part celebration. Ellen Malcolm, the organization's CEO, was full of nationwide facts, election statistics, and outcomes.

At the close of the NGA meeting on Tuesday, I visited with Oregon Senator Mark Hatfield (R) and then with Representative Ron Wyden (D). As a former Governor of Oregon, Sen. Hatfield was interested in my reaction to my first NGA conference and my visit to the White House. Both Hatfield and Wyden promised to help support many of the issues on Oregon's challenging policy agenda. I knew the senator's offers were genuine but I also understood that we could face some potential conflicts on the spotted owl/timber solutions.

A week after I returned from Washington, D.C., I visited my home town of Sheridan. This was not, however, a celebratory homecoming, but a full working afternoon and evening. I toured the large new federal correctional institution on the edge of this small town, and then spent an hour with the publisher of the *Sheridan Sun*, the same paper where my mother had worked years before. The day finished with my delivery of the dinner speech at the West Valley Chamber of Commerce in Grand Ronde, about ten miles from Sheridan. In the audience were people I knew from Sheridan, Willamina, and Grand Ronde: old friends of my parents, former high school classmates of mine, men I had dated when we were all kids, and people who were new to the area.

These were rural communities in a predominantly timber-related area. I knew these small towns and many of these small-business owners. Yet they weren't so sure they still knew me. I had moved away. I now lived in the "big city." I was a politician! I supported the federal Endangered Species Act. They were respectful, but I could feel their doubts about who I had become and if I still remembered how tough times could be in their small communities. Perhaps there was some truth to the old adage, "You can't go home again." I certainly felt at home, yet I sensed their hesitation to fully embrace the person they thought I had become.

As I reached the end of my first month in office I could check off some items that were complete or nearing completion. The huge job of closing down the campaign had been wrapped up—the office move was done, final employee salaries had been paid, finance reports were filed with the Secretary of State's office, and government employer's filings were in the mail. That job was done for three more years. Hooray!

Patricia was close to filling the final staff positions for the Governor's office. I named Steve Peterson as Director of the Economic Development Department. One of the most pressing hirings was bringing Carole Morse to the position of Director of Executive Appointments. During the course of a four-year term, an Oregon Governor can be expected to fill over fifteen hundred positions on boards and commissions. Oregon's remarkable tradition of citizen participation is reflected in the tremendous influence of these policy-making bodies. We had an even more difficult job. Governor Goldschmidt had left office with over five hundred unfilled vacancies, so we were looking at finding over two thousand Oregonians willing to serve on these predominantly unpaid boards for four-year appointments. The added challenge was my commitment to bring true diversity to those boards and commissions, some of which had never had a woman or racial minority since their creation. We could do better. We *would* do better. Over four years, Carole's staff, including my sister, Pat, helped make an appointments record I could be very proud of: 2,013 appointments, 41 percent women and 14 percent from minority groups in a state with only a 7 percent minority population. These numbers were records for an Oregon Governor. Plus, in the first three years of my administration the state Senate approved every appointment I made. In my final year a natural-resources lobby group stopped four of my appointments, likely reflecting objections to my strong environmental leanings during my term in office.

Terry Ann Rogers, a leader on my Transition Team, came on our new staff as legislative director, responsible for our huge bill-tracking system, including keeping staff informed of upcoming committee hearings and votes in the House and Senate. She was a wonderful asset in dealing with legislators and committee staff. Terry also kept track of amendments added to legislation that might reverse my previous support or opposition to a particular bill. Her detail capability and her legal expertise were huge assets for our office. She was ably assisted by Marc Overbeck, whose interest in government and public policy transferred easily from the campaign to this new role on the Governor's staff.

Sarah Johnson took on another detail-oriented staff job with the title Citizen's Representative. This job is sometimes referred to as an ombudsman in other state governments. Using staff, student interns, and volunteers, and under Sarah's warm and knowledgeable leadership, my administration handled 29,377 cases during her four-year tenure. Some took only one or two telephone calls for resolution. Other cases involved months of investigation and research. From cases of domestic violence to lost unemployment checks to veteran's death benefits or adult literacy needs — the Citizen Rep.'s office usually saved the day.

One of the other positions that might be regarded as a behind-the-scenes role but is essential to the tone and public image of the Governor's office is one that has, quite frankly, an inadequate title. Barbara Allen was listed on our staff roster as Assistant to the

Governor but she was known in the office as BAAQ—Barbara Allen, Ambiance Queen. She was the person who chose and purchased flowers every Monday morning in Portland so that the governor's public reception area in Salem always greeted visitors with a touch of floral class. She arranged every reception held in the governor's public offices, the monthly changing of the office art displays, the caterers for every reception and dinner held at the governor's residence. She fussed over details regarding guests lists, seating, wine choices, cookie and punch orders, napkins, and timing. She did it all and made it look easy. She also made our office and me look professional, organized, and even classy.

Throughout the 1991 legislative session, I held dinners at Mahonia Hall for groups of seven or eight legislators at a time. I wanted the evenings to feel relaxed and social. I wanted legislators who had not previously had this opportunity to enjoy the house. Barbara Allen would select the caterer and menu. Arlene would be certain the dining room table was prepared with linens and place settings, glasses and flowers. Frank almost always joined in those dinners. To a degree, Frank was stepping out of his role as state senator and into his place as Oregon's "First Gentleman." We both enjoyed the dinners and felt that this house was intended for such social gatherings.

As the Legislature approached what I hoped would be its midway point in March, my staff and the state's agency leadership were pressed trying to keep up with major policy work, legislative hearings, proposed legislative amendments to my budget, and the outcry from citizens now becoming aware of the detail of the monetary impacts caused by the Measure 5 cuts. Oregon legislative sessions are usually a little crazy by this stage in the process, but the addition of my broad-based agenda of policy recommendations and the budget cuts resulted in a heightened level of activity and no small amount of policy conflicts.

I gave two major addresses in March, both related to crucial Oregon matters. On March 7, I spoke to the Western Environment Law Clinic at the University of Oregon. Obviously, the situation with the federal Endangered Species Act and Oregon's timber/wood products industry was creating a huge area of legal/environmental work being followed closely at the law school. The next day I spoke to the Governor's Tourism Conference. The status of Oregon's tourism industry was on an upward trajectory in our state's economic picture. Where the natural resources sectors of timber, agriculture, and fishing had long held the place of Oregon's economic trifecta, tourism and high technology were quickly climbing the economic ladder in the state. These industry transitions were creating both negative and positive waves. I again recognized how change could be perceived as loss as citizens and communities dealt with the shifts.

In late March I again traveled to Washington, D.C., this time to testify in support of a universal voter registration bill. During my two days in D.C. I met in their individual offices with every member of the Oregon congressional delegation—four Democrats and three Republicans. On my final evening in Washington, U.S. Representatives Les AuCoin and Ron Wyden hosted a reception in my honor. I returned to Oregon in time to greet the first Oregon National Guard members returning from the Desert Storm operation.

One of my final official acts for the month of March 1991 was one that I found exciting and extremely rewarding: I appointed my first judge to the bench. Judicial appointments in Oregon do not require state Senate confirmation, so this is a direct and clear power that belongs to the governor alone. I appointed Janice Wilson to the District Court of Multnomah County. A strong, intelligent woman with extensive legal skills and a calm professional demeanor, she would be an excellent judge, I knew. On April 10, I was in Portland to participate at her swearing in and robing.

As the legislative session continued, a slight upswing in the economy brought unexpected resources to the state budget. It was definitely not enough money to fill the hole caused by Measure 5, but it relieved some of the state budget pressures, allowing the Legislature to restore a portion of the most damaging of the cuts in human services and education that I had proposed in my January budget. In conjunction with those positive budget changes, I brought forward three additional budget matters:

First I requested the Ways & Means Committee to create a Rainy Day Fund as part of the session's ending balance, an amount that could not be touched without a special legislative session. Such an ending balance would help the state's bond rating and be entirely prudent considering the potentially large cuts coming in the 1993-95 biennium.

Secondly, I immediately froze the number of state manager positions and would not approve agency proposals for any new management positions. Records showed that from the end of the 1989 session until the beginning of the 1991 session, six hundred sixty new state managers had been added. I pledged to the Legislature and Oregon citizens that I would not allow a repeat of that hiring pattern during the next eighteen months.

Lastly, I encouraged thirty-five hundred eligible state workers to file for retirement; those position vacancies would be reviewed on a case-by-case basis to determine if the jobs truly needed to be refilled.

We were no longer in a "government as usual" mode in Oregon. I was hoping to convince our citizens that there were much better answers to tax reform and property-tax relief than Measure 5. Without that message being clear — and believable — Oregonians would be unlikely to vote for any improved tax overhaul.

On May 16, I announced the formation of a Governor's Task Force to Review State Government. The fourteen-member group was charged with reviewing central government systems (such as computer networks, accounting systems, and personnel depart-ments) and to determine if those support services could be improved upon. The second chore of this task force was to ask the tough questions: Do we need this agency? Could we merge those operations? Can this board or commission be eliminated? I gave this high-powered task force one year to complete its work, with an interim report to me expected at mid-point, in December.

The Senate Republicans had been attempting to start a management study of state government by an outside professional accounting firm, but even the Speaker of the House, also a Republican, had backed away from that proposal when it appeared that the cost would run between $1 million and $5 million and that it would take far more time than the year's work I had proposed for my task force. The Speaker felt we could operate my task force with about $250,000 for research and technical assistance.

At the time I announced the task force, I made comments about the reasoning behind directing this broad look at Oregon's state government.

I am convinced that our state government has done a good job in the past, and that state workers continue to do a good job. But that doesn't mean we should be complacent. Just because our state government programs and structure met the challenges of the past does not mean that we are ready to take on the future.

Our state structure has been evolving since 1859 – 132 years. Every two years the Legislature meets, bringing new ideas. However, most of these ideas tend to add to government and add laws and mandates. Bits of government have built up gradually, a commission here, a board there, a new agency. It is easier to create a new department or pass a new law than to get rid of an old one.

This is a huge job I am asking of this task force, one that has never been done before in Oregon. We need to do it well. When I retire from this office I want to leave state government in the best shape I can. This task force will help meet that vision.

Little did I know how much controversy would result over the next year from the ideas and proposals of my new task force. Obviously cuts and changes are never popular, but I heard from military veterans, minority groups, education leaders, recreational boaters, blind citizens, and two statewide elected officials, for starters. None of them was happy with the early proposals. I kept reminding those with strong concerns that these were recommendations only. My decisions would become clear with my State of the State address in January and my budget recommendations after that. We were facing a $1 billion cut in a $6 billion budget. There would be change. There would be loss. There would be pain.

In the middle of April, I testified in support of Senate Bill 708, which would make discrimination on the basis of sexual orientation a legal violation in Oregon. "It distresses me that in Oregon today it is legal to deny housing to a woman because she is a lesbian, or to fire a man because he is gay, or to refuse service to someone because they appear to be homosexual. It distresses me that it happens. It distresses me more that some find such discrimination acceptable and Oregon offers no protection to citizens treated in this manner," I told the committee. "Senate Bill 708 asks that we affirm our basic commitment to human and civil rights." The bill passed the Oregon Senate and died in the House Judiciary Committee without a hearing. A step at a time.

In early May I enthusiastically welcomed home a large contingent of National Guard troops from the Persian Gulf. These citizen-soldiers had been serving a world away from Oregon for months. Now they were safely home, back to their families and their jobs. That same month, I was back in eastern Oregon to participate in the opening of the new Pendleton Convention Center and to join in the exciting ground breaking for the new Oregon Trail Interpretive Center in Baker City. The museum would be part of the commemoration for the 150-year celebration of the Oregon Trail in two years. As a descendant of pioneers who had traveled the Oregon Trail, I was thrilled that this celebration would occur during my governorship. I found myself, however, feeling sad that Dad would miss this chance to celebrate with me this chapter in our family history. So many times in my role as Governor I thought of the joy he would have felt in elements of my service to Oregon.

Frank and I were hoping that the Legislature would adjourn in time for us to celebrate our seventeenth wedding anniversary on Saturday, June 29, but it wasn't looking too promising. A conflict had arisen between the House and Senate over a lottery bill that would allow operation of and state control over video poker machines. The legislation had been moving smoothly through the legislative process for weeks, having already passed the Senate; it was headed for a vote in the House when the first bipartisan opposition arose. New and vocal attempts to send the video poker machine amendment to the voters were gaining momentum. We had expected a Friday adjournment, but a weekend session to resolve this conflict was now on the schedule. Everyone seemed tired and cranky. They were ready for adjournment.

Frank looked beat when he came home late Friday afternoon. His heavy schedule was wearing on him. We ate a light dinner, watched the television news, visited for a while, and then I went downstairs with Frank while he got ready for bed. He admitted he was feeling worn out and was disappointed the session hadn't completed its work so he could sleep late on Saturday morning. It was becoming clear that our wedding anniversary celebration would have to wait for a few more days.

Early Saturday morning Frank called my upstairs extension. He was having chest pains, and he felt the pain was getting worse. He said clearly that he needed to go to the hospital. He hadn't had this kind of an incident since his heart by-pass surgery in 1983. We were only blocks away from the Salem Hospital. I rode with Frank and checked him into the emergency room, where he was treated with anti-coagulants and finally transferred to the cardiac ward. It was obvious Frank was not going to be released. I notified Patricia that I was at the hospital with Frank and did not intend to come to the Capitol unless it was absolutely critical. I was about five blocks from the Capitol but I needed to be with Frank. I had her notify the Senate President's office that Frank would not be available for this final conflict vote of the 1991 session. The Legislature continued its video poker battle all day Saturday and adjourned to come back for a Sunday morning session. I was definitely focused on a different kind of battle on that Saturday afternoon as Frank was transferred by ambulance to the cardiac center at St. Vincent's Hospital in Portland. It was becoming a strong likelihood that Frank would, once again, face major heart surgery.

On Sunday afternoon June 30, the Legislature adjourned *sine die*. It was the first time either Frank or I had missed the closing of the session since 1975 — sixteen years. We were together at St. Vincent's Hospital. Frank was being prepped for an early Monday morning heart bypass surgery. I was, quite honestly, worried about this second bypass surgery. Frank was eight years older than when he had faced this operation in 1983. Heart surgery at sixty-eight is scary enough. The same surgery at seventy-six seems much more worrisome. Yet Frank's medical fate was in the skilled hands of Dr. Albert Starr, Oregon's premier heart surgeon, who had performed Oregon's first heart transplant. I cancelled my Monday and Tuesday schedules and planned to stay in Portland at the hospital.

Frank's quadruple by-pass surgery was described by the surgeons as "uneventful." He came through the surgery strong. I was so relieved. His surgeons understood Frank's recovery would be somewhat slower than most patients' due to his inability to walk. However, on July 14, two weeks after his surgery, Frank left the hospital in his wheelchair with a very broad smile, wearing a T-shirt bearing the words, "Takes a Licking and Keeps on Ticking." The press covered his release from the hospital, including his smiling photo. He would be in a healing mode for a while. I would be back to work full time.

The fact that I was away from the Capitol for the close of the legislative session meant that I was unable to do the post-legislative press conference that Patricia and my communications team were planning. By the time I was back in the Capitol full time, all the newspapers had written their wrap-up articles. Television and radio stations had reported the session's end. Editorial writers had ranked the session's successes and failures. But I had missed my chance to get the hoped-for press and media focus on the many successes of my administration's first legislative session. It was an opportunity I could not recapture ... until now!

There had been strong doubts whether any legislation of importance would make it through the session. Many skeptics thought we would never be able to balance the first Measure 5 budget without some major tax increases. Pundits and the press looked at the Democratic Senate, the Republican House, a brand-new Governor, Measure 5, and the timber crisis, and logically had low expectations for the session.

But we produced not only a balanced budget, but a budget with a responsible ending balance. Admittedly, the upswing in the state's economic picture helped and there were some minor fee increases and a four-cent-a-gallon gas tax jump for road repairs, but we all worked to prove Oregon government could live within its means. We would then plan to give Oregon voters an opportunity to help us reverse our pending budget crisis with long-term tax reform.

One of the most crucial of the proposals I had included in my initial budget was $25 million to create the Oregon Housing Trust. The trust would create the first significant targeted state program to provide affordable housing for Oregonians. The money would be used to both build and rehabilitate housing plus offer support to local communities who needed the technical assistance and information to increase funding leverage for such projects. Rep. Bob Repine (R), Chair of the Housing and Urban Development Committee, took a strong leadership role on the legislation and helped shepherd the bill through his committee and the House of Representatives. We were successful. I also proposed and won the merger of the Oregon Housing Agency with the state Community Services Division of the Department of Human Resources. This integration of state housing and community services was designed to help program clients move toward self-sufficiency and recognized the essential role that housing played in these transitions.

These were just two of the successful components to one of the strongest housing agendas proposed by an Oregon Governor in decades. When I began talking about critical affordable-housing needs during the campaign, almost no one was paying attention. However, the 1991 Legislature heard the message. They recognized the impact of our strong new population growth, soaring rents, and escalating housing costs, and acted to meet these pressures. The housing programs I promoted helped create thousands of new units of affordable housing in Oregon. I remembered three of the sentences I had delivered on housing during my campaign for governor: "Almost no human need is more basic than shelter. No family which lacks it can even begin to meet its potential. No community which neglects it is viable." I felt proud and positive regarding my leadership on Oregon housing.

Another human services need my administration pushed for in the 1991 legislative session was funding for teen health centers in Oregon high schools. The range of adolescent health issues being ignored or undiagnosed was tremendous. We began with seventeen high schools in areas with a high percentage of uninsured students. Some concern was raised by legislative members who wanted to prevent any discussions with students on reproductive health issues, but that was quickly overshadowed by unsettling discussions on teenage diabetes, sexually transmitted diseases, tuberculosis, and HIV-AIDS. My budget commitment to these high school health centers survived the legislative process, and services were made available to hundreds of students, some even by the time classes began in the fall of 1991.

The 1991 session produced several very successful and significant pieces of environmental legislation that I was enthusiastic to sign — a major recycling bill; a significant phase-down of field-burning acreage in the grass-seed industry; a revision of Oregon's Forest Practices Act dealing with reforestation, harvest practices, and clear-cuts; plus a bill that my office had played a major role in negotiating on cyanide heap leach mining. My office worked hard to hammer out a proposal that could be supported by both industry and environmental groups. That negotiated measure passed in the closing days of the session and was considered one of the strongest control bills on leach mining in the nation.

One of the successes I felt most proud of from 1991 was my proposal to create a statewide Workforce Quality Council. As we looked at the dislocated workers from timber-dependent communities, the huge cutback in the salmon-fishing industry, and the potential shutdown of Oregon's only nuclear power plant, it became evident that we needed to prepare the state's workers for a changing economy. My Transition Team's first assessment of resources to meet this growing challenge showed a maze of more than fifty agencies, programs, boards, and commissions involved in worker training on the local, state, and federal level. There was no coordination, no mutual set of guidelines or shared vision. This was not the framework to get such a huge job accomplished. Thousands of workers needed our help. The leadership from my Education and Workforce Policy Advisor, Marilynne Keyser, on this workforce agenda was an amazing combination of policy knowledge, determination, and superb legislative outreach.

My WQC legislation created a state-level council with representatives from the private sector, state and local government, and the education community. The WQC was charged with identifying strategies for achieving our state objective: "Create the best-prepared workforce in America by the year 2000." I wasn't thinking small on this tough mission. When I signed the bill I said, "Together we will build an educational and training system that will encompass our schools, our community colleges, our four-year higher education system, our new welfare reform program, our unemployment system, displaced workers programs, vocational preparation, and worker up-grading programs." I went on to say, "We don't care where the worker comes from, whether it's a dislocated timber worker, a student coming out of high school, a disabled worker, whether it's a worker injured on the job, someone coming out of the prison system who has no job skills, a welfare mom ... whatever the context of the worker, it doesn't matter. This WQC will recognize that everybody can be a worker. If we do *our* job, they can do *theirs*." My Workforce Quality Council bill had an important ally in the new Oregon Workforce Quality Act introduced by the House Committee on Trade and Economic Development, and the package of these two bills passed with only one dissenting vote in both houses. U.S. Labor Secretary Robert Reich cited the program as a "national model."

I was also rewarded with the successful passage of my proposal to fund the state portion of Oregon's Head Start program with a budget increase of $10 million that would double the number of children in this state-paid pre-kindergarten program. This was an effort that Frank had championed in the 1987 session, shepherding the first $1 million of state money to the program. Now my own priority for $10 million for Head Start would reduce waiting lists for children all over the state. As grandparents of young children Frank and I celebrated this outreach to some of Oregon's most needy pre-kindergarten children.

I suppose a cursory look at my 1991 legislative accomplishments may have caused the July 1 *Oregonian* to say, "Her agenda was relatively modest ..." Perhaps a complete coordinated design for preparing Oregon's workforce, millions of dollars of new affordable housing, control of the massive pollution from cyanide heap leach mining, a revised welfare-reform system, doubling the children in Head Start, controlling the expansion of new state management hires, health services for teenagers, gaining a multimillion dollar mass transit grant to pay for 25 percent of the West Side light rail, and devising a Measure 5 budget that was not only balanced but included a responsible ending balance was simply less exciting than, for example, building hundreds of new prison cells and creating the huge bonding debt to pay for them.

With the legislative session adjourned, most legislators back home to their families and their jobs, Frank at home getting well, getting stronger every day, and lobbyists cleared out of the building, I took on another brand-new responsibility in my role as Governor—my first vetoes. I had three choices: sign into law, let a bill become law without my signature, or veto the bill. A veto would show my clear disapproval of the action taken by a majority of both houses of the Legislature or could also reflect a drafting error or a constitutional problem. There was one other part of this process that was relatively new in Oregon: a veto amendment submitted to the ballot by the 1987 Legislature and passed by Oregon citizens in November 1988. This constitutional amendment required the governor to give a five-day notice of potential intent to veto a bill. This notice gave both proponents and opponents of the legislation an opportunity to lobby the governor on his or her final decision. Interestingly, this amendment had been introduced at the request of Senator Frank Roberts. Frank believed a governor should be subject to the same arguments legislators heard on all sides of a bill rather than acting in isolation or hearing only one side when making a veto choice. It had seemed like a brilliant and balanced idea when Frank discussed it with me in 1987. Now that I was Governor, it felt a little closer to just one more decision-making headache. Frank actually seemed to enjoy my complaining about this element of the process. He took this as an indication his idea was working as planned.

In the end, I vetoed four Senate bills and eight House bills. Four of the bills I vetoed concerned election or initiative-petition processes, and I deemed them to be unnecessary or damaging to Oregon's election system. Three bills related to medical liability or state pharmaceutical purchases and were flawed in terms of fairness to low-income patients or had unrealistic trade restrictions. Two bills dealt with crime, but not the usual violent crime issues that often surface during a legislative session. One was intended to clarify the penalty for forging a lottery ticket, but inadequate drafting actually *lowered* the penalties, an unintended change. The second was on the subject of the use of prerecorded music. Rather than legitimately protecting the recording industry, the scope of the bill was so broad as to negatively impact school plays, nonprofit groups, even the playing of the national anthem at a ball game. It was basically unenforceable.

I also vetoed HB 2359, which I believed reversed much of the positive work we had done on amending and improving Oregon's Workers' Compensation system over the previous four years. It focused on sanctions rather than education and cooperation. In a somewhat controversial decision, I also vetoed HB 2820, a major bill on home-schooling standards, which locked into law the current minimum standards defined by the state. I believed that the power to amend these minimum standards, like the educational standards in the public school system, belonged with the State Board of Education not the Legislature. Due to the mistrust between home-schooling parents and the State Board of Education, my veto message included clear instructions about future meetings, testing requirements, and a good faith effort to repair that damaged relationship. The House later overrode that veto but the Senate upheld my action.

My final veto, HB 3294, was a real disappointment. The intention of the bill was wonderful, but a serious drafting error made signing it impossible. The purpose of the bill was to permit manufactured dwellings to be used for seasonal farmworker housing. I vetoed the bill but with instructions to the Building Code Agency to promulgate an emergency rule to provide for the temporary siting of these manufactured dwellings to serve Oregon's seasonal agriculture workers.

I allowed four bills to become law without my signature. The most significant was a budget bill, SB 5561, the budget for the Indian Services Commission, which suffered a 33 percent cut from the previous biennial budget and reduced the staff to a single person. That office represented *all* of the Indian nations of Oregon and they worked closely and cooperatively with the state on children's needs and human service issues. The Indian commission had also been a key player in the recent salmon summit, representing the unique rights of Native Americans to the fisheries of the Columbia River. It was a harsh and unjustified cut. I was clear that I wanted to veto the budget bill, but unfortunately that would have left the Indian Commission with no budget at all, hardly a better alternative.

On the flip side of the veto process was my ongoing signing of over nine hundred pieces of legislation passed by the 1991 Legislature. These began during the late months of the session and continued into the late summer. Some signings were done in stacks, quietly, during my daytime work hours. Other bills were signed in very public ceremonial celebrations. Special attention was given to HB 3343, which phased down grass-seed industry field burning. When I signed the bill on Skinner Butte overlooking the city of Eugene, which had experienced blackened skies on summer days for many years, it was a real community celebration.

The Oregon Workforce Quality Council Bill, HB 3133, certainly rated a signing ceremony from *this* Governor, as did the package of bills labeled the Timber Response Plan, HB 2244, the heap leach mining bill, and the two major housing bills that had my strong support, the Housing Trust (HB 2779) and the Housing-Community Services Consolidation Bill (HB 3377). I also agreed to a public signing ceremony for HB 3565, the Education Reform Bill that had been the work of former House Speaker Representative Vera Katz. I was not a total enthusiast of the legislation but felt Vera's hard work and leadership deserved recognition. All across the nation, states were experimenting with new educational ideas and delivery systems. Oregon couldn't be afraid to step off the beaten path and try a new direction. However, I would watch the new effort closely for any signs that "different" is not always synonymous with "better."

The legislators had failed in the 1991 session to complete what is always a highly political chore. Every ten years, following the latest federal census, legislators are given the political "hand grenade" of redrawing all legislative boundaries and the state's congressional districts to reflect population shifts and keep districts equal in the number of citizens represented. Legislative redistricting is usually a highly politicized process, but in Oregon in 1991 it was complicated by the fact that the House was in Republican control and the Senate had a Democratic majority. The two houses were not likely to find agreement. Every line, every border, every street mattered in these highly charged debates. The conflicting Oregon House and Senate redistricting versions ended up in a Joint Conference Committee, where the effort on the bills finally died for lack of agreement or compromise by session's end. The legislative redistricting would now be done by Oregon's new Secretary of State, Phil Keisling. The congressional boundary lines would be decided by the federal courts.

Even in a packed-to-the-ceiling calendar in July, I was given the special treat of attending the International Pinot Noir Celebration and dinner on the campus of Linfield College in McMinnville. As Oregon's wine growers and wine makers continued to produce both quality grapes and quality wines, the state's pinot noir wines were receiving special acclaim in the U.S. and in Europe. This festival was both a wine-tasting extravaganza and a celebration of a young but increasingly applauded Oregon product of quality. On the same campus where I had competed in speech contests as a high school student, I was now mingling as part of a new Oregon competition — world recognition of fine pinot noir wines — where Oregon was excelling. Part of Yamhill County had been "dry," selling no alcohol, only a few short years ago. Now the county's hillsides were blanketed with row upon row, acre upon acre, of fine wine grapes. This was one of Oregon's fastest-growing segments of our already productive agriculture industry.

On August 8, two of my state police officers escorted me to Portland for an unusual appointment. I entered Providence Hospital and joined my younger son, Mark, and his wife, Susan, for the birth of a new grandchild. I was again privileged to witness the arrival of a new member of our family. In this home-like birthing center, I also shared this amazing experience with Susan's mother, who had driven across the state to be here for the baby's arrival. Robert Michael Sanders was born on a warm sunny day, arriving in Portland as a new sixth-generation Oregonian. Robert was a namesake for both my late father and also his maternal grandfather. Michael was a special honor to my older son. Uncle Mike was thrilled to have his first nephew carry his name. I was simply thrilled to have another healthy and beautiful grandchild.

As the summer of 1991 flew by, I was missing most of Oregon's beautiful outdoor weather. In August I was in Seattle for three days for the National Governors Association summer conference. In September I traveled to Washington, D.C., to testify in support of the Oregon Health Plan, which could only become a reality with federal support for policy waivers. Some congressional members insisted on referring to our plan as "rationing" medical services to the poor—as if we didn't *currently* do that across the country! The difference was most states drew the service lines between levels of poverty. Oregon drew a line between necessity and effectiveness of medically ranked *procedures*. I kept telling Congress and the national press, "We are not proposing 'rationing' medical care; Oregon is proposing 'rational' medical care." I gained a great deal of expertise in explaining and advocating for the innovative system that was the Oregon Health Plan. Jean Thorne, an expert on the plan and its proposed implementation process, traveled with me to D.C. and served as both mentor and coach as I prepared for my testimony. This experience was considerably more tense than my usual appearances before the committees of the Oregon Legislature. Plus I might have only a single chance to make Oregon's case. I had to get it right.

Oregon's next biennial session would not be until January of 1993. Now one of my two biggest challenges, the budget, was temporarily off the top of my crisis list. It was quickly overshadowed by the spotted owl/timber situation. If ever there was an issue that defined my strong belief that neither nature nor the economy are static systems, this was the prime example. My understanding of this and my recognition of the political fallout that accompanied these systemic shifts caused me to recall the line from my inaugural speech, "I will be tuned to the next generation, not to the next election." I needed to be certain that I made the right policy choices without consideration of my future political successes.

The legally mandated Northern Spotted Owl Recovery Team was required to develop what I believed must be a biologically sound, legally defensible plan to protect the threatened owl from extinction *yet* a plan that would thereafter allow Oregon to move forward with a responsible level of timber harvest in the future. This was a huge scientific and policy agenda. My senior policy advisor, Martha Pagel, represented Oregon on the team. Martha, Ann Hanus from the Department of Forestry, Dave Riley on loan from the Forest Service, and their support staff carried a huge burden for our state. It would be eighteen months until the Legislature returned to the Capitol in regular session but there was not any break in the workload, legal challenges, frustration, controversy, and political rhetoric that would accompany the spotted owl controversy week after week, month after month.

As the policy work continued, in June of 1992, another talented, able, and environmentally knowledgeable woman, Ann Squier, joined my staff. I had worked with her when she had served as legal counsel to the State Land Board. So when Martha Pagel changed positions from her role as my Senior Policy Advisor for National Resources to become the Director of the Oregon Water Resources Department, I immediately appointed Ann to fill the position. We were moving and leading in a huge and challenging environmental arena. The work could not falter while I made this major staff change. It was a huge expectation to place on the shoulders of any staff leader. Ann accepted the workload, the conflict, the heat, and the reality we both understood — "It ain't easy being green."

In July of 1991, I began including a block of information in every speech I delivered: all my audiences heard the first description of what would soon be known as the "Conversation with Oregon." This massive statewide outreach to Oregon's citizens was believed to be the nation's first and largest interactive electronic hookup between a governor and a state's voters. Its intention was to inform and educate Oregon voters on their state tax structure, its dollar impact on state and local government programs, and the detailed expenditures of the state budget.

It had become more and more evident, with the passage of Measure 5 and recent polling, that Oregon citizens were making decisions on major ballot measures with inaccurate or inadequate information. However, this extensive effort to bring "real" numbers and better understanding of taxes and budgets to thousands of my state's citizens was much more than Taxes 101 for these Oregon participants. We wanted them to *share* their newfound knowledge in their homes, at work, at the barber shop, bowling alley, PTA, and coffee shop. The knowledge these citizens would carry away from the Conversation could easily multiply into a million better-informed voters … or so I hoped.

I would announce the details of the plan across the state at six large meetings over four days in September. After those meetings were complete and, hopefully, well covered and reported by Oregon's press and media, the process of random selection of thousands of Oregon registered voters would take place. Those selected could choose, if they wished, to participate in this first-in-the-nation process. They would become the "students" and I would become the "teacher" in a series of electronic classroom experiences. I was excited to unveil the entire plan to my state. Behind the scenes, my chief of staff, Patricia McCaig, was masterminding the details of this creative government outreach. Patricia and her team of strategists had no model or blueprint to follow. They were both the inventers and the implementers of a brand-new national model for citizen participation.

The Conversation with Oregon was tagged with many labels: creative; inventive; a waste of time and money; interactive government; conning the voters; ingenious; a publicity stunt; award winning; democracy in action. From my viewpoint, the Conversation ranked near the top of my personal experiences as Oregon's Governor. It was, however, the forerunner to the largest *failure* of my political career. That said, I still believe that the Conversation with Oregon was a democratic (with a small "d") success. The failure of the tax plan component, in my estimation, rested on the shoulders of several players. I accepted then, and still today, the major share of the blame for the loss of my tax plan referral. I hand some blame to the Legislature. So let me tell you the story, from my perspective after almost two decades of reflection.

With the planning and printed material completed and in place, all arrangements and funding ready to go, my office announced the first major step in the Conversation with Oregon. I would host six kick-off meetings in cities around the state over a four-day period, beginning in Pendleton in Eastern Oregon. Looking out on a large crowd of both expectant and perhaps curious Oregonians, I presented my plan to the hundreds gathered to hear this very first presentation. I told them, "I feel good that the process I've chosen to build a strong future for Oregon will involve thousands and thousands of Oregonians. It will be like an old-fashioned barn raising! Pitching in, working together, and getting something done which is valuable and necessary." I described the fact that some didn't place much stock in this Conversation process. I defined the two other schools of thought: the "quick fixers" and the advocates for the "slow painful breakdown."

Had I chosen the quick-fix route, I could have referred a tax measure, and labeled it the "Roberts Reform Package." It would have looked like leadership, sounded like leadership, smelled like leadership. Editorials written across the state would have heralded my action. And, once again, when the voters said, "No thanks," those same experts would have said, "Nice try, Governor." But in this effort, there are no points for "Nice try."

For those on the other hand who counsel, "Wait for the pain to set in," have you ever noticed that the pain they are so willing to wait for is always someone else's?

I spoke about Measure 5, our budget situation, our outdated tax structure and citizens' lack of trust in their own government. I spoke of the times in the past Oregon had stepped forward with innovation, positive change, and common purpose.

The time has come to reassert our pioneer tradition of imagination and persistence. No people ever went backward to greatness. Oregon can remain a great state but only if we act like one. Yes, it will cost something, but the price of doing nothing would be far more costly.

I am here today to ask for your help for our state, to ask you to become a volunteer in the greatest experiment in democracy since statehood.

I closed my remarks with these words: "Our purpose must be to find commonality, to reach consensus, to set priorities, and then get on with the business of the future."

From Pendleton I moved on to Bend in Central Oregon, to Medford in Southern Oregon, to Salem, and Portland, ending in Eugene. I have, over the years, described the doubters as saying, "What if no one attends the community meetings?" At the end of those six large public meetings, over five thousand citizens had attended. When that step was obviously successful, the next question was, "What if no one volunteers to help?" After the meetings, we had over five thousand volunteers signed up to help with the practicalities at each meeting. We were off and running! So much for the doubters.

The next step was the random selection from the registered voters files in Oregon's county election offices. Voters were selected who are frequently referred to as *motivated* voters or *persistent* voters, those who had voted in the previous three primary and general elections. There was some complaint about the fact that only registered voters were allowed to participate. I had no patience with this criticism. "If they don't care enough to register, I'm not very interested in their opinions." Blunt—but my bottom line. Invitations were mailed to eighty thousand Oregon voters statewide with a postcard response enclosed to either accept or decline the invitation.

By the time the Conversation sessions ended, over ten thousand Oregonians had participated in nine hundred local meetings in thirty-two separate broadcasts linking those local locations and the Oregon Public Broadcasting studio in Portland where my participation took place. Using Oregon's Ed-Net system, our state's interactive telecommunications network, each local site saw and heard me via video feed. Each local site had a two-way *audio* connection. So anyone speaking from any site could be heard at each of about thirty sites across the state. (In today's communication world, all of the exchanges would have included both video and audio.) The agenda for each of the two-hour sessions was the same, as were all the printed materials we used and distributed. Our trained volunteers helped with check-in, material distribution, and other essential activities. This project could never have happened without those dedicated volunteers.

Participants were asked to discuss three questions: *How well is the government spending your tax dollars?* Volunteers passed out charts on Oregon's tax system. I presented information from these charts and then asked Question 2: *What level of government services do Oregonians want?* and Question 3: *How do we provide this level of service?* A discussion followed, then facilitators wrapped up at the local sites. At the end of each meeting, participants filled out a questionnaire and evaluation. People were allowed to take all their printed materials with them with the hopes that they might study them further or share them with others.

The two-way audio connection meant a participant on the southern Oregon coast in Coos Bay could stand up for the economic importance of international trade and shipping after a voter from the Willamette Valley had commented that the whole idea of a small state like Oregon basing its economy on international trade was just public hype and would fail. Different views of Oregon's economy allowed me to comment on the complication of being governor with so many conflicting ideas and perceptions among the state's citizens on big issues like job creation, taxes, and education.

When participants viewed a list of twenty-four services, only a portion of the total delivered by state and local governments, choosing priorities and levels of service became instantly more complicated. The complexity grew when we listened to alternative regional priorities. Answers to funding issues changed when a bar chart showed the state lottery as a small sliver at the bottom of the chart, obviously not the answer to funding the huge costs of schools or prisons or mental health services. And when I presented the chart on where Oregon stood nationally in terms of state and local taxes per person, it flew in the face of all the propaganda about Oregon being a high-tax state. Before the passage of Measure 5, Oregon had ranked number 21, just a little higher than middle place nationally, surrounded ,by Arizona, Nevada and Colorado. Once Measure 5 was fully implemented, Oregon would be number 39, in the bottom quarter of the fifty states.

I presented this two-hour program thirty-two times between November 4 and December 7. It was, first of all, an educational experience *for me* and, hopefully, for thousands of our citizens. It was a privilege to interact with so many Oregon voters who cared so deeply about our state. There were more than three hundred news articles on the Conversation between October and December, many of them, especially in nonmetropolitan areas, negative. What a merry-go-round this process had been. On the final Saturday afternoon of my Ed-Net presentation at the Oregon Public Broadcasting studios in Portland, the television crew and my staff and I celebrated together wearing our brand-new T-shirts that read, "Survived the Conversation With Oregon." Nonetheless, I want to make clear that the innovative process that was the Conversation with Oregon is an accomplishment that I will remain proud of. It was risky, but demonstrated my strong belief in citizen participation, communication, and collaboration.

Dr. Carolyn Lukensmeyer, Executive Director of America Speaks and former chief of staff to Gov. Dick Celeste of Ohio, wrote these comments about our innovation, "Governor Barbara Roberts broke new ground when she held the Conversation with Oregon. It is now widely recognized that rebuilding citizens' trust in institutions is a primary task for all leaders. The lessons learned in Oregon are now widely applied in reinventing government and citizen involvement work across the country." During December, we held more than a dozen brown-bag meetings around the state to share with some of the local Conversation participants the results of the ten thousand questionnaires. Using that information these second-round voters helped me think through the first design ideas for a new Oregon tax structure. As I finalized my new tax plan and prepared for my January 1992 State of the State address, I carried with me all that I had learned over an incredible month of statewide communication. The resulting tax reform would be the bundled thoughts and dreams and demands from ten thousand motivated Oregon voters. The big question was: would the Legislature recognize that citizen involvement with the credibility and respect it deserved?

In late 1991 I was given the rare opportunity to make a decision of great and potentially long-term impact — the appointment to fill a vacancy on the Oregon Court of Appeals created by the terminal illness and resignation of Judge Jonathan Newman. I appointed Robert "Skip" Durham to fill the position and was honored to speak at his November investiture in the Oregon Supreme Court Chambers. Judge Durham ran unopposed in the May primary of 1992 and continued to serve with distinction on that bench until I again appointed him, this time to the Oregon Supreme Court, in January of 1994 to succeed Judge Edwin Peterson. I consider my two appointments of Judge Durham as valuable gifts to the Oregon judiciary.

Sandwiched between my six large kick-off meetings for the Conversation with Oregon in September and my thirty-two Ed-Net sessions in November, I left on one of my longest international economic-development trips. Traveling for almost two weeks in Japan and Taiwan, our delegation met with government, business, education, and environmental leaders to expand and sometimes cement relationships with these two economically important Asian nations.

After an exceedingly lengthy flight, we landed in Taipei, Taiwan's capital city. The next two days were spent discussing issues of shared concern with Taiwan's President Lee Tung Hwei and Premier Hau Pei Tsun. I was the first Oregon Governor to meet with either of the top Taiwanese officials. It was considered a great honor. In addition to trade, two other policy matters were of particular interest. Taiwan's Council of Agriculture briefed me on their country's recent agreement to abide by the United Nations resolution calling for a moratorium on drift-net fishing. At the time, Taiwan maintained the second-largest drift-net fishing fleet in the world. The huge fleets were believed to have a negative impact on Pacific Northwest migratory salmon spawning grounds. This was no small matter. I commended President Lee on his leadership in changing his country's policies on this issue.

I also discussed with the President a proposal to provide technical assistance to his country to help clean up the Tam Sui River, which flows through Taipei. Later that day, I did a formal presentation to the ten-member panel of Taiwan's Environmental Protection Agency. I summarized the presentation as I closed, saying, "We can share the expertise Oregon gained cleaning up the Willamette River in our state and provide you with the experienced Oregon environmental technology companies to advise you with this crucial work." Back in Oregon I explained the proposal, saying, "We can export quality of life to Taiwan and at the same time generate Oregon jobs."

Our week in Japan included meetings with executives of Japanese companies already invested in Oregon — Fujitsu, NEC, Seiko Epson, Mitsubishi Materials, Toshiba and Kyotaru. These companies employed thousands of Oregonians and our state's relationships with these companies and their leadership executives were critical to job retention and expansion. The delegation also met with representatives from Matsushita Electric Works, who announced, as we were leaving Japan, that they planned a $28 million factory in the Oregon community of Forest Grove. While I was in Japan, I also met with Prime Minister Kaifu and with officials backing Kiichi Miyazawa, who was elected later that month as Japan's new prime minister. As a special surprise, Prime Minister Kaifu introduced me to his son, who had spent several months in Eugene, Oregon, as a high school student in the late 1970s.

One of the most enjoyable parts of this trip was the excursion to Toyama Prefecture, where I signed the first sister-state agreement between a Japanese prefecture and a U.S. state. Over two hundred of Toyama's leading citizens joined Governor Yutaka Nakaoki and me in a formal ceremony and celebration. Governor Nakoaki was considered the most popular and strongest governor in Japan. He had actively pursued our sister-state relationship. After four years of discussion, this was considered a major success for him. I felt honored to be a signatory of the historic document between our states, between our countries.

Seven months after I returned from this successful Asian trip, Governor Nakaoki of the Toyama Prefecture, our sister state, made an official visit to Oregon. We did a joint press conference citing the importance of this official new relationship in terms of economic development, educational and cultural interactions, and state employee exchanges. That evening, I hosted Governor Nakoaki and his delegation at the governor's residence.

There seemed no end to the exciting experiences on my first major international economic-development trip. I not only rode the amazing bullet train in Japan — I drove it! I met for dinner with the leaders of Taiwan's women's movement. I spent time in Taipei, a city of 3.5 million people. I spent most of a day with the leaders of Waseda University, one of Japan's most prestigious. Oregon's Director of

Agriculture, Bruce Andrews, was presented with five Japanese JAS certificates (the equivalent of an *enhanced* "Good Housekeeping Seal"). We celebrated what this JAS certification would mean for a variety of meat products, jams, and fruits from Oregon. I ate a great amount of beautifully prepared food, some of which looked back at me! I drank the necessary amount of sake. My Japanese expanded from ten words to almost seventy-five. I experienced the formal Japanese tea ceremony and the informal charm of the beautiful children of Asia. Our delegation boarded the return flight exhausted but feeling rewarded after a highly successful business, government, and cultural exchange. I returned home with a much-expanded knowledge base on our two major trading partners and a greater appreciation of the significance of these outreach efforts on the state's part. I also returned home ready to see Frank after the longest separation of our seventeen-year marriage. I had a hundred stories to share with him. I was also ready for my own bed, a glass of Oregon water, one of Arlene's wonderful dinners, and even for my office workload. I would also have to check myself to avoid bowing as I entered a room and reentered my home culture.

CHAPTER TWENTY-ONE

Challenges and Controversies

On October 17, Attorney General Dave Frohnmayer announced he would be resigning his office on January 1, 1992, to become Dean of the University of Oregon School of Law. Before his election as attorney general, Dave had been on the law school faculty for ten years. This announcement gave me the responsibility of filling yet another statewide elected office by appointment. Since the position would be on the 1992 ballot, I could choose someone who might seek the office at that time or a person who would fill out the remaining year with no intention to run for the post. However, because Frohnmayer was a Republican, I must appoint a registered Republican.

Just after Thanksgiving, I announced that retired Multnomah County Judge Charles Crookham had accepted my invitation to fill that appointment. His twenty-five years of experience on the bench and his reputation in the legal community made him a solid choice from the list of fifteen men and women suggested by my staff and others. Even though Judge Crookham and I discussed the upcoming election, I left the decision about his running in his hands. Charlie Crookham retired as attorney general at the end of his one-year tenure. Dave Frohnmayer went on to become the president of the University of Oregon for fifteen years until his retirement in June of 2009.

As a new year began with no indication it would be any easier than 1991, I did a number of interviews so the press and media could take stock of my first year as Oregon's Governor. While everyone agreed that I had faced a particularly difficult first year because of the budget crisis, there was disagreement about how well I had faced my challenges. One of my former House colleagues, House Democratic Leader Peter Courtney, expressed concern that I had been the target of unfair potshots. "It's been horrendous to see the criticism out there about her and I just don't understand it. I don't see anyone else coming up with a plan, so how can we point our fingers?"

So the first-year stories continued with reactions of both supporters and detractors, but as Representative Courtney indicated, no one else was "coming up with a plan," no better plan was on *anyone's* drawing board. However, in reality, the general expectation was that the leadership for this multifaceted crisis rested on the shoulders of the Governor. My shoulders.

After a year of being Governor, I prepared for yet another "first." On the evening of January 23, 1992, in the chamber of the Oregon House of Representatives, I delivered my first State of the State address to the assembled members of the House and Senate, to several personally invited guests, to the Oregon press and media, and to a number of Oregon citizens who had been participants in the Conversation with Oregon. The speech was carried live by several television and radio stations. I delivered a message I would have preferred to avoid. I would have much preferred to tell my state that everything was ship-shape, right on target. However, what I had to report was that Measure 5 had diminished Oregon's property-tax receipts and placed that burden squarely in state government's lap. The state of our state was clearly not a good-news story. *The Oregonian* called the $1 billion-plus budget loss from the state general fund "chilling." They labeled my 10 percent cut in state government workforce "dramatic."

"Government is going to work better," I told the assemblage. "Government is going to work smarter. And your government is going to work with fewer employees." I announced state workforce reductions of four thousand, half of which would be management-level employees. The majority of the cuts would occur through attrition, retirement, and unfilled vacancies, but there would also need to be at least a thousand layoffs to reach the goal of downsizing the state workforce by 10 percent. These personnel cuts would save $50 million in the remaining months of the 1991-93 budget cycle and over $200 million in the next biennium. Yet that wouldn't get us even near halfway to the projected shortfall.

I went on to describe further proposed consolidations and cuts, including the elimination of more than seventy of the state's three hundred boards and commissions. I described the important citizen input I had received from the Conversation, as well as some of the early recommendations from the Governor's Task Force on State Government, which had just completed the first six months of their year's assignment. I said clearly that I understood that many of the proposals I was making, and would continue to make, would upset and dishearten those who preferred the status quo. "But the time has come for change—change across the board. Change brings turmoil, but it is the only way we will bring progress in our current situation."

However, many of these changes would require legislative approval. They were far from a done deal. Pendleton's *East Oregonian* remarked on that point the next day. "Roberts has shown a willingness to take action. ... We can be sure that legislators and interest groups will fight every cost-reduction proposal, every step of the way."

That was the State of the State on January 23, 1992.

The next day's *Oregonian* quoted the good, the bad, and the ugly in reaction to my speech. Speaker of the House Larry Campbell (R): "We've been looking for a signal from the Governor—and she has given us a signal. More importantly, I think she has taken a first step. She is the first one who has taken the bull by the horns." John Kitzhaber (D), president of the Senate, "She has taken the problem head on ... very responsible." Others were not so complimentary. Don McIntire, major sponsor of Measure 5, was reported as saying, "I'm not sure her grip on reality is reflected in the numbers she's talking about." The *East Oregonian* perhaps most accurately reflected the speech and its aftermath: "Roberts knows that those she once called friends will attack her. She knows that head-in-the-sand types will turn away from the reality of change. Few politicians are willing to challenge the interest groups that help put them in office. Roberts has indicated that she is willing to put the welfare of the state ahead of the desires of any one powerful interest group that feels it is owed a special favor." A week following my State of the State address, I flew to Washington, D.C., to get a clearer picture of the state of the nation and also the state of the *other* forty-nine parts of the union. Meeting with the nation's governors, I listened to Ira Magaziner speak on education reform and Ambassador Bob Strauss elaborate on Russian and American international relations. I met with both the NGA committees on which I served, dined at the White House, and attended the Women Executives in State Government reception prior to the Democratic Governors annual fundraising dinner. Yet, unlike the year before, it felt a little less glamorous and I was frankly mentally distracted by the budget issues waiting at home.

Early in the New Year Fred Pearce announced that he would be resigning his position as director of the Department of Corrections effective April 1. Fred had come to the state corrections position in early 1989 following the murder of Corrections Director Michael Franke. Working with Governor Goldschmidt, Fred Pearce oversaw the biggest building boom in prison beds in Oregon history. He saw those three thousand-plus new beds as a great success. Pearce and I had not always seen eye to eye. When I asked for the Measure 5 cuts in my first budget, his department reached a major portion of their reductions by eliminating all the alcohol- and drug-treatment programs. I sent the proposal back and told him to start again. When I announced the cuts coming in 1993-95, Pearce was one of my strongest critics. When he announced his retirement, he commented to *The Oregonian*, "I came to oversee the building of the prison system, not the dismantling of it."

With a national search under way to fill the position, Assistant Director Sally Anderson was promoted to the interim post, and she became one of the semifinalists for the director's position. It was certainly unusual both in Oregon and nationally to see a woman as the head of a state corrections department. Sally was a personal friend, and I was excited to see her in this role. But in mid-May I announced the appointment of Frank A. Hall to fill the post. I was a little sad that Sally Anderson hadn't made it into the finalist list but was quite proud of her for competing in this nearly all-male domain.

Frank Hall came with strong corrections experience in California, Massachusetts, New York, Maryland, and North Carolina, as well as another asset that carried a lot of weight with me—he was a *rehabilitation* advocate. In his previous position in Santa Clara County, 75 percent of eligible inmates were participating in alcohol and drug programs and seventy to eighty inmates every month completed their GED requirements. Frank Hall believed that corrections departments should be about "correcting" not just warehousing. He believed offenders could be changed for the better. For the next two and a half years, Frank's expertise and my support for his work brought positive changes to Oregon's Department of Corrections and the lives of hundreds of offenders behind the bars of our state institutions. I described it as getting Oregon Corrections out of the "recycling" business. Frank Hall wisely described the same philosophy, saying, "Oregon cannot build its way out of the crime problem."

An ongoing challenge began in March of 1992 and spanned the calendar until October of 1993. For the first time in Oregon history, a recall petition was filed against a governor! In early February, a recently retired building contractor and former lumber-mill worker decided I needed to be recalled because of my environmental positions and my lack of support for the timber industry. The cover sheet on the recall petitions faulted me on three accounts: I hadn't done enough to stop environmentalists from locking up the forests and throwing thousands of Oregonians out of work; I was more willing to raise taxes than cut government spending; and I had not been working for or listening to the majority of the people. In order for the recall measure to qualify for the ballot, 166,928 *valid* signatures from registered voters had to be submitted to the secretary of state's office by the qualifying date in May. Generally speaking, 10-15 percent of signatures are disqualified, so the recall effort leader stated his intention to gather two hundred thousand signatures to assure a safe margin.

So the petition began to circulate across the state. In addition to the strong signature gathering taking place in timber communities, the recall campaign gained a new support group in early May — Oregon Right to Life. They spent $5,000 to mail twenty thousand recall petitions to their members statewide who were opposed to legal abortion and other reproductive services. It seemed a rather strange coalition, but it was quite likely to add to the signature collection totals. My pro-choice positions were very public and long-term. Press stories quoted petition circulators: "lacks family values," "Barbara is short of moral and social values," "strident views," "lack of leadership,""she's ruined the timber industry!" Wearing "Bye Bye, Babs" T-shirts, the signature gatherers worked street corners, shopping malls, barber shops, road-side stands, taverns, bowling alleys, and worksites. In May, they turned in their petitions. They had 162,000 raw signatures, short of the required amount even without a verification that would likely have invalidated over 10 percent.

The largest financial contribution to the recall effort came from the lumber magnate Aaron Jones, owner of Seneca Sawmill Company. He contributed more than $58,000. However, regardless of anger and money, the recall failed. But two weeks later, the same Myrtle Creek retiree — again with funding from Aaron Jones — Hershel Taylor, launched a *second* recall effort that he labeled "USA Voters Club II." The flyers were printed on pink paper. That may have been a message about giving me a "pink slip" to indicate my job was ended or maybe represented the fact I was a female. Maybe both!

The Sunday *Oregonian* of May 31 editorialized against the new recall effort. "This smacks of the industry's glory days of the past, when King Timber expected to rule Oregon's political roost." This time, instead of ignoring the recall effort, I, at least, made a plea to my supporters for contributions in order to be prepared if the second effort was successful and I had to face an election fight. My campaign sent a fundraising letter headed, "THEY'RE BACK" to eleven thousand former contributors and supporters. The mailer raised $45,000.

In July, a new committee with timber industry leadership, labeled "Committee to Save Oregon Jobs," was unveiled as a support effort for the recall campaign. The organizer, Rick Re, vice-president of Seneca Sawmill, indicated "he was acting as a private citizen." The same week this new committee was organized, the Oregon Citizens Alliance (OCA) announced it was joining the recall bandwagon. The OCA was well known in Oregon as a conservative political action committee focused on anti-gay issues. Immediately, conflict arose about whether OCA was a help or a hindrance to the recall effort. A spokesman for the USA Voters Club II group was quoted in *The Oregonian* saying, "We do not have any ties with or support for the hatred and hypocrisy of the leaders of the OCA."

I now had anti-gay groups, anti-choice groups, and timber community leaders working to recall me from office. This was a perfect example of the old adage, "Politics makes strange bedfellows." Yet, despite this unusual coalition, the second recall effort also failed. This time the organizer, Taylor, chose not to even submit the petitions for an official count. Later, Taylor said he only had 115,000 signatures in his possession at the deadline, according to an *Oregonian* story on September 1, 1992.

A third and final recall effort failed a year later on October 13, 1993. I had a number of "firsts" in my political career, most of which I was proud and honored to have achieved. These three recall efforts against an Oregon governor were another "first," but one I could have done without.

The spring of 1992 felt almost as if I were back on the campaign trail, and perhaps in many ways I was. I was on the road in every part of Oregon speaking to newspaper editors, teacher groups, civic organizations, state employee groups, local government leaders, and participants from the Conversation. I reported what I had learned from the Conversation process, the efficiencies and cuts I was making in state government, the ongoing work to design a much-improved tax structure for our state, and my plans to have the Legislature place that new tax proposal on the ballot. I met with both Republican and Democratic legislators as I visited their home districts in my travels. Despite the old adage, "You can't please all of the people all of the time," sometimes it felt as if I couldn't please *any* of the people *any* of the time. Those who were focused on service levels (teachers, mental health workers, law enforcement, senior citizens) were loath to see any further cuts at all. Those who believed government simply needed to tighten its belt or those who simply wanted less government didn't believe the cuts were deep enough, hadn't seen enough pain yet. I shared numbers, budget projections, the reinvention work in state agencies, lowered management levels, salary freezes, outcome measurements, and the views of the ten thousand Oregonians from the Conversation. I sometimes took my charts from the Conversation and shared them with audiences at local Rotary Clubs, Chamber of Commerce groups, Kiwanis, and even high school student audiences. The schedule and travel were tough, but the attempt to find common ground was even more challenging. Many times my remarks would receive what I described as "the nod test," yet I often felt that once I was an hour away or a day away those nods would once again become shrugs of doubt. This was a hard sell — part education and part persuasion. I wouldn't know if I had closed the deal until the voters had spoken at the ballot.

With my sense of personal and political accomplishment with regard to our state's impressive 1991 housing legislation, I would soon after insert myself *smack* in the middle of a new housing controversy in 1992.

The city of Woodburn, a small community only fifteen minutes north of the Capitol, owned eleven acres of land that was originally planned for senior citizen housing. The senior development fizzled and the city was left with the acreage, a $252,000 federal grant, and an unpaid loan. Over several years the state urged the city to use the federal-state grant to benefit lower-income residents. Time passed; the land sat vacant; the grant was unused.

In 1991, the nonprofit Farmworker Housing Development Corporation (FHDC) was incorporated and stepped forward with both a plan and money to build desperately needed housing on the site. The city refused to even hear the details of the plan. In a community surrounded with agricultural lands and workers planting, irrigating, harvesting, and working in the fields and canneries almost year round, the mayor and city council had no interest in or intention of supplying housing within the city limits for those workers and their families. A former Woodburn mayor, Nancy Kirksey, was quoted in *The Oregonian* from an earlier letter she sent to the state Department of Housing: "I believe this action is racially motivated and Woodburn's mayor and city council are reflecting the bigoted attitudes in this community."

With litigation and several formal discrimination actions filed, I felt it necessary to step forward and find a resolution to the growing conflict. No one could argue that the housing was unneeded. There was no other viable plan or buyer for the eleven acres. The location was quite near the local high school and public elementary-school buildings—perfect for these families. FHDC had a detailed plan for fifty family units and a child-care center. I endorsed the plan and the site. I directed the Oregon Economic Development Department to offer Woodburn forgiveness for the outstanding loan it held on the land if the city would transfer the land to FHDC. To my surprise, the city immediately refused. I was losing patience with Woodburn and its political leadership. I informed the city that all future economic development funds for Woodburn would be frozen until this issue was resolved.

Finally, the city caved—but only partially. It continued to refuse to deed the land to the farmworkers' housing group and instead deeded the eleven acres to Marion County. The county government took quick action in signing the legal documents to transfer the land to FHDC. This could have been such a positive action for the city but was instead turned into a mean-spirited, stubborn conflict with strong racial overtones.

In December of 1992 when the groundbreaking ceremony took place, I stood with my shovel beside my state housing director and members of the FHDC board. Not a single member of the city of Woodburn government responded to the invitation to attend the ceremony. We stood ready to turn the earth for a $2.8 million housing project—the first fifty-apartment phase of the plan—that would become Nuevo Amanecer, "New Dawn." I have remained involved with Nuevo Amanecer over all the years since that initial conflict. Forty additional units were opened in 1999, a beautiful new education center in 2003, and expansion has continued right up to the restoration and remodeling work to update the original units and rededicate New Dawn in August of 2009.

I spoke at the rededication ceremony of Nuevo Amanecer in 2009. Photo by Jaime Arredondo.

Today the City of Woodburn and its elected leaders are enthusiastic partners in Nuevo Amanecer, including unanimous sponsorship of a $600,000 community development block grant for construction of the new Cipriano Ferrel Education Center.

At the August 2009 rededication ceremony I delivered the keynote remarks. "This facility and all of its programs stand as an example to our entire state. You have built wisely, protected and conserved your assets, shared your knowledge, enhanced your skills and invested for a better tomorrow.

"Oregon would do well to follow your lead."

In December of 2009 Larry Kleinman of PCUN, the farmworkers' union, mailed me some materials and news clippings about the history of Nuevo Amanecer. Included was a statement about my history with FHDC and that Woodburn farmworker development: "Barbara Roberts has well earned the title of *madrina* or godmother of Nuevo Amanecer as bestowed on her by FHDC. She was present—

and instrumental — at the birth in 1992. She believed in us when few others did. She used her power to do the right thing for us. She kept us in her heart and urged others to do so as well. So many of us are much the better for it. So is Woodburn. So is Oregon."

In the early spring of 1992, the first election season following the legislative redistricting, there was a certain amount of confusion and inter-party competition caused by the new district boundaries and political residency shuffles. It was also a presidential election year, with Governor Bill Clinton of Arkansas (D) the front-runner in his challenge to the seated president, George H. W. Bush.

The race that was garnering much of the press and political attention in Oregon was the competitive Democratic primary race for the U.S. Senate seat held by Republican Bob Packwood. Congressman Les AuCoin and businessman Harry Lonsdale of central Oregon had been trading leads in the last weeks. In the last week before the primary, Packwood, the Oregon Republican Party, and the National Rifle Association all joined an attack on AuCoin. It was quite obvious the Republicans wanted Lonsdale to win the Democratic primary and felt that outcome would better suit Packwood's chances in the November election. The Democratic primary outcome was so narrow that it forced a complete statewide recount. The outcome: AuCoin 153,029, Lonsdale 152,699, a 330-vote margin.

The other race I was following closely was the Democratic race for secretary of state. My appointee, Phil Keisling, was being challenged by state Labor Commissioner Mary Wendy Roberts, my stepdaughter, as well as two other candidates. Phil gained 46 percent of the Democratic electorate with Mary Wendy coming in second with 39 percent. As noted earlier, the race was an awkward one for our family, with Frank supporting his daughter and my endorsement going to my appointee. Anyone for Thanksgiving dinner?

I spent more and more of my energies gaining an in-depth understanding of the size and impact of the budget deficit I would face in preparing my 1993-95 budget. During the first half of 1992, I continued to travel extensively statewide, meeting with citizens who had been part of the Conversation with Oregon and local leaders and opinion makers across Oregon. I began to evaluate what elements might be part of a tax-redesign package and what would be necessary to build equality and fairness into a new system. I also considered where I would need to propose changes to the balance between personal tax responsibilities and business portions of the tax system. As I worked with my staff I would test out various ideas. I wasn't trying to pad the state budget but rather to get us back to some level of financial stability following the passage of the Measure 5 tax initiative. Some elements began to emerge: there had to be changes in the property-tax assessment process and in property-tax levels; a small constitutionally limited sales tax was possible but only with some reductions in the state personal income tax levels; voters needed to see a balance of responsibility between homeowners and business property owners in the arena of property taxes.

As I continued to think out loud about what tax reform might look like in Oregon, I also continued to be clear about what steps we were taking to downsize and bring greater efficiencies and measurable outcomes to the agencies across the breadth of state government. I tried to make certain those two messages were delivered to every audience as the two sides of a single coin. There was certainly no secret about where I was headed. I wanted an opportunity, after almost a year's efforts, to develop a quality, balanced tax-reform package to place before Oregon voters. I was willing to take the heat about agency downsizing from both the agencies themselves and advocates of the services that would be negatively affected. I was also willing to publicly talk about elements of property-tax reform, even a possible sales tax, and changes to our income tax system. The 1991 Legislature had not taken on these issues beyond the bare necessities of the budget cuts I had proposed. As 1992 passed, as we edged closer to the billion-dollar budget "cliff" we would face in 1993-95, I saw little indication of any major tax proposals under discussion by the interim committees of the House or Senate. I was willing to be the "bad cop" if it meant a chance to reform our tax structure and avoid the ugly cuts. My interest in seeking tax reform was no secret in Oregon. There would be political risks.

I stop here — and take a deep breath. I can't decide if I should simply give it all to you in one or two ugly sentences or spread the story of my tax proposal, the special legislative session that followed in July 1992, and the greatest public loss of my political career over several painful pages. However I tell this story, there is, in my mind, enough blame to go around. But since this was my tax-reform package, my special session, and my governorship, I must clearly take the lion's share of the blame for the failure of the reform package to reach the

Oregon ballot. Additionally, there may be lessons to learn and some details seem demanded here.

My tax package consisted of a constitutionally protected 3.5 percent sales tax on goods, a split-roll property tax that levied a higher rate for commercial property, a reduction to the graduated personal income tax, and a fast-track for the Measure 5 property-tax relief rather than waiting for the full five-year implementation period. Also included were a number of tax-relief measures to benefit low-income Oregonians. This was a fair and equitable reform measure for Oregon's citizens. The package would raise $950 million per biennium, closing much of the billion-dollar budget gap.

With the tax package completed, I called a special session of the Legislature for July 1, 1992. I presented the full tax-reform package to a joint session of the Senate and House revenue committees and made the full tax-package elements available to the ninety members of the Legislature, asking them to refer the package to the ballot for a September vote of the Oregon electorate. The July 1 session date was only an eleven-day notice for the Legislature but certainly enough time to examine *one* measure and decide on a referral to the voters. I gathered supporters from education, labor, human services, law enforcement, senior citizens groups, and businesses.

When the session began, HJR 70, the constitutional amendment that was my tax-reform package, came out of the Republican-controlled House Revenue Committee without recommendation. By 2:30 p.m. on the first day of the session, HJR 70 failed on the floor of the Oregon House on a 26-Aye to 33-Nay vote. Eight Republicans and eighteen Democrats voted in favor of the ballot referral. I lost ten members of the House Democratic caucus. Several of those Democrats were *pledged* to vote for my plan but decided to wait and see if a "reasonable" number of Republicans would vote in favor of the referral. A reconsideration vote was expected later in the afternoon.

Speaker Larry Campbell and I became embattled over the date of the election. He wanted a November vote at the General Election. I wanted the voters' attention to be undiverted. I stuck to my guns about a September stand-alone date with every voter receiving a vote-by-mail ballot. We were nose-to-nose and nobody blinked!

When the House went back into session, the Speaker's determination *and* his power were both evident. When the vote for reconsideration was taken, the Speaker had held every single Republican member and one conservative Democrat. The reconsideration vote failed on a 31-28 vote. My eight Republican supporters stayed loyal to their Speaker on a procedural vote. My "second-chance" Democrats were not given a second chance.

The state Senate worked hard to keep the measure alive and showed me great support, even refusing to adjourn for two days. But in the end, my entire tax-reform effort had failed. I lost not only the tax package but also a great deal of political credibility.

Speaker Larry Campbell and Senate President John Kitzhaber then turned to their own newly created "Oregon's Future" panel, a panel they co-chaired to seek a bipartisan agreement regarding needs and money. The panel's intended product fell far short of providing any answers for Oregon. My answer had been rejected. Theirs never materialized. I moved forward to prepare a budget with 16-20 percent cuts in services.

There were several lessons to be learned from this costly political experience. It certainly reinforced my knowledge that legislative egos can outweigh good public policy. I also learned that the *second* vote counts as much as or more than the first vote. Everyone in Oregon now clearly understood that two stubborn leaders do not create even one tax vote, regardless of date. I found the press uses a lot more ink on *failure* than they do on *success,* and ten thousand Oregonians from the Conversation and hundreds of citizens rallying outside the Capitol in favor of tax reform do not add up to "Nice try, Governor."

Almost twenty years later I still wince at the memories of that defeat, yet a few positive memories have stayed with me. I remember the House Republicans with the courage to vote for my tax referral: Mary Alice Ford, Ted Calouri, Stan Bunn, Tom Brian, John Schoon, Tony Van Vliet, Jerry Barnes. I remember the many and loyal supporters who stood with me at the press conference the morning the session convened. I remember the strong support of Grattan Kerans, Bill Bradbury, and the fourteen Senate Democrats who joined them in attempting to create an alternative bill to send to the ballot. I remember turning around to a very familiar voice at the end of a 4:30 p.m. press briefing, after the reconsideration vote had failed, and seeing my mother. She gave me a long, warm hug when I needed it most.

I could say much more about this huge story; there are editorials, negative and positive quotations, political analysis, and partisan predictions. Yet I can best end this tale of woe with two comments.

My quote to the press when it was all over still stands today — "I've given this my best effort. The only issue before us is the issue of Oregon's future." My second comment is a sad commentary on Oregon's political leadership: Almost twenty years later, with the exception of the 1993 Legislature, neither the years of legislative sessions nor the two Oregon governors who have served in those years have stepped forward to truly try and reform our state's inadequate and outdated tax structure. As I said early on, "There is plenty of blame to go around."

Nonetheless, the summer months of 1992 also brought a fair amount of both interesting and fun political activity to my calendar. After all, 1992 was a presidential election year. In early June, the Democratic Governors Association met in Aspen, Colorado. Governor John Waihee of Hawaii, the DGA Chair, and Governor Roy Romer (D), the National Governors Association Chair, made certain the program and free time allowed ample opportunity to talk not only gubernatorial politics but the exciting realm of presidential politics. That subject was hard to avoid with one of our own, Governor Bill Clinton, moving ever closer to becoming the presidential nominee of our party.

On July 11, I arrived in New York City for the Democratic National Convention. National political conventions are always hectic and crazy, but attending my first as a state's governor added a series of additional events where my attendance was expected. Yet those added calendar expectations were made much easier with the assistance and transportation that my state police security detail provided. I presented two sets of remarks to the convention floor during those four days in Madison Square Garden. I was co-chair of the Credentials Committee and presented the completed credentials report, not exactly a simulating address but a report required before the convention can actually conduct business. I also had the fun of introducing Montana State Representative Dorothy Bradley to the huge convention. Representative Bradley was running as the Democratic nominee for Montana governor and her introduction was part of the evening's program to introduce women candidates running for major offices across the nation. In the early fall I traveled to Montana as the headliner for a huge outdoor event for Dorothy. My mother, who was born and raised in Montana, was excited about my new connection to the state.

One of the most stirring moments at the convention, at least for me, was to be present as the keynote speaker, former Texas Congresswoman Barbara Jordan, stepped to the microphone. The applause was deafening. Her gentle voice and powerful words stirred pride, hope, and recommitment to a better and more inclusive America. But the convention was not without controversy. Pennsylvania Governor Bob Casey wanted a speaking role at the convention. Two things stood in the way of Governor Casey receiving an invitation to address the convention: his very lukewarm support of the ticket and his intention to deliver a speech in opposition to abortion. In the end, the convention leadership turned down Casey's request but not without some hard feelings and a certain amount of press controversy.

Bill and Hillary Clinton and the vice-presidential nominee Senator Al Gore of Tennessee and his wife, Tipper, were all four very popular with the convention delegates. The foursome as a *political team* met with solid excitement. The convention was considered a success and Clinton-Gore were off and running, while the Bush-Quayle team were still awaiting their August convention. I left the convention feeling excited and very hopeful about the outcome of the November election. I had been a worker in the "political vineyards" since the campaign of John F. Kennedy in 1960. I was accustomed to actively supporting my party's presidential candidate every four years. However, 1992 was different because I *personally* knew Bill Clinton. The governors of America are a small group of political leaders. We are only half the number who serve in the U.S. Senate and this adds to our camaraderie. In the fall campaign I would actively support the Clinton-Gore ticket across Oregon, and I also joined other Democratic governors from the western states as we campaigned with Governor Clinton in Seattle and Las Vegas. Those traveling political rallies were both fun and successful. The polling numbers looked good nationally and in Oregon.

During 1992 I had the fun and excitement of participating in the ceremonial openings of three important new cultural/educational/historical sites in Oregon. In May I did a "kelp-cutting" for the opening of the beautiful and expansive new Oregon Coast Aquarium in Newport. Two days later I was on the far eastern border of the state for the grand opening of the impressive new Oregon Trail Interpretive Center on Flagstaff Hill overlooking historic Baker

City. From that vantage point we could see the valley floor below where wagon ruts from the Oregon Trail still scarred the land after a hundred fifty years. This ceremony felt especially emotional for me as a descendant of Oregon Trail ancestors. In October I attended the opening night gala at the new riverfront facility of the Oregon Museum of Science and Industry (OMSI) in Portland. These major public facilities take years to plan, site, and fund, and such special openings are usually few and far between. I was fortunate to be Governor in such a unique year of significant openings.

Before Oregon's beautiful summer season disappeared, I had the opportunity for a relaxed, casual, and rather unusual three days. My chief of staff and I joined four state police officers, including two fish and game officers, on a river trip and camping excursion in eastern Oregon on the Snake River. I received an on-site lecture on fish management and river patrol as we motored up the river. It was an opportunity to watch how fish and game officers did their work, to actually do a little fishing of our own (I caught the largest fish!), cook over a campfire, share a few beers, and explore the beautiful rural setting. Near our camp, I picked some wildflowers, arranged them in an old coyote skull, and they became the centerpiece on the rugged old camp picnic table. The whole group made fun of my need to be domestic in the wild but it satisfied my love of flower arranging, which was sadly neglected in my current lifestyle. The most energetic debate around the campfire in the late evening was my objection to being referred to as *ma'am.* The state police, especially Sgt. Rick Geistwhite, saw the term as respectful, just like the term *sir.* We debated this useless argument for far too long. Finally I ended it by saying, "I worked too hard to earn my office to simply be *ma'am.* You may call me Governor or you may call me Barbara, but drop the damn *ma'am!*" We all laughed and the next morning I never heard a single *ma'am* out of any of the officers. The trip was a great way to end a summer *and* to end an ongoing debate.

There are numerous gubernatorial activities that occur on a somewhat regular schedule. There are, however, major responsibilities that come to a governor on the timetable of others. Let me take the opportunity here to describe two such important roles that I undertook with the least initial understanding but the most respect and concern for the long-term imprint my decisions would leave on my state. The two areas were negotiations with Oregon's Native tribes on the matter of Indian gaming and the selection of judges to fill resignations from the bench.

Oregon had nine federally recognized tribes in 1991. The smallest of these was the Burns Paiute with fewer than three hundred members, the largest was the Warm Springs with almost thirty-five hundred members and over 640,000 acres of tribal land. The 1998 congressionally passed Indian Gaming Regulatory Act (IGRA) required my office to negotiate "in good faith" to create gaming compacts between the state and the individual Oregon tribes. The state was required to allow the tribes to participate in any type of gaming that the state did not completely prohibit. Oregon's lottery was somewhat limited in 1991, but two other issues affected the negotiations. The Oregon Constitution prohibited "casinos" but allowed one very short-term gambling activity called "Happy Canyon" games during community and nonprofit charitable fundraising events. That regulation, which allowed casino-style games, put every kind of gaming on the negotiation table with the tribes. As the first Oregon administration to conduct these negotiations, I was uneasy and somewhat unhappy with the idea of negotiating this broad expansion of gambling in my state. We had to negotiate in good faith, yet I wanted to create reasonable limits for these new operations. We explained to the tribes that we would move forward to negotiate the gaming compacts with the understanding that the Oregon constitutional provision would mean limitations on the size and scope of gaming. I felt I had a strong legal responsibility to express the public policy of the state and believed that by limiting which games were played, the number of games, and the overall size of the facility, I had met my legal responsibility to both the state and the tribes. This framework became the successful transitional phase for Indian gaming in Oregon; the tribes began to generate revenue and the Oregon State Police were able to assist them in creating appropriate security protections for their new, and later expanding, operations. Kerry Barnett led my negotiating team for almost three years, assisted by Pamela Abernethy, special counsel from the Oregon Attorney General's office.

Dozens of great stories came with the unusual negotiating climate between Oregon and our tribal members from around the state. Tribal representatives showed off their prospective gaming sites, which at that time were generally empty fields. Yet tribal members viewed the sites with different eyes. They saw economic development, the dreams of financial stability for their members, and visions of health clinics, child-care centers, and hotels. Sue Schaeffer of the Cow Creek Band of the Umpqua Tribe showed my negotiation team an empty, drafty, small metal structure that would be the tribe's initial location for their video gaming machines. Today, the tribe's dream has blossomed: a huge convention hotel, gaming tables, hundreds of gambling machines, cafés, a fine restaurant, an RV park, a new community water system, big-name entertainment in the theater, and hundreds of employees. The Grand Ronde's gaming operation complex is now Oregon's number one tourist destination. The Warm Springs and Umatilla have both added extensive history museums to their facilities.

Outside interests tried to insert themselves into Oregon's negotiation process with our state's tribes. I remember receiving a telephone call from former Chrysler CEO and casino investor Lee Iacocca as he and his associates worked to be part of the Confederated Tribes of the Coos negotiations. I didn't accept the telephone call. A few weeks later I was in Coos Bay on another matter. As my small plane took off from the Coos Bay airport, Iacocca's personal jet landed on the other runway. He had planned to "head me off at the pass" before I could finish my business on the southern Oregon coast. He had the jet but I was too fast for him. From my perspective, Oregon had only *one* negotiating partner—the Native tribes of our state. My business was with *them*, not the out-of-state movers and shakers. It turned out just fine for Oregon and for our tribes. Oregon tribes invest their gaming profits for the betterment of tribal members: housing, health, education, natural resources, new land, and cultural awareness. Some also invest in charitable work for the broader community.

The governor's role of appointing judges to fill positions vacated by resignations, illness, or death placed huge decisions in my hands. I filled more than fifty judicial vacancies in four years, more than any other Oregon governor in a four-year period. I was able to change the face of the Oregon judiciary. Rarely has a nonattorney had so much impact on a state's legal history.

When I took office in January of 1991, there was a single woman serving on the Oregon Supreme Court and one on the Court of Appeals. There were sixteen women out of 152 judges seated on the combined lower courts—circuit and district—statewide. That added up to eighteen women judges out of 168 on the Oregon judicial benches. If my count is correct, there were at that time five racial minorities serving on the combined courts of the state. When I left office, I had made appointments of twenty women and five racial minorities to judicial seats in Oregon. Like the entire list of fifty-two judges I appointed, they were all elected when they reached the Oregon ballot.

My office went through a stringent interview process with a small, dedicated, knowledgeable committee. My Legal Counsel, Kerry Barnett, and Art Johnson of Eugene as regulars, and later Danny Santos when he became my Legal Counsel in the fall of 1993. Also, my Director of Executive Appointments, Carole Morse, sat in on most of these judicial interviews to reflect both a woman's and a lay person's reactions. We searched out strong, diverse candidates prepared to serve and willing to seek election. Attorneys with strong skills, balanced temperaments, good reputations, and a commitment to justice and the law. In some areas of the state only a few attorneys lived in the judicial district. In other jurisdictions there was an abundance of legal talent. We paid close attention to the bar preference polls, but they were not the only factor in my choices. I believe I personally interviewed every attorney I appointed to the bench. Plus, I *always* made the final call offering them the appointment. It was not something I delegated. It was too much fun!

When I was ready to appoint the brilliant and energetic Anna Brown to the Multnomah County bench in early 1992, I was traveling by car and Kerry called Anna at her law office, reached her, and then asked her to hold while he connected me to her office extension. By mistake, we were disconnected. Anna loves to tell the story about running madly through the halls of her law firm telling the receptionist and every secretary to stay off the phones and keep the lines open because the Governor was going to be calling her at any moment.

Finding minority members to appoint to the bench was not always easy. We put a panel of seated minority judges together, including Judges Ancer Haggarty, Mercedes Deiz, and Roosevelt Robinson, and invited every minority attorney they could identify, most of whom were younger attorneys at that time, to meet with them. The current judges explained about aspiring to become a judge and preparing yourself professionally. My staff made it clear we were seeking diversity but above all the appointee had to be superbly qualified. We hoped this would be an important first step to increasing judicial diversity.

In early 1993, two vacancies became available on the State Court of Appeals. One of the applicants my committee interviewed was a professor of law from Willamette University, Susan Leeson. The committee was quite impressed, and she was high on their list. Then, suddenly, she withdrew her name. We were quite surprised. We asked her if she was willing to talk about her reason for withdrawing. She said she had gotten considerable feedback from various members of the bar that her lack of traditional trial court experience would make it very difficult for her to be accepted in an appellate judicial position. We believed that appellate courts needed diversity of thought and background. There was no reason a highly respected law school professor shouldn't be able to make impressive contributions to the work of the court. In the end, Professor Leeson resubmitted her name and I was honored and pleased to see her carry her new title — Judge Leeson.

My work and commitment to diversify the Oregon courts was exciting, satisfying, and sometimes challenging. Kerry Barnett, at the time my legal counsel, told about appearing at the Lane County Bar Association early in my term to discuss the judicial appointment process our office would be following. Kerry said he was very careful to emphasize that, while we were very interested in diversifying the bench, our first and most critical priority was finding candidates of exceptional quality. He also explained that bar preference polls would be given proper weight in indicating an attorney's standing in their legal community. The district and circuit courts in Lane County had fifteen judges, only one of whom was a woman. Both their county bar and their bench were considered dominated by older, traditional attorneys. After Kerry finished his balanced and respectful presentation, feeling he had made his case well, one of the more senior judges raised his hand and asked pointblank, "Is it even worthwhile for white males to bother applying?" Two years later, the Lane County Bar Association was still grumbling over the same issue. I finally sent them the entire statewide list of my appointments that, by anyone's count, still remained dominated by white males. The other area of diversity I opted to give attention to was the appointment of openly gay and lesbian attorneys to the bench. I found some really superb talent in that arena and proudly appointed five outstanding lawyers who have served with distinction on the Oregon bench.

When Kerry left to become director of the Oregon Department of Consumer and Business Services in October of 1993, I reached out to Danny Santos, whom I had appointed Chair of the Oregon Parole Board only three months earlier. His three years' experience as a member of the Parole Board, his strong work and commitment to diversity, and his tremendous ability to work well with others were, in my estimation, strong assets to complement his legal ability. I knew he would be a good fit for both the job and my office. Little could I have anticipated the "excitement" Danny would bring to my administration!

A few weeks after Danny became my Legal Counsel, a former prison inmate, Russell Obrimski, who had served twenty-five years on a murder conviction and had been released on parole while Danny was still Parole Board Chair, was arrested for allegedly molesting his fiancée's four-year-old daughter. The public outrage was almost instantaneous. The story was in every Oregon newspaper and filled radio and television newscasts. The National Rifle Association ran a full-page ad in the Sunday *Oregonian* asking all Oregon citizens to call the Governor and tell her to fire Danny Santos. On Monday, the telephones at the front desk in my office were going crazy! One television station even came by to film the receptionist trying to take all the calls. Danny Santos was standing next to the desk, worrying about the poor receptionist. The television reporter asked, "How many calls have come in this morning regarding Mr. Santos?" The receptionist replied, "About eight hundred, but they're not all in opposition to Danny. About fifty calls were to support him." Without missing a beat, Danny added, "You mean my dad has only called fifty times?" We laugh now when recalling that funny line but we all knew there was nothing funny about the story. There was outrage. There was anger. There were death threats against Danny Santos. Danny offered to resign his position as my legal counsel. I refused to accept that offer. The parole board had acted under the requirements of the law. Danny Santos had performed his duty. Obrimski was later found not guilty on the charge. Today, Danny Santos has just completed serving his *fourth* Oregon Governor. All of us were proud to work with him.

Later in my term, I was interviewing lawyers for a vacancy on the Jackson County District Court. Since the county is several hours drive from the Capitol, the four finalists had arranged to ride together for the trip to Salem. One of the lawyers was quite worried because a skunk had "let loose" under her house the night before, and she feared that the smell might have lingered on her. She checked with her three fellow finalists. "No problem," they said. She even asked Danny Santos before she entered my office. He said she was fine. But her worry was too strong—it was almost the first thing she asked after she entered my office. I told her I didn't notice any smell. Danny remembers me turning and quietly asking him, "Is this a lawyer joke?" After fifty judicial appointments I was still trying to understand legal humor!

After Frank and I moved into the governor's residence it became necessary to begin a serious conversation about putting an elevator in this very large house. Frank could easily enter the front door on the main level of the house. This gave him access to the kitchen, dining room, library, and great room. However, the small bathroom on that floor would not accommodate his motorized cart, and any visitor with need for wheelchair access would also find that same limitation. Plus Frank had no access to the second-floor bedrooms—including mine. Frank's bedroom and bathroom were located in the basement. He could only reach the basement by going outdoors, and clear around the house to the backdoor access ramp, where he could gain entry. This long outdoor trip was the equivalent of over three city blocks in length and had to be traversed even on cold and rainy nights. The house—and Frank—needed an elevator.

In early 1992, after a year in the house, we were supplied with the first estimate for installing an elevator—$40,000-$45,000. I was clear that no public funds could be expended on the project, and we began a rather quiet fundraising campaign for private donations to make Oregon's governor's residence handicapped accessible. Truthfully, the obligation should have belonged to the state to make this state-owned building accessible, but in that Measure 5 climate I didn't want to turn Frank's situation into a potential controversy. Oregonians were still getting accustomed to even *having* a governor's residence.

So we raised over $33,000, the ACME Elevator Company donated the installation costs, and with close management of the carpentry and electrical work, we met the revised budget numbers. On December 26, 1992, Frank drove his cart into the brand-new elevator, I walked in beside him, we posed for a "photo op," and then rode down to the basement. We then reversed the trip and went from the basement to the second floor and Frank toured the whole set of bedrooms, including getting out of his cart and lying down with me on my big bed in the master suite! It was a real celebration. The next day we left for a ten-day vacation to Hawaii. When we came home to Oregon, Frank moved his bedroom from the basement to the second floor.

In the midst of constant pressure, conflict, and calendar craziness, one must find a source of joy or solace. During 1991-94, I found a great deal of that joy with my granddaughter, Katie. As a still-practicing grandparent I discovered that every new word she uttered, every silly behavior, every small hug, was brilliant and darling. Arlene and I found excuses to bring her to the governor's residence for overnight stays. She had two bureau drawers of her own in my bedroom, toys and books, and the full attention of three adoring adults.

As Katie reached ages three and four and was easier to travel with, I sometimes took her on weekend road trips for speeches, receptions, ribbon cuttings, and parades. She loved my state police officers, and they spoiled her almost as much as I did. Katie was a good-natured, happy little girl and would sit quietly working in her coloring book while I delivered a speech to the League of Women Voters, the Oregon Education Association, or a local Chamber of Commerce luncheon. I loved buying cute outfits for her and showing her off as we spent happy public time together. She found nothing unusual, with her limited life experience, in a grandmother giving speeches or being interviewed on television. She also loved riding with Frank on his motorized cart and that seemed equally normal to her.

In thinking back on that time, I feel certain that the hours I spent with Katie were perhaps equivalent to having had a full-time mental health counselor! She made me laugh and smile. She lifted my spirits and lowered my blood pressure. Having raised two sons, I found this feminine, pretty little creature to be a new and charming experience.

In October of 1992, Frank and I were in Portland for a follow-up medical appointment for him. His PSA levels had recently been tested, which is standard for former prostate-cancer patients. Dr. Halpert asked both of us to come in for the report on the test, a not-unheard-of request, but still rare. His request made me uneasy, yet

Frank seemed unconcerned. It would turn out that my worry was more than founded.

Dr. Halpert told us that Frank's prostate cancer had metastasized and was now in his lungs. He further informed us that this was a terminal condition. His prognosis was that Frank had about a year to live. In the four and a half years since his original cancer treatment, these six-month reports had become somewhat routine. We had begun to feel that the earlier radiation treatments had "killed" that cancer. Now instead, the exact reverse was apparently true. I took Frank's hand. No one spoke for a few minutes. I noticed Frank's eyes were closed. He squeezed my hand — hard. Then his doctor told Frank he would go ahead and set up chemotherapy appointments beginning the following week.

Now Frank spoke. "Will this treatment extend the time I have left?"

The doctor said, "Yes, it will."

Then Frank asked the more telling question, "For how long?"

The doctor said quietly, "For a month, perhaps even six weeks."

Frank shook his head. "No, no." Frank was clear that he would opt for protecting whatever quality of life he had *now* for as long as possible rather than hoping for an extra month at the very end of this medical ordeal. He felt fine now and was unwilling to give that up to gain a few extra weeks of nonquality time at life's end.

We left the doctor's office with my two security police, got in the car and looked at each other as the car door closed. We were stunned. Where did we go from here? How would we handle this crushing news?

That night Frank made a very clear decision. He did not want this diagnosis to be made public. He did not want to be treated as if he were dying — even when he was. Except for our immediate family and a few very close friends, this would be a confidential medical matter. I respected Frank's decision, but I could already imagine how difficult it would be to go on with our life as if everything was normal. I could already feel the pressure of this huge secret. Frank and I wept together that night, sensing what was to come, sensing what was to end. We talked and talked and finally decided we would need to get away right after Christmas to have some private time together. We had decisions to make. We had taken a blow today, but we also had the gift of time. We would try to use the time wisely and well.

During the next months even a casual observer could discern the pressure I had as Oregon's Governor: creating the new 1993-95 biennial budget with the huge Measure 5 gap, working through the legal and economic matters related to the spotted owl/timber crisis, the ongoing work on the Oregon Health Plan, the growing issues surrounding Oregon's threatened salmon runs, just for starters. Yet, behind the curtain loomed a personal crisis that ballooned as the months passed, adding pressure and pain that far overshadowed my political and policy challenges. My husband was dying, and I couldn't tell anyone.

In the last weeks of October, the U.S. Senate contest between incumbent Bob Packwood (R) and his Democratic challenger, Congressman Les AuCoin, showed narrowing poll numbers as the election date approached. Even with Packwood's huge $8 million campaign fund stacked against AuCoin's barely $2 million, the gap was closing quickly. Yet Oregon voters were kept in the dark on a disturbing story being investigated by the *Washington Post.* Rumors began to leak from behind the walls of political smoke-filled rooms. Packwood was the subject of an investigation by the *Post.* Reporters were contacting former Packwood employees now living back in Oregon … so the rumors said. It was said *The Oregonian* had the story about Packwood as well — a serious accusation of sexual harassment — but did not intend to publish it. In spite of the growing evidence to the contrary, the state's largest newspaper had apparently decided the accusations were simply an attempt at a last-minute political smear. After the fact, on December 2, *Oregonian* Editor Bill Hilliard told the *Washington Post* that his paper "should have been more aggressive. … We were worried about ruining a man's career." I guess Les AuCoin's career and his service to Oregon didn't matter even in terms of journalistic balance. They simply buried the story. I have no verification of what pre-election decisions took place on this subject at *The Oregonian.*

Mark Zusman, editor of Portland weekly newspaper *Willamette Week,* was also aware of the Packwood sexual-harassment story. One of the women who had experienced Packwood's unwanted physical attention told her story frequently but made it clear she would not go public. Zusman said that incident was "not a big secret." He explained that "he had tried to pin the story down but didn't have the resources." Had *Willamette Week* printed any part of the story, they would have likely forced the much larger *Oregonian* to move further on an investigation. The accusations of serious long-term sexual harassment against Senator Packwood stayed unpublished until after the election. That fact changed Oregon political history for decades.

A *Washington Post* reporter had confronted Senator Packwood in October with the allegations of ten women claiming unwelcome and many times aggressive sexual advances, including the fact that the senator had often been drinking prior to the incidents. Packwood categorically denied the accusations. His then Chief of Staff, Elaine Franklin, called the *Post*'s inquiry a "witch hunt." Packwood and Franklin began supplying documentation to the *Post* to discredit the women who had submitted the statements. Because of this exchange of materials the *Post* informed Packwood on October 31 that the story would not be ready for publication in advance of the November 3 election.

Voters in Oregon deserved to read the Packwood story. They deserved the right to weigh and balance the evidence. There were written statements by reputable Oregon women who claimed serious sexual advances by Packwood. There was a long history of such behavior now being revealed by brave women, brave enough to come forward to tell their story. It was all there, but Oregon voters would cast their votes for Oregon's U.S. Senate seat, choosing between Packwood and AuCoin, while they were shielded from the evidence that might have changed the outcome of the race.

When the votes were counted, Bob Packwood had won the Senate contest 52 percent to 48 percent. Within days, on November 22, the *Washington Post* released the entire story in its Sunday edition, exposing the facts, the sexual aggression, *and* the senator. The *New York Times* carried the *Post* story that same day in their late edition.

The story became an Oregon and a national scandal. Oregon citizens had missed the opportunity to choose between an experienced, committed, intelligent leader and a powerful but abusive womanizer. It was Oregon's loss. The scandal dragged on for almost three more years until investigations and ethics charges finally forced Packwood to resign his Senate seat in September of 1995. The election "upset" story that should have been the headline of the 1992 election became merely an historic political asterisk. Les AuCoin never sought election again, not even the special election to replace Packwood in 1995. *That* was indeed Oregon's loss.

There was, however, considerable good news in 1992 for Oregon Democrats. At the top of the ticket, Governor Bill Clinton of Arkansas defeated President George H. W. Bush. Closer to home, Secretary of State Phil Keisling (D) defeated Representative Randy Miller (R), 53 percent to 42 percent. In the Oregon treasurer's race State Senator Jim Hill (D) defeated money manager David Chen (R) 51 percent to 46 percent to become Oregon's first-ever African American statewide elected officeholder. In the remaining statewide partisan race on the ballot, attorney general, an impressive victory of 62 percent to 31 percent went to Democratic former legislator Ted Kulongoski. This was a major return to politics for Kulongoski following defeats for the U.S. Senate (1980) and Governor (1982). It would prove to be only a first step as Ted was later elected to the Oregon Supreme Court and then became a two-term Oregon Governor (2003-2011).

In Oregon's five congressional races, Oregon voters returned four incumbents to office and elected longtime peace activist Elizabeth Furse to the First District seat vacated by Les AuCoin in his run for the U.S. Senate. When the 1992 election results were final, Oregon's six state officeholders included three women and three men (one African American), and our federal delegation of seven members once again included a female. In the same election, Portland elected its third woman mayor in history, former Oregon Speaker of the House Vera Katz.

In legislative races the partisan balance in the Oregon House (thirty-two Republicans and twenty-eight Democrats) was unchanged, but the number of women members increased from fourteen in 1991 to seventeen. In the Senate, the Republican Party increased their numbers from ten members to fourteen. This obviously meant the Democratic caucus lost four Senate seats. Two of the seats were lost when Democrats retired. The real disappointment and surprise in the Senate contests was the defeat of Democratic Senator Wayne Fawbush of Hood River to Wes Cooley (R). Cooley seemed to come out of nowhere in this huge, sprawling, rural district. He would later return to nowhere after a short stint in the Legislature and then Congress, when the revelation came that he had lied about his residency, his marital status, his military service, and even a long list of adventure stories he had shared with great animation with his political colleagues. Frank listened to Wes Cooley's sailing adventures with enthusiasm and would later learn Cooley had invented the stories after reading about sailboats and sailing lore. Frank felt really burned that he hadn't recognized Cooley as a phony.

Although I was not on the ballot in 1992, that election year gave me two personal wins. The Oregon ballot included a measure initiated in the spirit of bigotry and discrimination. Measure 9, sponsored by the Oregon Citizens Alliance, declared homosexuality a "perverse behavior" and would require schools to teach students that homosexuality was abnormal and wrong. The OCA indicated they were working to halt a "homosexual agenda." Oregonians who disagreed with Measure 9 formed a large and impressive coalition across the state. Prominent civic, business, and political leaders stepped forward to oppose the measure. Grassroots groups to oppose the measure formed in thirty of Oregon's thirty-six counties. Newspapers editorialized against the measure, the meanness, the divisiveness, and the harm to Oregon's reputation. Labor unions and many church leaders also spoke out against the measure. As Governor, I made my opposition clear from the first day the initiative was filed until the election. I spoke against Measure 9 at rallies, civic organizations, Chamber of Commerce meetings, labor union gatherings, at every opportunity. I wore my "No on 9" button openly and proudly.

The harsh public argument over Measure 9 divided the state for weeks and weeks. It split Oregon voters along urban-rural lines, along party lines, by income, education, religion, and gender. But when the dust settled and the angry voices stilled, Oregon had defeated Measure 9 — 57 percent to 43 percent. My state had spoken and I was proud of my fellow citizens.

The other exciting election experience for me was traveling to Little Rock, Arkansas, on election night to be at the evening festivities where Bill and Hillary Clinton and Al and Tipper Gore would receive the results of the 1992 presidential election. Forty thousand people filled the streets of Little Rock. I stood outside on the Capitol lawn, feet cold and damp but spirits warm, and thrilled as I heard my new President accept his landslide victory in a voice hoarse from campaigning. "My fellow American, on this day, with high hopes and brave hearts, in massive numbers, the American people have voted to make a new beginning." The crowd cheered, flashbulbs went off at every angle, and you could hear honking car horns from across the city. Everyone was singing patriotic songs. I've never experienced anything like it. I had worked with Governor Clinton for the past two years. Now I would see this bright, energetic, charismatic leader make the huge jump from Governor of Arkansas to President of the United States. Many of his fellow Democratic governors, including the six of us who were his national co-chairs, had come to Little Rock to celebrate in person. We all knew Bill. He had been one of us. Now he would be *our President.*

When I returned, the press was quite curious about my trip and my experience. Rumors were circulating that I was under consideration for an appointment in the new Clinton administration. I immediately set that straight. "I haven't talked to anyone about any offers. I'm not seeking to move to Washington, D.C." I did, however, elaborate that my working relationship with the President-Elect was quite good and that it would help Oregon secure our needed federal waivers for the Oregon Health Plan and also in resolving the contentious spotted owl/timber situation. In my heart I knew I could not walk away from Oregon at this difficult time in our state's history. And of course, I also understood with Frank's current medical situation, a move away from Oregon was next to impossible.

Two days after the election, I reported to the Marion County Courthouse to attend a jury assembly session for the court. I had been summoned for jury duty and would be oncall for the next two weeks. I could easily have been excused from jury duty, but if I was willing to serve I could make a strong statement about citizen responsibility. And, beware, the next Oregonian who told me they were too busy for jury duty! I read briefing papers, newspapers, and edited speech drafts while I awaited the morning and afternoon call-ups to fill that day's juries. Once the jury pool was excused for the day, I simply returned to my office four blocks away and completed my day's work with a little more privacy. Other jurors were quite fascinated that I was part of the process with them. When I was actually chosen for a jury, the judge looked quite surprised but pleased. While I was appointing judges to the bench in Oregon, I should definitely believe the value of our own justice system warranted my willingness to report for jury duty.

When the July 1992 special session failed to refer my tax-reform package to the ballot, it was evident that I would need to prepare a 1993-95 state budget that included somewhere between $1 billion and $1.2 billion in cuts. I could not plan on any significant new revenues to save Oregon from the cutbacks and program losses. At that point I opted to make a somewhat historic budget process change. I instructed all state agencies, commissions, and boards to submit their upcoming budgets with a 20 percent cut. Actual across-the-board cuts would have been closer to 16 percent. The difference would create, on paper, a multimillion-dollar pool of money that would be allocated based on the state's priority system — the Oregon Benchmarks. My predecessor, Governor Neil Goldschmidt, had designed a creative system called the Oregon Progress Board. Chaired by the governor, this board would define "success" for the state and then measure gains or losses toward meeting that success. Those were the Benchmarks. Measuring educational outcomes, economic expansion, teen pregnancy rates, air and water quality, affordable housing, personal income, health care access, new AIDS cases, adult literacy, high school and college graduation rates, infant mortality, voter participation, new job creation, and much more, Oregon was clearly defining its state goals and would spend the next twenty years measuring our progress. We were not simply measuring state government; we were measuring Oregon, as a whole. During the 1991 legislative session, the Progress Board Executive Director, Duncan Wyse, and I had presented the first Oregon Benchmarks document and its extensive details to every legislative committee in the Capitol building. We received support and strong interest at almost every presentation.

Those Oregon Benchmarks' highest priorities would become my budget priorities both in appropriating the 4 percent pool in my budget but also in determining other agency cuts. If agencies wanted any of the budget add-back, they had to link their request to a specific Benchmark and show how their agency or commission could produce outcomes for that priority goal. These Benchmarks were not simply a published list gathering dust on agency bookshelves. The 1991 Oregon Benchmarks publication, the state's first, became dog-eared from overuse by agency directors and staff. I was grateful to have a solid tool that at least aided me in choosing the painful cuts that would define my 1993-95 budget.

The other major money issue that would be before the 1993 legislative session would be about additions rather than subtractions. Even though I had never been an advocate of the lottery as an acceptable means for government to raise revenue, I found myself with $244 million in lottery resources in the 1993-

95 budget, an amount constitutionally dedicated by a vote of the people to economic development. I would successfully propose funding for international trade, film and video work, for the state's tourism budget, for regional economic projects, workforce development, education reform, and the state's contribution to the expansion of light rail in the metro area. The lottery was not a panacea for filling holes in the budget. It had to meet the test of the voters — economic development. I was careful to meet that test. In a special election in May of 1995, Oregon citizens passed a legislatively referred ballot measure to constitutionally expand the lottery's purpose to add public education. However, in 1993, I did not have that flexibility.

With the early budget preparation under way, every state agency was feeling some level of unrest and disruption. To add to the mix, on September 14, 1992, Fred Miller, head of the Executive Department, announced his intention to leave his position. This was a huge leadership loss for state government at an unusually challenging time, both budget wise and policy wise. Fred had great respect among state agency managers, and his departure would be felt. On November 3, I filled the vacant position with long-term state manager and fiscal expert Dan Simmons.

On December 1, 1992, as required by Oregon's constitution, I publicly released my 1993-95 budget, or more correctly — *budgets*. By law I had to present a balanced budget and I did that, releasing what I called my "mandated" budget, which cut the current level of services by $966 million. My second version I labeled the "mandated-plus" budget. It included increases in beer and wine taxes that amounted to about 5 cents per drink, a cigarette tax increase of 10 cents per pack, and a new tax on health care providers that would raise $216 million and would help fund the Oregon Health Plan. The third version of the budget was focused on restoring most of the $500 million in cuts to elementary and secondary education and community colleges. This budget would rely on the passage of a major tax-reform package, both in the Legislature and at the ballot. Three budgets — three different price tags!

Quoted in *The Oregonian* the next day, I said it plainly and simply, "The choices are laid out clearly, this is the starting point for budget debate."

Beyond the overwhelming pall that Oregon's budget shortfall cast on the 1993 legislative session, there were plenty of other policy matters to fill the 207-day session—Oregon's longest in history to that time. My major priority, beyond the budget issues, was the passage and funding of the Oregon Health Plan. I also knew after my experience during the 1991 session that this year it was likely we would have to address some issues in Oregon's statewide land-use laws if we were to keep the system truly statewide. The state's new corrections director, Frank Hall, had also presented some corrections and parole changes that I felt were crucial. By bringing forward my proposal to eliminate dozens of outdated and unnecessary state boards and commissions plus downsizing state government employees by 10 percent—four thousand positions—I had also created what was jokingly referred to as the Lobbyists' Full Employment Act. Every legislative hearing room was soon full of lobbyists arguing to save boards and commissions that most legislators and citizens had never before heard of. Legislation would also be proposed to create a new five-member Economic Development Commission, appointed by the Governor and confirmed by the Senate. Several legislators were also preparing to create a tax measure referral to send to the ballot. Now that had a familiar ring to it! State Superintendent of Public Instruction Normal Paulus was even talking about starting an initiative petition tax measure—a sales tax dedicated to education. There seemed no end to the creativity now that my tax reform measure was dead and buried.

The Legislature convened on January 11, 1993, and at that traditional morning ceremony, I also delivered my State of the State remarks. I spoke about Oregon's budget crisis and the contents of my 1993-95 budget, yet I kept that message brief. It was not new to this audience. I also added this thought: "History, however, will not define this Legislature or this Governor solely by the budget we build in this Capitol. This legislative session is *not* just about managing today's crisis. Oregon's national image, our reputation, and our place in history have been carved, not by budgets, but by legislators and governors who captured an idea, took a risk, and turned it into a reality." I reminded them of past policy leadership, creative legislative plans and ideas, and collaboration on new innovations. I added this reminder in this currently conflicted assembly, "Remember, innovative public policy in Oregon has never had a partisan label."

I asked for their strong support on my legislative package for rural economic development. I focused on the need for the new Human Rights Commission I was proposing. I placed strong emphasis on my new watershed management strategy. "It is time for all Oregonians to treat water as the finite and fragile resource that it is." My remarks were somewhat brief for a State of the State, but my focus and priorities were clear.

A week later, I left Oregon for Washington, D.C., for five days to attend the inaugural festivities for President Bill Clinton and Vice-President Al Gore. I had been involved in political activities for over twenty years but never before had I been involved beyond simply television viewing with the inauguration of a President of the United States. I was accompanied by two of my communications staff, Gwenn Baldwin and Sarah Carlin Ames, and Sergeant Rick Geistwhite and Darrell Berning from my state police detail. I purchased a beautiful emerald green gown for the ball, the most expensive piece of clothing I had ever owned. I also bought two new suits to add to my wardrobe for the other afternoon and evening events I would be attending. I was excited and anticipating a hectic but impressive three days. I was *not* disappointed.

The Democratic Governors Association attended a brunch with national and state leaders of the AFL-CIO, and later that same day spent two hours hobnobbing in the beautiful home of one of Washington D.C.'s most famous hostesses—Pamela Harriman, widow of Governor Averill Harriman of New York. On Tuesday, all of the governors in attendance joined the President-Elect and Mrs. Clinton for a beautiful luncheon in the Great Hall of the Library of Congress. I was honored to introduce Reverend Horne, the new president's minister, to give the invocation.

Wednesday, January 20, was clear but cold in D.C. This historic day would be packed full of memorable moments from start to finish. The governors had breakfast together and then began their drive to the Capitol for the inauguration. Each car in which a governor rode was given a special inaugural license plate showing the state's order of joining the union. The governors were seated together. I cannot tell you how proud I was as I sat on the dais, looking out at thousands of Americans gathered for the ceremonies. I felt the awe and wonder of a small-town kid from a tiny town in Oregon.

That evening, dressed for the Western Regional Presidential Inaugural Ball at the Kennedy Center, one of several huge formal balls across the city that night, I felt a little like Cinderella. Every one of my group members looked so beautiful, so handsome that night as we left for the Kennedy Center. However, part way to the event our little group from Oregon recognized that we were unlikely to be able to get to the catered food tables at the huge crowded ball. We were all hungry and knew every decent restaurant in D.C. would be packed. So we pulled over to the curb, the five of us emerged from the car in our elaborate finery, and we went into McDonald's and ordered hamburgers and drinks. Those Oregon folks really know how to celebrate! We attracted quite a bit of attention in the fast-food establishment, and the story stayed with all of us for years as a fun and special memory from our inaugural night on the town in Washington, D.C. The ball was beautiful, the music loud, the Kennedy Center filled to overflowing—and we were among the few revelers who arrived well fed! We watched on tiptoes as the new President waltzed with the new First Lady!

The Oregon contingent at the inaugural party. Left to right: Darrell Berning (Oregon State Police), Gwenn Baldwin, Barbara Roberts, Sarah Carlin Ames, unidentified man identified only as "military support," Sgt. Rick Geistwhite (Oregon State Police). From Portland State University Collection.

I came home to Oregon still feeling the glow of that inaugural week, but that blush wouldn't stay with me long. The battles between the Republican-controlled House and the Democratic Senate seemed to make every Oregon issue worthy of a war. I could already hear the first legislative grumbling about my proposed elimination of employee positions. Even legislators who made frequent press comments about "downsizing" government were hesitant to step up to the plate and do the required cuts. I recalled campaigns that were generously sprinkled with phrases like "tightening belts" and "tax-and-spend liberals." Now here was the chance to downsize by four thousand positions, and I began to see the hesitation mounting. I had kept my promise in my budget document. Now, we would see if the Legislature was willing to follow my lead. I was also beginning to suspect I would find some of the same reaction to my proposed eliminations of outmoded boards. Would I find strong legislative advocates for the Advisory Committee for Hair Design Schools or the Woodstove Emissions Control Advisory Committee? Time would tell.

As January came to a close, I would be off to Washington, D.C., once again, this time for the winter meeting of the National Governors Association. However, for this trip, I was stealing Frank out of Oregon for a long weekend away from his legislative duties. We flew to Washington on Friday afternoon, both of us anticipating our Sunday evening dinner at the White House with President Clinton and Hillary. On Saturday and during the day Sunday, Frank attended a number of meetings and events with me. He had a grand time surrounded by governors, new administration leaders, and politics! Frank was especially interested in the meeting of the NGA Task Force on Health Care. He had served on the legislative committee that had helped develop the Oregon Health Plan and was quite knowledgeable on the subject. Frank also sat in and watched the C-Span interview and call-in show I did. Finally, he went back to our room to rest and skipped my last committee meeting. I worried that the flight and all this exciting activity might be draining for him, but I also recognized how important sharing this week was for both of us. It was not likely we would ever get another week to match this one before Frank's illness controlled his choices — and mine.

On Sunday evening Frank, looking so handsome in his tuxedo, and I, in my formal attire, arrived at the White House. This was the first formal dinner in the Clinton White House and the NGA members and spouses were excited and honored to be there. I sat at the President's table. Frank was seated across the room with other governors and other spouses. As always, the tables were splendidly set, the food was gourmet, some of the fine wine was from Oregon, and the conversation was stimulating. I was so grateful to be able to include Frank in this extraordinary evening.

On Monday Frank flew home to Oregon to get back to his legislative responsibilities. I had three more days in D.C. packed with meetings, a governors-only session at the White House with President Clinton, and a couple of Western Governors' meetings. On my final day in Washington, I met with the entire Oregon delegation. This gave me an opportunity to talk about some of our shared concerns: securing the Oregon Health Plan waivers, ongoing light rail funding for the metro area, the huge importance of adequate monies for communities and dislocated workers in the Clinton forest plan, and other significant issues facing Oregon on both the state and federal agenda. It was an issue-packed hour.

I left on an evening flight to Portland and was back in my office for an 8:30 a.m. meeting with legislative leaders the next morning. After only four days home, I was in downtown Portland on Monday for an NGA work session on welfare reform. Staff and policymakers from more than twenty states attended the two-day work session, and Oregon's JOBS program from the 1991 session was cited over and over as a model for moving people from welfare into family-wage jobs that included adequate child care and health insurance.

On February 12, I was involved in two of what would soon be dozens of ceremonial events as part of the state's celebration of one hundred fifty years since the Oregon Trail brought the first settlers to the territory. On that day, we unveiled the new Oregon Trail postage stamp and that evening celebrated at a huge Pioneer Ball in period costume in the Capitol Rotunda.

As the legislative session moved into full swing in the spring months, I testified before the Senate Judiciary Committee in support of Senate Bills 34 and 35, which would ensure equal rights for Oregonians regardless of sexual orientation. Later in March I testified again, this time in strong support of SB 128, which would create the state Human Rights Commission, which would help identify and remove barriers to equal opportunity, mediate community tensions, and take the lead in decreasing the number of hate crimes in Oregon.

In a conference call on March 19 with Representative Ron Wyden and myself, Health and Human Services Secretary Donna Shalala called to inform us that the Clinton administration had given Oregon the waiver, the green light, to begin the Oregon Health Plan. Secretary Shalala's official words were, "The American people want, need and deserve the peace of mind of knowing that their health care needs will be covered. In Oregon, citizens and state officials have come up with an approach to provide that security for state residents." After the long and complex journey Oregon had taken to arrive at this moment, it was a complete thrill for me to hear those words. Every news photo of me speaking on the telephone, and as I hung up, showed me smiling broadly, fists clenched in excitement. It was a big day for Oregon. The story was covered broadly in Oregon and across the nation. The next step would be to find the state funding in this current legislative session. I hoped such broad smiles would also be evident at the end of that critical effort.

On March 22 and 23, I was back in Washington, D.C., for several significant events. I participated in a news conference announcing the formation of a new organization, the Alliance for Redesigning Government; I would be serving as vice-chair of the Alliance along with reinvention leaders from across the nation including David Osborne and Ted Gaebler, co-authors of the new and popular civics and public policy book, *Reinventing Government*. The following day I testified before a House subcommittee regarding Oregon's top-priority projects in the Federal Transportation Bill. After the hearing, I went directly to the White House to meet with President Clinton. Joining me for this special gathering were Michael Hollern, Chair of the Oregon Transportation Commission, Irv Fletcher, President of the Oregon AFL-CIO, and Paul Schlesinger, Vice President of Ralph Schlesinger, Inc., in Portland. That meeting was immediately followed by a meeting with Labor Secretary Robert Reich. Following more meetings on transportation issues, it was back to the airport, back to Oregon, back to the legislative session. I was grateful for these expanding ties in D.C. and the positive outcomes I felt Oregon would experience, but I was envious of the quick travel access East Coast governors enjoyed to the federal power base.

In the early morning of March 25, at 5:34 a.m., I was startled awake by what felt and sounded like a freight train rumbling right through the house from east to west. I jumped out of bed, calling Frank's name as

I ran to his room. He was fine but equally surprised about what we had just experienced. Arlene came rushing down the hall to check on us. Having been raised in California, Arlene was quite clear. "Wow, we had a real earthquake!" The state police officer on duty called in to the house to make certain everyone was safe.

It turned out the quake measured 5.6 on the Richter scale and the epicenter was in Scotts Mills, only twelve miles from the Capitol. The three hardest-hit counties — Marion, Yamhill, and Clackamas — had early estimates of $14 million of uninsured loss. There were no deaths and minimal injuries. However, Oregon was shaken, not only by the quake itself, but by the fact that the state so rarely experiences an earthquake. The small aftershocks the next day had Oregonians very edgy.

Interestingly, the most newsworthy story about the earthquake was centered squarely in the state Capitol, in fact in the Capitol Rotunda. The Rotunda dome, towering 106 feet overhead, had visible signs of damage, and the Capitol Rotunda was immediately cordoned off with yellow crime scene tape. The greater worry, however, was the eight-and-a-half-ton, twenty-three-foot-tall, Golden Pioneer statue that sits atop the state dome and whose gilded presence symbolizes the state. The statue had been rocked until it cracked free from its base, shifted, and was then left dangerously unanchored above the rotunda floor. The rotunda would be closed for months, and repairs to make the area secure again would run into the millions. With the Legislature in session, I joked that I had been waiting for something to move in the Capitol but this was not what I had in mind.

Less than a week following the earthquake excitement, the Oregon media were experiencing yet another unusual story. The President and the Vice President were coming to Oregon, accompanied by several members of the Cabinet. This impressive delegation from Washington, D.C. was in Portland for the Pacific Northwest Forest Conference. The *Washington Post* of April 2, 1993, described the conference as "coming face to face with a political and environmental tar baby." Several of the cabinet secretaries had been visiting Oregon over the previous few days to gain further insight on the spotted owl/timber controversy. Among the impressive list of participants beyond the President and Vice President were Secretary of Labor Robert Reich, Carol Browner, administrator of the Environmental

Protection Agency, U.S. Forest Service lead biologist, Jack Ward Thomas, Secretary of Interior Bruce Babbitt, Agricultural Secretary Mike Espy, and Commerce Secretary Ron Brown.

In my prepared remarks, I welcomed our distinguished guests and told them, "The citizens of this region know change is coming, and they are preparing for change. But as they adapt, they also seek predictability, as we plan together for our communities, our industries, and our workers."

When the conference was over, as the Sunday *Oregonian* of April 4 stated, "Nearly everyone pronounced it a smashing success." But every quote from both industry leaders and environmentalists showed that neither side had budged much by the end of the conference. President Clinton stated that he "wanted to make the current environmental laws work and had no plans to seek changes in those laws ... In the end, we can't run the country on lawsuits." Forest Service biologist Jack Ward Thomas said profoundly, "Both sides speak the word 'balance'! They all mean different things." There rested the challenge in an issue that seemed devoid of middle ground and where polarization had become the norm.

In April, an important new staff member joined my administration. I was extremely excited to be able to appoint a strong Portland business leader, Bill Scott, as the new director of the Oregon Economic Development Department. Bill's background in government, law, education, and business gave him exceptional credentials for this position. In addition to his professional background, his willingness to give back to his community and state were evidenced by his service on the Portland School Board and his commitment over the past two years as an active member of the Oregon Progress Board. In mid-June I took a break from the Capitol building and the 1993 legislative session to spend a long weekend with the Democratic Governors Association in Woodstock, Vermont. It's a beautiful little town and our conference hotel was a visitor's ideal of charm and elegance. This was our first DGA policy conference since the Clinton presidency began, and the new administration was well represented at the event. At this time I was also serving on the DGA executive board, so I would have some additional meeting responsibilities over the four days of the conference. There was notably more press in attendance than we usually experienced during these policy weekends. The Vermont location and summer weather were likely incentives, but the presence of political notables from the Clinton White House was clearly the bigger draw.

Thursday afternoon I participated in the opening news conference. On Friday the program turned to big policy and even larger politics. The day was kicked off with a keynote address on health care reform from First Lady Hillary Clinton. Her presentation was impressive and highly informative. She had a strong grasp of the subject matter and of the mountain of opposition that would soon rise to try and stop changes in health insurance, hospital and physician practices, reimbursement policy, and government insertion into the nation's health care policies. She spoke without text or notes. I was strongly impressed with her knowledge and her presentation skills.

The evening program was pure politics. I served as moderator for a lively discussion between DNC Chairman David Wilhelm and Paul Begala, political strategist and counselor to the President. The politics were predominantly nationally focused, but with a room full of governors and "all politics being local," the outcomes of the national policy agenda often turned to the resulting impacts on the states. Governors are not a shy group, and it is always fun to watch them take on the "national experts"!

Two experiences remain with me from that particular DGA conference. One was sharing lunch with Education Secretary Dick Riley and his family as we played tourists in the friendly Woodstock community just before the conference opened. I had the opportunity to share some of my personal experiences as a ten-year local school board member and a four-year community college board member. The second memory from that weekend remains vivid after all these years. Hillary Clinton and I took a walk into Woodstock to find the local Ben and Jerry's ice cream store. We walked back to the hotel, talking, savoring our tasty ice cream, relaxed in the Vermont summer atmosphere. To some it may not have been their imagined picture of a First Lady and a Governor. Observing our casual appearance and our ice cream cones, one would not know that our consuming issues were health care reform and the impact of the Endangered Species Act protections! These were changing times.

I flew from Vermont to Washington, D.C., after the DGA meeting to discuss with Secretary of Interior Bruce Babbitt and other federal officials the forest alternatives under consideration by the Clinton administration and to press strongly for adequate accompanying economic packages. It was a tough day's work but certainly an improvement over trying to negotiate with Secretary Lujan and the Bush administration.

Through 1992 and 1993, through two federal administrations, through the federal court system, throughout my calendar and across my desk, there was a continuous army of memos, reports, legal documents, staff updates, press coverage, and editorials relating to the ongoing conflict surrounding the endangered species listing of the Northern Spotted Owl. Federal agencies, state agencies, lawyers, judges, scientists, legally appointed committees, no less than twenty-two environmental organizations, federal cabinet members — the list of participants and players was broad and frequently combative.

I tried to remain consistent and clear about my agenda. No matter the political fallout, I remained a supporter of the federal ESA law. I sought a scientifically credible plan for the owl's survival. I didn't believe denial would do anything but keep Oregon *in* the courts and *out* of the woods in terms of responsible harvest options. The Bush administration, particularly Secretary of Interior Manuel Lujan, had presented added conflict and constant attempts to short-cut the ESA legal process. When the Clinton administration took office, I was rewarded with the environmental knowledge and philosophy of both Vice President Al Gore and the new Secretary of the Interior, Bruce Babbit of Arizona. Yet, before that political transition took place, the spotted owl cases were filling federal court dockets, plus viable plans for both the owl species recovery and economic recovery for our timber workers and timber communities were being lost in mountains of legal briefs and political rhetoric.

The legal cases supporting the requirements of the ESA had been piling up. In December of 1991, a federal judge in Seattle had refused to allow the U.S. Fish and Wildlife Service to delay designating critical habitat for the owl until the federal recovery plan was finished. That same month, the U.S. Circuit Court of Appeals for the 9th Circuit had upheld a ban on timber sales, basically blocking all new national forest timber sales until the U.S. Forest Service completed a new owl management plan and environmental impact statement. The appeals court had agreed with U.S. District Court Judge William Dwyer that the Forest Service violated the National Forest Management Act by failing to adopt a scientifically credible plan for protecting the owl from habitat loss due to logging. The viable recovery plan finally produced by the Spotted Owl Recovery Team in 1992 was not implemented. Secretary Lujan ignored it, shelved it, in an attempt to call together the powerful federal "God Squad," a committee of seven cabinet-level members that has the authority to exempt federal agencies from protecting an endangered species. Secretary Lujan moved to outflank science and the law by using the "God Squad" to permit the Bureau of Land Management to begin forty-four timber sales in Oregon without protections for the spotted owl. The so-called God Squad could grant such an exemption only if they had met strict legal requirements. *They had not.* The recovery plan had been ignored. Federal court injunctions were in place to prevent those sales and such harvests. Secretary Lujan was grandstanding. It was pure politics.

At that point I met with my natural resource policy advisors and legal counsel. I felt I could not stand quietly by and let this federal charade continue. I knew we must have a long-term resolution to this crisis before Oregon disappeared in a further quagmire of legal delays. I authorized state agencies to intervene in a court action declaring that the state did not believe the BLM had met the legal criteria necessary for the "God Squad" exemption. I released our legal brief at a news conference on February 18. The brief concluded it was "doubtful the exemption process should have been invoked at all. It falls short of the high standards required." Pro-timber groups and Oregon Senator Bob Packwood swiftly denounced the state's position. However, not all informed observers and opinion leaders agreed. On February 27, *The Daily Astorian* editorial noted: "If Governor Roberts is guilty of anything, it is speaking the truth about the Bureau of Land Management and Interior Secretary Manuel Lujan ... Lujan and the BLM are breaking the law." *The Oregonian* supported me: "This is a realistic state response. It addresses the situation squarely. Yet for suggesting it, Governor Roberts has incurred open hostility. ... The refusal to face the threat of the Spotted Owl directly and promptly, not anything the Governor has done, is what has produced the chaos in the federal forests."

The debate would continue under the new administration but with new direction and priorities. I would remain front and center on the controversy in Oregon, gaining more scar tissue than friends. Sometimes that is the role required of a leader.

CHAPTER TWENTY-TWO

Personal Struggles

In my private role as wife, I was struggling as Frank's quality of life began to diminish. He was starting to be short of breath on occasion, the strength of his voice was noticeably diminishing, and his pain level was increasing. He tired more easily and, had it not been for his motorized cart, his growing weakness would have been even more evident. Frank had become a Hospice client four months into the 1993 legislative session, partially to receive pain assistance but also for both of us to have the needed emotional support as we faced his terminal cancer. This new support was making his situation easier and it certainly gave additional support to me and to Arlene, who was helping with his care. Now that the elevator had been installed in Mahonia Hall, our bedrooms were side by side and during the week I spent hours with Frank as he prepared to go to sleep each evening. The two of us never ran out of conversation. We talked politics, grandchildren, reminisced about our past sailing trips, laughed over our early relationship years, talked of friends, music, movies, and a future together that now grew ever shorter. He was determined to finish this final legislative session. I was committed to helping him do so. I now believed it would be a very close call.

For eight months his diagnosis, as he wished, had remained hidden except to family and a few very close friends. But the silence was becoming an increasing burden for both of us. Frank's pain meds were beginning to affect his alertness during legislative committee hearings. He hated for observers to assume that he was simply a sleepy-eyed old legislator. At this point, Frank decided the time had come to release the information on his medical situation. He reasoned he should simply prepare a press release stating his diagnosis plus his intention to resign his Senate seat on September 1, after the Legislature had adjourned for the session. I supported his decision, and he came to my office to ask my communications staff to help write the press release. He wanted it done well. When the press release was completed, one of Frank's staff simply dropped the copies off at the Capitol press room. Frank believed the chore was now behind him and re-focused on his legislative work load.

Within minutes the telephones in his office and at the governor's office began ringing off the hook. It seemed that every newspaper and radio and television station had questions … lots of questions. Frank became increasingly frustrated that he couldn't accomplish any work. He called my office. He was going down to the press room. He clarified for me that he would answer their questions, once and for all, and be done with it so he could get back to work. "Could you join me?" he asked.

I stood quietly to the side as Frank began to field press questions.

"Are you currently taking treatment, Senator?"

Frank said he was not.

"Do you have a surgery planned?"

"There won't be any surgery," Frank answered. The press began to look puzzled. Perhaps the carefully prepared press release had not been fully digested. Finally, Frank put the situation in total clarity. "I have terminal metastasized lung cancer. I have chosen to undergo no further treatment. I am currently under Hospice care."

The room was totally still. Finally a reporter broke the silence and asked, "Senator, when did you get this news?"

Frank responded, "My doctor told me I had a year to live in October of last year, eight months ago."

The same reporter then added a follow-up question. "Senator, when did the Governor learn of this diagnosis?"

"At the very same moment I did. She was seated beside me when the doctor delivered the news," Frank added softly.

I walked over to Frank, took his hand, and we left the press room together. Not one reporter moved as we exited. There was nothing more to ask. I wondered if some of these press and media folks might be thinking back over the stories they had written and aired over the last eight months on Frank and me. Had they been unkind, even harsh, at times? Had they possibly added another straw to the camel's back without knowing the personal burden we already carried? Yet they were simply doing their job. It was Frank and I who had chosen the silence for all these months. I actually felt an amazing relief at finally having the story out. Frank had never wanted to be "treated like he was dying," even when he was. Yet that choice had meant that we gave up a thousand kindnesses and broad support from those who cared about us. There had indeed been an emotional price for keeping the secret.

Photo by Mike Lloyd from The Oregonian

Once the story became public, both of us were given the rare opportunity of shedding light on our personal journey with Hospice and the reality of facing this end-of-life experience. We did interviews. The press and media did informational stories on Hospice: how it works, whom it serves, what it costs. We learned that some Hospice programs around the state were receiving expanded charitable contributions following all the press coverage about Frank. We both felt this was a small but deserved reward for Hospice, considering the caring and professional support they delivered to Frank and to patients across the state.

As the 4th of July weekend approached, I knew I needed *at least* a small break. On Sunday the 4th, I planned to ride in the fun holiday parade in the southern Oregon community of Ashland. Ashland was also the home of the Oregon Shakespeare Festival, and Frank and I decided we would treat ourselves and our friend Nancy Wakefield to a play on Saturday night. The two days before the holiday weekend I would be doing meetings in several timber communities explaining the details of the newly released Clinton forest plan. I knew it would be controversial and very hostile work. And boy was it! As soon as the plan was released, Republican state legislators went bonkers. Speaker of the House Larry Campbell said adamantly, "Instead of being offered a balanced approach, Oregon has received a bullet between the eyes." Representative Fred Girod stated, "If this is a decision by the best and the brightest, then heaven help this country." Senator Rod Johnson of Roseburg, in the heart of the timber region, added, "The President has fulfilled his promise to his wacko preservationist friends of turning Oregon into a national park the eco-freaks can come visit."

In that political climate, I would visit several timber communities as I headed south for my two days off. By the time I reached Ashland, I was worn out, too tired to even eat a late dinner in one of my favorite Oregon communities. My friend Nancy would be arriving the next morning and we planned a leisurely day shopping and sight-seeing until Frank arrived from Salem with one of my state police officers. The three- to four-hour drive would be wearing for Frank, but he was looking forward to dinner, a play, the parade on Sunday, and our shared ride back to Salem. All I needed was a good night's rest.

When Nancy arrived the next morning, we ate breakfast and then began our shopping tour down the main street of Ashland, my two security officers following discreetly behind. We looked at shoes, spent time in an amazing bead shop, grazed through a bookstore, and continued down the street. I began to understand that something was amiss. I wasn't feeling normal. I spoke quietly to Nancy, "Do not look around at my officers. We are going to walk two more blocks to the park and seat ourselves on a bench. I am going to hand you my purse right now. I can't carry it. I may be having some kind of heart trouble." Nancy's eyes widened but she didn't turn around, as instructed. We reached the bench and sat down, and my two officers sat down several benches away. I looked around at the area and saw an ambulance parked at the curb. I asked Nancy to calmly walk over to my officers and tell them I was going to get up and walk toward the ambulance. No one was to run or attract any attention. They just needed to be sure there was a driver in the emergency vehicle when I got there and help me step unnoticed into the ambulance. I didn't think what I was feeling was life threatening but I needed to remain calm until I could reach medical help. It all worked quietly and smoothly. I checked into the Ashland Hospital emergency room under my middle name and former married last name. I didn't want the press picking this up until I understood the situation. Once the medical staff had examined me, they indicated they might need to transfer me to the larger Medford hospital only a few miles away.

My first worry was Frank. We needed to figure out how my officers in Ashland could call the officer who was driving Frank without alerting Frank that I was in the hospital. I wanted them to bring Frank to the hospital, but I didn't want him worrying for the last thirty to forty-five minutes of the drive. The officer handled it perfectly, only informing Frank as they arrived in Ashland's city center. He was immediately upset, which was why we had delayed informing him. He entered my hospital cubicle on his cart, his eyes wide and his face pale with worry. I assured him I was going to be fine, but I would miss dinner, the play that night, and the fun of Ashland's parade the next day. I would be in the Medford hospital having some additional testing done.

The long and short of this story is that I was drinking too much coffee, eating too much chocolate, living under too much stress, and tests showed some minor narrowing in my arteries. At age fifty-seven, I needed *less* of all of the above excesses. I also knew from my Hospice reading that end-of-life caregivers are at risk for health issues due to emotional stress, interrupted sleep, diet changes, and the worry over their loved one. If I combined that with the spotted owl, the lengthy, bitter legislative session, and the schedule of being governor, the scare I had experienced shouldn't have surprised anyone. It did, however, ruin a wonderful two-day break.

Frank was able to continue serving through the entire legislative session, the longest in state history, right up to adjournment *sine die* on August 5, 1993. He called on every ounce of strength and endurance he could dredge up to complete those last few days, including the 4 a.m. dropping of the final gavel of his legislative career. I can't remember ever being so grateful to see an Oregon legislative session adjourn. Frank could now go home. He could get the rest he needed and deserved. He had fulfilled his duty to his district constituents and to the state. It was time for him to focus on his own needs in these final months, or weeks, of his life.

The 1993 legislative session had brought both successes and failures to my legislative agenda. One of the personal disappointments for me had been the loss of SB 128, my proposed Human Rights Commission. Even after a strong 26-to-4 vote in the Senate, I had to give up any chance of the measure getting out of the Republican-controlled House. I had refused to accept a committee amendment to strike sexual orientation from the list of nondiscrimination policies that the commission would undertake. It was made clear to me that the amendment was required before the House would act. I made it equally clear that I would rather see the bill die than allow the state to make such a bigoted legal decision. The bill died in committee. The House also let SB 34 fail, a measure that would have prevented discrimination in housing and employment.

I was especially pleased to see the passage of my $10 million budget request for watershed health. The funds would now be used to identify and implement watershed restoration on the south coast and in Eastern Oregon's Grande Ronde Basin, both areas facing significant degradation and potential listing of endangered fish species. The previous December I had testified before U.S. Senator Mark Hatfield at a Portland hearing of the Senate Appropriations Committee on evaluating options for salmon and steelhead restoration. That same month I had keynoted the first Coastal Salmon Recovery Conference, which I had initiated. Discussions on this issue, much like those on spotted owl recovery, were full of diverse views, conflicting options, and no small amount of finger pointing. This $10 million budget commitment would put feet on the ground, or perhaps in the water, as public agencies and private citizens worked to bring back ecological health to two major Oregon watersheds. I was proud of the work of my natural resources agencies and staff in putting together this essential plan and budget package.

Much of the long, hard work involved in creating my three budget options resulted in a high percentage of legislative acceptance. The disappointing exception was the unwillingness of the Legislature to bite the bullet on my proposed cutback of four thousand positions; the final legislatively adopted number was closer to a cut of twenty-seven hundred. Oddly enough, this failure was, on several occasions, described by the press as *my* failure to reach the goal. I can only say I handed them the blueprint. They ignored the directions. My proposed elimination of forty-six unneeded boards and commissions unfortunately became a notable opportunity for the House and Senate to find disagreement. The Senate first retained eight of my proposed eliminations. The House added back twelve — but not a match for the Senate list of eight. The conference committee debated the list and in the end eliminated only twenty-eight boards. Eighteen fairly useless boards survived the debate and the lobbying efforts. Frustrating!

During the 1991 legislative session we had struggled with the issue of land use, particularly what was known as "secondary lands." These are lands determined to be of lesser agricultural and forest production value. Secondary lands do not, for instance, receive the protection from development that high-value farmland does. Taking into consideration issues of soil drainage, steepness, and crop potentials becomes highly contentious when designating secondary lands. The Legislature had been unable to come to agreement on the issue. After the 1991 session ended, I instructed the Division of Land Conservation and Development (DLCD) and its commission (LCDC) to resolve the issues of conflict on secondary lands administratively.

Yet once the 1993 session was under way, legislation was introduced that, in its original form, would have *gutted* Oregon's land use program. Policy Director Ann Squier and policymakers from DLCD went to work to help create a responsible answer to the bill, working with members of the Legislature and some outside advocacy leaders. I made clear that I would veto the original legislation if it reached my desk. House leaders, during this period of intense debate, went so far as to threaten to "zero out" the budget of DLCD. I told them to go for it! I would let the agency stand idle for two years before I would so severely damage our state's nationally respected land use system. This battle was breaking a generation-long tradition of bipartisan support for land use in the Oregon Legislature. I would not be bullied by budget threats into harming this essential growth management tool. In the closing days of the session a new version of House Bill 3661 passed both chambers of the Legislature by solid margins. It wasn't everything I wanted to see in the bill, but I felt we had perhaps dodged a bullet.

When I considered all the legislation that came out of the 1993 session, I took special pleasure in the final passage and funding of the

Oregon Health Plan. I had felt so rewarded for all my efforts when the federal waivers were secured. It would have been devastating to lose the plan in the bitter political climate of the '93 session. Yet—that almost happened.

On what was expected to be the final day of that very lengthy legislative session several major matters were still unresolved with no agreement in sight. One of the critical issues still hanging in the balance was the Oregon Health Plan. During the lunch break I walked into a meeting of Senate and House leaders, *uninvited*. The meeting was loud and angry, with threats from Speaker Campbell that he was ready to adjourn right away and allow the whole pile of unfinished business to simply be left—period. No compromise seemed possible. Campbell was ready to throw in the towel.

I listened, then made a few suggestions about possible ideas for compromise; the room quieted down and new discussions began. I then said calmly to the legislators from both parties and both houses, "As far as I know we are all getting paid for the whole day. How about we all put in a full day's work?" The Salem *Statesman Journal* of August 5 commented on the meeting, "The crucial moment in Wednesday's drive toward adjournment came .... when House and Senate leaders and Governor Barbara Roberts emerged from a closed-door meeting." Senate Majority Leader Dick Springer (D) said, "The agreement to continue negotiations signaled to everyone that a chance remained to find common ground. Both sides were looking for a way to back themselves out of a corner." In the end, they did that full day's work, including passage of the Oregon Health Plan, which would provide health insurance coverage for 120,000 low-income Oregonians in the first phase beginning early in 1994, plus they passed a dime-a-pack cigarette tax to launch the plan. I felt a real sense of accomplishment on this one, both the passage of the issue and the outcome of my leadership as an uninvited "guest" in a closed legislative leadership meeting. Sometimes there are matters far more important than an invitation.

The other weighty issue to come out of the 1993 session was a sales tax measure that would be referred to the voters in a special election on the November ballot. The proposed 5 percent sales tax would raise about $1 billion a year for public schools and remove public school funding from Oregon property tax bills. I wasn't thrilled with the measure. I didn't feel it was nearly as balanced or equitable as the tax reform measure I had proposed only a year ago. However, I supported the measure in hopes of creating more financial backing for our schools and fewer funding crises for the state government.

The session ended on its two hundred seventh day—a state record at that time. Speaker Larry Campbell told the press in the wee hours, awaiting the session's final bills, that he did not intend to seek reelection. He was quoted in the next day's *Oregonian* saying, "It's a tough, tough ballgame. It's just not fun anymore." Surprise! It never occurred to me that the work of the Oregon Legislature was supposed to be about entertaining its members, particularly its leadership.

I was so glad this session was over. If a miracle occurred and the sales tax measure passed in November, perhaps the next legislative session would at least not have the burden of such huge program cuts. I hoped that was the case.

Four days after the legislative adjournment, I was in Portland, headed to a meeting, when I received a call on the state police telephone. I needed to return to Salem. Frank had been unable to breathe, and Hospice had an oxygen unit delivered to his room. He was quite upset, and Hospice felt he needed my support and reassurance. Patricia cancelled my Portland meeting as we headed directly back to Salem. On that return trip, my sister called. She was in tears. Pat had gone to the Salem Hospital for a routine exam. While she was there she asked her physician about a sore spot under her collar bone. The doctor checked it out and asked questions. Further examination gave strong indications that she could have lung cancer. Her husband, Don, was working out of town, and she was upset and scared. She needed me! This began to feel like a nightmare.

I told Pat I was on my way back to Salem and would be at the hospital in an hour. I didn't tell her about the situation with Frank. I was now only ten minutes from the governor's residence. I found Frank quite worried but now calmed and wearing an oxygen mask. We both understood the message in this physical change. We knew his cancer was worse, his lungs were more compromised, and his time was narrowing. It was such a hard day for both of us. We were hit with the power of this new reality. The Hospice nurse encouraged Frank to sleep for a while. I sat beside him until he dozed off. I didn't tell him about Pat. He had experienced enough upset for one day. I tiptoed out of his room. I had ten minutes to keep my promise to my sister. By the time I found Pat they had taken X-rays and a biopsy.

The early indications were definitely not encouraging. I held her and we cried together. If ever I needed a good cry, this was that moment!

From that day forward I would watch two people I deeply loved struggle through the effects of lung cancer ... one dying, the other trying to stay alive. Pat was given only a 5 percent chance of survival. I told her over and over, "Somebody has to be in the 5 percent." She began chemotherapy and went on disability.

On August 17 a celebration of Frank's twenty-five years of legislative service was held in the state Capitol. Frank was honored for his work on behalf of people in need. Our family members were there to hear Terry Rogers of Legal Aid say, "The definition of 'champion' for human services advocates in Oregon has always been Frank Roberts." Two days later, the Campaigners Club and the Democratic Party of Oregon held a sold-out dinner honoring Frank. Five hundred people attended. Frank, looking frail but happy, loved the tributes. It would be his last time out of the house.

So late summer brought a number of endings: the 1993 Oregon legislative session *finally* adjourned, Frank's legislative career was over, and Pat's health forced her to retire. However, endings are usually balanced by new beginnings and a number of those were reflected on the pages of my over-scheduled calendar.

August 12—I was part of the groundbreaking ceremony for the West Side's light rail tunnel. It was exciting to see this next step in the Portland metro area light rail system.

August 18—I signed three important bills for the Corrections Department: their new budget, SB 139, the new boot camp proposal, and HB 2481 on sentencing guidelines. Director Frank Hall now had more tools for his priority changes in the Corrections Department.

September 9—I signed the budget bill for the Oregon Health Plan, followed a few days later, on September 14, with the signing of the actual Health Plan legislation. I was excited to see my signature on those two bills.

September 7—I was in McMinnville on the acreage of the beautiful Sokol Blosser vineyard and winery as I signed into law HB 3661, the new secondary lands bill.

There was another September item on my calendar that I do not know if one could define as a beginning or an end. On September 4, in pioneer period dress, my granddaughter Katie and I rode in a covered wagon for the last leg of the journey of the official Oregon Trail Wagon Train. I had so wanted to spend several days on the trail

Signing HB 3661, the secondary lands bill, at Sokol-Blosser winery, surrounded by legislative leaders. From Oregon Archives Collection.

with the wagon train, but with Frank's health situation I didn't want to be away from him unnecessarily. It would have been so thrilling to experience the trail for several days and better understand what my ancestors James and Almeda Boggs had endured for six months on the trail. However, Katie and I had a several-mile experience that I wouldn't have missed, arriving at the end of the trail in Oregon City to crowds, music, cheering, and a 150-year celebration. This would be one of the few times that fall that I could just relax and have fun with Oregon citizens.

During the rest of August and September Frank continued to deteriorate, becoming pretty much bedridden. He was continuously on oxygen and used liquid morphine to try and keep his pain under control. Close friends and family began to help more and more, even taking turns sleeping in Frank's bedroom through the night. In times of personal struggle, caring friends and family can keep one afloat. They all did that for me—they and Arlene. Arlene's presence in our home, her support, her kindness, her friendship, kept me going. Not only did Arlene manage the governor's residence for me, but her loving care of Frank in those last months and weeks was a priceless gift. We were also grateful for the personal attention and medical support of Frank's Hospice team. They helped us through every step of this emotional journey.

Over the previous few weeks, Frank and I had completed the task of putting his personal affairs in order—his retirement accounts, an updated will, arrangements for his cremation and interment, a notification telephone tree, and finally, fulfilling his wishes about a memorial service. He chose the music he wanted, the speakers, and the location. When the last planning detail was in place he seemed to feel a sense of comfort, perhaps even some control in a life that now offered him very little self-determination.

In these trying months Frank and I sometimes had conversations about *my* future. 1994 was fast approaching, a reelection year for me. Frank was quite clear he expected me to run for a second term as governor. I wanted him to understand that after his death my grief could well keep me from facing a heavy-duty campaign. Frank joked that what I needed, after becoming a widow, was to then become unemployed! We laughed about it but, in truth, I needed him to tell me that if I found I was unable to run again, that he would understand my choice. I *needed* to hear it! Frank told me what a solid and brave governor I had been. He told me Oregon needed my strength and openness. Yet, he finally recognized I wanted his understanding that losing him might change my reelection plans. Frank finally told me that I was the only person who could make that decision and, as always, he would respect my choice. I breathed easier and reaffirmed why I loved this man so.

At the office I was nearing the end of a process of acting on—both signing and, on rare occasion, vetoing—each of the eight hundred-plus bills passed by this recent legislative session. My staff and a variety of agency leadership had evaluated the bills, carefully weighing the impacts on the state budget, on individual citizens, on other agencies of government, on the environment, and on Oregon's economic picture. At home, I was surrounded by another closing process—the end of life. We began limiting Frank's visitors to family and only his closest friends. Frank slept more each day. I would come home from the office and lie beside him on his bed, watching him sleep, watching him breathe. Sometimes he would open his eyes, and we would communicate without a single spoken word.

On September 16, I was scheduled to deliver the keynote address to the Dallas, Texas, Human Rights Campaign dinner. This formal gala was one of the largest gay rights events in the country every year, and I was thrilled to be their speaker. But as the event grew closer, Frank grew more frail, and I began to panic that he might die while I traveled out of the state for the speech. Finally, I knew I couldn't go. I videotaped the speech, and it would be shown at the dinner. In my closing paragraphs, I told the hundreds that would be gathered in Dallas, "We have stood together and spoken out for racial equality, women's rights, religious freedom, and rights for the disabled. Our message tonight is no different from any of those, for … if any group of Americans face the loss of their civil rights, their dignity, … their job or their housing — that we might be in the next group chosen by those who judge by self-appointment. We cannot afford to be silent." A friend reported that he had never witnessed a standing ovation for a video until that night in Dallas.

Well, in keeping with the old adage about things coming in threes, while I was home checking on Frank one lunch hour in late September, my office called. My staff said a very upset woman was calling from California about my ex-husband. She needed an immediate return call. The caller did not even know my name, only that I was Oregon's Governor. I then learned from Neal's brand-new fiancée, Belinda, that he was in intensive care, in a coma. He was on life support. There was no one there who had legal authority to make medical decisions for him. He and his second wife, Karen, were awaiting their final divorce date, only days away. She was in Virginia. My younger son, Mark, needed to fly immediately to California. The state police even got the airline to hold the flight for ten minutes so Mark could make the plane. I couldn't believe this was happening!

Only the night before, while Mark was in Salem visiting Frank and me, my son, who had been estranged from his father for several years, told me he wanted to mend that relationship. Watching Frank slowly dying had helped Mark understand that he needed to act. Time is not always our friend. Mark planned to call his father the next evening after work. I was relieved to see his positive decision.

Now, my younger son was on the way to his father's bedside with the recognition that his intended reconnection with his father might never happen. For two days Mark's phone calls kept me apprised of Neal's condition. Neal had suffered a brain stem hemorrhage. I grieved for Neal and for my sons. There was no good news. Mark listened to the doctor's grim medical reports. He met and comforted his dad's fiancée. Mark talked to his dad for hours. He sang the songs his father had taught him as a child. He was now singing to an unresponsive audience. Finally, Mark said good-bye to his dad and shut off the machine that had been keeping him alive. My thirty-five-year-old son made the ultimate and loving decision for his father. When that step was done, Mark called me. We cried together, and then, for the first time in his life, Mark made the decisions that follow death. There was no one else to take that responsibility. He decided to bring his dad home to Oregon. Mark flew back to Portland with a suitcase full of Neal's papers and photographs and a receipt for his father's cremation and the shipment of his remains to Oregon.

I finally had to explain to Frank what had been happening over those four days. It seemed unfair to me that I was experiencing grief for anyone but Frank. Yet, the grief was there, and it was very real. It was such a vulnerable time for me to face Neal's death and to give the needed support to my two sons. My husband was dying and he had earned every ounce of my love and attention. But my sons also needed me now. Plus Mother and Pat were grieving Neal's death as well. After all, he had been family to them for almost twenty years. I felt stretched very, very thin.

Two political things were happening that fall of 1993 that mattered to me and to Frank. We were following the circulation of a citizen initiative petition referred to as the Death with Dignity measure. Frank had introduced the equivalent legislation in two previous legislative sessions. His two bills did not even receive a hearing, although Frank, the sponsor, was a senior member of the body. In this most recent session, a related bill had been scheduled for a hearing. In the hearing room that day was the cadre of brave leaders who would decide to take the Death with Dignity legislation directly to the Oregon voters. During the last months of his illness, Frank knew the petitions were circulating, and his interest in the success of the measure remained strong. He had no illusion that he would, himself, live long enough to use the potential new law, but his belief in the right to a dignified death had been evident long before his own terminal illness. Every few days he would ask, "How's my petition doing? Are they collecting enough signatures?" I would report to him about the efforts . Frank would tell me each time, "If it qualifies for the ballot, Oregonians will pass the law." It was his final political wish.

The second thing we were watching was the growing rumor that John Kitzhaber, a Democrat, was intending to challenge me in the

1994 governor's race. Kitzhaber, after four terms as state Senate President, had not sought reelection in 1992. He was considered the "father" of the Oregon Health Plan, for which he deserved much credit. Yet that credit did not, in my mind, give him any entitlement to challenge a seated governor of his own party with whom he shared almost every policy position in the state. Still, Kitzhaber had made it clear: he was giving the idea serious consideration.

During September, media and the political rumor mill carried more and more stories about Kitzhaber testing the waters for a run for governor. He was raising money, traveling statewide, holding meetings with movers and shakers. While many observers thought he was just being coy, Kitzhaber insisted he had not yet made the decision.

In late September, or it may have been very early October, John Kitzhaber came by my office asking to see me. I made myself immediately available. He came into my private office, not even taking a seat, informed me he intended to run against me in the 1994 primary election, and turned to leave the office. I asked him to sit down so we could have a conversation about his decision. He just kept walking. I spoke to him several more times, asking him for the courtesy of a conversation. He kept walking, never responding, never turning, as I followed him down the hall, through my outer reception area, into the Capitol corridor, and about twenty feet further—before I stopped and watched him disappear down the hall. He simply walked away.

At home my husband was dying. Frank had served as a colleague of Kitzhaber's for over a decade in the Senate. Yet John didn't even ask about Frank. He also didn't have the guts to talk with me, face to face, about the decision to challenge me. Behind the scenes he reportedly had the help and support of former State Senators Mike Thorne and Ted Hallock and the rumored support of former Governor Neil Goldschmidt. I found myself thinking that perhaps "the boys" wanted the governorship back! I wondered if in the halls of power women would continue to be seen as outsiders, as interlopers.

On October 13 Frank had a stroke. This is not uncommon with terminal patients. It is just one more sign of a body shutting down. For several days Frank was unable to speak—only a jumbled mess of disconnected words came out. He was confused and upset. This articulate Senate orator, a college speech professor, now without communication skills. Total frustration!

The day after Frank's stroke, for the first time in two months, I put out a press release on Frank's medical situation. The stroke and his increased deterioration would likely signal that he was in very serious condition. He had not been seen since August and it seemed right to share at least this much information about his condition.

Each morning after the stroke, as he awakened, I would explain to him that he had experienced a small stroke and it had affected his ability to speak. After four or five days of this morning routine, I was seated on his bed explaining, once again, his situation. With a twinkle in his eyes and a small smile, he reached his hand to my cheek, gently touching me with his fingers and said clearly, "Stroke, stroke." I could feel my tears. I could feel the tenderness and the love. Just as he had charmed me twenty years ago, again that day he moved my heart.

Three days after Frank's stroke, Kitzhaber announced his bid for Oregon Governor. Obviously, this announcement was no surprise to me or to anyone else who had been paying attention. An *Oregonian* story the next day commented: "The announcement came at an awkward time, as Roberts cancelled a scheduled appearance in Portland Saturday night to stay with her husband, Frank, who is dying of cancer. His condition worsened after he suffered a stroke on Wednesday." That same *Oregonian* article quoted Kitzhaber as saying "he was suspending his campaign appearances until it is appropriate to resume." Whatever that meant! I thought it translated into: "It's okay to *announce* while the Governor's husband is dying, but I have to wait to *campaign* until he actually dies!" Harsh reaction on my part, but my heart was breaking.

As late October arrived it was evident that the end of Frank's life was near. He had not eaten for days, took little water, and was in a coma-like state. Frank seemed unaware of the people at his bedside who watched him closely and spoke in whispers. He was surrounded by pillows to keep him comfortable and physically supported. Frank looked small and pale in his nest of pillows. An oxygen tube helped him to breathe. His pain medication was by his bedside, but seemed called for less and less. Our Hospice nurse was in attendance, and she felt Frank would not survive until dawn.

Nine family members held vigil at Frank's bed. We waited and watched. We took turns holding Frank's hand. Quietly, we also took turns comforting each other. The swish and click of the oxygen machine was often the only noticeable sound in the room.

Frank took another labored breath. We waited for him to breathe again. My eyes left Frank's face to glance at the Hospice nurse. She looked at her watch, then our eyes met. She smiled gently, nodded to me, and then walked across the room and shut off the oxygen machine. The silence was deafening. Frank would not breathe again. I reached down and removed his oxygen tube. Then the silence was filled with sobs as we all understood the meaning of the quiet.

It was October 31, 1993, and the love of my life had died. After months of knowing and preparing and dreading, the end had come. The calls went out from our telephone list—family, friends, the mortuary, the press, the announcement of the memorial service. Once again, a very private experience would turn public.

Frank's memorial service, held in the chambers of the Oregon House of Representatives and televised into several overflow hearing rooms, was attended by hundreds of people—political leaders, state employees, faculty members, disabled citizens, labor union members, nonprofit groups, ACLU members—all of whom Frank had advocated for during his long political career. The memorial Frank had designed was a warm, historical, inspiring program. Finally, the Portland Gay Men's Chorus' Cascade Choir sang the Peter, Paul, and Mary ballad, "One Hundred Miles." "If you miss the train I'm on, you will know that I am gone, you can hear the whistle blow a hundred miles."

Senator Frank Roberts was gone. His record of progressive politics, of advocacy for civil rights, human rights, higher education, and children was unmatched in the Oregon Legislature. Frank was sometimes referred to as the "conscience of the Senate." He was a dedicated public servant and proud to be a liberal. The legislative process would strongly miss him. My life would never be the same.

A week later I went back to my full-time schedule. I faced a mountain of work, a tough primary campaign, and a heart full of grief.

With fourteen months left in my term, seven and a half months until the May primary election, and several very big policy issues, including the state budget, still on my platter, I concentrated on getting refocused on both policy and politics. My staff and I began preparing a list—an action agenda—for the items I wanted to make certain were completed by the end of my term. If I ran for reelection and was defeated, the list might become my final legacy as governor. If I decided to forgo the reelection campaign, this itemized agenda could turn into a work blueprint for my last year in office. If I ran successfully for a second term, the completion of this list would be a solid foundation to build on. Choosing priorities would be important, exciting, and productive ... perhaps even a little fun.

One of the priorities I wanted to see on the list was a re-focus on the policy position I had taken in my inaugural address on a Livable Communities Initiative. Flashier and more controversial issues had tended to overshadow this agenda but the fundamental goal had influenced many decisions over the past three years. Now, with Oregon's fast-growing population (now just over three million), I felt it was essential that we reemphasize this agenda. Yet my staff and I recognized that Oregon's outstanding land use system could not do stand-alone duty on this huge set of challenges. We desperately required interagency cooperation and cross-agency planning. A few months earlier, I had convened the first-ever joint meeting of the state's Transportation, Land Conservation and Development, and Environmental Quality commissions. I told them, "[W]e have no hope of achieving our visions if we stick to old habits. If we believe that air quality is solely the responsibility of the DEQ, or that planning for transportation systems can be left only to ODOT, we will fail. The two are inextricably linked, and both are inevitably tied to our land use efforts."

From that meeting and others that followed, an expanded agenda on the impacts of growth on livability began to take higher priority. Late in 1993, I brought Bob Stacey on staff as Senior Policy Advisor for Urban Growth. He worked with a broad swath of interest groups, including state, local, and federal agencies, to assure wise transportation and growth policy choices. His biggest early challenge was the proposed West Side Bypass Freeway in the Portland metropolitan area; we had strong evidence that the bypass would increase sprawl, destroy farming communities, and do little, long-term, to alleviate traffic congestion. With Bob's diligent leadership we were able to defeat the proposal. I also worked with Bob Stacey to put in place an executive order requiring new state offices and state office relocations to seek downtown locations, encouraging more vibrant downtowns and avoiding suburban sprawl. This was the state putting its money where its mouth was on planning and healthy downtowns. Stacey had a tremendous impact on Oregon's livability agenda during his year's tenure with my administration.

At the end of each day, in late 1993, I would return home to a very large house that felt exceedingly empty. Arlene, who was also feeling somewhat lost after Frank's death, seemed glad for my arrival home. We would eat dinner together, visit for a while, compare our next few days' calendars, and then I would begin to tackle two briefcases full of reading and work. After an hour or two I would take a break and walk up the stairs to Frank's bedroom. I would look at all the photos, pace around for a few minutes, and then sit down in his big chair and have a good cry. When I arrived back downstairs to finish my evening's work, Arlene would often have a cup of tea or a small dessert on my table. I honestly don't know how I would have survived those first months without her. We had been close friends for many years. Now we had truly become family.

In mid-November I flew to Seattle to attend the Asia-Pacific Economic Cooperation (APEC) trade conference. In addition to this opportunity to converse with many international trade delegates, I was also able to have conversations with Secretary of Commerce Ron Brown, Washington Governor Mike Lowry, Seattle Mayor Norm Rice, and Washington's Secretary of State Ralph Munro. On the second day of the meeting I literally had a front-row seat for President Bill Clinton's major policy address to the full conference and to a huge number of national and international press corps members. The President acknowledged my presence in his welcoming remarks and gave me a warm embrace after the speech. President Clinton asked how I was doing since Frank's death. He hoped he would see me at the White House when the Governors Association met in January. I was grateful for his recognition of my difficult personal situation.

When Thanksgiving arrived, I invited both my family and Frank's family to the governor's residence. My two sons, my daughter-in-law, and my two young grandchildren as well as Frank's two daughters, his son-in-law, and his three grandchildren all came to the house for that first holiday without Frank. I prepared a large traditional holiday dinner right down to the pumpkin pie. When dessert was finished I announced that I had arranged a display of special gifts and mementos that Frank had selected for each family member. As my family left in the evening, they carried with them a piece of art, a special political memento, a sailing replica, a piece of jewelry, the items Frank had chosen as a lasting reminder of his life and his love for his family. This holiday without Frank was already difficult. The sharing of these gifts left me feeling emotional and lonely. I was certainly discovering that I could not surround myself with enough people to erase the loneliness.

As December began, Patricia and I were preparing and expanding fundraising call lists for the 1994 campaign. We were working on outreach to potential endorsers and major contributors. We were also making arrangements to put an in-depth political poll in the field. After three years of Measure 5, the ongoing controversy of the spotted owl decisions, the highly publicized legislative loss of my proposed tax reform measure, and the recent press attention Kitzhaber had been getting since his announcement, I was bracing for some bad numbers. It reminded me of the first poll we had conducted when I entered the race against Dave Frohnmayer in 1990. We hadn't expected good numbers then, and we definitely didn't get them. Whatever the numbers showed this time, I needed to see them. The results would be ready in mid-January.

With the governor's race, even this early, attracting attention, I had constant requests for interviews. I also had a heavy travel schedule in December, beginning in Pendleton with a visit and tour at Eastern Oregon Correctional Institution. The inmates at EOCI produced high-quality jeans under the label "Prison Blues." I observed the jeans operation, toured other parts of the remodeled facility (a former mental health hospital), and met with staff. Late that afternoon I also visited the Nash Industries facility in La Grande, where they manufactured recreation vehicles. With the help of the Oregon Economic Development Department, Nash Industries would soon have a new manufacturing center at the La Grande airport. My day in eastern Oregon also included two newspaper interviews and an evening dinner reception with local friends and supporters.

The next day I left for Spokane, Washington, to meet with Governor Stan Stephens of Montana, Washington Governor Mike Lowry, and Governor Cecil Andrus of Idaho. Our four states made up the Northwest Power Planning Council. We were meeting to discuss the salmon recovery plan being developed by the National Marine Fisheries Service for the Columbia River Basin salmon species then listed under the federal Endangered Species Act. Every step of this recovery process, big or small, created controversy, raised scientific questions, economic concerns, and political unrest. Today, nearly twenty years later, those questions, concerns, doubts, and controversies still exist … and those salmon species are still at risk.

My week was almost done except for a fun Saturday morning event, the long-awaited grand opening of the Terwilliger Boulevard overpass across the I-5 freeway in Portland. After twenty years of planning and $12 million, the old 1927 wooden bridge had been replaced with concrete and steel. Pep bands, Boy Scouts, bicyclists, a fire engine, and local students were all part of the parade across the brand-new span. The usual December Oregon rains held off for the morning's celebration and ribbon cutting.

On December 17 Patricia publicly announced that she was taking a leave from her position as my chief of staff to take the leading role with my campaign once again. We also announced that Kevin Smith would return from his work at the state Economic Development Department to assume the position of acting chief of staff.

I was beginning to move toward my double role as full-time Governor of Oregon and nearly full-time candidate for reelection. I had no illusion this would be easy. The campaign would have been tough for me in the usual way that primary elections are: splitting friends and allies, dividing Democrat from Democrat, losing the support of issue partners. However, this election came so close on the heels of Frank's death, while my sister, Pat, was under treatment for advanced lung cancer, with my mother in failing health, and with my sons still experiencing the loss of both their father and stepfather. I felt the weight of all this and I felt the grief … so much grief.

I had always been an energetic, tough campaigner. Now that would be tested under the most difficult of burdens.

On Tuesday, December 21, my first appointment was a 7:30 a.m. call-in radio interview. At 9 a.m. that day I began a series of budget briefings with small groups of legislative leaders. The last briefing meeting for that day ended at 3 p.m. I was scheduled to be at the Marian County Courthouse in Salem at 4 p.m. for the investiture of Circuit Court Judge Paul Lipscomb.

Oh, did I forget to mention that this very day, December 21, was also my birthday? I turned fifty-seven on a day filled with budgets, meetings, interviews, and public appearances. The next day I would leave Salem at 8:30 a.m. for the hour-plus drive to Eugene for a full day's schedule. Did I remember to mention to my staff that it was only three shopping days until Christmas? I apparently forgot to send that memo again!

Yet, in spite of my schedule, Christmas came. On Christmas Eve Mark and his family arrived early at the governor's residence. Leslie, Frank's younger daughter, her husband, and their children arrived a couple of hours later. I had brought Mike back from Portland with me the evening before. The house looked beautiful with two large decorated trees, one with professional ornaments, one with my own personal decorations. The main floor of the house was filled with candles, holly, and fir boughs. I was extremely happy to be surrounded by my family on this special night.

Before we opened gifts, we shared a new family ritual in Frank's honor and his memory. Each family member brought a special tree ornament and one by one we hung them on the tree — a crystal heart, a blown-glass seashell, a small sailboat, a beautiful blue bird, a silver anchor — reminders of Frank.

As 1993 came to an end, I felt I was leaving behind the most difficult year of my life. I could not predict what 1994 would bring but I felt it was unlikely it could contain as much loss or pain as the previous year. Both 1993 and 1994 would have in common my extraordinary honor of being Oregon's Governor. Beyond that, the rest was three parts speculation and ten parts guesswork. So I took a deep breath, crossed my fingers, and turned the page on my calendar.

CHAPTER TWENTY-THREE

New Tests and New Transitions

As 1994 began, Pat's chemo and radiation treatments were leaving her weak and with a number of negative side effects. I sometimes joined her at the hospital during her treatments, hoping this extra support would make these tough days somewhat easier. For the first few months of her treatment, a number of my staff members had donated vacation days to her to help her financially until she could go on disability. It warmed my heart to see their support for my sister.

I was also worried about my mother. Her health was slipping, and I fretted that the attention she needed now that she was widowed sometimes fell short, as Pat dealt with her own health situation and I worked to keep on top of my governor's responsibilities and to handle my grief after Frank's death. Mother needed our attention, and I often felt guilty about not being there enough for her. Thank goodness Arlene and Mother were close friends. They shopped together and went out to lunch, and Arlene would drive clear across town to get Mother so she could spend time with us at the governor's residence. Three widows learning to cope with a changed personal world. We were lucky to have each other.

After I had had a number of in-depth meetings with the staff and leadership of one of Oregon's mental health facilities, Dammasch State Hospital, and further meetings with advocates for the mentally ill, it become obvious that the facility needed a change of direction and a change of leadership. There had been five patient deaths at Dammasch over the previous four months. It was time to step in and take the action needed to protect patients both short term and long term. My press conference on January 3 set a clear direction. I announced that Dammasch would get a new director, Dr. Marvin Fickle, who was currently serving as chief medical director at Eastern Oregon Psychiatric Center. I had given the order to downsize the patient load from the current 274 to only 132 patients by the end of June. These would be the first steps toward full closure of that institution. I couldn't help but think how easily my older son could have been one of those endangered patients. Psychiatric hospitals are about more than numbers. All of these patients were someone's children, someone's family.

Once again, as I had done for the past two years, I delivered a January State of the State speech, but this address was delivered before the Portland City Club, one of Oregon's most prestigious civic organizations. With the Legislature not in session in an even-numbered year, this Portland audience seemed an opportunity for a larger crowd and full media coverage. The City Club audience was well informed and sophisticated. I felt they were much more interested in results delivered and new agendas proposed than in what the well-publicized problems of state government were.

I shared some impressive numbers as the result of my administration's policy focuses: In these three years, Oregon had added more than one hundred fifty thousand jobs to our economy. We had helped more than sixteen thousand Oregonians move off welfare and into jobs. Oregon's affordable housing stock had increased by thirteen thousand new units. And in ten days, the first of one hundred twenty thousand Oregonians would be enrolled in the Oregon Health Plan. My remarks made very clear that these were more than impressive numbers—these were people's lives. A new job, safe, affordable housing, a doctor's appointment for a child, the chance for a better life and a better future.

However, I also spoke of some of the places where Oregon was failing—failing badly. Our juvenile crime numbers were sky-rocketing. Gang membership was growing. More felonies, more sex crimes, more homicides. We weren't talking about teenagers knocking over garbage cans or stealing candy bars from a convenience store. This was dangerous, violent crime. I explained that the day before I had signed an executive order creating a nine-member Governor's Task Force on Juvenile Justice that would be chaired by Attorney General Ted Kulongoski. We would develop an action plan to change the direction for these kids *and* our state crime rates. I was disappointed to find my new task force had not even been mentioned in *The Oregonian* the next day.

One of my other areas of emphasis in the State of the State address was the issue of teen pregnancy. I explained to the City Club that, in 1993, five thousand young women in Oregon aged between fifteen and nineteen, had given birth, and 70 percent were unmarried. I pointed out further, "The costs of failing to curb teen pregnancy are high: low-weight babies, more delinquency, more school dropouts, and more families that can't support themselves." Teen pregnancy frequently damaged the lives of two generations. I would actively move forward to combat this "epidemic." I announced my plan to appoint a special assistant to help Oregon combat unwanted teen pregnancy. I explained my intention to double the number of school-based health centers in the next budget. I also spoke to the City Club about the impressive work that was happening around Oregon's Benchmarks and the exciting new cooperative work we were doing with the Clinton Administration.

At the end of the *Oregonian* story on my State of the State presentation was a quote from my Democratic challenger in the upcoming governor's race plus two statements by Republican candidates in the race. It seemed to be an odd way to end the article. No quotes from anyone in the City Club audience. I guess the reporter considered those three candidates' quotes as "equal time." It reminded me of what the next months might be like.

John Kitzhaber had already challenged me to five debates. He indicated his choice of location and dates and subject matter for the debates. John had a little to learn about statewide campaign negotiations. I remembered back to the race with Dave Frohnmayer in 1990 and our ongoing battle over the debate schedule. No candidate gets to decide unilaterally, *especially* the one challenging an incumbent governor. When I made my campaign fundraising numbers public, Kitzhaber was pushed into the position of releasing his own financial numbers, which were somewhat lower. Included in my contributions were over $100,000 from Emily's List members. What an asset they were for Democratic women candidates. However, a recent newspaper poll had shown Kitzhaber running ahead of me. He had received a great deal of press from his entrance into the race. It was quite rare in Oregon to have a seated governor challenged by a member of their own political party. The press had given the story lots of ink.

During the grey rainy month of January, I found myself feeling restless and sad. Carrying the heavy load of my role as Governor without Frank's constant support was difficult. I missed seeing my sons and grandchildren. My life was always about being overscheduled, and the campaign season would clearly add to that time pressure. I missed having lunch or dinner with my close friends, time to just laugh and gossip and reminisce. I knew there were some rough spots in Mark's marriage. I was falling a little behind in help-ing Mike keep up to date on his medical appointments. Mother was definitely growing more frail. My sister's health situation remained a big question mark. I had always been such a high-energy person and felt worried about the huge load on my horizon. I needed to get reenergized, re-inspired.

Well, that re-inspiration did *not* arrive with the poll that we had commissioned, which showed Kitzhaber with a comfortable lead. I had faced numbers quite similar to those as I entered the 1990 race. I understood they were not insurmountable — uphill, but far from impossible. Perhaps the question was not the numbers but rather the candidate. The four of us in my office weighed and balanced the possibilities. Patricia, usually up for a good fight, sounded less determined than usual. She was a skilled political strategist but not, perhaps, a miracle worker. God, how I wished for Frank's input at this juncture. Part of me was ready to hit the campaign trail. Another part of me simply wanted off the merry-go-round.

To drop out of the governor's race would be a major life decision. However, maybe it was time to stop and listen to what I was feeling. I cared deeply about my work as Oregon's governor. But I also loved my family, and they needed me. My whole family had been there for me during Frank's illness and death. I truly owed them. Could I do justice to those highly important obligations if I was focused on campaigning, fundraising, television spots, and polling numbers? The more I thought about my priorities, the easier the decision became.

On that Monday, in my office, I made the choice to withdraw from my reelection race. I decided to let the decision settle for a couple of days to see if I was still in the same place by mid-week. Patricia didn't try to talk me out of it, which said a lot for such a highly competitive campaign manager. By Wednesday, I knew it was the right decision. I suddenly felt like I could breathe easier, Almost everyone close to me felt it was the correct choice for me, for my health, for my life.

On Friday morning, January 28, I walked into the governor's ceremonial office to a crowd of cameras, microphones, reporters, staff, and the politically curious. I read my prepared two-page statement as cameras rolled and reporters scribbled notes on writing pads. I began: "Today, I am announcing my decision to withdraw from the race for reelection as Oregon's governor." I added that I did not believe I could do justice to my job as governor if I diverted time and energy to a reelection campaign. "In ordinary times, being governor and a candidate has clearly been done. But these are not ordinary times for Oregon and these are not ordinary times for me." I went on to explain the family challenges I was facing and the obligations that came with those challenges. "I thought I could do it all — Barbara Roberts the Governor, Barbara Roberts the candidate, Barbara Roberts the mother, the sister, the daughter, the grandmother, and even still, the wife. But I can't do justice to my family or myself if I spread myself that thin." Several paragraphs later, I made one priority very clear: "No honor I have ever been given means so much to me as being Oregon's governor. But with such an honor goes the responsibility to put Oregon first. Today I am doing just that."

I finished my prepared statement with these words: "I watched Frank give everything he had to complete this past legislative session. He was unwilling to quit until the job was done. Well, today I am making a commitment to stay focused on the work I've been given until the job is done. It allows me to dedicate myself to this state, to a job I love, and to the family I love."

After the press conference, I switched hats and headed over to the Supreme Court chambers for the swearing in of Robert "Skip" Durham as the newest member of the Oregon Supreme Court. I had appointed Skip Durham to the Oregon Court of Appeals just over two years before. Now I had been able to elevate Judge Durham with this recent appointment to Oregon's highest court. During the ceremony, as I walked to the podium to deliver my remarks, the entire assembled audience rose to their feet applauding. That standing ovation, that show of respect here in these hallowed chambers, almost brought me to tears. I was already feeling quite emotional after my news conference. This unexpected show of affection touched me deeply. I would miss being Oregon's Governor.

That afternoon and evening, Oregon's television stations were filled with the story of my leaving the race. The next day's newspapers in every part of Oregon carried the news in large headlines. It is amazing the warmth and kind words displayed when friend and foe alike see a major political status change take place. I certainly experienced that for the next few days. Even President Bill Clinton made a statement of regret. Attorney General Ted Kulongoski said,

"Barbara Roberts is genuinely the kindest person who served as governor of Oregon. Fate dealt her a cruel hand."

The *East Oregonian* from Pendleton wrote: "Roberts, in our view, remains an impressive public servant. Few state leaders can match her intelligence, insight, energy, wit, grit, compassion and political skills. She leaves office with her integrity intact and the right to say that she worked hard to do the right thing. In today's mean-spirited public arena, that's something. She has given Oregon her best and for that she deserves much credit."

The next day, I stopped by a women candidates' workshop being held by the Oregon Women's Political Caucus. I received a standing ovation from the women gathered there, as well as lots of hugs and a few tears. Many of the people in that room had been dedicated volunteers during my 1990 race and my exit from the '94 race was a huge disappointment to them. That evening, I attended the NARAL dinner. I had worked with the organization for years on family planning and abortion rights, and the five hundred people in attendance were well aware of my strong advocacy for their agenda. When I stepped to the stage, several voices called out, "Don't go!" I waited for the applause and the voices to die down, and then I pointed to the huge banner hanging behind the stage that simply said: "Choice." I told the audience that if you believe in a woman's right to choose, it must extend beyond the issues of pregnancy and abortion. "Unless you have walked in my shoes over these challenging three years, you cannot know the personal cost of the choices I have made. This is the right choice for me and for Oregon." At that moment, the decision clearly felt *behind me*. I would look forward to my work, my gubernatorial duties, my expanded time with family, and savor being governor for the next eleven months.

To emphasize my new sense of freedom, I left that evening on a red-eye flight to Washington, D.C., for one of my last NGA meetings. But in the spirit of this new commitment to family time, traveling with me were my younger son Mark and his wife. They had never been to D.C. and the plane tickets I had purchased for them would give them four days to play tourist in this amazing and historic city. The added twist was that Mark would be my escort at the White House dinner on Sunday evening. It was customary that only a spouse could attend this dinner with the governors; however, the Clinton White House felt that, so soon after Frank's death, it was important

I have the support and company of a family member. I would be taking my son to the White House for dinner!

In addition to all the normal NGA committee meetings, plenary gatherings, and speakers, this particular trip offered two other events that I expected to enjoy—and did. Emily's List held a reception and dinner with Governor Ann Richards as the main speaker. Women Executives in State Government also had a special reception where I received the organization's highest award, "Breaking the Glass Ceiling." They also honored retiring Governor Joan Finney of Kansas and welcomed our newest woman governor, Christine Todd Whitman of New Jersey. At least for the next eleven months, the NGA would have four women governors, the largest number to serve simultaneously in the nation's history. I thought about 1990, when Ann Richards, Joan Finney, and I had all been elected on the same night. Now, two of us would not be returning for a second term. Hopefully Ann Richards would survive her reelection race in Texas, but in her state's rough-and-tumble political climate, nothing was a sure thing.

When Mark and I entered the White House for dinner with the President and First Lady, I could see Mark's excitement and awe. I have a special photograph that sits in my bedroom showing my younger son shaking hands with the President of the United States that night. It was so rewarding to be able to give Mark that amazing opportunity. President Clinton gave Mark some personal time and attention which, of course, brought out my motherly gratitude and pride. To dine at the White House is always a stimulating treat. To be able to share that experience with my son was a gift few mothers can hand to their offspring. I truly loved it.

Before leaving D.C., I met with Senator Mark Hatfield and with four members of our congressional delegation. Of course, each of them expressed their regret at my recent decision. That courtesy out of the way, we then talked about several pending federal issues affecting Oregon, including light rail funding, the re-invention work Oregon was doing with the Clinton administration, and ongoing steps in the job training package that was part of the Clinton forest plan.

In the middle of February, I held a press conference at the Teen Health Center at Grant High School in Portland to announce a new member of my staff, the special assistant on teen pregnancy. Allie Stickney would lead us in the development of a teen-pregnancy prevention program for Oregon and a method for bringing that message to Oregon's young people. She was ready to go to work. We hoped to have some answers within three months, at least, a starting point for our efforts to reduce teen pregnancies.

On March 1 it became official, and public, that Patricia McCaig would be leaving my staff. After my late-January announcement, she had been dismantling the fairly new campaign office. Things had grown tense between us since Frank's death. I had needed time to heal. She had needed a full-time enthusiastic candidate. I had needed sympathy and support. She had needed "moving on" and action. Neither of us was happy. She did not rush back to her position as chief of staff. I did not push her to return. I believe she truly saw me now as a lame duck governor. She did not find that appealing. Her most telling comment, from my perspective, was in an *Oregonian* interview where she described the failure of my 1992 tax measure as "getting through the biggest public humiliation of my life." Funny, but I thought the failure and loss were mine. There seemed in that statement a confusion of roles and perhaps even power. Therein lies the problem of drawing lines between delegating authority and assuming power. One cannot govern without delegating. The heavier the load, the more delegation takes place. It was time to clarify my role as governor. I knew it. Patricia knew it. She never returned to my staff, and Kevin Smith removed the word "acting" from his title.

As Patricia told columnist Steve Duin in a March 1 *Oregonian* interview, she envisioned only "a maintenance mode" as chief of staff. "A treading water mode. And I don't do that very well. I would end up causing trouble." So I had a new chief of staff, Kevin Smith, and we were working closely together with the newly appointed Director of the Executive Department, Gary Weeks. We would be a good team. We had a heavy workload. We moved on.

On March 8, Oregon's political communities celebrated filing day, the final day for filing as a candidate in the 1994 elections. There were not many surprises. In the governor's race, John Kitzhaber was the only viable Democrat. I had walked from the governor's office to the Secretary of State's office, a few days before, side by side with Kitzhaber, as he officially filed for the office. I would stand by my party's candidate. There were six Republican candidates for Governor; businessman Craig Berkman and Denny Smith, former congressman, were the perceived leaders in that primary. In the

Labor Commissioner's race, Frank's daughter Mary Wendy Roberts had drawn three strong primary opponents. I was sorry to see her with a tough race after her difficult loss to Phil Keisling in the 1992 Secretary of State's race. Norma Paulus, running for reelection as Superintendent of Public Instruction, looked like a sure thing to me.

In two of our congressional districts, we had experienced, skilled women seeking federal office. However, both were Democrats in less-than-progressive districts. They were both smarter and more prepared than their male opponents, but their races would still be very challenging.

Another particularly exciting race for me was seeing that Frank's son-in-law, Rex Armstrong, had filed for judge of the Oregon Court of Appeals. There were five candidates in the race, and I had high hopes for Rex's success. Talk about a political family. It just got better and better.

As spring approached, my duties went on, my schedules were put together, my statewide travel continued, and I began the process of my third Measure 5 budget. I unveiled my guidelines for the 1995-1997 budget at a press conference on March 10. This biennium would be the toughest yet under the constraints of Measure 5. My budget guidelines gave the greatest protection to the K-12 education system, kept the state police at current levels, and cut Corrections 10 percent, Higher Education 13 percent, and the Department of Human Resources 11 percent. These proposals represented only the beginning of a long decision-making process from that day, through a new governor, and into the next legislative session, when I would, after so many years, no longer be part of the process. Yet I hoped and believed I could offer Oregon's incoming political leaders a roadmap to tackle the new budget. I did note that I was labeled, "the lame duck governor" for the first time in the *Oregonian* story about my proposals. That would take some getting used to.

On the last day of March, I had the pleasure of attending the investiture of one of my newest judicial appointments, Judge Joseph Ochoa, who would become Marion County's first Hispanic judge. I was extra proud to make this appointment in a county with one of the highest Hispanic populations in the state.

In mid-May, Oregon's primary election took place. It turned out to be a good election night for major women candidates. Superintendent of Public Instruction Norma Paulus won her reelection bid by more than 50 percent and would not face a November contest. Mary

Wendy Roberts defeated her three opponents and was off to a general election race. In the Second Congressional seat, Sue Kupillas won the Democratic nomination and, in the Fifth District, Catherine Webber was the Democratic nominee for Congress. My son-in-law, Rex Armstrong, won his race for the Court of Appeals bench, and John Kitzhaber would face Denny Smith (R) in the fall governor's race. All in all, a good set of outcomes from my point of view.

On May 16, I led an interactive telecommunication program using Oregon's Ed-Net system. This time, rather than talking with voters about state spending and taxes, I would be speaking with over two thousand middle, junior high, and high school students on the subject of teen-pregnancy prevention. The parents of each child had signed an approval form for his or her participation in this conversation. And, believe me, there was a two-way conversation. I asked how they viewed teen pregnancy and what influenced their decision to have sex or not. And they answered—honestly, openly, and seriously. I can't believe any governor had ever spoken to two thousand teenagers about sex and pregnancy. I felt honored to be trusted enough by these young people to have this conversation.

The release we had sent to press and media pointed out that, in 1992 alone, nearly three thousand females ages ten to seventeen got pregnant. And age "ten" is not a misprint. Almost one hundred fifty of those 1992 pregnancies were of girls fourteen or younger!

We did the Ed-Net Program twice that day and once again on May 23. The third program, however, had a different group of participants, including health service providers, those involved in teen-pregnancy prevention, teens, business leaders, local governments, school leaders, and religious organizations. Allie Stickney had done a tremendous job of preparing the agendas for these programs, which both garnered the information and input we had hoped for and allowed us to share pertinent information. So far, our efforts were going even better than we had anticipated.

On June 28, we took one of the final steps in our teen-pregnancy prevention effort. I led a forum where three hundred Oregonians, working together, crafted a series of solutions to reduce the rate of teen pregnancy in Oregon. We had leaders from education, health, business, community, and religion from around the state. The day-long conference was a marvel to watch as participants discussed such topics as girls' low self-esteem, contraceptives for sexually active teens, teaching parents to talk to their children about sex, and sexually transmitted diseases.

At 12:30, the working groups came back together for a special keynote address via satellite from U.S. Health and Human Services Secretary Donna Shalala. At the end of her remarks Secretary Shalala took questions from the Oregon participants. It was exciting to me to have a Cabinet secretary who believed teen pregnancy was an issue worth her time and attention. She didn't hesitate when presented with our request for her participation and perspective on teen pregnancy nationally. Our participants took that national perspective back to their afternoon deliberations. When that day's work was complete, Allie Stickney prepared to compile the final report on these months of work. I looked forward to receiving the report in the fall.

One afternoon in late May, the executive director of the Oregon Progress Board and I met in Portland with a representative of the Ford Foundation and Harvard's Kennedy School of Government. Oregon's innovative Benchmarks program, used for measuring the outcome of our state's efforts for creating a healthier economy, a more environmentally sound natural atmosphere, and a culturally improved state, had just been named as a semifinalist for the 1994 Innovations in State and Local Government award. We were very excited to be recognized even at this semifinalist level. We knew that the uniqueness of our program might be a liability or could be an asset. The complexity of the program might make competition and presentations more difficult. But we were excited and planned to compete actively for the award.

In the ongoing spirit of government innovation, I left two days later for a conference in Denver. This was an important meeting of the new Alliance for Redesigning Government organization. The meeting featured the Oregon Benchmarks program and the expansion of the program to some of Oregon's local governments. I was joined by Portland Mayor Vera Katz and Multnomah County Commission Chair Bev Stein. The three of us did a detailed presentation on the collaborative, intergovernmental work we were involved in. It was an exciting and informative two-day meeting with tremendous sharing of ideas and strong potential for expanding on Oregon's creative blueprint for measuring outcomes. In this arena, Oregon was certainly leading.

In early June, I found myself feeling sad and emotional. Usually as summer approached I'd feel happier. This year seemed to be an exception. Perhaps it was the approaching of Father's Day now that Dad was dead, and I was unable to personally honor him on that holiday. With Frank and Neal both gone, my sons were also without a father to celebrate on that special day. I simply felt disconnected. Both Dad's birthday and what would have been Frank's and my twentieth wedding anniversary were in June. Before Frank's terminal diagnosis, we had discussed a possible trip for that significant anniversary. My grieving for Frank, mixed with these June dates, felt like simply too much sadness.

On June 11, I left for San Francisco to deliver a long-scheduled speech. By the time the date arrived, I felt a weekend in San Francisco might be just the break I needed. Well, it turned out to be even more of a break from my usual schedule than I could have anticipated. I was in that beautiful city to deliver a speech to a formal gala for the San Francisco Human Rights Campaign. My friend Terry Bean was there with me. I was looking forward to a wonderful evening. Suddenly, the music stopped, police officers with dogs entered the premises, and they began evacuating the hall. There was a bomb scare. Everyone assumed that some extremist had created this event crisis as an objection to HRC's agenda on gay rights. We were wrong. It turned out the bomb threat had centered around me *personally* and my pro-choice stance on family planning and abortion. San Francisco HRC found it a surprise, even a little laughable, that *I* and not *they* had been the focus of the threat. I was terribly apologetic to have caused a disruption in the evening's festivities.

On June 29, my wedding anniversary, I found a way to divert my attention from sadness to joy. I flew with the Oregon National Guard and my old friend General Fred Rosenbaum to the National Guard's Camp Rilea on the Oregon coast. Once a year that facility became "Camp Rosenbaum." It was an operation founded by Fred for low-income kids living in public housing in Portland and Salem. Over the decades, it grew to include children from a number of other locations in the state and added the support of several police and fire departments. Most of these children had never been to a camp, never seen the ocean, never had the fun that we associate with being children. They came to the camp and ate well, learned to work with wood, leather, beads, paint, and adults. They rode a horse, "lawn surfed" down a grassy hill, decorated dorm rooms, learned camp songs, and were given an anti-drug, anti-gang education. They had a wonderful week of just being kids. They left with new Nike tennis shoes, a camp sweatshirt, and a new backpack filled with school supplies, as well as wonderful memories. I attended the camp almost every year I was Secretary of State and Governor, and I continue to make the effort to "go to camp" even after all these years. General Fred Rosenbaum died in 2010, but he left behind the legacy of thousands of children who had experienced Camp Rosenbaum and a dedicated team who won't let the camp die.

On July 6, tragedy hit in the forests of Storm King Mountain in Colorado and immediately ricocheted to Oregon. Fourteen young forest firefighters, all in their twenties, died as a wind shift resulted in a "blow-up" fire condition trapping them without exit. The fire blew up behind them to a height of over a hundred feet and reached two to three hundred feet as it crossed over the forest ridge. They ran for their lives—the fire was faster. Nine of the fourteen firefighters were from Oregon. In their community, they were known as the Prineville Hot Shots. They were a daredevil squad that battled some of the nation's most dangerous wildfires. They fought fires together, partied together; they were proud and tough. They were a team. Before that fatal July 6, there were nineteen Prineville Hot Shots. Now there were ten.

On Saturday July 9, I traveled to Prineville for what was usually the annual Crooked River Roundup rodeo and parade. Joining me was Governor Roy Romer of Colorado. Prineville was bedecked with American flags—all at half staff. The parade began with nine riderless horses. Governor Romer and I walked behind the surviving Hot Shots, arms stretched across the shoulders of their grieving comrades. The town was somber and emotional. Following the parade, Governor Romer spoke first at the memorial recognition service at the high school football field. When I spoke, I referred to Frank's recent death and to the grieving process. I urged people to reach out to one another. "My husband told me when he knew he was dying, there are only two things, two assets we have that matter in this life. They are love and time. It is how you spend this time, and how you spend your love that tells you who you are." When the memorial service was over, Governor Romer visited the home of each set of parents, each spouse, each fiancée. He spoke to each of them personally and expressed his sympathy and grief about the tragedy of their loss. I couldn't do what

Roy did. I gave him kudos for that kind bravery. I knew, with my emotions already so close to the surface, these face-to-face meetings would have left me a sobbing mess. Sometimes, the better part of valor is to know what you *can't* do.

With less than six months left in office, I tried to be more aware of each day's work, to be able to savor the contacts, the decisions, the experiences that were part of my unique role.

In mid-July, I left for Boston for five days of activities that carried personal and policy priority status for me. I began at the campus of Harvard's Kennedy School of Government, where the official presentations were being held for the finalists in the Innovations in State and Local Government awards. I was always excited to be back on the JFK campus, but this time, I came as a competitor in a tough national award process. It was not unusual to have a mayor or county commissioner make one of these presentations at the Kennedy School; more frequently, it was an agency director. Everyone believed that my prepared remarks, as a governor, were a first for this award. Yet the Oregon Benchmarks were a state program under the Progress Board, chaired by the governor. I had committed myself to this effort since my first week as Governor. I believed in it. I was an advocate and salesperson for the Oregon Benchmarks. I really coveted the opportunity to speak for the Oregon Benchmarks in this prestigious competition. My presentation went smoothly. The audience was very attentive. I handled the questions easily. However, we wouldn't know the outcome for several weeks.

The next day, the eighty-sixth annual National Governors Association conference began in the same city. Boston is one of America's most historic cities and also well known as a great convention city. Governor Bill Weld (R) of Massachusetts was a tremendous host. I was grateful to have my final NGA meeting in such a hospitable setting. Yet, last meeting or not, I was not seen as a lame duck at this conference.

I offered a new policy statement on teen-pregnancy prevention. It was one of only six new policy statements brought forward for consideration of the full NGA membership. I felt very rewarded by the NGA's acceptance of this new policy to prevent adolescent pregnancy and to address risk factors such as poverty, abuse, and low self-esteem. I have long held the philosophy that what we can talk about, we can make better. Knowing America's governors had talked about this issue gave me hope for more attention to the problem, more support for these at-risk teens.

The governors dined at the stately Massachusetts State House. We listened to addresses by President Clinton and Senator Bob Dole. We were updated at a DGA breakfast on the governors' races taking place in November 1994. We had at least two incumbent Democratic governors running behind in the polls. I reported that John Kitzhaber was looking strong in the Oregon race.

With less than a week's turnaround time, I was back on the East Coast for an exciting Washington, D.C., presentation with Portland Mayor Vera Katz and Multnomah County Chair Bev Stein on the Oregon Benchmarks. Top-level staff from the White House and the Cabinet filled the conference room. It was a much larger and higher-level crowd than our hosts had predicted. At the end of two hours, we had completed detailed explanations of the Benchmarks process at both the state and local level. We had answered dozens of policy questions and even a few questions that fell into the political category. Perhaps the most *fun* question was: "Do you have any male officeholders in Oregon?" The crowd had a good laugh, but truthfully, this high-level audience had just witnessed an extremely professional presentation by three of Oregon's strongest female political leaders. There is no reason to shy away from that leadership recognition when it is a fact. Coyness is not the sign of a leader.

On Monday August 1, I began a new week and a new month doing a service I was proud and honored to perform. I administered the oath of office at the official swearing-in ceremony for Oregon's new Adjutant General of the National Guard. Major General Raymond F. ("Fred") Rees was returning to Oregon from the national head-quarters of the National Guard in Washington, D.C. General Rees had been A.G. when I was a brand new governor. Now he was returning home to the state he loved and the Guard he loved. I was truly happy to have him back and said so in my remarks. Oregon had struggled with some National Guard leadership matters over the past couple of years and I was most grateful to have Fred Rees back in charge.

For five days in early August, I set off with my security officers to one of my favorite parts of Oregon, the far-eastern segment of the state. Even though this was a working trip, being in this expansive, dramatic, rural part of Oregon always felt more like a vacation to me. The added sense of vacation came from sharing this week with my dear friend Arlene Fall and my executive appointments staff leader, Carole Morse, neither of whom had ever toured Eastern Oregon extensively. This week, they would get the "royal tour" from the Governor. On the way east, we stopped for a visit to the Deschutes County Fair, and I rode in the parade in Redmond. We took a breather in John Day for a newspaper and radio interview, and lunch and a neighborly visit with Grant County Judge Kevin Campbell and Commissioners Sondra Lino and Charlene Morris. Local government leaders in these rural counties carried a heavy responsibility for their citizens. I tried to be supportive where I could.

That afternoon, we headed off for an unusual tour. In the tiny former ghost town of Sumpter, I was given the grand tour of the newly restored gold dredge that had worked the local streambed over a hundred years before. Surrounding the small community of Sumpter are hundreds of piles of rocks, removed from the river and left to stand as mute evidence of what man is willing to destroy in his search for gold. The restoration of that old gold dredge and the renovation of the community's narrow-gauge railroad were bringing back a tiny town that for years had been known as the "liveliest little ghost town in Oregon."

The next day, we were off to the far northeastern corner of Oregon and the charming old town of Joseph in Wallowa County. The Wallowa Mountains are sometimes described as the "Alps of the West." It is an apt description. The mountains are rugged; the forests are rugged; for decades, the people have needed to be rugged as well. But Joseph and Wallowa County were in a period of transition. Where cowboys and loggers had populated the area even before statehood, now bronze foundries, sculptors, artists, and gallery owners were a growing part of this unique corner of Oregon. In a community that still reenacted an Old West shoot-out on the city streets, artists and cowboys, gallery owners and loggers are practicing the art of sharing a community. We marveled over a "herd" of bronze horses being prepared for shipment to New York City.

The rest of our day in Wallowa County was a tour of the riparian- and watershed-health projects that I had actively supported in my 1993 budget, giving me a rare opportunity to see this work firsthand. So often a governor depends on the reports of staff to try and understand this crucial work. This time, I was on the ground, seeing the early results for myself. It was a highly satisfying experience.

That Eastern Oregon week was such a treat for me. I felt more relaxed and happier than I had felt in a long time. We loved every ghost town, every pioneer cemetery, the mountains, the ranches, the coffee shops, and the adventure. My two security officers thought we were three giggly girls for much of the trip, but it was hard to ignore the joy of sunshine, mountain ranges, grazing cattle, wheat fields, and rock mesas. I worked every day of the trip, but we played an equal number of hours each day. I was an enthusiastic tour guide.

From August 21 to August 27, I traveled across the International Date Line on a trade mission from Oregon to Indonesia. Our delegation of state and private sector officials hoped to create new markets for Oregon products. I participated in the Asia Pacific Business Network Conference as a guest of the U.S. ambassador to Indonesia, attended the U.S. Food Showcase, and spoke at the closing ceremonies of the showcase. It was a wearing trip, and I was glad when I arrived back in Oregon to once again have clean and safe water, more direct communication in my dealings, and a little more reality in Oregon's economic outreach. I did not consider this trip to have had the same level of success that Oregon had experienced in other international trade missions.

With only four months left in office for me, September was a highly positive month. Two wins were especially significant to me.

On September 23, Interior Secretary Babbitt officially announced that an eleven-mile stretch of the Klamath River had been designated a National Wild and Scenic River. After four years of work, the state had won this critical designation. The U.S. Department of Interior press release said, "This designation will preserve the nationally significant resource in this beautiful stretch of the Klamath. Governor Barbara Roberts took the lead in seeking to protect the Klamath and we are pleased to join forces with her and the people of Oregon in this effort." The press release went on to describe that the lengthy study made by the National Park Service had found that the river had seven classes of significant resources that should be protected, including Bald Eagles, outstanding fishing and whitewater boating, and seven thousand years of Native American traditional use. The battle to protect the river was finished. There would be no power-generating facility constructed on this stretch of the Klamath River.

The second big win for Oregon was our designation as a winner in the Innovations in State and Local Government competition. On September 29, I flew to Washington, D.C., to accept the award.

Another satisfying duty in September was to travel statewide to award the current round of regional strategies monies for economic development to communities across Oregon. This highly successful economic framework, and the huge community involvement it entailed, were bringing Oregon back economically.

When the calendar reached October, I began to speculate that my schedule would soon slow down. After all, wasn't I supposed to be a lame duck? Didn't that imply something about lost power and diminishing influence? I think state government missed that memo.

That month I made economic-development trips to Germany and Italy, and we planned for an early-November trip to Japan. The highlight of the visit to Germany was my ride on their high-speed train from Stuttgart to Hanover. The new tilt-system model Germany was finalizing seemed worth examining for some positive applications in Oregon. My time in Italy was productive and enjoyable. As a first-time visitor to Italy, I was charmed and awed by the beauty of the architecture, the warmth of the people, and the history of that part of Europe. In Milan, I toured a show that brings suppliers of American travel products together with European buyers to develop packages to encourage Europeans to visit the United States. Oregon was hosting a booth at the conference. We were also able to show a twenty-minute video on Oregon to the seven hundred delegates at the luncheon, and I delivered the keynote address on behalf of the U.S. and Oregon. Oregon's presence was quite obvious.

By the time I returned from Europe, the general election was in its final month. Causing much confusion and an equal amount of heated debate was the "pile" of ballot measures Oregon voters would be contending with — eighteen measures, sixteen of which were citizen initiatives. The measures were all over the board — crime, education, taxes, equal rights, mining laws, inmate labor, and legislative vacancies. I was focusing much of my personal and political attention on Measure 11, a harsh, inflexible mandatory-sentencing law for juveniles fifteen and over (I opposed the measure); Measure 13, an anti-gay rights measure that I also opposed; and Measure 16, a vote to create Oregon's Death with Dignity law (I supported this ballot measure). It was turning into a very cranky election season. I was actually feeling grateful not to be on the ballot.

On October 11, Timothy Egan of the *New York Times* released a feature article on Oregon's current economic climate. I was thrilled with the story. Egan weighed predictions of disaster against the reality of outcomes. "Although economic calamity was predicted as the result of logging restrictions in Oregon aimed at protecting the spotted owl in 1991, Oregon in 1994 has posted the lowest unemployment rate in a generation, just over 5 percent." Egan shared this quote from George Bush as he was campaigning in Oregon in 1992: "We'll be up to our neck in owls and every millworker will be out of a job." In truth, as Egan reported, by 1994, thousands of Oregon millworkers and loggers were completing retraining programs for dislocated workers. They were now auto mechanics, accountants, cabinet makers, even nurses. "So many people say this is the best thing to ever happen to them." One former millworker expanded on the change, "I was brain-dead at the mill, never thought I'd do anything else. Now, it's like the world has opened up." One of the final quotes in the lengthy article was from Mayor Bill Morrisette of the timber-town of Springfield: "Owls versus jobs was just plain false. What we've got here is a quality of life. As long as we don't screw that up, we'll always be able to attract people and business." We had added nearly a hundred thousand jobs in Oregon over this last year alone. Right on, Mayor Morrisette!

On the morning of October 20, in my ceremonial office, I was excited to release our long-anticipated teen-pregnancy action plan. Now labeled the STOP program (Sex, Teens and Oregon's Plan), it listed action steps for the state, for schools, for families, and for teens. Allie Stickney detailed a number of the plan elements for the press. I also got to share one of my favorite components of the plan. The state would develop a video for parents to give them the skills and language to talk with their children about responsible sex and personal choice. The video would be available at every video store and library in Oregon. We had found from our Ed-Net outreach to students that they wanted to learn about sex from their own parents; 68 percent of them had said so. We would offer parents statewide a tool to help with this delicate personal conversation in the family.

One last comment on the month of October 1994: I was extraordinarily proud to be honored with the 1994 Salmon Festival Stewardship Award. The sponsoring organizations presented an extensive list of my accomplishments and work to "protect and enhance Oregon's rivers, wild places, and native fish." Their declaration of my award stated in its final paragraph, "You can be proud of your legacy. Not since Governor Tom McCall has an Oregon Governor made such a large contribution to the national resource heritage and wildness that makes Oregon unique. It is our responsibility to carry on in the tradition you have defined."

On November 1, I left Portland International Airport on a flight to Tokyo, Japan. This was a large economic-development trade mission but definitely had an unusual twist. The National Basketball Association, the Portland Trail Blazers team, the Oregon Economic Development Department, the Port of Portland, and Delta Air Lines, were joined by a number of Oregon business and political leaders to jointly promote Oregon and NBA professional basketball in Japan. The Trail Blazers would be playing two regular season games against the Los Angeles Clippers in Japan. Both games were already completely sold out. A blitz of media advertising had preceded our arrival.

Now, this is my true confession: I am Portland Trail Blazer "nut." I love basketball and have been with the Blazers through thick and thin, season after season. My mother was the same kind of Blazer fan. Every game night, before the television coverage of the game began, mother was attired in one of her Blazer jerseys or sweatshirts. She was never too frail to see a televised game. Well, can you imagine a crazed basketball fan discovering she would be flying from Portland to Tokyo as the only other passenger joining the Trail Blazers in first class? I thought I might have to wrestle my own mother for my plane ticket! So there I was, seated in the same cabin with Clyde Drexler, Cliff Robinson, and Rod Strickland. I watched the team play cards, read, eat, and nap. Buck Williams dozed and read a tourist book on Japan. Chris Dudley and Cliff Robinson did stretching exercises every few hours. Jerome Kersey and Clyde had a discussion about some of the public relations activities they were doing in Japan. I was truly flying "first class"!

On our first full day in Tokyo, we held a beautiful reception in the posh Imperial Hotel. I was joined by U.S. Senator Mark Hatfield, Oregon Senate President Bill Bradbury and State Senator John Lim as well as the U.S. ambassador to Japan, Walter Mondale, but Blazers Kersey, Dudley, and Robinson were definitely the celebrity "heavy hitters" in the room. *The Oregonian* reported that the Japanese business leaders "behaved like schoolboys, eagerly collecting autographs and having pictures taken with the players.

The Japanese were happy because they got to mingle with celebrity athletes, the Oregon economic developers were happy because they got to drum up a few more business contacts, and the players were happy because they were the center of attention." I would definitely label that much happiness a success. But, following some business and political meetings, after all the publicity and fanfare about the Trail Blazers in Japan, I had to return to Oregon before their two games actually took place. I was very disappointed. However, for a Blazer fan, the good news was we beat the L.A. Clippers in both games, and Clyde Drexler scored a huge 41 points in the first!

I arrived back in Portland for the final weekend of the 1994 election season. When the Tuesday election ended there was some good news and some bad news.

The most disappointing losses for me came in the defeat of three bright, skilled Democratic women. Mary Wendy Roberts lost her reelection race for Labor Commissioner on a 49 to 51 percent margin to Republican Jack Roberts; no one really knew how to analyze the "name familiarity" factor. The two Democratic women congressional candidates lost their races. The other major women's race that kept us holding our breath through a whole recount was Democratic Congresswoman Elizabeth Furse's race, which was settled in her favor by barely four hundred votes. Too close for my comfort.

John Kitzhaber won the governorship. The Democrats lost the state Senate, which went Republican for the first time since Dwight D. Eisenhower was U.S. President. My son-in-law, Rex Armstrong, won his Court of Appeals seat with a strong 58 percent. The anti-gay ballot measure 13 was defeated 51 to 49 percent, the second such defeat in two years. It was a win Oregon needed and deserved, and my state's voters came through. In another 51 to 49 percent outcome, Oregon passed the first-in-the-nation Death with Dignity law. I immediately thought of Frank and his faith in the Oregon voters: "If we get it on the ballot, Oregonians will pass it." He would have been so thrilled about this election result. I was thrilled. After final numbers came in on the Oregon House of Representatives, the Democrats had lost another two seats, leaving them in a thirty-four to twenty-six minority position. At that moment, I didn't envy the challenge Kitzhaber would have as a new governor: both houses in Republican control, the ongoing Measure 5 budget impacts, a national trend toward more conservative Republican politics and policies. My choice looked better every day.

As Thanksgiving approached, I informed my family that I would be gone for the holiday weekend. I had been invited on a sailing trip, a very special sailing trip that had been designated as the "Frank Roberts Memorial Sail." Frank's old friend and sailing partner Chuck Mendenhall, his wife, Celia Mason, and another fun couple with long state government ties, Peter and Jean DeLuca, had made all the arrangements for this trip. This Thanksgiving, there would be no turkey and no dressing. We were going to the British Virgin Islands for a week of sailing, eating well, rum drinks, sunshine, and sand. When Frank and I had made this trip several years ago, Chuck had sailed with us. This would be a bittersweet but warm memory for me.

We had a grand week in this tropical paradise. We laughed, sang, told old sailing stories, felt the wind in our faces, the sun on our bodies. I am a nonswimmer but even I went overboard in my life jacket with a long rope attached to the boat. I was grateful, for once, to be without the protection of my security team. In forty feet of water, I bobbed in the waters of the Caribbean. For me, this was a very brave feat. New adventures for a changing life.

When I arrived at the Portland airport at the end of that fabulous week, my glow didn't last long. My state police officers were there to pick me up but standing with them was my son Mark, and the look on his face made it clear he didn't have good news. During the week of my absence, Mark and his wife had separated. He was clear that this wouldn't be a temporary parting. He had been sleeping in his car for three nights. He looked tired and stressed. Even though there was no furniture in the apartment I would be moving into in Portland the next month, it had heat, a bathroom with a shower, a stove, and a telephone. Mark could throw his sleeping bag on the carpeted floor for a few days until we sorted things out. I gave him the keys to the apartment. This was not the welcome home I would have wished for.

On Monday, December 5th, Oregon made a little history. I was in Washington, D.C., with Vice President Al Gore, U.S. Senator Mark Hatfield, and several Cab-inet members. We were joined via satellite hookup to Oregon; Mayor Vera Katz and Multnomah County Chair Bev Stein joined us for an official ceremony. We would simultaneously sign documents creating the "Oregon Option," a first-in-the-nation agreement. In D.C., at the old Executive Office Building and in Oregon at the studios of Oregon Public Broadcasting four officials from four governments laid pen to paper. The cheers and applause went up from two coasts of America.

The Oregon Option was a five-year experiment to test and possibly redesign intergovernmental delivery systems and focus on achieving results. The state and local governments committed to reaching better outcomes as the federal government, in exchange, offered greater flexibility in the use of federal funds. They would loosen the red tape. We would give them better results. The partners initially chose three broad goals: healthy children, stable families, and a prepared,

With Al Gore. From Portland State University Collection

developed workforce. For each of these goals, we agreed on a cluster of benchmarks by which to measure success. Each detailed benchmark would assist in identifying best practices, barriers to success, and removing those barriers. We set out on an effectiveness experiment in good government and intergovernmental cooperation. It was indeed a day for applause and photos!

Finally, the slowing down I had anticipated actually happened. My longtime friend Donella Slayton, who had returned as my scheduler earlier in the year, even added some scheduled time for my Christmas shopping. Arlene and I decorated the residence for the holidays. This would be my last Christmas here, and I wanted to savor it. A staff party was in the planning stages for a week before Christmas. I was also planning a family party for Mother, my sister, all our kids and grandkids. Then on December 14, Mother had a stroke and was rushed to the hospital. Thank goodness the stroke did only minor damage, and her medical team expected a full recovery. However, Mother was disappointed to miss my tribute dinner in Portland.

On December 15, at the Oregon Convention Center, a huge dinner celebrating my four years as Governor was held. Former Governor Bob Straub attended as did Governor-Elect John Kitzhaber. U.S. Senator Mark Hatfield also came to honor me. I was so touched when the planners decided to make the dinner a benefit for the Frank Roberts Community Service Scholarship at Portland State University. I opened my remarks with these words, "As I've approached tonight and the end of my term as Governor, I've thought a great deal about how I would feel. Finally I found an Abraham Lincoln quotation that says it so well. 'No one, not in my situation, can appreciate my feeling of sadness at this parting. To this state and the kindness of these people, I owe everything.'"

The Christmas holiday finished, my decorations packed away to move back to Portland, I was anticipating one last gubernatorial ceremony of significance. I was headed to California for the Pasadena Rose Parade and the big Rose Bowl New Year's Day game. The University of Oregon would be playing against Penn State. The city was full of crazed Duck fans from all over Oregon and across the country, as well as Oregon business sponsors and supporters. My friend Terry Bean was at the top of the "crazed" list. He was a fanatic Duck fan. For two days, we did receptions, pep rallies, parties, and press events. I rode on the Portland float in the Pasadena parade. I had ridden in almost every parade in Oregon from the Portland Grand Floral Rose Parade to the Pendleton Round-up Parade, the Albany Veterans' Parade, and the Tillamook Dairy Parade. However, the Pasadena Tournament of Roses Parade was a massive first-class display of floats, bands, marching units, color, and festival. The Portland float showed off a number of Oregon products and actually won the mayor's trophy as the outstanding entry from a city. Without a doubt, the funniest happening of those two days was the Sunday pep rally, where ten thousand "duck call" sound-makers were passed out to Oregon Duck fans and at a given time, after the speakers, including me, had all made their remarks, on cue ten thousand Ducks blew on those sound-makers for a full thirty seconds. It was billed as the "quack heard 'round the world." I did my part but I was reminded *not* to buy one of these duck calls for my grandchildren!

Unfortunately, the University of Oregon lost the game, 38 to 20. But as one of the Duck T-shirts I saw at the game read, "Every 37 years. Just like clockwork."

In the middle of my final full week as Governor, I found myself humming the melody to the rather melancholy "September Song" and repeating the lyrics, "It's a long, long time from May to December." It hadn't felt like a long time. It had rushed along with too little time for reflection. The one-year anniversary of Frank's death had taken place on Halloween and I decided, for this last time, to open the governor's residence for trick-or-treaters. I had presided over my last Progress Board meeting and my final State Land Board meeting. I had one more important speech as Governor, but this time as the "warm-up act" for a new Oregon Governor. I was packing up at home and also at the office. I guess the melancholy song I was humming was exactly right for these final few days.

However, I had a final few decisions tucked in my belt. It wasn't over until it was over.

On Wednesday, January 4, I appointed veteran administrator Gary Weeks as director of the Oregon Lottery. It was a good appointment of an outstanding state administrator, but it left me feeling highly frustrated. Gary had been the director of the Department of Administrative Services since 1993, but the incoming governor had already announced his replacement. Kitzhaber was appointing Jon Yunker, whom I had removed as state budget director when I became Governor. I felt the new governor might be settling some old score on this one. But the choice was no longer mine. Moving on.

When Friday arrived, my last full working day in office, I felt as if it were a stamp-of-accomplishment day to end my four-year term. As I headed to the Supreme Court Building, I remembered that I had appointed four judges in my final month: a woman, an Asian American, an Hispanic, and a white Jewish male. A nice balance, I felt, as I walked to the Supreme Court Building for a very important swearing-in ceremony. I was one of the featured speakers at the ceremony as my son-in-law, Rex Armstrong, took his oath of office as a new judge of the Oregon Court of Appeals. It was one of those perfect "lasts." I had done many "firsts" in my public career. Now I was experiencing some "lasts." To see Rex on the bench, watch Leslie's pride at her husband's accomplishment, and see Frank's three grandchildren in that courtroom was an especially nice combination of an ending and a new beginning. In the court that day was Leslie's sister, Labor Commissioner Mary Wendy Roberts. This was also her final day in statewide office.

The Governor-Elect had done a press conference that same morning to unveil his proposed 1995-97 budget. I hadn't watched the press conference.

Two more important decisions were finalized that last Friday: I signed the compact for Indian gaming with the Warm Springs tribes, plus I jointly signed with Governor Mike Lowry of Washington the final portions of the application to include the lower portion of the Columbia River Estuary in the National Estuary Program.

The compact between the state of Oregon and the Confederated Tribes of Warm Springs was signed by the chairman of the Warm Springs Tribal Council and myself, as Governor. It set the agreed-to conditions for a gaming facility at Kah-Nee-Ta Lodge on the Warm Springs Reservation. Tribal members had already approved $6 million to build and operate the facility for five years with a reevaluation at the end of that time. Interior Secretary Bruce Babbitt still had to approve the compact, but no delays were expected since it was so similar to our already-approved Oregon compacts.

The estuary application was actually a third attempt to protect the Columbia River Estuary. On two previous attempts, Oregon had urged the inclusion of the Columbia River in the federal program but lacked the support of either Washington State or local port officials. This time, Mike Lowry supported the application, and port and industry officials indicated they would not oppose the listing. Inclusion in the National Estuary Program could easily mean about $2 million in federal funds to help begin the cleanup on the Columbia. Tests had shown the river was polluted with both urban and farm runoff. The cleanup was essential and already long-delayed.

Over the weekend, Arlene and I prepared Mahonia Hall for its new occupants. It was a grey, rainy, cold January and we were packing and cleaning the huge house we had shared for four years. However, for Arlene and me, this was not simply the governor's residence or Mahonia Hall—it was home. It would be a hard parting in so many ways. I had no guarantee I would ever be back in the house or could ever again stand in the room where Frank died. We cleaned and checked each room, one by one, from ballroom to basement. Every room received a personal note with fun facts and a little history. I left a note in the small west-side apartment wing saying, "This is referred to as the Carter Suite because former President Jimmy Carter stayed here while visiting Governor Goldschmidt on a trip west." Arlene, at my request, went to the florist and came home with an armload of flowers. Bouquets were arranged and placed in the bedrooms, the dining room, kitchen nook, library, and great room. We packed, scrubbed, vacuumed, and arranged every room for the new residents. We worked until the wee hours of the morning. Two of my security were there to load items in Arlene's car and the truck that was moving things to my storage unit in Portland.

I knew the state agency in charge of the residence would fully check it out on Sunday. We left them little to do but remove a few garbage bags and perhaps wash a few windows if they wished. The house was in perfect shape.

Years later, I sometimes remember that huge home, its many bedrooms, hardwood floors, miles of white woodwork, and six bathrooms, and wonder why I need a housekeeper now for a two-bedroom condo. The tendonitis in my shoulder makes vacuuming and scrubbing fairly painful. Plus, my housekeeper, Dave Behrend, is a friend and totally trustworthy. We gossip while he cleans. I am his political consultant on all races and ballot measures. The cleaning services are a luxury. His company is a bonus.

On Monday, before the new governor was sworn in, I took three final actions. I issued two commutations and turned down every request to commute the death sentences of each of the nine men on death row.

I granted clemency to a woman who had served two and a half years of a five-year sentence for manslaughter. *The Oregonian* reported that I was the first Oregon Governor to commute the sentence of an inmate diagnosed with battered women's syndrome. Shelly Ann Brimberry, twenty-eight, was housed in the California Institute for Women and would be released as soon as the legal paperwork was processed.

I also commuted the sentence of Sandra Pollard Shook. Shook had been convicted of growing and selling marijuana and sentenced to sixteen months in prison. Before that arrest, she had a spotless record. She contended she was trying to raise money for her sister's care, a sister dying of a brain tumor. Her sister died. Shook adopted her eleven-year-old niece. The now-daughter needed Shook much more than Oregon needed her to spend the final months of her term behind bars. I commuted the sentence to time served.

Those two actions for those two women felt right and fair to me. I wish I could have felt the same comfort and satisfaction about my final decision. I turned down commutation requests from the nine men on death row. It was a "wrenching choice and I was not entirely comfortable with the outcome of my own private deliberations," I reported to the press. I went on to say, "I want to make it very clear that I am personally, adamantly, opposed to the death penalty. I believe it is morally wrong and I do not believe that it is effective or useful as a deterrent to crime." I had examined each of the nine cases individually. All of the inmates were pursuing appeals or had other legal avenues still available. If some of them had applied for clemency after all appeals had been exhausted, my decision might have been different. I was grateful to never have that ultimate decision for a life fall on my shoulders, my head, or my heart.

My record in this unique area of gubernatorial powers was that 171 people had appealed for pardons or commutations of their sentences during my four-year term. I pardoned or commuted the sentences of fifteen people. Most of my pardons had gone to individuals who had served their prison sentence and parole and were seeking to wipe their record clean.

As the final hour of the morning began, Oregon officials and citizens were gathering in the Capitol for the inauguration of a new governor. Once again, I was escorted down the center aisle of the House of Representatives — for the last time as Oregon's Governor. Following the presentation of the colors, the national anthem, and the singing of "Oregon, My Oregon," I was introduced and I walked to the podium to deliver my farewell address.

I told my audience that the challenges we had faced during my four years as Governor had been a real test for me and for the state. "And I'd like to believe that history will show that we passed that test and are both better for it." I ended my address by saying:

Four years ago, I took the oath of office, not from this podium, but on the House floor so Frank could be by my side. I knew then I stood beside my greatest supporter and best fan. He was with me then, he is with me now.

I return to private life today and the outward patterns of my life will change. But the greater change that has come from these four years means that I will never again return to the person I was.

The people I've met, the insights I've gained, the experiences I've had, the kindness and generosity I've been given — have changed me forever. Mine is a permanent bond with Oregon and Oregonians.

I leave the governorship knowing that Oregon has had my full energies and my total commitment for these four years.

Where we experienced real Oregon successes, I feel proud of what this administration was able to accomplish. Where we fell short, it was never for lack of trying or an unwillingness to take risks.

I have been privileged to be your Governor.

I have been honored to serve you.

When Governor Kitzhaber had been sworn in and delivered his inaugural address, we were again escorted out of the House chambers. At that moment, I recalled a funny line that former Republican Governor Victor Atiyeh had shared with me several months ago. "On inauguration day, you arrive in the Capitol as a peacock and you exit two hours later as a feather duster!" I smiled and knew Vic had hit the nail on the head. Feather duster it was. I could live with that. I had accomplished a "first" for Oregon women. It was now okay with me to become a "has been." It seemed, by far, a better option than being a "never was."

CHAPTER TWENTY-FOUR

Good Guys with Guns

There are several questions I was asked hundreds of times about being governor:

1. Did you like living in the governor's mansion?

2. Did you get paid a lot of money for being the governor? (This is the question that children in the classroom *always* ask!)

3. What was it like to have bodyguards?

Asked by both children and adults, this final question is, by far, the most interesting to answer.

So let me start with *semantics*. The group of state police officers who provided security for me for four years while I was Governor is correctly called a "dignitary protection unit." Not only are they top-of-the-line state police officers with an outstanding record on the force, but they also receive special training from the FBI for this duty. Six officers were assigned to the team and began their duties on the morning of election day 1990, awaiting the outcome of the governor's race later that night. For the next four years a total of ten members of the state police protection unit were a continuous part of my life, professional and personal.

Sergeant Rick Geistwhite was the officer in charge of the unit. Rick was in some ways, a stereotypical cop ... macho, military leaning, sometimes stern, and usually serious. He expected his security colleagues to be well groomed, always prompt, prepared in every detail of my day, and alert to my safety at all times. When we first met, Rick was a little macho for my taste. My God ... John Wayne was his hero! But over four years I discovered a committed man with respect for family, quiet warmth, a willingness to expand his thinking, and a dry "aw-shucks" sense of humor.

The first time Rick and I met together, he explained clearly the role he and his officers played. Their job was to protect the constitutionally chosen governor of the state, to respect the choice the voters had dictated. Their job was not to protect Barbara Roberts. Their job was to keep the Governor safe. It was a very important distinction.

I determined very early that my job was not to make their job more challenging. My cooperation with and respect for the professional work these officers did not only kept me safer but helped keep these dedicated officers out of harm's way. Many governors who have constant security protection find it stifling and intrusive. I made up my mind that I would avoid this frustration. I would do my job. They would do theirs. I would never think of them as "in my way." For me, that turned out to be a wise decision. I was rewarded with mutual respect, friendship, enlightening "war" stories, and hundreds of hours of great conversation as we drove throughout the state and traveled internationally. Very soon, I felt privileged to have their protection plus their companionship.

However, you can't spend four years in close connection with any group without collecting some stories worth telling, and my dignitary protection guys were no exception to that rule.

First of all, there was only one woman, Pam Pederson, in the unit. Pam was strong and determined and was a member of the class of the first ten female sworn officers in the Oregon State Police. However, quite realistically, with only one woman in my protection unit, most times I was accompanied by only male officers. For years I had been active in women's rights work. That commitment didn't end when I became governor. So my officers sat through events for the Oregon Women's Political Caucus, the League of Women Voters, and Planned Parenthood. Often they were the only men in the room. It was a little difficult to "blend in." Believe me, the women in attendance didn't miss the humor of those situations.

I also had years of involvement in the disability community and would sometimes be recognized in public by someone from that community. The first few times an excited disabled citizen came running toward me, arms flailing, voice shrieking, their awkward gait making them appear out of control, my officers were immediately on guard. But as time passed, my security crew grew accustomed to my diverse assortment of fans.

One of my other longtime areas of political and civil rights work was focused in the gay community. I attended dinners, made speeches, and received awards from the gay and lesbian community throughout my term as Governor. And where I went, my security detail went. For some of the officers, this was no big deal. For other members of the unit, there may have been some social adjustment. However, after four years, my officers were recognized in the community and gained the support and respect of a number of Oregon's gay leaders. The best story to come out of this experience took place during the 1992 Democratic National Convention in

New York City. I had been asked to deliver a speech to the first-ever official evening reception for all of the gay and lesbian delegates at the convention. I arrived with two of my officers and my friend, Terry Bean, an Oregon and national gay leader. We were slowly working our way toward the stage in a shoulder-to-shoulder crowd. Officer Glenn Chastain was leading the way through the crowd with me following at his elbow. The next morning when the daily convention newspaper was released, the front-page story contained Officer Chastain's up-close photo under the headline "Gay Delegates Meet." By the time we returned home to Oregon, Glenn's photo *and* the headline were on every state police bulletin board in Oregon!

The photo I always *wished* I had, however, would have brought real laughs from the bulletin boards across the state. The unrecorded incident took place between my November 1990 election and my swearing-in ceremony in January 1991. I was Christmas shopping with my mother at a mall in Portland and was looking for a gift that was on my daughters-in-law's Christmas list. Mother and I ended up at the Victoria's Secret store accompanied by two of my security officers. The two officers were trying to look invisible as they moved along the walls of the lingerie store. Focused on shopping, I walked behind a rack of bathrobes, and since I am barely five foot three inches tall, I was suddenly out of view of my officers. When the officers could not make a "visual," they became concerned. They had "lost" the new Governor! They asked my mother where I was. She looked around, equally unsure about where I'd disappeared. In the quiet but fast-paced confusion, Officer Gregg Lockwood backed into a metal rack of bras, spilling them across the floor. Hearing the noise, I stepped out from the bathrobe rack to see what had happened. Spotting me and knowing I was safe, Officer Lockwood uprighted the rack and began retrieving a rainbow of bras off the floor, rehanging them on the rack. His bright red face fit in perfectly with the colorful bras. How I wished for a camera! We never let Gregg forget the day he "lost" the Governor in Victoria's Secret.

Over the four years of my tenure as Governor my officers did security in some fun and exciting places. From my perspective, there were three assignments I believe they enjoyed the most: my visits to the White House for dinners, receptions, and meetings; economic-development travel to Germany, Korea, Japan, Italy, and Indonesia; and the nights I attended NBA basketball games at the Trail Blazer arena. My security detail never seemed to balk at Blazer duty!

That good duty however, was offset by some much tougher assignments. Walking into timber rallies and protests in timber communities at the height of the spotted owl controversy definitely did not make the "fun" list. Our trip to Central Oregon for the memorial parade for the young Oregon forest firefighters who had lost their lives in the Colorado King Mountain fire was an emotional day that disturbed the strongest among us. And the phrase "I love a parade" did not apply to the officers trying to keep me safe when thousands of parade-goers stood only feet from me in the Portland Grand Floral Parade, the Pasadena Rose Parade, the Pendleton Round-up Parade, and dozens of smaller parades. These events are demanding assignments for security officers.

When I hear people refer to these fine state police officers as "your drivers," I always cringe. I've been surrounded by a hostile crowd with four officers moving me to safety. I've been confronted by an emotionally disturbed woman with a gun in a Portland hotel. My officers were there and alert. I've watched them arrest a man with a large knife in a paper bag right in the state Capitol Rotunda, headed in my direction. For the most part, these stories aren't made public. The Governor remains safer if the threats are not sensationalized. But the reality of that danger is something these officers never forget. My state police protection officers were not simply "driving Miss Daisy." They were protecting Oregon's Governor, and every day they and I lived with this reality.

My security unit, with spouses. From Portland State University Collection

I savor so many wonderful stories about my security detail. They were there in the hospital waiting room while I was in the delivery room for the birth of my grandson Robert, in August of 1991. They were in the car with Frank and me when we drove home from the medical appointment where we learned of Frank's terminal cancer. They were with me when I learned of my son, Mark's, separation and pending divorce. They were with me as Frank's body was put in the hearse after his death on Halloween of 1993.

Officers Dave Frye and Darrell Berning helped me load the truck to move all of my personal possessions out of the governor's residence on my last night in office. In the cold, pouring-down January rain, until two in the morning, they were there, on their own time.

Officer Tim Steiner was there helping when it became necessary to move my mother into a senior care center. They were there *with* me and *for* me for four amazing and challenging years.

But, for me, this state police story wouldn't be complete without sharing a final special memory.

After Frank's death and his cremation in October and November of 1993, I decided not to inter his ashes until his birthday on December 28. Once that decision was made I felt sad that Frank's beautiful urn and his ashes were stored in the dark mausoleum vault in Portland. I decided to bring Frank home for Thanksgiving and Christmas. My state police always waited outside while I did business at the mausoleum. This day was no exception. As I walked out of the door of the funeral home, I was carrying Frank's urn wrapped in a black velvet bag. The urn and ashes were quite heavy and Officer Darrell Berning jumped forward to help. He gently took the urn from me, set it carefully in the back seat, reached up and grabbed the seat belt, locked it securely and then sweetly patted the urn and said, "There, Senator, everything looks comfortable."

So much for tough guys with guns! But this final story represents the special place these officers held in my life for four years. They made a tough job easier. They made me feel safe in some very threatening situations. They felt like family. They had my back.

In Appreciation

For your warmth and kindness to the members of my family and especially your "fatherly" behavior toward my grandchildren Katie and Robert;

For your ability and willingness to drive smoothly while I freshened my makeup in the car for my next public event;

For your patience in driving the back roads of Oregon when I couldn't stand one more mile of freeway;

For making my "chocolate runs" to a local grocery store after a long road trip;

For giving up time with your own families to keep my hectic schedule and late-night commitments;

For your incredible sensitivity during Frank's terminal illness and following his death;

For keeping me safe, physically and emotionally;

For all this and thousands of other kindnesses … you have my thanks, my gratitude, and my permanent respect.

To the good guys and gal:

Rick Geistwhite

Glenn Chastain

Darrell Berning

Fred Ackom

Pam Pederson

Tim Steiner

Gregg Lockwood

Dave Frye

Dick Hart

Dave Boitz

CHAPTER TWENTY-FIVE

The Next Step

With all the attention and recapping that comes as one leaves the position of governor, there is some sense that you may have died rather than simply finished a four-year term in office. Editorials, celebration dinners, speeches, flowers, media coverage, notes, hugs—it goes on for weeks. Yet no matter how much attention comes your way or how dramatic the personal life change, the fanfare finally ends. I now felt ready for a little down time and for contemplating my next steps in a changed lifestyle.

Having been unwilling to leave office before the end of my term, I had already turned down a position at the Kennedy School of Government at Harvard and later said "no" to an exciting offer from President Clinton to become his AIDS Czar. Those were both extremely impressive offers. I hoped they were signs of future opportunities.

Since Mark was living in my Portland home, I moved into a great apartment near the downtown Portland area. It was fun to be in the city and have honest-to-goodness free time for lunches, dinners, and coffee appointments. It had been so many years since my life had been this relaxed. However, having this much free time constantly reminded me of how much I missed Frank in my life.

In early February the first serious and tempting job offer came from, Harvard's Kennedy School. The executive director's position for the State and Local Government Programs was again coming open. Once again, they offered me that role. The salary was more than my income as Governor. The university would pay for my relocation and give me three months of temporary housing, the benefits were very good, and the position itself was one I knew I would love. However, relocating so far from Oregon meant a number of difficult considerations for me. Never before had I lived that far away from my two sons. It was a tough time for Mark with his marriage ending. Plus, would Mike be okay with me living across the country? I loved being a grandparent and hated the thought of being parted from Katie and Robert. My mother's health issues continued to be a challenge. My sister's cancer treatment aftermath meant she was far from her healthiest. I really wanted and needed to keep working, but these family concerns weighed on my mind. I had several conversations with the Kennedy

School regarding my personal situation. We reached an agreement that would allow me to fly home to Oregon for three or four days every three months. I also understood that my three annual vacation weeks could be timed around important visits like holidays and birthdays. It began to feel feasible.

I had not lived outside of Oregon for forty years, since moving to Texas as a bride in 1955. This was such a wonderful professional opportunity, but in my heart I knew I would miss my state as well as my family and friends. I finally agreed to go to Cambridge and take the position. My first day in my new role would be April 17.

In the next six weeks I spent a lot of time with my family. I also tried to put everything in order for my family before I left. Finally, I purchased a *train* ticket, not a *plane* ticket, to Boston. I felt this was such a major life transition for me that I should *feel* the change over the three-day trip rather than simply spending a few hours in the air. With my first-class train ticket and my own traveling compartment, I could get all the comfort and rest and privacy I might need or want on my way to Boston.

I have never kept a diary and have only journaled on three or four occasions in my life. One of those times was that train trip from Oregon to Massachusetts. Extracts from my journal express my mixed feelings about this new adventure:

At 7 p.m., two hours late, the Empire Builder pulled out of Union Station in Portland. In two days I'll arrive in Chicago, then one more day to Boston.

[S]aying goodbye at the station felt more like a tragedy than an adventure. Saying goodbye made me question if I had made a very large mistake.

Leaving my only sister, even with her cancer now in remission, made me think I might be giving away precious time between us.

Arlene cried and held me close, thanked me for our four special years together in the governor's residence. It was I who should have been thanking her.

Mike, even my special Mike, hugged and clung a little. Not like him. He bought me a book about Boston and a map for my train trip.

My mother told me how proud she was of me. She seldom cries and told Arlene she wouldn't cry today. But by the time she and I walked from the train station to the train itself, she was red-eyed and weeping. She looked frail and already lonely.

Katie and Robert, my wonderful, special grandchildren: right in the midst of all the disruption with Mark's pending divorce, their closest grandparent moves away!

And my Mark: I couldn't be certain if he held me and stood close with his arm around me to give me support and comfort or to give him courage for our parting. His life is so unhappy right now and I have tried to be there for him in these last months and weeks. He held me, looked in my eyes and said, "I'll be okay, Mom." Please let that be so.

Leslie and Rex had to be at their law offices that afternoon, so they sent flowers to the train. What a wonderful, thoughtful thing to do. I went to the mausoleum today to say goodbye to Frank and Neal and Dad. I hated to leave Frank behind. I still go to his crypt and take flowers every week. I never dreamed I would be that kind of a widow. I had a good cry when I asked Frank to watch over our family and then turned and walked away. I know that more than anyone else Frank would be exceedingly proud of what I am about to do.

Tonight, departing the train station and crossing the Columbia River, I watched Portland disappear from sight. We rode through the Columbia River Gorge down the Washington side of the river. Even in the darkness I could see the lights on the other side and knew my Oregon was there.

The next day, at a brief stop in Havre, Montana,

I ran for the single phone booth at the depot and called Mother. I was only twenty miles from her place of birth in Big Sandy. Mother answered the phone sounding almost weak. She revived when I told her I was calling from Havre. I felt I did just the right thing in calling her. She now knows I haven't disappeared from her life, only relocated for a while.

Two things would await me when the train reached Chicago's Union Station Depot: I would change trains for the final twenty-four-hour trip to Boston and my friend and roommate from the Harvard summer program, Amy, would be there to meet me. I stepped off the train with my luggage, and there stood Amy with a big sign reading, "Going to Harvard," a bottle of wine, and a small lunch basket. By the time we finished the wine and I stepped on the Lake Shore Limited to New York and Boston, I had moved from the sadness of *leaving* Oregon to the excitement of *arriving* in Boston. I waved at my wonderful friend Amy as the train pulled out and then stared out at the passing landscape as the train headed east.

On Saturday, April 15, at 5 p.m. the train pulled into Boston's South Station. I had arrived! I pulled on my coat, grabbed my luggage and purse, and stepped off onto the platform. I immediately heard a voice shouting, "Barbara, Barbara!" Running toward me was Persis Whitehouse from the Kennedy School. She had been a staff member when I was part of the State and Local Program in 1989. Now we would be working together on that same program. Persis had given up part of her weekend to meet me and get me settled in. She would deliver me to my furnished apartment at the Harvard Business School. It was wonderful to see a *familiar* face.

After hugs and greetings, Persis suggested, since she had a car, that we make a grocery store run before going to my new residence. Living without a car, I would learn to take advantage of such offers. The shopping completed, we arrived in the parking lot of my new dormitory building at Soldier's Field. We trudged upstairs with several grocery bags and my three pieces of luggage. Persis handed me my apartment keys and we entered the living room. My initial glance around reminded me of a highway Motel Six — sterile, cheaply furnished, and institutional. I knew it was only temporary but remembering that only three months earlier I was living in the Oregon governor's mansion, this was a little unsettling. "It's only for two or three months," I reminded myself. By then I would have found a more permanent home in Boston.

Perched right in the middle of the living room were the two antique trunks I had shipped ahead. They contained items I had packed to help me get by until the moving van arrived later: bedding, towels, framed photos, my alarm clock and radio, and a pretty shower curtain ... a few comforts from home. Once Persis left, I walked to the sliding glass doors and looked out at my view. A large open grassy area, some scattered trees, and a vista looking toward the Charles River, two bridges, and the main campus of Harvard University. It was spring break and the campus was abnormally quiet. I couldn't hear *any* sounds in my five-story building. Was I here all alone? I checked my door locks, then opened the first trunk. I desperately needed my radio. I needed some sound in the quiet of my new space! Before I went to sleep that first night I had completely emptied my three suitcases and the two old trunks. I knew I wouldn't have long-distance telephone service until Monday (this was pre-cell phone days), and there was no television. I felt cut off from my familiar world. Tomorrow I would explore the Business School campus, walk across the river to the Kennedy School, and re-explore all the stores in Harvard Square. Tomorrow.

Early on Sunday morning I was awakened by the sound of what seemed like dozens of church bells. I had forgotten this was Easter Sunday. My body was still on Pacific Time, and I wasn't ready to get up, but it became clear that this church bell serenade would continue for some time. I walked to the living-room sliding door and looked outside. It was a dark, grey, very rainy morning. I stepped out on the little third-floor deck and immediately turned back and slid the door shut. It was icy cold out there! Welcome to Massachusetts.

That Easter Sunday was one of the longest, loneliest days I had ever experienced. The weather was definitely not inviting, but I had to escape the quiet. It was raining hard, and the wind blew all day. I soon discovered that, on the Easter holiday, Boston shuts down. The campus buildings were closed and locked. Few local businesses were open. Harvard Square, usually bustling with activity and fun, was almost empty. I bought two newspapers, a candy bar, and a crossword puzzle book and headed the one mile back to my new "home." I just wanted this day to be over. I wanted to go to my new job and my office in the morning. I wanted people! I wanted to call my family. I found myself wondering, once again, if I had made a mistake in coming to Harvard. Friends had said how great this position would look on my resume. Strange, but I thought that Governor of Oregon looked pretty damned impressive on my bio!

I shook myself awake when the alarm went off on Monday, still obviously on West Coast time. I am not a morning person, and the three hours time zone change would challenge me for a few more days. I dressed, bundled up, and headed for the first day on my new job. Getting accustomed to being without a car would be a big challenge. I grabbed a cup of coffee to go in the Kennedy School cafeteria and headed to find my office in the same building. After six years, this JFK campus building felt a little like home even from that very first morning. Right now, anything familiar was important. I was glad to see Persis … I was glad to see anyone!

In just over ten weeks my first class of state and local government leaders from across the nation would arrive for their three-week July executive program. I had a desk-full of decisions to make. The class selection had to be completed. Fellowships still needed to be awarded. Letters of acceptance must be prepared for mailing.

Rejection letters would also need to be sent. It was a particularly tight set of timelines with my mid-April arrival on campus. Next year the process should work a little more smoothly.

Once all the dozens and dozens of program letters went out there were still piles of details to be taken care of while we awaited the replies and tuition checks from our class members: faculty teaching schedules, housing for the students, menus for three meals a day for an entire three weeks, ticket purchases for the one night our class members could see the Boston Red Sox play, arrangements for our special visit to the Presidential Library of John Kennedy, and visiting speakers' accommodations.

Within less than three weeks I was feeling quite settled and at home in my new position. In addition to the upcoming State and Local Government programs, I took my first shot at managing two other Harvard programs: the Child Welfare League of America's five-day seminar and the Hispanic Women's Program for thirty-five leaders from around the country. Both went well.

In May and June, Persis and I spent some weekend time searching for my permanent housing within walking distance of the Kennedy School campus. Everything was outlandishly expensive compared to housing costs in Portland, Oregon. We found a number of less-expensive apartments but they were obviously intended and acceptable as *student* housing. They were not for me! Finally in June we found a wonderful old home that had been converted into four condo units. One would be available on July 1. It was on the second floor, had two bedrooms, a nice kitchen, lots of window light, and even a small deck off the master bedroom. The informal name of the tree-lined street was "Professor's Row." My walk to the office would take me directly through Harvard Yard. Who could ask for a more romantic and picturesque walk each day? I signed a lease and contacted the moving company to set a date for the delivery of the van full of my household belongings. If all went well, I would move in just before the July class arrived on campus and be fully settled and ready for Mike's planned visit the last week of July. The mile walk to campus seemed very comfortable in June. I hadn't really thought yet about what a long walk it would be in the middle of the Massachusetts winter season. Within a few months I would own two full-length down-filled coats! So much for romantic and picturesque!

From my arrival in April of 1995 until my move back to Oregon in late 1999, I lived a life quite different from that of my past. My job and career were on the East Coast; my heart was way out West. My job was stimulating, varied, and expanded my world in many ways. My social life, on the other hand, was often lonely, devoid of the number of friends and activities that had made my life so full and happy in Oregon. If it had not been for Persis and my other wonderful Kennedy School friend, Joe Ryan, I might never have remained for the four-plus years. We did brunch some Sundays, antiqued together, and made trips to the shore.

That first July, Mike arrived in Boston after a very exciting train trip that included an unintended overnight stay in Chicago. I almost panicked when I found out Mike was stranded all by himself in the huge city of Chicago. The next day I was biting my fingernails, waiting for his safe arrival in Boston. My friend Nancy Wakefield came a few days later, and the three of us toured the New England states. My next visit was from Arlene, who brought Katie out on the plane; they stayed with me for ten days in the late summer. My dear friends Terry Bean, Amy Coen, and Rod Patterson each made a trip to Boston. Those visits and others from Oregon friends were like manna from heaven. I tried to get Mother and Pat to come and spend some time with me but it was just too much for them to manage. I was also excited to have several Oregon government leaders participate in my programs over those years. For four years my close friend Rod Patterson sent a weekly package containing all of the previous week's essential sections and articles from *The Oregonian*. I devoured every word of news from Oregon right down to the end of the obituary columns.

Throughout my time in Cambridge/Boston I sent out a newsletter every two or three weeks called *Barb Does Boston*. It was fun and creative and a way to keep family and friends up to date on my new activities. It also resulted in a constant flow of letters arriving in my mailbox ... obviously my ulterior motive.

There were so many new experiences and adjustments and changes in my new location. Imagine living in the home of the Boston Pops, the Red Sox, and the Celtics! Yet I was also living in the city with the highest auto accident rate of any city in America. No wonder they have such good mass transit in Boston. It is not safe to drive there! They seem to drive with only two parts of the vehicle ...

the gas pedal and the horn. And pedestrians beware. Crossing the street is a battle zone between driver and walker.

The weather was another *huge* adjustment. The snows lasted for months. In January of 1996 we had forty-one inches of snow in thirteen days. Easter Day of 1996 brought five new inches of snow. Pretty hard on Easter bonnets. When I returned to Boston after three months in Oregon at the end of March 1997, I awoke to fourteeen inches of new snow on April 1. April Fools!! When the snows finally disappeared I knew the humidity season would soon follow. The summer of 1995 set a record for Boston heat and humidity. Miraculously, I learned how to do without those undergarments we women have come to think of as "required." New situations sometimes create unusual solutions.

This may sound as if I was unhappy with my choice to go to Harvard, but that is not really the case. It was just a huge personal and social adjustment. I was still grieving Frank's death and adjusting to living alone for the first time in my life. I went from a very active social life to a community that had a more structured and closed social environment. The long, harsh winters in the Boston area kept me more confined than I wanted to be and that added to my sense of being somewhat isolated.

Yet some special opportunities came from my time at the Kennedy School. So many leaders passed through our campus: Senator Ted Kennedy, Yasser Arafat, President Walesa of Poland, Senator John Kerry, Arthur Schlesinger, Jesse Jackson, members of the Clinton Cabinet, Governor Mario Cuomo, Governor Michael Dukakis, Robert McNamara. The list went on and on. I marveled at the power and brains evidenced on Kennedy School platforms and programs. I felt privileged to hear and meet these national and international figures. Persis and I also traveled around the nation as we marketed our programs. The travel was fun and usually productive for our Kennedy School programs.

Another asset that came from my time in Cambridge and may well have been a direct result of those long Massachusetts winters was a manuscript I wrote almost in its entirety during my four years back east. Once I returned home, that manuscript would be published and become my first book, *Death without Denial, Grief without Apology*.

However, my greatest gifts during those four years were the hundreds of bright, talented, dedicated government officials I worked with in our programs. They may have been the "students" but I learned about the programs, policies, budgets, campaigns, and ethics of the more than forty states represented by the leaders I was exposed to. I spent not only class time but meal time, free time, and social time with a wide variety of government leaders. I asked questions and gained knowledge. I recognized I had become a skilled program manager for the university. Now my expanded knowledge of governments across America made me an extra asset in the classrooms and in policy discussions. I could manage, market, teach, and even inspire. I felt I was more than earning my keep at Harvard.

Finally, I cannot omit here how privileged I was to work with and learn from the remarkable Kennedy school faculty … an amazing cadre of teaching talent. I don't believe an equivalent faculty existed at any other school of government in America. I was honored to work and teach in the same classrooms where they taught and served.

After arriving at the Kennedy School of Government in the spring of 1995, I had accepted the fact that my elected career was ended. However, in September of that year I was tempted again. U.S. Senator Bob Packwood, a powerful and long-term member of Oregon's federal delegation, had been caught in a nasty scandal involving a lengthy history of aggressive sexual harassment. Starting in late 1992, creditable and respected Oregon women began to step forward and speak out. The numbers and the accusations grew … and they stuck. In a *Washington Post* story on November 22, 1992, ten women accused Packwood of sexual misconduct. The accusation and public process continued through the Senate Ethics Committee investigations, with subpoenas for the senator's diaries, accusations of influence peddling, and anti-Packwood pickets in Oregon. The senator was plagued. Under the leadership of Sen. Barbara Boxer of California and four other women senators, the Senate moved to take action. At first, Packwood ignored, then denied, and finally faced this political juggernaut. On September 7, 1995, he announced his resignation from the U.S. Senate.

Immediately, I started receiving calls from Oregon asking me to return home and run for the Senate seat. I had barely settled into my new job and home. This was, however, exceedingly tantalizing. My interest in women's history made me aware that no American woman had yet held both the positions of governor and U.S. senator. It would be a new "first" for women if I ran successfully. The idea of becoming a U.S. senator was *strongly* appealing. I listened to my enthusiastic Oregon supporters on the phone. I considered another statewide campaign and my strong potential Democratic primary opponents, none of whom had, as I had, won three statewide elections. I weighed the pros and cons of the race. In the end, the realities that had kept me out of a reelection race for governor were also strong deterrents for this new opportunity. I was still grieving Frank's death and just couldn't find the needed enthusiasm and energy to take on such a demanding campaign. I put the political temptation behind me and refocused on my work at the Kennedy School.

Unbelievably, within only three months, I found myself again weighing a run for the U.S. Senate. On December 1, 1995, Oregon Senator Mark Hatfield, after five terms, announced his intention not to seek a new term in the 1996 election. I understood immediately that there might not be another vacancy for years. Yet I also recognized that I would have to resign my $100,000-plus position at the university and move home to Oregon. I had financial responsibility for my mother's care. I also helped my son Mike every month with his expenses. As a widow, I was obviously self-supporting. A U.S. Senate race would last about a year. During that year, as a full-time candidate, I would be unemployed, living solely on my retirement and savings. At almost sixty, it was a big financial risk — without any guarantee of a successful outcome. I finally had to make the painful but practical decision to skip the race. I experienced some regret at missing this exciting political opportunity, yet I knew from decades of experience that timing could definitely be a deciding factor in life's choices. On several occasions in my life, it had simply not been "my turn." In other situations I had been at the right place at the right time. Two years later I might have made a different decision. Timing can be everything.

In the spring of 1997, I was planning a special trip home to Oregon. The invitations had been sent out. The ceremony was planned. I purchased my airline ticket unusually early. Two years had passed since I left office as Governor. Now it was time for the unveiling of my Governor's portrait.

I had sat for photographic "sketches" months before but, living out of state, I had not seen the painting as it progressed. The young woman artist, Aimee Erickson, had been wonderful about including

Four Oregon governors in front of my official portrait. Left to right: John Kitzhaber, Ted Kulongoski, Barbara Roberts, Victor Atiyeh. Photograph by Gerry Lewin.

items in the painting that held personal significance for me. I chose to have the portrait be a standing image, believing there is more strength in a standing figure. I chose a beautiful dark green wool suit, with a long jacket. The artist ended the portrait just short of the bottom of my skirt to avoid the viewer seeing the skirt length, which can date a woman's photo or portrait. I hoped this decision would help keep the painting more timeless.

The background showed a set of large double glass doors opened to an outdoor scene. Looking beyond the doors one viewed a background of tall fir trees representing the huge impact the spotted owl listing had had on Oregon's largest industry *and* on my governorship. To lighten the dark forest area outside of the window, I had asked Aimee to add some touches of the beautiful white dogwood that grows wild in Oregon's forested lands. My father usually brought me a bouquet of these glorious dogwood blossoms every spring and they now reminded me of Dad.

The artist placed a small art piece on the wall. It was a replica of a painting done for me by the son of the Japanese Consul in Oregon. It was a suggestion of my international economic-development travels during my term, especially my many trips to Asia. Since I frequently use my hands actively when speaking, we decided the portrait should reflect that personal trait. So, my outstretched left hand seems to be a welcoming gesture as one views the large painting. Even more than three years after Frank's death, my wedding ring shows clearly. That felt important to me. It was a small way to include Frank in this historic art piece.

I had begun to worry more about my mother's deteriorating health. She had recently taken a very bad fall. She expressed to me her concern that the portrait might not be unveiled while she was still able to come to the Capitol building. She was now in a wheelchair and growing more frail. When the unveiling ceremony was finally planned, Mother was thrilled and relieved. She knew I would be coming home for the ceremony, and she also understood she would rightfully have a front row seat for the big moment when her daughter's portrait was unveiled on April 25, 1997.

The day of the event I was excited and a little anxious. After being away for two years I really wasn't certain what to expect regarding attendance at the ceremony and how Oregonians would react to having me back home. I need not have worried.

A large crowd was already gathered in the Rotunda when I arrived. Secretary of State Phil Keisling had done a wonderful job of planning the event, and he acted as master of ceremonies as the program began. My whole family was in attendance, and I spotted many friends and former staff members among the crowd. Aimee Erickson was the first woman in Oregon to have been the artist for a governor's official portrait. That seemed appropriate for the first woman governor of our state! Phil shared that fact as he introduced Aimee, and the crowd was very responsive.

Once my family had been introduced and remarks made by Secretary Keisling, I made a brief thank-you speech, and then the time had arrived to remove the drape from the covered painting on the big brass easel. I was very nervous. I felt like I was in one of those dreams where one is caught in public in one's underwear … or less! Everyone was focused on the draped painting. My two grandchildren, Katie and Robert, and Frank's grandchildren, Iain and Morgan, each held a piece of the large drape, then they pulled the drape aside. I took a deep breath, feeling a little like a historical artifact. A large sound of approval was emitted from the gathered crowd as the drape fell. They liked it! So did I.

It was so much fun to be back home and part of a large gathering of supporters. My trips home over the past two years had been focused on my close family. That day's outpouring of affection and support was a little of a surprise for me. In Boston, I was usually a stranger in most places. Here, in Oregon, I was treated, once again, to the attention and respect of being Oregon's Governor. It felt very good.

On my next trip home during that 1997 summer I would visit the Capitol for two reasons: to see my portrait hanging on the second-floor marble wall just outside the House of Representatives and to visit the beautiful tupelo tree planted in Frank's honor on the state Capitol grounds. For many years those two special honors have given me real pleasure. Frank's tree has grown taller. The portrait hangs in the Capitol reminding visitors that Oregon once had a woman governor — and, hopefully, will again.

During my time at Harvard, I walked hundreds of miles, absent owning a car. I traveled by car with friends to see more of the region and the New England states. I used the trains to travel up and down the eastern seaboard for business and pleasure. I definitely knew America's East Coast in far more detail than when I arrived in 1995. I could name all the buildings in Harvard Yard. I could identify all the businesses in Harvard Square. I knew the train schedule to New York City, Washington, D.C., and Rutgers University in New Jersey. But I also knew exactly when every United Airlines flight left Logan Airport in Boston and took off for Portland, Oregon!

Over the Christmas holidays of 1997, I returned to Oregon but, this time, for a three-month leave from the university. According to my new contract terms with the Kennedy School I would return to campus on April 1, 1998, and lead the July and August programs. During that three-month leave I was in daily contact with Persis and the program staff by computer, fax, and telephone. I was on part-time salary and still maintaining responsibility for my programs. This was a period I would spend in Oregon reveling in the winter season and being quite grateful for every drop of rain. My down-filled coats, ear muffs, winter boots, and snow gloves were in my closet in Cambridge. I wouldn't miss them for a second. I had spent two winters tromping through feet, not inches, of snow to get to work, to the store, to the pharmacy, to a taxi cab. Oregon rain would be a walk in the park.

I can't complete this recounting of my time at Harvard's Kennedy School of Government without one final "timing is everything" story. I had already negotiated a new part-time contract with the university that would permit me to be in Oregon for five months a year. I had rented a nice apartment in Portland and shipped part of my furnishings home. I would be living bicoastal after three years full time in Boston. No more Boston winters for me! My heart and my head were in Oregon. With my computer and fax I would be connected and working for Harvard, but my view out the window would be of Mt. Hood. Then, for the second time in less than four years, I had a call from the White House ... President Clinton was again offering me an opportunity to come to Washington, D.C., and fill the role as his HIV-AIDS policy person. Oh God, how could the timing be any worse for me? My Harvard arrangements were already made. My mother was ill and needed me to come home. I tried to imagine taking on this huge new responsibility with less than two years to make a difference as the President's term ended. I faced what it would mean to rearrange all my newly made plans and move to D.C. full time. I wanted to do the AIDS work, and I had amazing support from the HIV-AIDS community to take the position. A year before I would have jumped at this exciting offer and accepted this chance to help my nation with this huge tragedy of the AIDS crisis. But now, I needed to go home ... now I *wanted* to go home. I turned down the offer. So once again, I found myself repeating, "timing is everything." Today, I volunteer time and support in Oregon assisting with HIV-AIDS work. I am on the advisory council for the Cascade AIDS Project and have a long-standing volunteer relationship with Our House, Portland's unique AIDS hospice. I have certainly learned that there is more than one way to do the work on HIV-AIDS. I have been very public about my support and involvement for this community. There are currently seven thousand people in Oregon living with HIV. There are 1.1 million people in the United States with the disease. The opportunities to help are over a million, and they exist across our country ... and the world.

So, back to Harvard University. Just before my final week's work at the Kennedy School, the school threw a very special late-afternoon "retirement" party in my honor. In the tradition of the Kennedy School of Government, they don't do anything half way. The food was plentiful and the attendance large. Several speakers extolled my contributions to the school and my dedication to the JFK mission. I was then presented with one of the famous Harvard chairs—beautiful cherry wood and black lacquer replicas from the colonial period of New England. It was perfectly matched to the Harvard chair that had been a gift from Massachusetts Governor Bill Weld when the National Governors' Association met in Boston. To own a pair of these special chairs would be a memorable record of my years on the East Coast. They would soon look charming and lovely in my Oregon home.

As the going-away reception drew toward a close, the final speaker made his comments. Those remarks would give me a story worth retelling for years after I returned to Oregon. The speaker, a faculty member I had worked closely with for over four years, made reference to my return to "Or-e-gone," a pronunciation I had corrected over and over. For one last time, I corrected the Harvard professor. "Oregon is pronounced Orygun," I said.

He stopped, looked at me, and seriously responded, "Are you sure about that?"

Finally, after four years, my frustration came out. "Yes, I'm sure! My family came on the Oregon Trail. I was born in the state, and I served as Oregon's Governor. I'm pretty damned sure!" The audience took great pleasure in what they thought was a joke between us. However, at home, in Oregon, my fellow Oregonians *loved* the story after years of hearing radio announcers, television newscasters, and speakers mispronounce our state's name. It was time to go home.

I had visited historic sites on the East Coast and felt the thrill of standing where George Washington, Paul Revere, Benjamin Franklin, and Betsy Ross had once stood. Now I would fly home to Oregon and marvel at the views of Mt. Hood and the Columbia River that had greeted Lewis and Clark and Sacajawea. I had traversed the continent in a journey of discovery much as my ancestors had done so long ago as they traveled the Oregon Trail.

CHAPTER TWENTY-SIX

Home to Oregon

Here I was, back home. I had come home to the state of my birth, the state of my Oregon Trail ancestors, the state of my governorship. My heart was full.

Yet, a full heart can cause one to be extra vulnerable to pain. I returned to a very difficult situation with my mother. She faced one health crisis after another. Her macular degeneration had stolen most of her vision. A bad fall and two recent surgeries (including a brain surgery) had weakened her and perhaps permanently confined her to a wheelchair. My sister and I shared an emotional and sometimes physical burden trying to help her regain her strength and some level of improved health. At age eighty, in a family of long-lived family members, we felt she could have a few more good years. We tried to provide both comfort and encouragement. Yet, in truth, she was tired of the struggle. She had never fully recovered emotionally from Dad's death. Her ongoing heart problems added to her discomfort and to her fears. I ached for her. She had always been such a fighter, such a competitor. I felt the extra pain of knowing she was ready to give up. It was understandable, but painful.

I now had three major responsibilities: my one-hundred-mile round-trip to Salem to be with my mother several times a week; getting my Portland house ready to put on the market; and completing the manuscript for my book on death and grieving ... *and* finding a publisher! I was so happy to be back home, but I certainly wasn't facing a period of laid-back retirement.

My son Mark was still living in my house, and he and I started spending every weekend redoing the house, room by room. We had a wonderful time working together. We talked constantly while we worked, laughed a lot, and became reacquainted as adults. The end product, in addition to our enhanced relationship, was a house ready for prospective buyers. We marveled over the job we had completed together.

With a falling market in the area, it might take a while to sell the house. Mark kept everything "real estate ready." In the meantime, I started looking at houses in a nice old neighborhood where I had worked and lived many years before. The Sellwood-Moreland neighborhood had always felt like home to me, much like my small town of Sheridan. My house hunting changed when my older son, Mike, and I decided we would try living together. It would be cheaper for Mike, and we both needed the company that a shared household would give us. My house hunting was now focused on a somewhat larger home that would give Mike his own bedroom, living room, and bath.

My search for a new home paid off. I found just the house I wanted. It was a home I would not have chosen before my years in Boston. I had lived almost entirely in suburban ranch-style houses since moving to Portland in 1958. *Now* I wanted a house with more "personality," more history. I purchased a big, old 1911 two-story house. In this city neighborhood, it was the tallest house on the block. The backyard included a pond and lovely wooden decks in place of a lawn. The front yard was small with oodles of flower beds and lovely old rose bushes. I fell in love with the house on my first tour. I immediately made a serious offer, and within hours the deal was done. For the first time in my life I had purchased a home totally on my own!

We turned the big second-floor sun porch into a bedroom for Mike, and one of the upstairs bedrooms became his "music room" with his television and wall-to-wall music equipment and bookcases. He was a happy camper.

Most of my furnishings worked perfectly in my new abode. I purchased a new craftsman bedroom set more in keeping with the age of the house, and rehung art that had been in storage since I moved into the governor's residence. My other large bedroom became my new home office. Arlene took her two antique wicker chairs out of storage and gave them to me for my front porch. They looked perfect there. My paternal grandfather's antique Duncan Phyfe table and chairs looked right at home in my dining room. I knew I had made the right choice.

In January of 1998 Pat called to say Mother had once again been taken by ambulance to Salem Memorial Hospital with serious heart pains. It was her third trip to emergency in the past few weeks. Things were reportedly quite grim in terms of Mother's survival. I called Arlene. I called Mark. Arlene rode with me to Salem. Mark drove from his job to the hospital. We arrived at the emergency room to find Pat and part of her family surrounding Mother in the curtained cubicle. I immediately thought about Mother's often-expressed fear of ending up as "a vegetable" on life support. She had a Do Not Resuscitate order filed with the hospital as well as an Oregon POLST form (a form Oregon has had since 1991 called a Physician Order for Life-Sustaining Treatment, which describes precisely how much care a patient wishes to receive if they are stricken and unable to express their wishes). In the next few hours those wishes and documents would come into play.

Mother was in a coma-like state. The doctor expressed his belief that she would not live more than forty-eight hours. The end of her life was approaching. I reminded the hospital staff about the documents she had on file and about our own wishes. We just wanted to be certain Mother was without pain, that she was comfortable in her last hours. We surrounded the bed. One of us talked directly to her at all times. We told stories, shared special family memories, and told her how much she was loved. We never quit speaking to her, holding her hand, caressing her forehead. We knew she heard our voices and felt our presence. She knew she was not alone.

That afternoon, on January 16, 1998, Mother died, two days before her eighty-first birthday. She died in exactly the same cubicle in the same hospital where Dad had died in October of 1990. Maybe she even *felt* that connection. I know I did.

January is such a gray, cold month. Mother was born in Montana during a January blizzard. She died in Oregon on a wet, windy January day. Yet, strangely, the sun shone brightly on the day of her memorial a few days later, and a beautiful rainbow seemed to fill the sky as we left the services. I had chosen "Over the Rainbow" as one of the songs for her memorial. At Mother's services, I watched with great emotion and pride as my younger son, Mark, delivered a very personal eulogy to his grandmother, to all the things she had taught him, from making piecrust dough to fly fishing.

Within the next few days we emptied Mother's room at the care center, her belongings were sorted, things donated, shared with family, stored in my garage. I was the executor of Mother's small estate. I paid her last bills and put her final affairs in order. I did what a good daughter does, and then I grieved. I soon understood for the first time that the term "orphan" does not refer only to a child. I was a mature adult, over sixty years of age, and I was experiencing what it meant, emotionally, to become an orphan. I actually felt abandoned! The feelings were unexpected and strong. I finally shared these emotions with my sister and found that what I was feeling was not unique. I felt certain the feelings would diminish with time but, for now, I was experiencing an enhanced "aloneness."

As spring neared I was offered something to feel happy about. Mark and his girlfriend, Tammy, were getting married! They had set the date—March 26. That date was *both* Mark's and Tammy's birthday. (Talk about never forgetting your wedding anniversary!) They wanted a home wedding and asked if they could do the ceremony and a small reception at my home. I was honored to be such a large part of their special day. They asked my son-in-law, Rex Armstrong, to perform the wedding ceremony. (It is very handy to have a judge in the family.)

I rearranged the furniture in my big dining room and sun room, adding seating for the guests. There were about twenty people in attendance, exactly the small number they had invited. The sun was shining through every window, and the guests seemed to be all smiles. Many years ago, in their early twenties, Mark and Tammy had dated seriously. Then, as sometimes happens, they had parted. After many years and a failed marriage for each of them, they had once again found each other, and now they were marrying. It was a fun and romantic love story.

Tammy had a grown daughter, Melissa, who no longer lived at home. Mark's two children, ages nine and six, lived with their mother and stepfather. We joked that, with no children in the household, Mark and Tammy could now have a perpetual honeymoon. Well, hold that thought and recite the old adage about life being full of surprises! Before the end of the year, they had temporary legal custody of Katie and Robert. In mid-1999 a judge would award Mark permanent custody of his two children.

These legal battles are never easy for anyone, and this one was no exception. I made every effort to act as a safe house for my grandchildren, keeping anger and conflict to a minimum and making sure adult issues remained in adults-only conversations. Katie and Robert stayed overnight with me often. They loved my old house. We went to dinner, watched movies, played cards, and just had fun. I held them, loved them, reassured them, and answered questions when they became worried or confused. I never promised what I was not in a position to deliver. Their father knew personally the hurt and damage that divorce, false promises, and adult failures can create in a child. He had been there. I admired my son's commitment to put his children's feelings before his need to vent and strike back in anger. He set the example for the rest of our family and we worked hard to follow his lead.

At the same time Mark and Tammy were adjusting to being full-time parents again, I became a part-time employee at Portland State University. My impressive new title was Associate Director of Leadership Development at the Hatfield School of Government at PSU. I was working with professors Doug Morgan and Craig Shinn and executive staff member Jennifer Chambers; we were creating a new program for the Hatfield School: a five-day intensive leadership experience for public officials from state, city, and county governments. We spent six months designing every aspect of the program, including elements and tools to aid in policy work, enhance press and communication skills, build collaborative models, right down to appreciation for our form of government and for the privilege of being a public servant. With the program design complete, we labeled it the Legacy Program and began selecting faculty for the various elements, both university faculty and experienced government leaders. I was personally active and visible in the marketing work. As a former Governor my personal contacts carried some weight and were important in promoting a brand-new university program for government agencies and elected officials. With our first class scheduled to begin in September of 1999, we needed at least a dozen participants to make it workable and affordable.

We ended up with sixteen class members from all around the state. There were two members of the Oregon Legislature, two county commissioners, three chiefs of staff, several agency directors, a law enforcement leader, a state racial minority board executive, and even the executive director of a prominent nonprofit environmental agency. It was a great mix in terms of issue areas, political philosophy, geographical locations, ages, race, and gender.

Over four years, the Legacy Program occupied much of my time and commitment; I enjoyed directing the program, teaching, and marketing to governments in both Oregon and Washington. I even developed a new graduate-level class called "Politics, Policy, and Risk Taking" that I taught in 2003. I stretched myself intellectually and professionally for that new academic experience.

During this time I found myself more and more connected to PSU. Years before, in the 1970s, I had visited the campus often during the time Frank and I dated and following our marriage. Frank was one of Portland State's original faculty members from the first days when it was still called Vanport College and teaching packed classrooms of World War II veterans attending on the GI Bill. Frank taught for thirty-seven years at PSU before his retirement in 1982. The longer I was associated with Portland State, the more I felt like "family" on the campus. Frank would have been amused and very pleased at my strong identity to his institution.

As the world approached the millennium, my personal world was at peace. I was engrossed in and enjoying my work. Mike and I had become very compatible roommates. I was spending large amounts of time with my grandchildren. I was supporting Katie's dance classes and transporting her to the dance studio most weeks. I was excited about the work Robert and I were doing together to help him learn to read. I was accepting quite a number of public speaking opportunities. This was a period of real contentment for me. I even held a millennium party at my home for my family members and close friends with party hats, noisemakers, and lots of photos to commemorate this landmark. I was feeling so positive and upbeat.

By January of 2001 I had one more reason to feel upbeat. I had a publisher for my book—an Oregon publisher. A few months earlier Maureen Michelson of NewSage Press and I had met briefly at a Montessori event where my grandchildren and her daughter both attended classes. We, oddly enough, shared a conversation about difficult deaths we had experienced over the previous months. I had no idea she was a publisher. She had no reason to know I was working on a book. A few months later an author whom both of us knew connected the two of us. We met for tea in a little Japanese tearoom. She wanted to read my manuscript. I was absolutely thrilled—and nervous at the thought of her reading my first attempt at writing a book. However, the results were highly positive. We soon had a signed contract.

On February 28, 2001, I got in my car and drove the fifteen miles to the next county to deliver a luncheon speech to a large Chamber of Commerce group. Just as I arrived and put my feet on the parking lot surface, I felt the jolt of an earthquake. This was not a large quake, but Oregon has few earthquakes, so folks here have a major reaction to even a small tremor. The gathered crowd inside was buzzing as I entered the auditorium. I ate lunch, delivered my address, took a few questions, and headed home. My telephone was ringing as I unlocked my front door. Suddenly I knew something was wrong — terribly wrong! I ran to the phone, picked up the receiver and heard my son Mark say, "Mom?"

"Oh no, oh no, it's Pat isn't it?" I wailed.

"Mom, she's gone — a heart attack about two hours ago. She was dead when Don found her on the floor." My knees buckled. I sank to the floor. I think I screamed. "Mom, just sit down, don't move. I've taken off work already. I'll be there in less than fifteen minutes and I'll drive you to Salem. Don't do anything until I get there. Just sit down and wait for me," Mark said quietly. "I'm coming *right now."*

When Mark arrived, I was still sitting on the floor, my front door standing open with my keys hanging in the lock. I hadn't moved. I was stunned. Mark bent down and took me in his arms. "Come on," Mark whispered, "let's go help Don and the boys. They need you."

When we arrived at my sister's home, all four of Pat's adult sons were standing in the driveway looking lost and shocked. In the house, Pat's husband, Don, told me what he knew about what had happened. Pat had been packing for a vacation she and Don were leaving on the very next day. Don was working in his backyard shop and he felt the slight tremor from the earthquake a little before noon. He thought Pat might come rushing out to the shop since she was quite fearful of earthquakes. She didn't show up, so Don assumed her packing for the trip was a higher priority than her fear of quakes. Thirty minutes later, he went inside the house. As he crossed the kitchen, he saw Pat lying face-down on the hall carpet. He knelt down and was quite sure she was dead … but he called 9-1-1 anyway.

Don later speculated that, as she felt the quake, Pat had left the bedroom and started down the hall toward where he was working. She was likely frightened and made it only a few steps before she collapsed. I hated that she had died in a moment of fear. I ached that my little sister had died alone.

The next day I went with my brother-in-law and my four nephews to the funeral home while they went through the painful process of making final arrangements. I needed to share something important with my sister's sons. I reached into my purse and took out a white envelope, now yellowing with age, that contained two dark locks of hair, each tied with a small pink ribbon. I explained that many

Me and Pat

years ago I had been given these small treasures by a funeral director to save until the time was right to give Kimberly's dark curls to Pat. But the right time never seemed to come. Pat would be pregnant again, have a new baby, be going through a divorce, or be ill. I could never seem to find the time when she was at peace enough to give her the envelope that contained her baby girl's hair.

On that day, the time had finally come. From *that* emotional family revelation and our shared tears came two decisions that felt so right for the whole family—and for Pat. The envelope with the tiny locks of hair would be cremated with Pat and then Pat's urn would be buried with her daughter in McMinnville. After almost forty years, Pat and her baby daughter would be together again.

The day after Pat's memorial service I called my book publisher and told her I wanted to add an epilogue to my book, a short section honoring my sister. I poured my heart out on paper and then shared with the reader the promise I had made earlier to my sister: when the book was published she would get the very first autographed copy. A few months later, just before the formal launching of my book, I wrote Pat a very personal message on the new book's opening page, placed the book in a clear plastic bag and sealed it, and then left the package on her headstone at the cemetery.

The book remained there on the headstone for several months in spite of the Oregon rains. Then one day I came with flowers to visit Pat and the book was gone. It didn't really matter *why* or *who*—the book was simply gone. So I placed my flowers, trimmed around her and Kimberly's double headstone, walked back to my car and got a copy of my book and then sat down on the grass and read the epilogue aloud to Pat. I had kept my promise.

In 2002 my book was publicly released. I did hundreds of book readings. I shed tears while reading emotional passages from my book. My audience understood and shared my tears. Then, I signed copies of my book—as the author! I felt so proud. I couldn't wait for more sales, not for the money, but to hear my readers' reactions to my writing, to my story, to Frank's story! The reactions came. Letter after letter, they poured out their stories, their pain, and their gratitude for my book. I have never been so humbled.

Being an author has been a satisfying role for me. I have found a reward in my hundreds of book readings and knowing that I have brought some comfort to my readers and listeners. My book on death and grieving has led to several years of service on the Oregon Hospice Board, the advisory board of Compassion and Choices, and invitations to testify in California, Vermont, and the state of Washington as they considered Death with Dignity legislation in those states.

Right after I bought my big old house, my dear friend, Arlene, moved into my neighborhood, only blocks away from me. I was thrilled to have her so close again. She sometimes traveled with me when I did out-of-town book readings and speeches. I took Arlene to lunch or dinner several times a week. She came to my house and cooked with me occasionally, and she and Mike and I ate these jointly prepared meals. She was a better cook than I, and I looked forward to her special dishes. With both of us widowed and with my mother and sister both gone now, Arlene and I were "family." Not only did she have my deep friendship and affection but my grandchildren and Mike adored her. Our closeness, both in the neighborhood and personally added so much to both of our lives over those years.

As the months of 2002 passed, I became aware of a new concern. Though Mike and I were very compatible housemates, I saw more and more signs that Mike was becoming increasingly dependent on me. I did almost all of the shopping, cleaning, laundry, and yard work. After years of planning and work to make Mike independent, I was now guilty of reversing those positive results. It was becoming clear that Mike needed to once again be on his own and also that the big house I loved so much was beginning to be too much work for me as a single woman at age sixty-five.

I began to chat with Mike about his needing more space of his own for his music, books, videos, and even some new furniture. Then I took the next step and started looking at apartments in the neighborhood without yet taking Mike on these first scouting trips.

Like many autistic folks, Mike does not take easily to change. He needed to feel as if he was the decision maker. I allowed him to reject several places without any argument on my part. Finally, as fall moved toward winter, the apartment search turned more serious. One Saturday I took Mike to look at a little court apartment right on the bus line (since Mike doesn't drive), only three blocks from his grocery store, and ten blocks from my house. I could see Mike was impressed. He liked having both a front door and a back door, though I was not certain why. When the landlady told him she would knock $40 off the rent since he didn't need the garage, he was sold! I breathed a sigh of relief.

In late 2002, Mike and his cat, Princess, moved into the new apartment. I would miss sharing my house with Mike, but my responsibility was to give him the independence to make it on his own. Parents hope for that for all of their children, but it is an extra requirement for those of us raising adults with disabilities.

As 2003 ended, my world felt in order. Mike was all settled. Mark and his family were doing well. My book readings and sales were adding some excitement to my schedule. My calendar was full. The only thing missing in my life was a new relationship. It had been nine years since Frank's death, and I now felt the growing desire for male companionship in my life. But it was becoming clear to me that was easier said than done. I was out and active all the time. I knew thousands of people in my state. I always tried to be friendly and warm. Yet I was never asked out on a real date. I finally came to a couple of conclusions. First, I was a very public widow. Everyone seems to remember when a governor's spouse dies. I knew it had been nine years. Others remembered Frank's death as more recent. Plus my image as a widow was not the only thing that was interfering with my eligibility as an appropriate "date." As my younger son reminded me, "How would you like to be the guy working up the guts to ask a former governor out?" While I might not think of myself as all that frightening, that didn't necessarily reflect the reaction of men looking in my direction. So—I moved on.

CHAPTER TWENTY-SEVEN
A Decade Alone

My big old house felt very empty with Mike gone. I started watching in my neighborhood for something smaller. I wasn't rushed. I could certainly wait until the right property showed up.

In June I received a telephone call from the chair of the Multnomah County Commission, Diane Linn. She had just listed her new condo. She wanted to know if I might be interested. I was indeed! It was Saturday and Diane was home. She encouraged me to come and take a look before the new listing hit the market. I had actually looked at her condo building the previous year, but all the units had only two bedrooms and, with Mike still living with me at that time, it simply wasn't enough space. It was immediately clear. I loved Diane's condo. The space was perfect. The location was just what I was hoping for. The price range fit my budget. Without Diane's real estate agent even being present, we verbally settled on a sales price.

The condo purchase was contingent on the sale of my house. I had to get my big house ready to go on the market. I had a basement full of things. My garage had dozens and dozens of boxes. There were things from my mother's final home, extra furniture, even items that Arlene had stored from her last move. I had to sort through everything and downsize. Within a couple of days I began to understand that I was sorting through "the boxes of my life." High school yearbooks and mementos, my children's old school papers, items from my first marriage, academic papers from my time at Marylhurst College, old Democratic Party materials, and papers from every office I ever ran for or served in.

Stacks began to accumulate in such a way as to clarify for me that these were, in fact, the personal papers that were my history. These papers told so much of my life story. They needed to be saved and not tossed. I came to understand they were a collection and not simply old papers to be junked. I called the library at Portland State University to inquire whether they would be interested in having these papers. Two weeks later, staff from PSU came and picked up the first forty cardboard boxes. Those papers have now become the Governor Barbara Roberts Archives Collection. It really helps one downsize when one's "junk" turns into an archives collection! There was some suggestion from a couple of women friends that I should donate my papers to the University of Oregon where the Oregon Women's Political Caucus had donated all their old records, but I felt Frank's long academic career at PSU and my own five years on staff made this choice the right match. I felt at home here.

I "archived." I repainted three rooms and cleaned ceiling to floor throughout two floors and a basement. Arlene helped me and kept me supplied with iced tea. I called my realtor and listed the house. It sold in two days! I had sixty days to move from house to condo. During this moving marathon I took a two-day break to travel to the Oregon coast for an overnight stay and a morning speech. I had invited Arlene to come with me. She had seemed very tired lately, and I hoped a change of scenery would do her good. She loved the beach and a dinner of seafood was always a treat for her. We were staying at a charming bed and breakfast; we checked in and then Arlene admitted she was too tired to go out for dinner. I was quite surprised but our hostess whipped up a light meal for us and we went off to bed early.

Arlene still seemed worn out the next morning. We headed over to the convention center, and I asked a friend to keep an eye on her until I was finished speaking. I was getting worried about her. I didn't feel comfortable about how she was acting and decided that once I had finished my commitment here we would drive directly back to Portland. I watched Arlene closely all the way home. She seemed easily distracted and even a little confused. She was gesturing with her hands in ways I had never seen her do before. I was getting more frightened as we drove into the city. I knew by now she needed to have medical attention.

Before the next forty-eight hours had passed, we had a medical answer but certainly not one I would have expected and a diagnosis that was sad and painful. Arlene had a large malignant brain tumor that was inoperable. Her condition was terminal. She came home and was given a Hospice nurse. A hospital bed was moved into her apartment living room. I was there several times a day. She was so brave. I tried to follow her lead but I wasn't sure I could face another death in my life so soon after Mother and Pat. I felt like all I did was bury people I loved. I took Arlene to her medical appointments, picked up her medications, cleaned her apartment, took her laundry home with me. And I spent hours just visiting with her about people and events in our shared history. Arlene had the same birthday as my sister, Pat. I knew Arlene's late husband, and she had helped care for my late husband during his final illness. She had been a next-door neighbor to my parents nearly forty years before. We had shared the governor's residence for four years. She had taken piano lessons on my piano. We had traveled to almost every part of the state together. We now looked at photos from so many of those great trips. We talked about her childhood, something she seldom did. We talked and talked and talked. Then I went home and wept almost every day. It was a cross between losing my sister again and losing a huge piece of my own history.

On July 7, 2003, Arlene died. Only weeks before we had planned all the great fun we would have in my new condo. Now she was gone without having visited there even once. According to her strong wishes, there were no services of any kind, not even an obituary in the newspaper. Nothing. I went home and sat on the wicker chair on my front porch, the chair Arlene had given me. Her death would leave such a big void in my life. I knew I would miss her terribly for a long, long time.

Two weeks later I began the move into my new condo. The last things to be moved were the two wicker chairs Arlene had given me. They were carefully placed on the small second-floor deck outside my bedroom sliding glass doors. They are the first thing I see every morning. They remind me of Arlene.

My new condo building has been such a wonderful place to live over these last eight years. It is full of window light, comfortable, just the perfect size for me, and an attractive place to spend this part of my life. I am so lucky to have moved into a building with so many bright, caring, fun people. The women of the building hold several potluck events a year. I feel fortunate to have landed here. I sometimes miss being able to go out in my front yard in the old house and pick a beautiful bouquet of roses. But most of all I miss the wonderful neighbors I had for my five years in that house. One of the bonuses of my condo is that it is located in the same neighborhood.

My activities at Portland State University soon expanded beyond my work with the Legacy Program. A new program called New Leadership Oregon began at the College of Urban and Public Affairs in 2003, and I assumed the role of chair for the first three years. The program was patterned after a program at Rutgers University at the Center for American Women and Politics where I had spoken a number of times during my tenure on the East Coast. NLO is a leadership program for Oregon college students statewide that brings about thirty young women to our campus for an intensive one-week workshop each June. The leadership work is focused on all elements of the political arena. It has been a highly successful program, and we have watched many of the women alums become active in Oregon politics, working on campaigns, active in ballot measure elections, even becoming candidates for public office. Every year their expanded political activities have shown clearly that New Leadership Oregon has fulfilled our expectation, for these participants.

I also became active with PSU's "Walk of the Heroines" project, which created a park-like setting on the campus with fountains, gardens, benches, decorative walls, special trees, and the names of hundreds of women being honored by their families, friends, and community. An informational kiosk will give the bio of each woman whose name is inscribed in the park setting. The program also offers scholarships to women students. I am very proud that the Walk's stage has been named in my honor.

The third campus effort I've worked on since it was launched in 2003 is the College of Urban and Public Affairs's annual Urban Pioneer Awards event. We have honored elected leaders, community activists, and business, public, and nonprofit organizations. It has been exciting to help with the selection process for these "pioneers." We have given special recognition to those who have championed diversity and community inclusion. When I made the decision in 2004 to retire from my position as associate director of Leadership Development at the Hatfield School and give up my lead role with the Legacy Program, I knew I wanted to stay involved with New Leadership Oregon, the Walk of the Heroines, and the Urban Pioneer project past the time of my official retirement. But at age sixty-eight I felt it was time I actually retired. I had worked for a full decade in higher education since I left office as Governor. It had been a wonderful and expanding period of my life, but I was ready to move on, to relax a little more, to try some new interests. Those new opportunities in my life were not likely to happen if I stayed tied to even a part-time employment commitment. Just the fact that I had determined that, told me the time for retirement had arrived. I submitted my letter of resignation feeling a little sad but slightly more free.

One of the first projects I became fully involved with in 2005, after my retirement, was fun and full of memories. I was one of a handful of longtime friends working on our fiftieth class reunion for Sheridan High School. Gad … fifty years! As we had done for a number of years we invited all students who had been members of our class during any of our four high school years. Most of us had graduated together in 1955 but in such a small high school that was not the only important factor that connected us during those years. When we started our first planning for the fiftieth reunion, in 2003, we decided we would make a special effort to find some of our classmates who were long-lost. We would locate them and urge them to attend. We were aiming for 100 percent attendance, which we had never accomplished before.

I was in charge of the series of mailings and the "search party." Our list included thirty-seven names from the class of 1955. (Fifteen members of our class were already deceased.) We worked hard at updating married names, mailing addresses, and then trying to track down classmates with whom we had lost touch. We began an active campaign to get five or six members who had never attended a single one of our earlier reunions to come to the fiftieth. We put out a class mailing with the list of the few people we were still searching for. We followed the leads that mailing gave us. While we searched, we went ahead with plans for a gathering on the Oregon coast, secured a hotel and banquet rooms, and decided on our menus.

With 1955 classmates. From left: Vietta Anderson, Barbara Roberts, Nadine Stuck, Alene Peterson.

We found every classmate but one who, sadly, may be a murder victim. I made dozens of personal phone calls to encourage our last stragglers to attend. I used all of my charm, humor, and negotiating skills.

As the decades had passed toward this fifty-year landmark our class members had learned some valuable lessons. When one-third of your classmates are deceased, a reunion is certainly not about showing off financial success, touting brilliant children and grandchildren, clinging to your high school status, or worrying about waistlines and hips. It becomes about shared memories, old friends, and gratitude just to be alive.

Decades ago they tore down our old high school building. Our elementary school building burned down just a few years ago. The movie house is gone. Our two after-school cafés now house an accounting office and a veterinary clinic. A good deal of the bricks and mortar of our youth is pretty well gone. What we have left are memories of those places and the people with whom we shared them. That was the tone we set for our fiftieth class reunion as the late-September weekend event neared.

On the afternoon of September 1, my daughter-in-law, Tammy, called. My son Mark had been in an accident on his motorcycle, and they called from the scene to tell her the ambulance was transporting him to Oregon Health Sciences University. I told Tammy I would meet her there. She told me not to worry. The ambulance EMT said Mark just had a broken leg. I understood that the ambulance was passing several closer hospitals to bring Mark to OHSU. I knew we were dealing with a bigger medical trauma than a simple leg fracture. I was so scared I could barely keep calm as I drove over the river and up the steep hill to the emergency center at the hospital. I arrived at the same time the ambulance was unloading my son. He was surrounded by medical personnel. I heard him cry out in pain as they moved him. He disappeared into the emergency room entrance just as Tammy drove up to the parking area.

We soon learned that Mark's right leg had been crushed between his Harley and the Ford Explorer that turned directly into him. His leg was broken in several places. Large areas of tissue and flesh were deeply gouged away. The leg was so badly damaged that on that first night the lead surgeon informed us that they might have to amputate. He said even if that didn't happen tonight or over the next few days, it was still unlikely Mark would ever walk on the leg again.

For the next six weeks, surgical teams worked to save Mark's leg. They surgically inserted metal rods, did large skin grafts, and his vascular doctors created new blood-flow paths. I lost count after thirteen surgeries. Tammy and I were at the hospital every day. Tammy slept over almost every night. The threat of amputation continued throughout those weeks. Mark was in constant pain. I would have to step out of the room whenever they moved him. I couldn't bear to see ... or hear ... his level of pain.

I took Katie and Robert, now sixteen and fourteen, school shopping for clothes and supplies. I made certain they had everything they needed to register for the new school year. I wrote checks for Mark and Tammy's household bills. The whole family worked together to try and keep things afloat. We were tired and worried about what would come next.

Three weeks after Mark's accident the weekend of my fiftieth class reunion approached. Mark insisted I had to attend and stay overnight for the festivities. He reminded me how long I had worked to make the event successful and to be certain *every* classmate was there. He was stable and didn't have any new surgeries scheduled for the next few days. Everyone had adjusted to the changed family routine by then. I finally took a deep breath and agreed to attend the reunion. Later, as I looked back, I was so grateful that I hadn't missed that landmark celebration. The reunion was a complete success. Classmates from 1955 arrived from across the nation. We squealed and cheered as each new arrival checked in at the hotel desk. We took hundreds of photos and shared dozens of stories of our youth. A memorial board of deceased classmates reminded us how lucky we were to be here together. We made our 100 percent goal! Maybe you *can* go home again.

Mark eventually left the hospital in a wheelchair. He was still unable to walk, was not allowed to even bend his leg or ankle, and was certainly a long way from returning to work. He progressed enough within a few weeks to take slow cautious steps with the aid of a walker. I remember the first time I picked Mark up so we could attend Robert's basketball game at the middle school. It took Mark fifteen minutes to walk up the sidewalk to the gym! Here was my six-foot son, still in his forties, moving at a snail's pace, leaned over on his metal walker. If I found this a painful adjustment, I could only imagine how Mark was dealing with this life change.

Five years later, Mark earned his black belt in karate! He had gone from walker to double canes to a single cane and eventually used a cane only on rare occasions walking long distances on rough terrain. He worked out and exercised for hours every week rebuilding his leg muscles and endurance. He took up karate to help him regain the balance he had lost with the difference in his two legs. Today if you watched Mark walk across a room, and were unaware of his terrible accident, you might not even notice his very minor limp. In the summer when Mark wears shorts, his scars are certainly evident, but compared to how his leg looked for the first two years, the scars have faded remarkably. What *hasn't* faded for me is my extreme gratitude that my son's life was spared, that Mark survived that horrendous motorcycle accident without any head or spinal injuries. The other memory that remains vivid for me is the strength and caring my daughter-in-law Tammy demonstrated during the months of pain and medical attention that Mark faced every day. She was a rock!

I had expected 2005 to be a relaxed year. This first full year of retirement was supposed to be about long lunches, a few vacations, less pressure, more fun. I apparently needed more practice at this retirement business! Hopefully, the future years of retirement would be easier, with less worry, and some positive life experiences. I crossed my fingers and planned for that better future.

CHAPTER TWENTY-EIGHT

Senior Statesperson

There are some unique lessons associated with being a state's governor. Some years ago, former Oregon Governor Victor Atiyeh (1979-1987) related a charming thought to me. "Once you have been the Governor of Oregon, the people own you forever." And believe me, there is much truth in that statement. Even after more than fifteen years out of office, I am recognized in every part of my state. Citizens speak to me, shake my hand, and even hug me. Adults introduce me to their children and grandchildren and point me out in the grocery store, on the beach, at basketball games, even in the women's restroom!

I am still in constant demand as a speaker, at public events, and in political settings. My email and mail box are packed every day. You would think after all these years, people would forget. It amazes me, but I must admit it also pleases me. I feel cared about, remembered, even a little special. All of us want that. I am very fortunate to have it. I was extremely proud to be Oregon's Governor. I remain honored to be an Oregonian and to be treated with such warmth and respect in every part of my state.

So what precisely *is* a senior statesperson? Several factors can make one "senior": aging; outlasting others in your field; refusing to disappear quietly into the sunset. However, defining statesmanship or statesperson is a little more challenging. The term may simply be used to refer to someone who has held high public office. It can label a person who demonstrates ongoing leadership. It is sometimes a term of respect or admiration for a former leader.

It is, perhaps, up to the citizens of Oregon or perhaps, you, the reader, to determine the appropriateness of my applying this label as a self-description. Yet, of *this,* I have little doubt: fifteen years after leaving office, I have certainly *not* ridden quietly into the sunset. I have been publicly, politically, and socially active.

I have served on a very lengthy list of nonprofit and unpaid state and national boards and commissions, which have not only given me a chance to contribute but also an opportunity to expand my knowledge on a wide range of subjects and community needs. I have donated thousands of hours of time plus financial resources to these efforts. Just a few examples: I served for six years as a board member of the Human Rights Campaign in Washington, D.C. HRC is the leading national organization working for civil and legal rights for gays and lesbians across America with focus at the congressional level. I also served for nine years on the national board of Population Action International, an advocacy, education, and research organization in the areas of international family planning and maternal health, HIV-AIDS prevention, and elimination of poverty. The list also includes Oregon Hospice Board, Northwest Osteopathic Medical Foundation, Children's Relief Nursery Board (child abuse prevention), and, by appointment from Governor Ted Kulongoski in 2009, the Columbia River Gorge Commission—this is the bi-state commission responsible for the Columbia River Gorge National Scenic Area spanning almost eighty miles of this tremendous river.

I also have a heavy and long-term public-speaking schedule. I average five major speaking commitments monthly that require thoughtful and time-consuming preparation. These are addresses that fall into the categories of keynote and policy speeches. My major focus areas are leadership, women's history and leadership, environmental management, human and civil rights, and citizen advocacy. In addition, I address such topics as affordable housing, tax reform, child abuse prevention, Death with Dignity, and HIV-AIDS. I enjoy public speaking and have worked hard to become a skilled and interesting speaker. I have a strong philosophy that, if someone offers you a podium, they deserve your serious preparation. An unprepared speaker, who tends to ramble on, unfocused and scattered, is one of my pet irritations. In the past three or four years I have begun to limit my public-speaking commitments to Oregon groups, with only an occasional out-of-state address. This change has come partly as a result of how complicated air travel has become and partly to allow me to focus on my writing.

I also frequently emcee a number of events. I have acquired some skill at fundraising from the stage. I have been known to auction off the shoes I am wearing for a large enough contribution to a good cause! I once sang an unrehearsed solo from the stage that raised $20,000. My lack of singing talent allowed us to raise that same amount the following year if I agreed *not* to sing!

The other area that keeps me active and highly visible is my love of politics and my commitment to help elect Democratic officeholders. Since my return to Oregon from Boston, I have been a regular fixture at Democratic events, political fundraisers, campaign gatherings,

Standing beside Governor Kulongoski at the signing ceremony for Oregon's Domestic Partnership bill, May 2007. Photograph by Chris Ryan.

and even candidate press conferences. I have assisted in recruiting candidates for the House, been featured at fundraisers in almost every part of the state, publicly endorsed candidates, and appeared in their campaign brochures and ads. I appear in almost every voters' pamphlet taking positions on ballot measures and in support of candidates. I don't believe there is any other public official, past or present, in my state who has so openly done this level of political endorsements. But I believe that if my support or opposition carries weight with Oregon voters, I have an obligation to come forward and speak out. I don't win them all, but I also don't stand quietly on the sidelines and hope things work out for the best. I choose the people I think are best and give them my strong support. I don't believe that democracy is a spectator sport.

In 2008, for instance, I took on four major political races in Oregon that were highly competitive and equally visible. They were all far from "sure things."

In the Oregon primary election, I accepted the position of co-chair of the Women for Obama campaign in my state. Because I have been an activist for women candidates for many years, this endorsement was one that surprised many Oregonians. However, my strong belief in the mind and heart and stature of Barack Obama led me to support his candidacy and I spoke publicly at rallies and on radio ads on his behalf in many parts of Oregon. I was in the front row at a huge rally for Sen. Obama on May 18, the largest in the nation to that point, where seventy-two thousand supporters filled the Willamette River waterfront beyond capacity! It was thrilling!

With U.S. Senator Jeff Merkley

The second 2008 campaign where I took a leadership role was the race against incumbent Republican U.S. Senator Gordon Smith, who was considered close to invincible. Democratic members of Oregon's federal delegation, other statewide elected Democrats, and a former governor all opted out of challenging the incumbent senator. But Jeff Merkley, serving his first term as Speaker of the Oregon House, felt this challenge was necessary and realistic. Jeff announced for the U.S. Senate, and I was, from day one, his state co-chair along with Oregon Governor Ted Kulongoski. I was there every step of the way, at dozens of events, fundraisers, and press conferences. Most people in Oregon didn't give Jeff Merkley much of a chance of winning. I always believed in Jeff *and* in his electability. In November he defeated the incumbent senator by almost sixty thousand votes. Today, Jeff is U.S. Senator Merkley of Oregon!

The third 2008 race where I jumped in early was for Oregon Secretary of State, an office I had held for six years. My own state senator, Kate Brown, decided it was her time to stand for election statewide. I had followed Kate's career closely and had sometimes played a mentoring role with her. I knew Kate's intelligence, her skills, and her ethical standards. She ran in a tough primary race that included two other Democratic state senators. She won an impressive victory and went on to defeat her general election opponent. Kate is already being recognized as a strong new statewide leader.

My fourth very public endorsement in 2008 was my support for Nick Fish in his race for the Portland City Council. I had endorsed Nick in an earlier race for council when he came in second. I respected Nick and felt certain he would be a strong, able member of the city council. He would bring great credentials, leadership ability, and progressive values to the position. I endorsed him early and I think I appeared on every piece of printed material his campaign distributed. My position was clear. Portland voters shared that position and elected Nick to the city council.

My 2008 electoral activities are not complete without sharing one more story about that remarkable election year.

I had intended to skip the opportunity to become a delegate to the Democratic National Convention in Denver. I had been a delegate at so many of these conventions that I felt I should step aside and give that opportunity to another committed Democrat. However, I became so involved and enthused about the candidacy of Sen. Obama, that I felt compelled to attend just *one more* national convention.

Truly, there is nothing quite like a national political convention. Each one is exciting and stimulating. Every convention seems unique. From my perspective, all national party conventions have special and memorable moments — highlights that stay with you, last for years. The 2008 Democratic convention gave delegates memories galore.

When Senator Hillary Clinton was introduced by her daughter, Chelsea, and walked onto the stage, the convention floor came alive with cheers, thunderous applause, and thousands of "Hillary" posters held high and proud. Senator Clinton was no longer a candidate for President but she had earned the respect of her party. It was an incredible moment in politics and in U.S. history that set the bar high for future female presidential candidates. Hillary's speech was strong, stirring, and, above all, a class act. She threw herself fully behind Senator Obama, her former opponent for the presidential nomination.

In Hillary's twenty-three-minute speech two statements stayed with me. "I haven't spent the past thirty-five years in the trenches advocating for children, campaigning for universal health care, fighting for women's rights here at home and around the world, to see another Republican in the White House squander our promise of a country that really fulfills the hopes of our people." She was determined and clear. However, for me, Senator Clinton's most memorable four sentences were encompassed in this moving and descriptive historical comparison: "Eighty-eight years ago on this very day, the Nineteenth Amendment gave women the right to vote and it became enshrined in our Constitution. My mother was born before women could vote. My daughter got to vote for her mother for President. This is the story of America, of women and men who defy the odds and never give up." History in action!

There was also the emotional moment when Senator Joe Biden's son, Delaware Attorney General Beau Biden, stepped to the stage to introduce his father as the Vice Presidential nominee. That speech brought tears to almost every delegate in that huge Pepsi Center. Captain Biden was leaving for Iraq in just a few days and would not be in the country to help on the campaign or to witness the 2008 election, but he pled with the delegates to "be there" for his father. When father and son embraced on the stage you knew you were witnessing the strong affection and respect between two dedicated Americans — and between a very close father and son.

Yet, the totally unexpected arrival of Senator Ted Kennedy, terminally ill with cancer, as he came to the convention podium for what most of us understood would be his final convention speech, was more emotional than any convention appearance I had ever witnessed. The convention audience, on their feet, offered him more than respect; they showed him love. I had heard Ted Kennedy speak at the 1980 Democratic convention in New York City when he knew his race for the presidential nomination was over. I had been a Kennedy delegate to that 1980 convention, and even his great speech on that long-ago night did not temper my sadness for his loss. Tonight, the senator's remarks brought me to tears from his first words. This Lion of the Senate, with his remarkable history, his decades-long service to his country, his commitment to those in need, had kept him a hero to me over these three decades. From the days I wore my bright yellow "Run, Teddy, Run" T-shirt until that very moment, when I witnessed his courage and personal strength delivering one last message to his fellow Democrats and his country, I remained a Kennedy enthusiast. Senator Ted then told us he would be there in January to see Barack Obama become our President — and he was there. I will always hold the memory of Teddy's last great convention speech. In his words, "The dream lives on."

Yet the dream we dreamed and the convention we shared definitely saved the best 'til last. On the final night when the entire convention was moved outdoors to the huge NFL Mile-High Stadium in Denver, I became one of thousands of on-site witnesses to an amazing and moving moment in American history. The night climaxed with a stirring and inspiring address by presidential nominee Barack Obama, and almost as one, the crowd rose to its feet, American flags, thousands of them, waved in the hands of delegates and guests. People were cheering, weeping, hugging. Fireworks lit up the night sky, and these synchronized displays played tag with the stars in a brilliant Colorado sky.

My heart swelled. My eyes filled with tears. I was overcome with emotion, with hope, with the promise of a better America. Thank goodness I had not skipped this convention! Never had I felt such pride in being a Democrat. Never had I believed so enthusiastically in America's future. I was convinced this would be my last national convention but talk about leaving on a high note! I was so excited about our nominee. I felt certain he would prevail in the November election. If Barack Obama won, I believed America would win. I do *love* politics!

I have described some of the ways in which I have continued to serve. However, those are *my* choices, *my* priorities, about how I spend my time. This next list represents the recognition by *others* of the work I have done, the service I have given to my state and beyond. I share this list feeling strong gratitude toward the organizations and groups that have honored me over the last number of years.

My most notable recognition was awarded in 2005 by the Oregon Legislature. The Oregon House and Senate named the Human Services Building in the Capitol Mall in my honor. It was the first time a state Capitol Mall building in Oregon had ever been named for a governor. On March 22, 2006, I attended the special naming ceremony and saw, for the first time, the lettering on all four entrances to the building: "Barbara Roberts Human Services Building." What a thrill!

When the presentations were complete, I delivered brief remarks, but my emotions were very close to the surface as I approached the podium. I had to swallow hard a couple of times as the audience applauded and I tried to regain my composure. I quoted the late U.S. Senator Hubert Humphrey in the first part of my remarks. "The moral test of government is how it treats those at the dawn of life (the children), those in the twilight of life (the aged), and those suffering in the shadows of life, the ill and 'disabled' … To have my name associated with a state agency that meets that difficult moral test every day of every year, is one of my life's great honors." Several years ago a mental health program was started in Portland named the Barbara Roberts House. The clients, mostly women, were former longtime residents of one of the state's secure mental health facilities. It was moving to know they were taking steps back into the larger society.

I was the first recipient of the Governor's Gold Award for Extraordinary Service to Oregon in 2005 given by Governor Kulongoski at what has continued to be a major charity event for Oregon Special Olympics. I received the Oregon Statesman Award from the Oregon Business Association that same year. I was particularly excited to return to Harvard University and be recognized by the Kennedy School of Government with the institution's Alumni Achievement Award in 1996.

In March of 1996 the Salem-Keizer School District named its alternative school the Barbara Roberts Secondary High School Program. I was extremely honored by the school's naming as well as several comments in an editorial by the Salem *Statesman Journal:* "Roberts was a strong advocate for education, especially education for those who needed tailored programs. She realized Oregon … cannot afford to lose even one young person. When you hear of graduates of the Barbara Roberts High School, salute them and their model." Today the school serves teen parents, GED students, students with learning challenges, and those with behavioral issues.

In 1995, I received two coveted national lifetime achievement awards, one from the Center for Policy Alternatives and the other from Women Executives in State Government. Those are heartwarming honors that recognize decades of work and leadership.

I have been honored several times by both the national and local Human Rights Campaign for my leadership on LGBT issues and for standing up and speaking out on issues like gays in the military, hate crimes legislation, AIDS funding, domestic partnership rights, and gay marriage, plus my history of fighting against anti-gay ballot measures. I treasure that recognition.

My resume lists honors from the ACLU, environmental groups, disabilities organizations, the Democratic Party, children's groups, minority and women's organizations, and two honorary degrees, one from Portland State University and the other from Willamette University in Salem. No matter how many times these honors come my way, each one feels special, unique, and emotional.

Another interesting honor came without ceremony, a plaque, or a framed certificate, but I think of it as an honor, nonetheless. Western Oregon University and the Governor Robert Straub Archives housed on that campus did a complete video oral history of my life. There are hours and hours of taping that capture my personal life and political history. They supplied a set of the finished CDs to their own university, a set for my personal collection (and my family), and a final set to the Millar Library at Portland State University, where my personal papers are housed. This oral history was done in my home by a wonderful, skilled videographer, Michael O'Rourke, whose patience and great questions brought out information and stories that will be available for research and political and historical interest for years. For me, it felt like a two-way gift, both giving and receiving. I know now that my history will not be lost, just as I know this book captures my words, feelings, and memories about that same history.

In the last three or four years I have learned the importance of not losing history. I recently made a historical "find" of great personal value to me. My family came to Oregon on the Oregon Trail in 1853. My great-great-grandparents, James and Almeda Boggs, both from Pennsylvania, left Iowa that spring with a wagon full of their worldly possessions, an ox team, three children ages ten, eight, and four, and, yet unknown to them, a baby on the way. They arrived in October of 1853 to accept their donation land claim in Polk County. Almeda was seven months pregnant when she reached Oregon. The child she carried inside for every mile of that arduous journey was my great-grandmother Anna, the first generation of my family to be born in Oregon, on January 1, 1854.

In 2007 Mark and I traveled to southern Oregon, searching for the headstones of my Oregon Trail ancestors. We knew that five years after reaching Oregon they had traded their Polk County farm for another land grant farm in Douglas County. We believed they were buried in one of the many pioneer cemeteries in the Roseburg area. Before his death, Dad had searched unsuccessfully for the markers in a number of cemeteries. My son and I decided we would search again.

On our second day of searching, in the heat of August, we found our family at the Civil Bend Pioneer Cemetery in Winston. We found the double headstone, the final resting place of the pioneers who had made Oregon "home" for the next six generations of my family. We cleaned and polished the headstone, cleared the plot, and took out our cameras to record this moment where past and present came together for our family. It was a very emotional "reunion" for me.

My great-great-grandparents lived to see Oregon become a state on February 14, 1859. Can you imagine what they would have felt knowing that one of their descendants would one day become, not only an Oregon governor, but the first woman governor in our state's history?

I believe they would have been almost as excited about my piece of history as I was to fill in the blank in our family's history.

A final thought on personal history comes to mind as I remember fondly my seventieth birthday on December 21, 2006. Year seventy certainly felt like a landmark. But instead of the sensational birthday party Terry Bean and Rod Patterson had thrown for me on my sixty-fifth, I asked for a much smaller private party for this latest event. So Terry held a lovely dinner party for close friends and family, with lots of laughter and chocolate. However, I also agreed to have my birthday converted into a separate fundraising evening for Planned Parenthood of Oregon. It was a highly special event for me. We celebrated my birthday while raising money for a cause I strongly support. My friend Amy Coen came all the way from Washington, D.C., to speak. My son Mark did a beautiful personal tribute that brought me to tears. My longtime friends Terry Bean and Gretchen Kafoury affectionately shared stories and personal praise. Senate Majority Leader Kate Brown told the audience what it had meant to her to have me as a mentor and friend. The printed dinner program carried a quote from a letter written by Governor Ted Kulongoski: "Barbara, you are truly a hero to the people of Oregon. Your selfless devotion to serving others and to making our state a better place to live, is unparalleled." What a remarkable way to reach age seventy!

My seventieth birthday will always be memorable for two other gifts that surpassed my wildest expectations. My close friend Terry went over the top by presenting me with a brand-new Toyota Prius.

My dependable Honda Accord was eight years old and Terry, a good friend of Al and Tipper Gore, thought I needed a car that was more environmentally friendly. I am seldom speechless, but seeing that new Prius in Terry's driveway, wrapped in a huge red ribbon, left me without words. I just kept saying "Wow!" "Wow!" Hardly my usual articulate response!

To add to Terry's remarkable gift, my dear friend Amy Coen and her husband, Gerry, presented me with an airline ticket to Paris (my first time ever!), a reservation to a wonderful little hotel on the West Bank, and their company for a week in that amazing city. We made the trip in the first week of July 2007, and I still look at my photos of the three of us on that trip and relive the fun and excitement we shared in the streets and museums of Paris. We were in Paris on July 4th for America's Independence Day. We were on an evening boat trip on the Seine and boated right past the replica of our Statue of Liberty that sits on an island in that river. Americans aboard the boat burst into our national anthem. It was surprising and stirring! Paris is everything it is romanticized to be — an amazing and beautiful city. It was perfect for an amazing and beautiful seventieth birthday trip!

I definitely do not believe senior statesperson is synonymous with Paris and Prius, but somehow, for me, that's where my life landed at age seventy. I marvel at the special affection of my friends … and their generosity.

Before I end my thoughts on being a "senior statesperson," I have a confession: I have failed miserably at retirement! In late January of 2011 I was appointed to fill a vacancy on the Metro Council. Metro is the only elected regional government in America. Covering most of three metropolitan counties in the Portland area, it handles matters on land use, recycling, mass transit, visitors' venues, air quality, and pioneer cemeteries. Until December of 2012, I will, once again, be a public official.

So, I continue to give my time, energy, and enthusiasm to Oregon and its citizens. I will stay connected to policy issues, politics, and social needs. I will speak out when I believe my voice will make a positive difference. I certainly don't sense a quiet period of retirement coming any time soon! Senior statesperson is not synonymous with simply observing from an ivory tower. For me, it is more closely defined as "up close and personal!" *That* continues to be my relationship with my state, with politics, with life.

A Few Final Thoughts
on Family, Friends, and Feminism

Family

I grew up in a home filled with love that set the standard of caring for the rest of my life. My parents, Bob and Carmen Hughey, gave me unconditional love. My sister, Pat, added beauty, sharing, and laughter.

The joy of being a mother and watching my two sons grow from infancy to manhood has broadened and deepened my life in ways I could never have imagined. Mike and Mark have given me my greatest pride and most tremendous sense of purpose.

My older son, Mike, has accomplished so many things the "experts" predicted he would never be able to do. He has just recently retired after thirty years on his job delivering the mail on the Mt. Hood Community College campus. He may sometimes march to a different drummer, but he has earned his spot as a "member of the band." Mike makes me beam with pride at his unpredicted successes.

My younger son, Mark, faced challenges as a teenager and young man as he dealt with the anger and disappointment at his father's abandonment. Yet his basic intelligence and very good heart won the battle. Mark has been a very hard worker all his life with a quick head for math plus sales and negotiating skills. When his first marriage failed after six years, he ended up with custody of his two

Mark and Tammy

children. My pride in watching Mark mature and grow as a father has given me the sense that I may have done my job of parenting with some success. Mark is a caring parent, a committed husband, a good provider, and a loving son. He warms my heart.

Tammy, Mark's wife, is definitely a special package. She is only four foot ten inches tall, part Native American and part Hispanic, was adopted at birth, and grew up in a family with the last name of Swanson. In spite of her long dark hair and her skin tone, she tells me she grew up thinking she was tall and blond! That image may have given her a little attitude. She's a hard worker, loves my son completely, worked diligently to raise her daughter, Melissa, as a single parent and then to be a good stepmother to my two grandchildren. Melissa is now the mother of two. I have tried hard to understand the boundaries of being a good mother-in-law. I hope she thinks I have succeeded.

I was in the delivery room when each of my two grandchildren, Katie and Robert, were born. I fell madly in love with them at birth. Robert, now twenty, and I have long shared our love of basketball and are Portland Trail Blazer fans. He has a wicked and dry sense of humor that totally entertains me. He is tall, slender, smart, and has the kind of charm that warms female hearts—including Grandma's. He

My grandchildren, Robert and Katie

is now serving in the U.S. Navy. Katie spent years in dance classes doing tap, jazz, and even hip-hop. She danced with skill and self-confidence. After high school graduation she gave up dance classes and joined the Army, an interesting transition. She was "my girl" for a long time, and it is hard when growing up results in growing away. Her return home to Oregon as a veteran and an adult will give us an opportunity to build a new kind of relationship. I can't wait.

Growing up in a family of very solid, long-term marriages, I had almost no experience with "step" relationships. Over the years I gained new insights as two stepdaughters, fourteen step-grandchildren, and two step-great-grandchildren gave my life new texture and new love. Most notable in this category are Frank's two daughters, Mary Wendy and Leslie. They are quite different women and I have very different relationships with them. Frank's elder daughter, Mary Wendy, has, over the years, been a very political person. She has held the offices of state Representative, state Senator, and Oregon Commissioner of Labor and Industries, impressive accomplishments. You might imagine that two statewide elected women in one family could occasionally create some political tensions, and it did. Today, Mary's daughter, Alex, is on staff at Metro and in my new position there, we cross paths often in our work world, a treat for me.

Frank's younger daughter, Leslie, and her husband, Rex Armstrong, are an important part of my life. These two brilliant attorneys have both been elected to the bench. Rex serves on the Oregon Court of Appeals and Leslie is a Circuit Court Judge. They are parents of twelve—yes, twelve—children. Their two birth children, Iain and Morgan, are now grown. However, Leslie and Rex have adopted ten children from China, four girls and six boys. I feel privileged to be treated like both parent and grandparent in their household.

My list of stepfamily members has another added component. During the years Frank was married to Betty, her four children were part of his life. Her two daughters, Di and Jo, and her two sons, John and Randy, remained special to Frank for all the years that followed. When I became part of Frank's life, I was included in this circle of affection. Betty's sense of family made it possible for Frank and me to attend weddings, graduation celebrations, and baby showers for her children and grandchildren. After Frank's death I was still included. This experience demonstrated the flexibility—and joy—possible when there is a willingness to expand the definition of family.

I am also an aunt. My sister's four sons still call me Auntie Barb. We don't do the large family gatherings I grew up with, and I miss the opportunity for that special kind of family fun. In addition to my four nephews, Craig, Scott, Bob, and Chris, I have also acquired an additional opportunity to be an aunt to Frank's nieces and nephew. His niece, Laurel, and her brother, Brian, live in the area and we make excuses to get together and share food and stories. Laurel is a fine storyteller, so every meal or visit resembles tales around the campfire.

Friends

I have loved and treasured many close friends. Some go all the way back to grade school, but newer friends have come into my life as recently as my sixties. What warmth and richness they have added to my life.

From my high school class of 1955, Nadine, Alene, Sharon, and Vietta keep me connected to my roots. Maintaining friendships over sixty years is part determination, part love, and a large dose of "art."

My dear friend Terry Bean has brought me into his life and his broader community in more inclusive ways than you can imagine. We have been friends for so long and because Terry is a gay man and we are seen together so often, we have been labeled as Portland's "Will and Grace." We both chuckle about the title but are quite proud of the recognition of our close friendship.

My close friend Rod Patterson covered my political career as a newspaper reporter while I held several public offices. There are always warnings that politicians and press folks should keep their distance. We worked at doing that but failed. We liked each other so much that we decided our friendship was more important than the risk. Rod is retired now, so that "stigma" has evaporated. Our friendship has not! Nancy Wakefield and I go back to my first race for Secretary of State in 1984. She was a teacher committed to the campaign and to me. I gained a life friend. She's fun to be with, smart, and just cynical enough for my taste and humor.

Three special friends have been mentioned often in writing this autobiography. These three women played vital roles in my life. Arlene Fall, Donnella Slayton, and Amy Coen gave me support, love, and encouragement over many years. They completed my life in ways that only close women friends can.

My list of political friends encompasses Oregon and the nation. I have friends from so much of my political life: the school board, the Legislature, my time as Governor, working with the Democratic Party. All of these active, dedicated people have added color and excitement to my life.

Feminism

Gender is not a small matter. One might think in this day and age, with women doctors, judges, engineers, CEOs, U.S. senators, and police officers, that gender would no longer be a defining characteristic. Don't you believe it!

I know from experience that women leaders are held to a different standard, a higher standard. Women face judgments about their dress, their hair, their marital status. Women leaders are assumed by many to have little or no knowledge on "boy stuff" such as economic development, transportation, or military matters. We are, on the other hand, expected to know about children and education, perhaps senior citizen issues, and that's about it.

Men can serve in leadership positions and no one seems to worry about their knowledge background or about who is caring for their children. This is not the case for women leaders.

Political women cannot cuss in public even if "I'll be damned" is the accurate way to describe a situation. A woman cannot pound on the podium during a speech without attracting frowns from the audience. For women politicians dangly earrings, skirt length, and any sign of cleavage will often mean their most brilliant ideas will not be taken seriously. Guys can be unpressed, unshaven, wear bad hairpieces or huge belt buckles, and no one doubts their knowledge, opinions, or seriousness. Gender too often defines leadership. This remains an unfinished equity agenda.

A Final Thought

The word politician is not synonymous with unethical, dishonest, or uncaring. I served with hundreds of elected officials, knew elected leaders from every state in America, taught dozens and dozens more in university leadership programs. Almost every one of these politicians loved the work they had chosen. They worked hard, gave up huge amounts of their time, and often worked for unimpressive salaries. Politics is, in large part, an honorable profession populated by smart, dedicated, hard-working elected citizens. For most politicians, it is about more than ego, recognition, and a title. It is about making policy decisions, making a difference, and, if you are lucky, making a little history.

Looking Back:
Four Years of Accomplishment

This line from my inaugural address still describes my view of leadership and feels apropos to my work, my struggles, my commitment, and my successes in the one term I served: "Each generation has but one chance to be judged by future generations, and this is our time."

The Economy

When my administration took office in January of 1991, Oregon was still feeling the effects of a national recession. As I left office in January of 1995, state unemployment was the lowest it had been in twenty-five years; there were over 150,000 new jobs with more on the way; and we had experienced the greatest amount of business investment in state history, with the Oregon Economic Development Department actively involved in the $4.7 billion in new private-sector investments alone in the first eighteen months of the 1993-95 biennium.

Our state had experienced dramatic increases in international trade, including a near-doubling of Oregon exports to Southeast Asia between 1990 and 1994. *The Oregonian* on October 24, 2010, reported that "[i]n 1994, Gov. Roberts' last year in office, there was actually more foreign investment in Oregon than in all of China." I'll take that!

More than 180 businesses located or expanded operations in Oregon, including notable high-tech companies. But beyond Oregon's Silicon Forest corridor, we brought new companies to more rural parts of Oregon where there was great need for expanded job opportunities.

Beyond the work and travel I did internationally and nationally to bring new high-quality business enterprises to Oregon, I was exceedingly proud of Oregon's Workforce Quality Council, our successful use of the Strategic Investment Program Reserve for grants and loans, and wise and well-placed decisions for investing Oregon's lottery dollars. We saw real return on our tourism investments, the upgrade to attract greater film and video activity to the state, and the upgrading of Oregon's training and workforce-preparation programs with strong support from Oregon's community colleges.

It is important to remember that all this positive economic change occurred during Oregon's timber/spotted owl crisis. While losing old-growth timber operations and thousands of related jobs, the state also helped timber-dependent communities create jobs in second-growth timber markets and aided new businesses centered around secondary wood products like high-quality hunting arrows and wooden furniture.

Housing starts in 1994 were estimated the highest in fifteen years including thousands of new units of affordable housing under Oregon's new Housing Trust.

I felt satisfied that I had contributed positively to Oregon's economic recovery and growth in my four years.

People

Just briefly, here are some ways that my administration team touched Oregon's people and made their lives better:

The success of Oregon's Housing Trust; the Oregon Health Plan funding and federal waivers that added 120,000 citizens to those covered with health insurance; doubling the state budget for HIV-AIDS; the successful work my administration did on teen-pregnancy prevention; the huge funding increase—nearly double—for state-funded Head Start; my successful commitment with the Progress Board to increase child immunization rates for young children; the defeat of Ballot Measures 9 and 13, two anti-gay measures; increased alcohol and drug and anger-management programs in Oregon's prisons; using education, literacy classes, and training programs to prepare prison inmates for success on the "outside." Adult recidivism dropped every year; we were no longer in the "recycling" business; Oregon's welfare rolls decreased by nineteen thousand through job training, education, and making child care and health coverage part of the package, and 80 percent stayed self-sufficient.

The Environment

Much of this focus has been covered in earlier chapters but just a reminder of the successful highlights I will remember with pride:

My support of the Endangered Species Act and protection of the Northern Spotted Owl under intense public, industry, and political pressure; my work with and strong support for the skilled team moving the federal government toward solutions on forest management and species protection for the spotted owl and salmon species; my successful work to bring eleven miles of the Klamath River into the National Scenic Rivers program; my strong support, both politically and legislatively, of Oregon's statewide land-use program; my joint application with Washington's Governor Mike Lowry to include the Columbia River Estuary in the National Estuary Program; securing inclusion of Tillamook Bay in the National Estuary Program; the successful $10 million budget request for watershed health on the south coast and the Grande Ronde watershed in Eastern Oregon; the December 1992 Coastal Salmon Recovery Conference and the cooperative work that followed that two-day meeting; my work with industry and environmental groups to win legislative adoption of one of the strongest mining laws in the nation; securing state funding to allow Westside light rail construction and the funding to begin preparing for north-south light rail; my last official letter, written just as I left office, was to ask U.S. Senator Mark Hatfield to change his position on the Elk Creek Dam on the Rogue River in southern Oregon and to help secure the federal funds to remove the partially complete, environmentally costly dam.

Government Reinvention

Here again, the previous chapters define much of my work, but I will highlight a few items important to me in those years:

The use of the Oregon Benchmarks for budgeting, prioritizing program work, measuring outcomes, and planning toward the future; the "E for Effort" award from *Financial World Magazine,* and moving Oregon's ranking from number 37 to number 7 in less than two years in that magazine's state efficiency rating; the Conversation with Oregon, a national first and winner of several awards; receiving the Innovations in State and Local Government Award from the Ford Foundation and the Kennedy School of Government at Harvard; being appointed to the National Alliance for Redesigning Government Executive Board; the completion and signing of the Oregon Option agreement between the U.S. government, the state of Oregon, the city of Portland, and Multnomah County; my selection as a fellow of the National Academy for Public Administration.

Other Successes

My appointment of more than fifty judges in a four-year term was the most by an Oregon governor in a four-year term. However, equally as important as the *number* of judges was the diversity among those new appointees—twenty women, five racial minorities, and five openly gay and lesbian members of the bar.

I was blessed with the talent and dedication of an extraordinary staff. They cared about Oregon, about good public policy, about the citizens of our state, and the ethics of good government. The previous pages might be left blank if it were not for their hard work, commitment, innovation, and collaborative work agendas.

This last item is not usually listed as part of a record of accomplishment but it is a success that mattered deeply to me. In my four years as Oregon's governor, there was not *one* ethics shortcoming, not a hint of inappropriate behavior, not a sign of dishonesty or corruption *anywhere* in my administration. I proudly add that to my record.

Notes

The names of the members who served in the Oregon House and Senate between 1971 and 1995, their partisan affiliation, gender, and committee assignments, as well as the identity of the House and Senate leadership, are from the 1971-1995 editions of the Oregon Blue Book, as are all statewide primary and general election results. Unless otherwise noted, the outcomes of measures and legislative races are from the Oregon Secretary of State. All campaign fund totals and contribution amounts for the 1984 Secretary of State and 1990 governor's race are from publicly available financial reports filed with the Oregon Secretary of State.

Information on Oregon House and Senate bill numbers, subject matter, sponsors, date of consideration, floor votes, vetoes, and veto statements are from the legislative record. References to and quotes from committee proceedings are from the committee records housed at the Oregon State Archives. The dates of each legislative session, the total number of bills passed by the Legislature, and the number of bills vetoed by the Governor are from the *Oregon Blue Book*.

In Chapters Twenty through Twenty-Four, unless otherwise noted, all dates and event details are from the Governor's daily calendars located in the gubernatorial records available in the Oregon State Archives.

Introduction
That may explain why I feel: Madeleine Kunin's memoir, *Living a Political Life*, was published in 1994 by Knopf.

Chapter One
The "memo" of the author's personal and political thoughts recorded during Feb 1990 is from the author's personal files.

Chapter Two
The family genealogies are from the author's personal files.

As I think of the adult: The quote from Suzanne Braun Levine was taken from Nancy Hass, "Hey Dads, Thanks for the Love and Support (and the Credit Card)," *The New York Times* (Jun 16, 2002). The quote from Terri Apter was taken from Helen Croydon, "Daddy's Girls," *The Sunday Times*, June 15, 2010.

My father had a good singing voice: "Paper Doll" was performed by the Mills Brothers and released in 1943; "Red Sails in the Sunset" was performed by Guy Lombardo and released in 1935; "Daddy's Little Girl" was performed by the Mills Brothers and released in 1950.

There was a great deal of freedom: "a village to raise a child" is a reference to the book by Hillary Rodham Clinton, *It Takes a Village to Raise a Child*, published by Simon and Schuster in 1996.

Chapter Three
By the time Neal graduated: "Too Young" was performed by Nat King Cole and released in 1951.

Chapter Five
I cannot share this story: Bruno Bettelheim's book, *The Empty Fortress: Infantile Autism and the Birth of the Self*, was published by Free Press in 1967.

I share now that long-ago: Poem is from the author's personal files.

Chapter Six
And then … Frank showed me: "The Impossible Dream (The Quest)" from the musical *Man of LaMancha* was composed by Mitch Leigh with lyrics written by Joe Darion in 1965.

As the legislative agenda: Information on the Women's Rights Coalition was taken from an interview with Gretchen Kafoury conducted by the author.

The Oregon Women's Political Caucus and *As the OWPC became more active*:

Information on the Oregon Women's Political Caucus and Camp Tamarack was taken from interviews with Betty Roberts, Gretchen Kafoury, and Jane Cease conducted by the author.

Chapter Seven
In the spring of 1973: Parkrose School Board election results were verified with the records located at the Multnomah Co. Elections Archive.

Chapter Eight
The ship's log from that trip: The ship's log is from the author's personal files.

Chapter Nine
Information on the date and time of legislative adjournment, comments by Governor Bob Straub, Jason Boe, and Frank Roberts, and the major issues present within the legislative session is from three *Oregonian* articles: Phil Cogswell, "2nd Longest Session Ends; 'Safety Net' Offshoot Okd" (Jul 6, 1977); Stan Federman and Phil Cogswell, "What Legislature Accomplished—And Left Undone" (Jul 6, 1977); and Stan Federman and Phil Cogswell, "What Oregon Legislature Accomplished in this Year's Session" (Jul 7, 1977).

When the 1977 Legislature adjourned: The details of Wally Carson's resignation and replacement were verified with Carson.

Just think how different the state Senate: The lapse in Republican women serving in the Oregon Senate since Dorothy McCullough Lee was verified in the lists of membership available from the Oregon State Archives.

Chapter Ten
Information on the appointment of the Multnomah County Commission seat is from Rod Patterson, "Barbara Roberts Fills Gordon's County Seat," *The Oregonian* (Mar 28, 1978).

Details of the light rail motion are from the meeting minutes available in the Multnomah Co. records.

Yet even the most mundane decisions: The content and date of the vote on the ERA resolution are from

the resolution text available in the Multnomah Co. records. The states that had not ratified the ERA at this time included Alabama, Arizona, Arkansas, Florida, Georgia, Illinois, Louisiana, Mississippi, Missouri, North Carolina, Nevada, Oklahoma, South Carolina, Utah, and Virgina.

The other new Democratic senator: The difficulties in the opening of the 1979 session are chronicled in three *Oregonian* articles entitled "Speaker Selection Unsettled" (Jan 8, 1979), "Attempt to Force Vote Fails; House Still Unorganized" (Jan 10, 1979) and "Democrats Unite, Settle on Myers as House Leader" (Jan 14, 1979).

Other major conflicts included: The summary of the major 1979 legislative session controversies are based upon seven *Oregonian* articles dated Jul 5, 1979: Phil Cogswell, "Squabble Settled; Legislature Closes"; Phil Cogswell, "Tax Relief Plan at Core of Legislative Session"; Julie Tripp, "Service Agencies Face Belt-Tightening Budgets"; Sandra McDonough, "Ten Measures Left to Voters"; Tom Brennan, "Businessmen Satisfied with 1979 Legislature"; Sandra McDonough, "Energy Issues Given Priority"; and Sandra McDonough and Phil Cogswell, "Legislature Hoed Tough Row within Tight Money Frame."

Chapter Eleven
Information on the 1980 Democratic candidates for the Oregon House is from the Oregon Blue Book and the author's personal files.

Since Oregon was one: The others were Alaska, Delaware, Montana, and New Hampshire. From *Significant Features of Fiscal Federalism*, 1987 edition, published by the Advisory Commission on Intergovernmental Relations.

When the rankings came out: The articles quoted regarding the author's performance in the 1981 legislative session are Ronald A. Buel, "The Good, the Bad, and the Awful," *Willamette Week* (Jul 27-Aug 3); Foster

Church and Sandra McDonough, "Lobbyists Rate Gardener, Myers Best Legislators," *The Oregonian* (Sep 27, 1981).

Looking back twenty-five-plus years: Information on the major issues in the 1981 session from the Democratic Caucus' "1981 Legislative Session Highlights Document" from the author's personal files.

The 1981 legislative session: The Oregonian's assessment of the session is from two articles by Sandra McDonough dated Aug 3, 1981: "Woeful Session Not Mourned" and "Legislature Ends Record Session."

The next special session: Information on this session from Foster Church and Leslie L. Zaitz, "Legislature Balances Budget, Adjourns," *The Oregonian* (Mar 2, 1982).

Well – one more time around!: Information on the Sep special legislative session from Leslie L. Zaitz and Foster Church, "Legislature OKs Plan to Assess SAIF Millions," *The Oregonian* (Sep 4, 1982).

Chapter Twelve
Information on the major issues within the 1983 legislative session from the Democratic Caucus' "1983 Legislative Session Highlights Document" from the author's personal files.

We were so busy adding numbers: The OEA endorsement balloting results are from a report in the author's personal files.

Chapter Thirteen
In mid-September: The press referenced regarding the poll release was J. Roy Bardsley, "Survey Finds Roberts Leading Rivals, Rutherford Out Front," *The Oregonian* (Sep 13, 1984); Ron Blakenbaker, "Poll Results on Two Races," *Statesman Journal* (Sep 14, 1984).

The controversy related: Information on the Rajneesh campaign issue was taken from five *Oregonian* articles: "Antelope Plans Vote to Kill City" (Mar 11, 1982); Foster Church, "Atiyeh

Picks Antelopers over Interlopers" (Mar 13, 1982); Jeanie Senior, "Antelope Awaits Its Fate as Faithful, Fearful Flock to Ballot Box" (Apr 15, 1982); Jeanie Senior, "Guru Followers Win Battle for Antelope" (Apr 16, 1982); Tom Stimmel, "Antelope Losing Fight with Rajneeshees" (Nov 14, 1982); "Roberts for Secretary of State" (Oct 21, 1984).

I was excited to be selected as a delegate: Information on Convention and the author's speech is from the Official Proceedings of the 1984 Democratic National Convention.

We were checking: The Secretary of State endorsement editorials dated Oct 25, 1984, were "Roberts as Secretary of State" (*Statesman Journal*), "Put Roberts in Number 2 Office" (*Corvallis Gazette-Times*), and "Rep. Barbara Roberts is Tops for Secretary of State" (*Eastern Oregonian*). A full list of newspaper endorsements is available in the Barbara Roberts Papers, Special Collections, Portland State University Library.

Chapter Fourteen
Today, I am still involved: The Portland Gay Men's Chorus program entitled "Brave Souls and Dreamers" was first performed on Jun 16, 2007.

As a fourth-generation Oregonian: Quotes from speech at the swearing-in ceremony are from the author's personal files.

With the ceremonial aspect of my new role: The requirement that the Secretary of State reside in the same county at the state Capitol building was from Section 5 Article VI of the Oregon Constitution. Information on the passage and voter confirmation of the constitutional amendment is from the 1985 legislative record and the Oregon Blue Book.

An Archives Building for Oregon: The speech announcing the intention of building a new Archives Building is from the author's personal files. The funding requests from the Department of General Services are from the Secretary of State files located in the Oregon State Archive. The amount of funds approved by the Legislature is from the 1987 legislative record. Additional information from Michele Matassa, "Archives Gets North Mall Site," *Statesman Journal* (Jun 11, 1988); Janet Davies, "Oregon History Will Have Home in New Archives," *Statesman Journal* (May 3, 1990); Nancy McCarthy, "State's Public Records from 1833 to Present Moved to New Home," *The Oregonian* (Dec 10, 1991); David Steves, "Archives a Showcase, Official Says," *Statesman Journal* (Jan 18, 1992).

Performance Auditing: The official letter regarding the performance audits and the press release regarding the veto of the performance audit legislation is from the Secretary of State files located in the Oregon State Archive. *The Oregonian* editorial regarding the performance audit veto override was "No Partisan Performance" (Jan 19, 1987). Information regarding the two pilot performance audits was based upon research done by former Deputy Secretary of State Marilynne Keyser.

Patricia McCaig took on: Information on the fine from Jeff Mapes, "State Hits Demos with Fines," *The Oregonian* (Dec 6, 1989).

A New State Motto: Information on the history of the Oregon motto before 1987 from an Oregon State Legislature publication entitled "State Motto Timeline."

Oregon had one of the most expensive: The report from the Governor's Policy Advisory Group on Workers' Compensation and the letter from Governor Goldschmidt are from the author's personal files. Further information from Michele Matassa, "Workers' Comp Plan Unveiled," *Statesman Journal* (Apr 4, 1987).

The second obligation I assumed: The speech given at the Hanford Waste Board meeting on May 2, 1988 is from the author's personal files. Additional information from Wanda Briggs, "WNP-1 Supporters Dominate Hearing," *Tri-City Herald*; Janet

Goetze, "Witnesses Urge Cleanup of Hanford Weapons Waste," *The Oregonian* (Dec 7, 1988).

You've certainly heard reference: Information on the number of women holding statewide elective office in 1985 is from the Center for American Women and Politics of Rutgers University. Information on the number of female United States senators and congresswomen is from the same source: "Women in the U.S. Congress 1917-2007" and "Women in the U.S. Senate 1922-2007."

Most of America's secretaries of state: Information on the responsibilities held by secretaries of state and lieutenant governors is from National Association of the Secretaries of State and the National Lieutenant Governors Association. Information on previous public offices held by governors is from two publications by the National Lieutenant Governors Association: "Analysis: Governors and Past Elected Offices (1980-2006)," (Dec 5, 2006) and "Analysis: Governors Who Once Served as Lieutenant Governor (1980-2006)," (Jun 28, 2006).

Chapter Sixteen
Information on the Goldschmidt resignation and sex scandal is from Jeff Mapes, "Governor Won't Run Again; Roberts Likely Candidate," *The Oregonian* (Feb 8, 1990); Harry Estive and Gail Kinsey Hill, "Goldschmidt Confesses to '70s Affair with Girl, 14," *The Oregonian* (May 7, 2004); and David Steves, "Former Governor Goldschmidt's Teen-Sex Confession Jars Oregon," *Register Guard* (May 10, 2004).

I began, "Today, I am announcing: The text of the author's statement announcing her gubernatorial candidacy is from the author's personal files.

Twenty-four hours later: Information on the author's announcement of her gubernatorial candidacy is from five *Oregonian* articles: Alan K. Ota, "Pullout Leaves Demos Shocked,

Republicans Surprised" (Feb 8, 1990);
Kathleen Monje, "Frohnmayer Says
Edge in Race Isn't Automatic" (Feb 9,
1990); Barnes C. Ellis, "Roberts Runs
for Governor" (Feb 9, 1990); Barnes
C. Ellis, "Democratic Candidate
for Governor Reports Donations
Pouring In" (Feb 10, 1990); and Jeff
Mapes, "Goldschmidt Offers Refunds;
Hatfield Endorses Frohnmayer" (Feb
13, 1990).

On filing day in March: The Oregonian
article naming Frank Roberts the
most diligent senator was Wayne
Thompson, "Session Produced Some
New Stars" (Jul 5, 1989).

U.S. Senator Bob Packwood became:
Information on the timber rally from
Rick Bella, Dave Hogan, and Don
Hamilton, "Timber Rally Leads to a
Truck-Drivin' Log Jam for Traffic,"
The Oregonian (Apr 14, 1990); Jeff
Mapes, "Protest Draws Thousands,"
The Oregonian (Apr 14, 1990).

I attempted to set a historical: The
text of the timber policy presentation
is from the author's personal files.
Additional information is from two
Oregonian articles by Jeff Mapes:
"Candidates' Tacks Differ on Owl
Crisis" (Apr 6, 1990) and "Owl
Issue Could Have Big Impact on
Governor's Race" (Apr 8, 1990).

A few days before the primary election:
The Oregonian story on fundraising
totals was "Frohnmayer Leads
Fundraising Race" by Jeff Mapes
(May 11, 1990).

It was way more than apparent:
The Oregonian story on the timber
controversy was Jeff Mapes, "Roberts
Calls for a Timber Tax Boost to Help
Oregon's Mills, Workers" (Jun 21,
1990).

In late July Dave and I were invited:
Information on the ONPA debate is
from four *Oregonian* articles by Jeff
Mapes: "Candidates Step Up Pace
of Gubernatorial Campaign" (Jul
20, 1990), "Roberts, Frohnmayer
Battle in First Debate" (Jul 22, 1990),
"Gubernatorial Debate on Nuclear
Plant Nears Meltdown Heat" (Jul
26, 1990), and "Trojan Nuclear Plant

Made Factor in Political Race" (Jul 29,
1990). Additional information from
Rick Attig, "Roberts Endorses Trojan
Closure," *The Bulletin* (Jul 22, 1990);
"Roberts, Frohnmayer Differ in the
First Debate," *The Daily Courier* (Jul
23, 1990); "Roberts and Frohnmayer
Debate Issues," *Weekly Reminder*
(Jul 26). The follow-up speech (in
Springfield) is from the author's
personal files.

Then in early summer: Information
on the nomination process for
nonpartisan or minor party
candidates is from the 1989 edition
of the Oregon Secretary of State
Elections Manual, Sections 249.732
and 249.735.

Over the last weekend of June:
Information on NOW's 1990
convention from Jane Gross, "At
NOW Convention, Goal Is Putting
More Women in Office," *New York
Times* (Jul 1, 1990); Diane Mason,
"Surge in NOW Membership May
Spur Bold New Political Course," *St.
Petersburg Times* (Jun 29, 1990); Diane
Mason, "Women's Role in Politics
Highlighted at NOW Convention," *St.
Petersburg Times* (Jun 30, 1990); Diane
Mason, "NOW Delegates Promoting
Idea of Third Political Party," *St.
Petersburg Times* (Jul 1, 1990).

In July my campaign people: Dave
Frohnmayer's comment regarding
the debate schedule from Steve Duin,
"At Least One of Her Dreams May
Come True," *The Oregonian* (Jul 17,
1990). Quote from Patricia McCaig
regarding Dave Frohnmayer's
leadership is from Jeff Mapes,
"Candidates Step Up the Pace of
the Gubernatorial Campaign," *The
Oregonian* (Jul 20, 1990). Quotes
from the Visitors Association speech
from Jeff Mapes, "Roberts Raps
Frohnmayer on Crime," *The Oregonian*
(Jul 13, 1990).

Chapter Seventeen
*In the summer of 1990: The Good, the
Bad and the Ugly* was directed by
Sergio Leone and released in 1966.

Then on top of the ongoing:
Information on the Salt Cave

hydroelectric dam is from a speech in the author's personal files and Gail Kinsey Hill, "Key Decisions Could Make or Break Salt Caves Plan," *The Oregonian* (Aug 22, 1990).

On the timber front: Information on the national trade bill is from Alan K. Ota, "Senate OKs Log Export Ban in NW," *The Oregonian* (Aug 2, 1990); Alan K. Ota, "House Sends Log Export Ban to Bush," *The Oregonian* (Aug 4, 1990).

The next good news: The Oregonian article on the poll was "Poll Shows Frohnmayer Lead Shrinks," by Jeff Mapes (Sep 2, 1990).

I began preparing for the first: Information on the first debate from Jeff Mapes, "Eugene Debate Will Preview Oregon Governor's Race," *The Oregonian* (Sep 12, 1990); Jeff Mapes, "Debate Spotlights Four Candidates for Governor," *The Oregonian* (Sep 13, 1990); Shawn Wirtz, "Candidates Aim at Frohnmayer," *Statesman Journal* (Sep 13, 1990); "Round 1: Roberts," *Eugene Register-Guard* (Sep 13, 1990).

I also received the overwhelming political endorsement: Information on the Oregon Public Employees Union endorsement from a press release in the author's personal files.

With Frank clearly on the mend: Information on the Oregon District Attorneys Association endorsement is from Jeff Mapes, "Frohnmayer Receives Endorsement of DAs," *The Oregonian* (Aug 23, 1990).

That day, I received: Information on the endorsements by the Oregon Women's Political Caucus, the Black Leadership Conference, and the Rainbow Coalition from Chuck Westerlund, "Political Endorsements Come Rolling In," Corvallis *Gazette-Times* (Oct 13, 1990); "Rainbow Coalition, Other Groups Forecast Voting Intentions," *Skanner* (Oct 17, 1990).

Also, just to make certain: Information on the IBEW endorsement from Jeff Mapes and Dan Hortsch, "Union Stung by Roberts, Switches to

Frohnmayer," *The Oregonian* (Oct 31, 1990).

Our next debater: Information and quotes on the second debate from Dan Hortsch and Jeff Mapes, "Sparks Fly in Governor Debate," *The Oregonian* (Oct 1, 1990); "Gubernatorial Debate," *The Oregonian* (Oct 1, 1990); "Spending, Crime Top Debate Issues," *Daily Astorian* (Oct 1, 1990); Brad Cain, "Frohnmayer, Roberts Spar on Spending," *Gazette-Times* (Oct 1, 1990); "Gubernatorial Candidates Trade Blows," *News-Times* (Oct 3, 1990).

Three days later I received: The Oregonian story on the October governor's race poll was "Roberts, Lonsdale Close Gaps" by Jeff Mapes (Oct 4, 1990).

So I headed to Pendleton: Information and quotes on this debate from Jeff Mapes and Dan Hortsch, "Frohnmayer, Roberts Spar Over Spending," *The Oregonian* (Oct 5, 1990); "Pendleton Debate Helps Roberts," *East Oregonian* (Oct 8, 1990); "Candidates Trade more Jabs in Pendleton Event," *World* (Oct 5, 1990); "Frohnmayer, Roberts Wrangle in Third Debate," *Gazette-Times* (Oct 5, 1990).

The day after the Pendleton debate: Information and quotes from the Portland City Club speech from Dan Hortsch, "Roberts Tells City Club She Never Will Take Oregonians For Granted," *The Oregonian* (Oct 6, 1990); Shawn Wirtz, "Roberts Solos at Portland City Club," *Statesman Journal* (Oct 6, 1990).

With my ever-improving polling: Information on fundraising sources is from Jeff Mapes, "Roberts Emerges as Top Fund-Raiser Since June 5," *The Oregonian* (Oct 9, 1990).

Perhaps the place for me to prove: Information and quotes from the fourth debate from Andrew LaMar, "Another One-on-One? It's Debatable," *The Daily Tidings* (Oct 10, 1990); Jeff Mapes, "Frohnmayer Wants to Debate One More Time," *The Oregonian* (Oct 10, 1990).

The statewide Oregon Voters'
Pamphlet: Information and quotes
from the editorial endorsements from
"Roberts Offers Oregon Sense of
Leadership," Dalles Chronicle (Oct 14,
1990); "The Race for Governor," Daily
Astorian (Oct 19, 1990); "Frohnmayer
Gets Nod in Gubernatorial race,"
Keizer Times (Oct 18, 1990); "Barbara
Roberts," Willamette Week (Oct 25,
1990); "Barbara Roberts for Governor"
(Oct 24, 1990); "Frohnmayer Will
Be a Better Governor," Graphic
(Oct 24, 1990); "Frohnmayer for
Governor," The Bulletin (Oct 25, 1990);
"Elect Barbara Roberts Oregon's
34th Governor," The Oregonian
(Oct 28, 1990); "Elect Barbara
Roberts Governor of Oregon," East
Oregonian (Oct 29, 1990); "Governor:
Frohnmayer," Register-Guard (Oct 30,
1990); "Frohnmayer for Governor,"
Democrat-Herald (Nov 1, 1990),
"Frohnmayer Is Best for Eastern
Oregon" Daily Argus Observer (Nov
1, 1990); "Give Frohnmayer Nod,"
Observer (Nov 1, 1990); "Frohnmayer
Would Serve Oregon Best," Daily
Courier (Nov 1, 1990); "Frohnmayer
Offers Best Hope in Governor's
Race," Herald and News (Nov 2, 1990).

All four candidates: Information and
quotes from the fifth debate from Jeff
Mapes, "Frohnmayer Agrees to Four-
Way Debate," The Oregonian (Oct 13,
1990); Jeff Mapes, "Heated Words Fly
at Debate," The Oregonian (Oct 24,
1990).

Of the eleven statewide measures:
Information on the 1990 statewide
ballot measures from Gail Kinsey
Hall, "Statewide Ballot Measures,"
The Oregonian (Nov 2, 1990);
"Statewide Measures Offer Tough
Choices," The Oregonian (Nov 4, 1990).
The Sunday editorial was entitled
"Oregon's Next Governor: Measure
5," The Oregonian (Oct 28, 1990).

The last week before the election:
Information on the final week of the
gubernatorial campaign from Gerald
Erichsen, "Union Chief Heads State
Sign Effort," The Dalles Chronicle
(Oct 17, 1990); Jeff Mapes and Joan

Laatz, "Frohnmayer Reaches for
Mobley Votes," The Oregonian (Oct
31, 1990); Dan Hortsch, "Roberts,
Frohnmayer Strike Familiar Themes,"
The Oregonian (Oct 31, 1990); "Poll
Gives Roberts Edge in Governor's
Race," Mail Tribune (Nov 1, 1990);
Shawn Wirtz, "Roberts Claims
Momentum in Her Favor," Statesman
Journal (Nov 2, 1990); Shawn Wirtz,
"Roberts, Frohnmayer Keep Busy
Campaigning," The Statesman Journal
(Nov 3, 1990); Jeff Mapes, "Hopefuls
Approach Finish Line," The Oregonian
(Nov 3, 1990); Jeff Mapes, Dan
Hortsch, "Frohnmayer Disputes
Roberts Ad," The Oregonian (Nov 4,
1990); Jeff Mapes and Dan Hortsch
"Governor's Race Now a Sprint,"
The Oregonian (Nov 5, 1990); Pat
Knight "Ad Gaffe Causes Campaign
Chagrin," The Oregonian (Nov 6,
1990); Jeff Mapes, "Roberts Ends on
Confident Note," The Oregonian (Nov
6, 1990).

Chapter Eighteen
The county-by-county: Information
on the 1990 election results is
from Rick Bella, "Republicans Eye
House Speakership, Await Tallies,"
The Oregonian (Nov 7, 1990); Jeff
Mapes, "Voters Put Their Faith in
Roberts," The Oregonian Nov 7,
1990); Holly Gilbert, "Voters Make
Choice: Abortion Remains Legal
in Oregon," The Oregonian (Nov 7,
1990); Janet Goetze, "Measure 4 Goes
Down: Trojan Will Remain Open,"
The Oregonian (Nov 7, 1990); Don
Hamilton, "Tough Campaign for
Senate Turns into an Easy Victory,"
The Oregonian (Nov 7, 1990); Cathy
Kyomura, "Most Oregon Incumbents
Keep Congressional Posts," The
Oregonian (Nov 7, 1990); Jeff Mapes,
"State May Face Gridlock in
Government," The Oregonian (Nov 7,
1990); Christopher Connell, "Women,
Blacks Score Notable Gains, Losses,"
The Oregonian (Nov 7, 1990); Maralee
Schwarts, "Women Hold Their Own
in Quest for State and Congressional
Posts," The Washington Post (Nov

8, 1990); Joan Laatz, "Dim Future
Predicted for Measure 7's 'Workfare'
Project," *The Oregonian* (Nov 9, 1990).

Then I stepped to the podium: Quotes
from the author's victory speech are
from author's personal files.

Once I stepped: Information on the
1990 gubernatorial race outcome from
Shawn Wirtz, "Roberts Claims Victory
in Gubernatorial Race," *The Oregonian*
(Nov 7, 1990); "Roberts Takes
Charge," *Mail Tribune* (Nov 7, 1990).

Before lunch I had made: Information
on the gubernatorial transition is from
Dan Hortsch, "Roberts Transition
Team Hones Axes," *The Oregonian*
(Nov 18, 1990).

Chapter Nineteen

On Monday, November 12: Quote
by Governor Bob Straub from
"Bob Straub, A Personal Portrait,"
television interview with Ted Bryant,
KATU Channel 2 News, Portland,
Oregon (Jan 6, 1979)

*Appearing early in the "delegation"
column*: Information regarding
the members, structure, and
recommendations of the Transition
Team are from the gubernatorial
records available at the Oregon State
Archives.

While these dozens: Information
on staffing changes in this and
subsequent paragraphs is from Dan
Hortsch, "Roberts to Retain Key
Official Fred Miller," *The Oregonian*
(Nov 14, 1990); Dan Hortsch, "Roberts
Appoints Campaign Director to be
Chief of Staff," *The Oregonian* (Dec
8, 1990); Gail Kinsey Hill, "Budget
Official Joins Insurance Agency," *The
Oregonian* (Dec 11, 1990),

With my Transition Team:
Information on the National
Governors Association New
Governors' Seminar is from the
program summary available in the
gubernatorial records at the Oregon
State Archives.

By the time I had digested the last part:
"(Get Your Kicks On) Route 66" was
performed by Nat King Cole and

released in 1946.

On December 24, I finally announced:
Information on the appointment of
Phil Keisling as Secretary of State
is from Holly Danks, "Roberts
Sets Date to Name Successor," *The
Oregonian* (Nov 8, 1990); Jonathan
Nicholas, "Candidates Kept on Pins
and Needles," *The Oregonian* (Nov
19, 1990); "Roberts to Delay Naming
Successor," *The Oregonian* (Dec 5,
1990); Don Hamilton, "Roberts
Appoints Secretary of State," *The
Oregonian* (Dec 25, 1990).

As I contemplated these cuts:
Information on other tax limitation
measures from "Massachusetts Voters
Cut Taxes as 42 States Decide Ballot
Issues," *The New York Times* (Nov
6, 1980); Laurent Belsie, "State Stirs
Up Embers of Tax Revolt," *Christian
Science Monitor* (Sep 28, 1989).

Every state agency: Poll on the
solution to Oregon's revenue crisis
was from *Oregonian* article, "Survey:
Oregonians Want Government to
Reduce" (Dec 16, 1990).

Since the passage of Measure 5:
Information on the aftermath of
Measure 5, projected budget cuts,
and the Sagebrush Coalition meeting
in this and subsequent paragraphs
from Jeff Mapes, "Roberts Girds for
Economic Battle," *The Oregonian* (Nov
11, 1990); Dan Hortsch, "Roberts'
Transition Team Hones Axes" (Nov
18, 1990); Robert E. Shotwell, "Roberts
to Meet with E. Oregon Coalition,"
The Oregonian (Jan 9, 1991); Rick Attig,
"1,000 Rally to Protest Measure 5's
Pain," *The Bulletin* (Jan 11, 1991); Gail
Kinsey Hill, "Roberts Outlines Plan
for Cuts in Spending," *The Oregonian*
(Jan 11, 1991); Jeff Mapes, "Roberts
Tries to Offer Fair Budget for All
State Services," *The Oregonian* (Jan 12,
1991).

*In the midst of all this December
budgeting*: The *Oregonian* article on the
projected job performance poll was
"Roberts Gains 60 Approval Rating"
by Jeff Mapes (Dec 9, 1990).

When my alarm rang: Information

on the inauguration is from the 1991 House Legislative Journal and the inauguration program from the gubernatorial records available at the Oregon State Archive. Additional information from Shawn Wirtz, "Roberts Looks Ahead," *Statesman Journal* (Jan 15, 1991); David Steves, "Lawmakers Convene in Harmony," *Statesman Journal* (Jan 15, 1991); Gail Kinsey Hill, "Inauguration Comes off Without the Frills," *The Oregonian* (Jan 15, 1991).

Chapter Twenty

On my first official morning in the office: Information on staffing and appointments in this and subsequent paragraphs from "Roberts Adds Pai, 2 Others to Staff," *The Oregonian* (Jan 19, 1991); Judy Rooks, "State Selects Development Director," *The Oregonian* (Jan 19, 1991); and from the gubernatorial records available at the Oregon State Archives.

Several years later: Quote from Ron Heifetz is from page 127 of *Leadership without Easy Answers*, published by Harvard University Press in 1998. Quotes from Ron Heifetz and Marty Linsky are from pages 11, 12, 14, 15, and 20 of their book *Leadership on the Line: Staying Alive Through the Dangers of Leading*, published by Harvard University Press in 2002.

Sarah Johnson took on: The "Citizens' Representative Office Report for the Administration of Governor Barbara Roberts: 1991-1994" by Sarah Johnson from the gubernatorial records available at the Oregon State Archives.

On May 16 I announced the formation: Comments from the announcement of the Governor's Task Force to Improve State Government and group membership from Dan Hortsch, "Roberts Orders Panel to Streamline State Government," *The Oregonian* (May 17, 1991).

The 1991 session produced several very successful: Additional information on the legislative session from David Steves, "Little Tax Changes Add up

for State," *Statesman Journal* (Jul 2, 1991); "Session Gets High Marks," *Statesman Journal* (Jul 2, 1991); Scott McFetridge, "Lawmakers Kill Most Bills Along the Way," *Statesman Journal* (Jul 2, 1991); "Highlights of the 1991 Legislative Session," *Statesman Journal* (Jul 2, 1991). The *Oregonian* article on the governor's legislative accomplishments was "Change Characterizes 66th Session" by Jeff Mapes (Jul 1, 1991).

My WQC legislation: Speech on the Workforce Quality Council from the author's personal files.

In July of 1991, I began including: The speech on the Conversation with Oregon and information on program participation, organizational structure, and outcomes in this and subsequent paragraphs from the gubernatorial records available at the Oregon State Archives. Further information from "Citizen Participation in Policy Formation: A Review of Governor Roberts' Conversation with Oregon" by Edward C. Weeks, Margaret Hallock, James B. Lemert and Bruce McKinlay (1992). The quote from Carolyn J. Lukensmeyer is taken from correspondence from the author's personal files.

Our week in Japan: Comments regarding the trip to Japan that were published by the Oregon Economic Development Department are from the gubernatorial records available at the Oregon State Archives.

Chapter Twenty-one

On October 17, Attorney General: Information on the retirement of Dave Frohnmayer and the appointment of Charles Crookham from Jeff Mapes, "Frohnmayer Takes UO Job," *The Oregonian* (Oct 18, 1991); Nancy McCarthy, "Crookham Appointed Attorney General," *The Oregonian* (Nov 28, 1991).

After a year of being Governor: The 1992 State of the State address from gubernatorial records available at the Oregon State Archives. Additional information from Gail Kinsey Hill and Dan Hortsch, "Roberts Vows Dramatic Cuts," *The Oregonian* (Jan 24, 1992); Gail Kinsey Hill, "Department Heads Learn How the Eventual Reduction of 4,000 Positions Will Affect Their Domains, and They See Rough Times Ahead," *The Oregonian* (Jan 25, 1992); Dan Hortsch, "Roberts Lays Next Cards on the Table," *The Oregonian* (Jan 26, 1992); Brent Walth, "Governor: State to Cut 4,000 Jobs," *Register-Guard* (Jan 24, 1992); "Roberts Rules," *The Daily Astorian* (Jan 27, 1992); "Roberts: Offending the Few for the Many," *East Oregonian* (Jan 24, 1992).

Early in the New Year: Information on the departure of Fred Pearce and the appointment of Frank Hall in this and subsequent paragraphs from Nancy McCarthy, "Pearce to Retire as Oregon Corrections Chief April 1," *The Oregonian* (Jan 8, 1992); Gail Kinsey Hill, "Acting Corrections Chief Named," *The Oregonian* (Mar 27, 1992); Phil Manzano, "Governor Appoints Corrections Chief," *The Oregonian* (May 19, 1992).

An ongoing challenge: Information on the first recall from Gail Kinsey Hill, "Roberts Recall Campaign Widens," *The Oregonian* (Mar 12, 1992); "Recall No Answer," *The Oregonian* (Mar 15, 1992); Harry Bodine, "Recall Campaign Opens Office," *The Oregonian* (Mar 31, 1992); Dan Hortsch, "Drive Draws in Signatures on Petition to Recall Roberts," *The Oregonian* (Apr 5, 1992); Dan Hortsch, "Recall Supporters Blame Roberts for All Problems," *The Oregonian* (Apr 12, 1992); "Roberts Recall Petitioners Say Drive for Signatures at Three-Fourths Mark," *The Oregonian* (Apr 14, 1992); Gail Kinsey Hill, "Roberts Recall Drive Points to Angry Electorate," *The Oregonian* (May 4, 1992); Gail Kinsey Hill, "Roberts Recall Drive Falls Short," *The Oregonian* (May 9, 1992). Information on the second recall from Nancy McCarthy, "Foe of Governor Launches Second Recall Attempt," *The Oregonian* (May 22, 1992); "Reject the

Recall," *The Oregonian* (May 31, 1992); Jeff Mapes, "Roberts Seeks Money to Fend off Recall," *The Oregonian* (Jun 11, 1992); Nancy McCarthy, "Roberts Recall Effort Gains Ally," *The Oregonian* (Jul 10, 1992); Nancy McCarthy, "OCA Joins Recall Effort," *The Oregonian* (Jul 11, 1992); "Recall Committee Disavows Help of OCA," *The Oregonian* (Jul 28, 1992); Anastasia Athon, "Second Effort to Recall Roberts Fails," *Statesman Journal* (Aug 21, 1992); Gail Kinsey Hill, "Recall Redux: Signature Effort Comes Up Short," *The Oregonian* (Aug 21, 1992). Information on the third recall from "Roberts Recall Backer Wants to Try it Again," *The Oregonian* (Sep 1, 1992); Nancy McCarthy, "Recall Roberts Campaign Backed by Timber Money," *The Oregonian* (Sep 2, 1992); Gail Kinsey Hill, "Roberts' Appeal for Help in Recall Fight Nets $45,000," *The Oregonian* (Sep 12, 1992); "Latest Effort to Recall Roberts Falls Short of Required Signatures," *The Oregonian* (Oct 14, 1993); "Third Roberts Recall Drive Fails," *Statesman Journal* (Oct 14, 1993).

The city of Woodburn: Information on farmworker housing development in Woodburn in this and subsequent paragraphs from Nikki DeBuse, "Migrant Housing Addressed, Agencies Rally, Form Nonprofit Corporation," *The Independent* (Feb 20, 1991); Cheryl Martins, "Woodburn Approves Farm-Worker Housing Development," *The Oregonian* (Aug 31, 1992); LeAnn Hamnik, "Governor Pays Visit to Nuevo Amanacer Site," *The Independent* (Dec 12, 1992). The letter from Larry Kleinman and the August 2009 rededication speech are from the author's personal files.

The race that was garnering much of the press: Information on the 1992 primary election from Jeff Mapes, "Packwood Wins Easily But Light Voter Turnout May Be a Major Factor in Several Tightly Contested Races Around the State," *The Oregonian* (May 20, 1992); Don Hamilton, "Keisling's Uphill Battle Overwhelms

Experienced Foe," *The Oregonian* (May 21, 1992); Bill MacKenzie, "Furse, Meeker Take Big Leads," *The Oregonian* (May 20, 1992); Gail Kinsey Hill, "Kulongoski, Rodeman to Face off in November," *The Oregonian* (May 21, 1992).

I spent more and more: Information on the 1992 tax-reform proposal and the special legislative session in this and subsequent paragraphs from the legislative record. Additional information from David Steves, "Tax Session Begins Today," *Statesman Journal* (Jul 1, 1992); Scott McFetredge and David Steves, "Even Democrats Show Little Enthusiasm for Helping Gov. Roberts Marshal Support," *Statesman Journal* (Jul 1, 1992); David Steves, "Roberts Stumps for Tax Vote," *Statesman Journal* (Jul 1, 1992); Gail Kinsey Hill, "Tax Package Front and Center," *The Oregonian* (Jul 1, 1990); Nancy McCarthy, "Governor Bends Ears for Tax Plan Before Loss," *The Oregonian* (Jul 2, 1992); Gail Kinsey Hill, "Tax Plan Cast Adrift," *The Oregonian* (Jul 2, 1992); Anastasia Athon, "Governor Rides Emotional Roller Coaster," *Statesman Journal* (Jul 2, 1992); Dan Hortsch, "Lack of Date Turns Tax Plan Into Wallflower," *The Oregonian* (Jul 3, 1992); Gail Kinsey Hill, "Tax Ball Rolls to Legislators' Court," *The Oregonian* (Jul 3, 1992); Scott McFetridge, "Round 2 Begins in Tax Battle," *Statesman Journal* (Jul 3, 1992); Scott McFetridge, "Gov. Roberts Firm on Vote," *Statesman Journal* (Jul 3, 1992); Scott McFetridge, "Lawmakers Give Up," *Statesman Journal* (Jul 4, 1992); Jeff Mapes, "House Rejects Try to Revive Tax Plan," *The Oregonian* (Jul 4, 1992).

On July 11, I arrived in New York City: Information on the Convention and the author's remarks from the Official Proceedings of the 2008 Democratic National Convention.

The governor's role of appointing judges: Information on judicial appointments and the gender breakdown of the members of the Oregon Supreme Court, the Court of Appeals, and the lower courts from the Oregon Blue Book.

After Frank and I moved: Information on the installation of the elevator in the Mahonia Hall from the gubernatorial records located at the Oregon State Archives.

In the last weeks of October: Information on the 1992 Packwood/AuCoin race from "Packwood Played Rough from Start," *The Oregonian* (Nov 5, 1992). Press coverage of the Packwood sexual harassment allegations from Florence Graves and Charles E. Shepard, "Packwood Accused of Sexual Advances; Alleged Behavior Pattern Counters Image," *The Washington Post* (Nov 22, 1992); "Senator Is Accused by Several Women of Sexual Advances," *The New York Times* (Nov 22, 1992); Dee Lane and Bobbie Ulrich, "Woman Told on Senator But Was Not Believed," *The Oregonian* (Nov 23, 1992); Jeff Mapes, "Packwood's Career in Question," *The Oregonian* (Nov 23, 1992); Steve Duin, "The Tip of a Dirty, Little Iceberg," *The Oregonian* (Mar 8, 1992); Foster Church, "Packwood Story Hunt Lacked Follow-Through," *The Oregonian* (Dec 1, 1992).

There was, however: Information on the results of the 1992 Oregon election from Sura Rubenstein, "Measure 9 Goes Down to Defeat by Wide Margin," *The Oregonian* (Nov 4, 1992); Dan Hortsch, "GOP Head Toward Gain in State Senate," *The Oregonian* (Nov 4, 1992); Nancy McCarthy, "Incumbent Keisling Keeps Seat," *The Oregonian* (Nov 4, 1992); Bill Graves, "Ted Kulongoski Wins Attorney General Race," *The Oregonian* (Nov 4, 1992).

When the July 1992 special session failed: Information on the content of the Oregon Benchmarks from the 1991, 1993, and 1995 editions of report from the Oregon Progress Board to the Oregon Legislature entitled "Oregon Benchmarks, Standards for Measuring Statewide Progress and

Institutional Performance."

With the early budget preparation: Information on the resignation of Fred Miller from Nancy McCarthy, "Miller Plans to Depart State Post," *The Oregonian* (Sep 15, 1992).

On December 1, 1992: Information on the 1993 Governor's budget from Gail Kinsey Hill, "Budget Proposal Spells Out Cuts, Some New Taxes," *The Oregonian* (Dec 2, 1992) and the gubernatorial records located at the Oregon State Archives.

The Legislature convened: The 1993 State of the State is from the Governor's speech files located at the Oregon State Archives.

In a conference call on March 19: Information on the granting of the federal waiver for the Oregon Health Plan from Alan K. Ota, "Oregon Health Plan Approved," *The Oregonian* (Mar 20, 1993); "Oregon Victorious," *San Francisco Chronicle* (Mar 29, 1003); "Oregon to Ration Medical Services," *St. Louis Post-Dispatch* (Mar 20, 1993); Robert Pear, "U.S. Backs Oregon's Health Plan for Covering All Poor People," *The New York Times* (Mar 20, 1993).

In the early morning of March 25: Information on the Salem earthquake from Diana Elliott, "Shaking up Oregon: Earth Quake Damage Assessments Could Take Weeks," *The Statesman Journal* (Mar 26, 1993); Bill MacKenzie and Cathy Kiyomura, "Quake Cracks Capitol Rotunda; Doors Closed," *The Oregonian* (Mar 26, 1993); John Snell, "Aftershocks Roll and Damage Mounts," *The Oregonian* (Mar 27, 1993); Cathy Kiyomura, "Roberts to Use Damage Estimates to Seek Federal Disaster Help," *The Oregonian* (Apr 2, 1993).

Less than a week following: Information on the Clinton administration forest conference from Tom Kenworthy, "The Owl and the Lumberjack: Can Clinton Break the Logjam?," *The Washington Post* (Apr 2, 1993); Timothy Egan, "Thunder of Debate on Owls and Jobs Rings in Forests as Opponents Face off," *The New York Times* (Apr 2, 1993); Katie Durbin, "President Aims High for Forest Solution," *The Oregonian* (Apr 4, 1993).

Through 1992 and 1993: Information on the legal issues surrounding the spotted owl from Roberta Ulrich, "Lujan Convenes the 'God Squad' on Timber Sales," *The Oregonian* (Oct 2, 1991); Katie Durbin, "Court Backs Timber Sale Ban," *The Oregonian* (Dec 24, 1991); Katie Durbin, "Governor Voices State's Opposition to BLM Exemption," *The Oregonian* (Feb 19, 1992); "Peddling Illusion," *The Daily Astorian* (Feb 27, 1992); Katie Durbin, "Judge Extends Administration's NW Forest Plan Deadline by 90 Days," *The Oregonian* (Nov 12, 1993); Katie Durbin, "Forests: New Plan, Old Fight," *The Oregonian* (Feb 24, 1994); "Roberts not the Culprit," *The Oregonian* (Feb 29,1992).

Chapter Twenty-two

As the 4th of July weekend: Comments from Republican state legislators regarding the Clinton Forest Plan from Cathy Kiyomura and Bill MacKenzie, "Roberts Says Change Coming; Republicans Rip Plan," *The Oregonian* (Jul 2, 1993).

I took special pleasure: Information on the implementation of the Oregon Health Plan in this and subsequent paragraphs from David Steves, "Session Grinds to an End," *Statesman Journal* (Aug 5, 1993); Diane Dietz, "Deal Gives New Life to Health Plan," *Statesman Journal* (Aug 5, 1993); Dan Hortsch, "1993 Legislature Going, Going, Going…," *The Oregonian* (Aug 5, 1993); Diane Dietz, "Health Reform Effort Is Blueprint for Brawling," *The Statesman-Journal* (Aug 6, 1993); Diane Dietz, "A Guide to Understanding How Oregon Health Plan Works," *Statesman Journal* (Aug 6, 1993); Bill MacKenzie, "Most of Oregon's Poor Will Get Health Care," *The Oregonian* (Aug 6, 1993).

The session ended: Information on the end and accomplishments of the 1993 legislative session from,

"Key Accomplishments of the 1993 Legislature," *Statesman Journal* (Aug 6, 1993); "A Successful Session," *The Oregonian* (Aug 6, 1993); Cathy Kiyomura, "Session Called a Success," *The Oregonian* (Aug 6, 1993); "Tax Breaks for Business, Needy Ok'd," *The Oregonian* (Aug 6, 1993).

On August 17 a celebration: Terry Rogers and Frank Roberts were quoted in "Frank Roberts Celebrated," *The Oregonian* (Aug 17, 1993).

On September 16: Speech to the Human Rights Campaign from the author's personal papers.

The second thing we were following: Information on John Kitzhaber's decision to run for governor in this and subsequent paragraphs from Jeff Mapes, "Kitzhaber Tests Waters Around State," *The Oregonian* (Sep 18, 1993); Jeff Mapes, "Kitzhaber to Challenge Gov. Roberts in Primary," *The Oregonian* (Oct 17, 1993); David Steves, "Kitzhaber Makes it Official," *Statesman Journal* (Oct 17, 1993).

On October 13 Frank had a stroke: Passages on Frank Roberts' death are based upon pages 56-59 from Barbara Roberts, *Death without Denial, Grief without Apology*, published by NewSage Press in 2002.

One of the priorities: Quote regarding livable communities from a speech in the author's personal files.

In mid-November I flew to Seattle: Information on the APEC conference from documents available in the gubernatorial records at the Oregon State Archives.

My week was almost done: Information on the Terwilliger Boulevard bridge opening from Kolani Roberts, "South Burlingame Neighbors Celebrate New Terwilliger Bridge," *The Oregonian* (Dec 19, 1993).

On December 17 Patricia publicly announced: Information on Patricia McCaig's move to the gubernatorial campaign from Jeff Mapes, "Roberts Aid to Head Re-Election Bid," *The Oregonian* (Dec 18, 1993).

Chapter Twenty-three

After I had had a number: Information on the Dammasch State Hospital closure from Cathy Kiyomura, "Governor Announces Dammasch Changes," *The Oregonian* (Jan 4, 1994); Cathy Kiyomura, "Hospital Director Foresees Closure by End of Year," (Jan 14, 1994).

Once again, as I had done: The 1994 State of the State is from the speech files available at the Oregon State Archives. Additional information from Gail Kinsey Hill, "Gov. Barbara Roberts' State of the State," *The Oregonian* (Jan 15, 1994).

John Kitzhaber had already challenged me: Information on the gubernatorial campaign fundraising, debate negotiations, and poll numbers in this and subsequent paragraphs from "Kitzhaber Challenges Governor to Series of Debates," *The Oregonian* (Jan 4, 1994); Jeff Mapes and Barnes Ellis, "Roberts, Kitzhaber Report Raising $200,000 a Piece," *The Oregonian* (Jan 13, 1994); Jeff Mapes, "McCaig Sets New Course for Roberts," *The Oregonian* (Jan 23, 1994).

On Friday morning, January 28, I walked: Speech withdrawing from the governor's race from the speech files available at the Oregon State Archives. Further information on the aftermath of the withdrawal from Jeff Mapes and Gail Kinsey Hill, "Roberts Won't Seek a Second Term," *The Oregonian* (Jan 29, 1994); Cathy Kiyomura and Barnes C. Ellis, "Roberts' Decision to Quit Race Wins Praise," *The Oregonian* (Jan 29, 1994); Alan Gustafson, "Roberts Puts Family First," *Statesman Journal* (Jan 29, 1994); Jeff Mapes, "Family Health Woes Drain Roberts," *The Oregonian* (Jan 29, 1994); Gail Kinsey Hill, "Roberts Greeted with Tears, Praise at Speaking Events," *The Oregonian* (Jan 30, 1994); "A Good Time for Roberts to Bow Out," *East Oregonian* (Jan 29, 1994).

On March 1 it became official: Information on the departure of Patricia McCaig from the governor's staff from Steve Duin, "McCaig and Metro: A Sneak Preview," *The Oregonian* (Mar 2, 1994).

On March 8, Oregon's political communities: Information on the filings for statewide office candidacy in the 1994 election from the Oregon Blue Book.

As spring approached: Information on the 1995-97 Governor's budget from Gail Kinsey Hill, "Roberts Vows to Protect Schools in Budget," *The Oregonian* (Mar 11, 1994) and the gubernatorial records available at the Oregon State Archives.

In mid-May, Oregon's primary: Information on the outcomes of statewide races Oregon primary election from the Oregon Blue Book.

On May 16, I led an interactive telecommunication: Information on the teen-pregnancy prevention efforts from the report entitled "Sex, Teens and Oregon's Plan," released by the governor's office in Oct 1994 and the calendars from the gubernatorial records at the Oregon State Archives.

On July 6, tragedy hit: Information on the deaths of the Prineville Hot Shots from Jeff Barnard, "Oregon Firefighters Remembered at Service," *Spokesman-Review* (Jul 10, 1994); Seth Mydans, "Town of Firefighters Weeps for 9 of them," *The New York Times* (Jul 9, 1994).

On September 23, Interior Secretary Babbitt: Information on the Klamath River designation from press releases from the gubernatorial records located at the Oregon State Archives. The press release from the Department of Interior is from the author's personal files.

On October 11, Timothy Egan: Timothy Egan, "Oregon, Foiling Forecasters, Thrives as it Protects Owls," *The New York Times* (Oct 11, 1994).

One last comment on the month of October 1994: The 1994 Salmon Festival Stewardship Award declaration is from the author's personal files.

On November 1, I left Portland: Information on the economic trade mission to Japan from Alan K. Ota, "Blazers Help Oregon Business in Blazing New Trails in Japan," *The Oregonian* (Nov 3, 1994); Jeff Baker, "Japan Is Getting a Full-Court Press from NBA," *The Oregonian* (Nov 4, 1994); Jeff Baker, "Drexler Scores 41 in Win," *The Oregonian* (Nov 6, 1994); Jeff Baker, "Blazers Find Tourist Routine Difficult Even in Japan," *The Oregonian* (Nov 6, 1994).

The most disappointing losses: Information on the issues and outcomes of the 1994 general election from the Oregon Blue Book and Jeff Mapes, "Kitzhaber Rolls to Victory," *The Oregonian* (Nov 9, 1994); "Ballot Measures at a Glance," *The Oregonian* (Nov 9, 1994); Ashbel S. Green, Bryan Smith, and Cathy Kiyomura, "State Senate Gets Republican Party," *The Oregonian* (Nov 9, 1994); "Oregon Congress," *The Oregonian* (Nov 9, 1994); Mark O'Keefe, "Assisted-Suicide Measure Survives Heavy Opposition," *The Oregonian* (Nov 9, 1994); James Mayer, "Furse-Witt, No. 8 Too Close to Call," *The Oregonian* (Nov 15, 1994); Jeff Mapes, "Jack Roberts Wins State Labor Post," *The Oregonian* (Nov 12, 1994); "By the Numbers Final Returns from Tuesday's General Election," *The Oregonian* (Nov 12, 1994); James Mayer, "Furse Squeaks in for a Second Term," *The Oregonian* (Nov 18, 1994).

On December 15: Speech at the Dec 15, 1994, celebration dinner from the author's personal files.

The Christmas holiday finished: Information on the 1995 Rose Bowl from Norm Maves, Jr., "Fans Party so Hearty," *The Oregonian* (Jan 2, 1995); J. E. Vader, "Ducks' Pep Rally Is All It's Quacked up to Be," *The Oregonian* (Jan 2, 1995).

In the middle of my final full week as Governor: "September Song" was composed by Kurt Weill with lyrics by Maxwell Anderson.

On Wednesday January 4r: Information on the appointment of Gary Weeks from Jeff Mapes, "The Top of it: Roberts Taps Weeks as New Oregon Lottery Boss," *The Oregonian* (Jan 5, 1995).

Two more important decisions: Information on the Indian gaming compact from "Roberts, Warm Springs Tribe Sign Casino-Gambling Pact," *The Oregonian* (Jan 7, 1995).

The estuary application: Information on the application from "Roberts Asks Protection for Lower Columbia," *The Oregonian* (Jan 7, 1995).

On Monday, before the new governor: Information on the commutations and pardons in this and subsequent paragraphs from John Snell, "Nine Killers Ask Roberts to Spare Their Lives," *The Oregonian* (Jan 8, 1995); Phil Manzano, "Roberts Denies Bid from 9 on Death Row," *The Oregonian* (Jan 10, 1995); Phil Manzano, "Roberts Commutes Woman's Sentence," *The Oregonian* (Jan 10, 1995).

As the final hour: The text of the farewell address is from the author's personal speech files.

Chapter Twenty-five

I have never kept a diary: Diary of the train trip from Oregon to Massachusetts from the author's personal files.

After arriving at the Kennedy School: Information on the resignation of Senator Bob Packwood and the special election for his Senate seat from Dee Lane, "Chronology November 3, 1992," *The Oregonian* (Sep 8, 1995) and Jeff Mapes, "And They're Off and Running," *The Oregonian* (Sep 9, 1995).

Unbelievably, within only three months: Information on the retirement of Senator Mark Hatfield from Jeff Mapes "Mark Hatfield Retires: 'It is Time to Come Home,'" *The Oregonian* (Dec 2, 1995).

I can't complete this recounting of my time: Information on the number of people in Oregon and nationally that are infected with HIV from the Cascade Aids Project.

Chapter Twenty-six

January is such a gray, cold month: "Over the Rainbow" was composed by Harold Arlen with lyrics by E. Y. Harburg in 1939.

Chapter Twenty-eight

My 2008 electoral activities are not complete: Information on the Convention and quotes from convention speeches are from the Official Proceedings of the 2008 Democratic National Convention.

In March of 1996 the Salem-Keizer School District: Information on the naming of the Barbara Roberts Secondary High School Program from "Salem Alternative School Renamed for Ex-Governor," *Statesman Journal* (Marh 26, 1996).

Appendix

Information not cited elsewhere is from relevant speeches and policy documents from the gubernatorial records located at the Oregon State Archives. Oregon state government was ranked seventh in the May 11, 1993, issue of *Financial World*. Additional information on judicial appointments from Rick Bella, "Capitol Notebook: What They Said," *The Oregonian* (Jany 10, 1995).

Index

References to photos are in italics.